Stakeholder Theory

In 1984, R. Edward Freeman published his landmark book, *Strategic Management: A Stakeholder Approach*, a work that set the agenda for what we now call stakeholder theory. In the intervening years, the literature on stakeholder theory has become vast and diverse. This book examines this body of research and assesses its relevance for our understanding of modern business. Beginning with a discussion of the origins and development of stakeholder theory, it shows how this corpus of theory has influenced a variety of different fields, including strategic management, finance, accounting, management, marketing, law, health care, public policy, and environment. It also features in-depth discussions of two important areas that stakeholder theory has helped to shape and define: business ethics and corporate social responsibility. The book concludes by arguing that we should re-frame capitalism in the terms of stakeholder theory so that we come to see business as creating value for stakeholders.

R. Edward Freeman is Olsson Professor of Business Administration and Co-Director of the Olsson Center for Applied Ethics at the Darden School of Business, University of Virginia.

Jeffrey S. Harrison is the W. David Robbins Chair of Strategic Management and Director of the Innovation and Entrepreneurship Program at the Robins School of Business, University of Richmond.

Andrew C. Wicks is Associate Professor of Business Administration, Co-Director of the Olsson Center for Ethics, and Academic Advisor for the Business Roundtable Institute for Corporate Ethics at the Darden School of Business, University of Virginia.

Bidhan Parmar is Lecturer in Business Administration at the Darden School of Business, University of Virginia.

Simone de Colle is a PhD candidate in management and business ethics at the Darden School of Business, University of Virginia.

Stakeholder Theory

The State of the Art

R. Edward Freeman

Jeffrey S. Harrison

Andrew C. Wicks

Bidhan Parmar

Simone de Colle

CAMBRIDGE
UNIVERSITY PRESS

University Printing House, Cambridge CB2 8BS, United Kingdom

Cambridge University Press is part of the University of Cambridge.

It furthers the University's mission by disseminating knowledge in the pursuit of
education, learning and research at the highest international levels of excellence.

www.cambridge.org
Information on this title: www.cambridge.org/9780521137935

First published 2010

A catalogue record for this publication is available from the British Library

ISBN 978-0-521-19081-7 Hardback
ISBN 978-0-521-13793-5 Paperback

To stakeholder researchers, theorists, and critics all over the world.
Thank you.

Contents

Part IV Stakeholder theory: some future possibilities

Figures

Table

Acknowledgements

The arguments in this book have been developed in a number of places over the years. We have drawn liberally from these sources, and we thank a variety of co-authors, editors, and publishers for their kind permission to allow us to keep the copyrights involved, or to use and recast some of the material here.

Chapter 1 is based on Freeman, Wicks, and Parmar, "Stakeholder theory as a basis for capitalism," (in press) in a volume from Palgrave, edited by Lorenzo Saccone, Margaret Blair, and Freeman, that results from the International Economics Association meeting in Trento, Italy, in 2006. It also owes a debt to Freeman, Harrison, and Wicks, *Managing for Stakeholders*, Yale University Press (2007); Freeman, "Managing for stakeholders," in N. Bowie, T. Beauchamp, and D. Arnold (eds.), *Ethical Theory and Business*, 8th edn., Prentice-Hall (2008); and B. Agle, T. Donaldson, Freeman, M. Jensen, R. Mitchell, and D. Wood, "Dialogue: Toward superior stakeholder theory," *Business Ethics Quarterly*, 18 (2) (2008), 153–190.

Chapter 2 is based on Freeman (1984, 2004, 2005).

Chapter 3 draws on Freeman and D. Newkirk, "Business as a human enterprise: Implications for education," in S. Gregg and J. Stoner (eds.), *Rethinking Business Management*, Princeton: Witherspoon Institute (2008); and Freeman and Newkirk's "Business school research: Some preliminary suggestions" working paper (2008), available from the Social Science Research Network. It also draws on Freeman, "The relevance of Richard Rorty to management research," *Academy of Management Review*, 29 (1) (2004), 127–130; and Wicks and Freeman (1998).

Chapter 9 draws on Freeman (2000); Freeman and Phillips (2002); Freeman, K. Martin, and Parmar (2006); and Freeman, K. Martin, and Parmar, "Stakeholder capitalism," *Journal of Business Ethics*, 74 (4) (2007), 303–314.

Many people have been involved with this project over the years, and have contributed in a variety of ways, especially in helping us to get clearer about what "stakeholder theory" really is and how it can be developed. The early pioneers at Wharton are detailed in Chapter 2, but personal thanks to Russell Ackoff, James Emshoff, Howard Perlmutter, Ian Mitroff, Alan Shapiro, and the late Eric Trist are still in order. More recently Robert Phillips, of the University of Richmond, has been our partner in much of this work, as he has pursued his own interpretation of stakeholder theory, found in Phillips (2003a and b). His colleague Doug Bosse at Richmond has been helpful as well. Our co-authors of other related works deserve special mention, especially Professor Kirsten Martin at Catholic University, Jared Harris at Darden, and Rama Velamuri at IESE. Gordon Sollars of Fairleigh Dickenson University has been our most persistent friendly critic since 1977. Patricia Werhane has been an intellectual force for those of us at Darden for many years; she has made this book better. We would like to acknowledge the contributions and support of former Darden School deans John Rosenblum, Leo Higdon, and Robert Harris, and the current dean, Bob Bruner. Darden, and the Robins School at Richmond, have been terrific places to work on stakeholder theory. We especially thank our Darden colleagues, Jay Bourgeois, Richard Brownlee, Robert Carraway, Ming-Jer Chen, James Clawson, Jacquelyn Doyle, Greg Fairchild, Mary Margaret Frank, James Freeland, Sherwood Frey, Paul Harper, Jared Harris, Mark Haskins, Alec Horniman, Lynn Isabella, Erika James, Andrea Larson, Mike Lenox, Jeanne Liedtka, Marc Lipson, Luann Lynch, Marc Modica, David Newkirk, Ryan Quinn, Peter Rodriguez, James Rubin, Saras Sarasvathy, Scott Snell, Robert Spekman, Lisa Stewart, Elizabeth Tiesberg, Sankaran Venkataraman, Elliot Weiss, Ron Wilcox, and others. We are grateful for having to make these ideas clearer to generations of graduate students, Ph.D. as well as MBA. The book is better for some of their skepticism and criticism. The ethics team at Darden, Dean Krehmeyer, Jenny Mead, Brian Moriarty, Karen Musselman, Lisa Stewart, Heidi White, and a number of others over the years have created an environment where research is fun. Jenny Mead is owed a special debt for actually helping us to get the book out the door and assuming the massive task of turning it into something that approaches readability. BluesJam has kept some of us sane, while our families have lived with the insanity of writing such a book. We humbly thank all of them.

For many years (since the 1960s) the Olsson family of West Point, Virginia, has supported the idea of putting business and ethics together. Without the generous support of the Olsson Center for Applied Ethics, this book could not have been written. In 2004 the Business Roundtable established the Business Roundtable Institute for Corporate Ethics at the Darden School, with the idea that we needed an organization dedicated to the express mission of putting business and ethics together, solving once and for all what we call in this book "the problem of the ethics of capitalism." The support of the CEOs of the Roundtable has helped us develop these ideas. Without the full support of John Castellani and Tom Lehrer our institute would not exist. We have also taken inspiration from the thousands of executives with whom we have had conversations over the years in seminars and consulting assignments, and in friendships. We would not have written this book if they were not out in the world bringing the ideas to life.

Outside our immediate environment we would like to thank Professors Brad Agle, Ellen Auster, Shawn Berman, Maureen Bezold, Norman Bowie, Archie Carrol, Andrew Crane, Tom Donaldson, Michele Dorigatti, the late Tom Dunfee, Laura Dunham, Dawn Elm, Heather Elms, George Enderle, William Evan, Valeria Fazio, Jose Luis Fernandez Fernandez, Tim Fort, Bruno Frey, Daniel R. Gilbert, Jr., Mattia Gilmartin, Paul Godfrey, Ken Goodpaster, Jenn Griffith, Terry Halbert, Ed Hartman, Jamie Hendry, Michael Jensen, Michael Johnson-Cramer, Tom Jones, Gilbert Lenssen, Thomas Maak, John McVea, Joe Mahoney, Joshua Margolis, Dirk Matten, Phil Mirvis, Ron Mitchell, Jeremy Moon, Mette Morsing, the late Juha Näsi, Salma Näsi, Richard Neilsen, Mollie Painter-Morland, Nicola Plessa, Jim Post, Lee Preston, Gianfranco Rusconi, Lorenzo Sacconi, Sybille Sachs, Grant Savage, Michel Schlosser, Jag Sheth, Raj Sisodia, Harish Srivatsava, Sandra Waddock, Jim Walsh, David Wheeler, and Donna Wood, and their students, with whom we have been privileged to meet and discuss these ideas all over the world. We are also grateful to the anonymous referees for Cambridge University Press. All of these scholars are engaged in developing what we have called in this book "stakeholder theory." It is to them and others who are too numerous to mention that we dedicate this book.

Finally we are most grateful for Paula Parish, Chris Harrison, Philip Good, and the team at Cambridge University Press. Good publishers are hard to find, and a great one like Cambridge University Press is a rarity.

Preface

For the past thirty years a group of scholars has developed the idea that a business has stakeholders – that is, there are groups and individuals who have a stake in the success or failure of a business. There are many different ways of understanding this concept and there is a burgeoning area of academic research in both business and applied ethics on so-called "stakeholder theory." The purpose of this book is to examine critically this body of research and assess its relevance for our understanding of business in the twenty-first century. In this volume we attempt to explain and assess stakeholder theory so that any scholar or doctoral student or interested reader can find their own way through this literature by reading this book.

The stakeholder theory literature seems to represent an abrupt departure from the usual understanding of business as a vehicle to maximize returns to the owners of capital. This more mainstream view – call it "shareholder capitalism," or "the standard account" – has recently come under much criticism, and the "stakeholder view" is often put forward as an alternative. Our assessment of this debate is that, despite a great deal of theorizing, there is little direct conflict between the shareholder view and the stakeholder view. In fact, we argue that the stakeholder view is a more useful way of understanding modern capitalism.

Our plan is as follows. The chapters in Part I, "The genesis of stakeholder theory," focus on our view of stakeholder theory as a whole. In Chapter 1 we explain how changes in the business environment necessitate a rethinking of the dominant conceptual models used to understand business. We suggest three main problems that something like stakeholder theory can begin to solve: (i) the problem of value creation and trade; (ii) the problem of the ethics of capitalism; and (iii) the problem of the managerial mindset. We call this the "basic mechanics of stakeholder theory." We then explicate the four dominant metaphors used by economists and business theorists to conceptualize how we create value and trade with each other. Business has been variously understood as relying primarily on "markets," "business strategy or industry structure," "agency relationships," and "transaction costs." We use Milton Friedman, Michael Porter, Michael Jensen, and Oliver Williamson as icons of these ways of understanding business. We suggest in Chapter 1 that each of these metaphors is compatible with a stakeholder interpretation, and suggest that the usual way of juxtaposing shareholders and stakeholders is, at best, disingenuous.

Chapter 2 recounts the history of the stakeholder idea, concentrating on its development during the last thirty years, primarily around a number of researchers who happened to be at the Wharton School in the late 1970s and early 1980s. These ideas, originally intended to revise our understanding of the business discipline called "strategic planning" or "business policy" or, more recently, "strategic management," were picked up and developed by a number of scholars working in some of the normative disciplines of business such as "business ethics" and "social issues in management" or "corporate social responsibility" (CSR). This history has led to the diversity of interpretations of stakeholder theory, from seeing it as a new way of understanding business to a more sophisticated way of understanding corporate social responsibility. We argue that the basic mechanics of stakeholder theory – the problems it was meant to solve, developed in Chapter 1 – require an integration of these two perspectives.

Chapter 3 is a brief reprise of our general approach to stakeholder theory and research in general. Since we do not do this in the way that is usual for management theorists, we need to explain the pragmatist approach that runs throughout our thinking. Chapter 3 is a brief introduction to such pragmatic theorizing.

The chapters in Part II, "Stakeholder theory and the traditional disciplines of business," trace the development of the stakeholder idea in the traditional disciplines of business, focusing on those disciplines that would claim to be "nonnormative." Chapter 4 picks up the story in strategic management and assesses the impact of the stakeholder idea in that discipline. Freeman (1984) intended to show how taking the stakeholder idea seriously would reconceptualize strategic management. Much recent work has begun to actualize that line of research. Chapter 5 looks at finance, accounting, management, and marketing, and shows how the idea has had a variety of impacts in these disciplines. Chapter 6 looks at some disciplines that may not be present in all schools of business but which inform important institutions in society. In particular, there has been a fair amount of work using the stakeholder idea in developing the disciplines of law, health care, public policy, and the environment as they are relevant to business. Our emphasis throughout this part of the book is to provide an explication and an assessment of the major ways in which "stakeholder theory" has been developed and used in the disciplines of business.

The chapters in Part III, "Stakeholder theory, ethics, and corporate social responsibility," take up the story in the more normative disciplines of business. In Chapter 7 we examine work in business ethics where the stakeholder idea has had a major impact. Indeed, most of the textbooks in business ethics juxtapose "stakeholder models of business" with "shareholder models." Many philosophers writing on business ethics call for a more explicit connection between stakeholder theory and the more traditional normative ethical theory. We examine these claims and others in this chapter. Chapter 8 looks at the idea of "corporate social responsibility" and the way in which stakeholder theory has been used to set out more useful models of this idea. We end with the suggestion that corporate social responsibility (CSR, as its advocates call it) can more usefully be interpreted as "company stakeholder responsibility," and thereby link the supposedly normative disciplines of business with the more traditional nonnormative disciplines.

The chapters in Part IV, "Stakeholder theory: some future possibilities," suggest some lines of research that we believe are necessary and likely to occur in support of the future development of stakeholder theory. Chapter 9 explains how we can understand stakeholder theory as a more complete theory of "value creation and trade" or "business" or "capitalism." It begins the process of outlining what "stakeholder capitalism" would look like, the result of putting stakeholder theory in the center of our mainstream ways of thinking about business. Chapter 10 suggests how we might develop stakeholder theory by asking a set of questions that have arisen as we have worked on this book. In some cases it may mean rethinking traditional disciplines of business with stakeholder theory in mind.

Throughout this book we are philosophical pragmatists. We aim to tell a new narrative about business, rather than to prove or disprove propositions and hypotheses. We try to assess the research that has been done, but our task will necessarily be incomplete. The stakeholder theory literature has become vast and diverse. We are certain that our interpretation is not the only one, and we hope to stimulate other scholars to offer their own. Throughout this book we are indebted to the many scholars who have devoted their time and attention to these issues, especially our critics, and we humbly dedicate this book to them.

Part I

The genesis of stakeholder theory

1 The problems that stakeholder theory tries to solve

We begin this chapter by outlining the problems that stakeholder theory was originally conceptualized to solve and the "basic mechanics" that we believe underlie the development of the theory during the last thirty years. We turn in the next sections to the arguments of Milton Friedman, Michael Jensen, Michael Porter, and Oliver Williamson, often cited as opponents of stakeholder theory, and suggest that all are compatible with the main ideas of stakeholder theory. We highlight what we also take to be key differences between stakeholder theory and these largely economic approaches to business. We suggest that while these approaches are compatible with stakeholder theory, it makes more sense to return to the very roots of capitalism, the theory of entrepreneurship. We suggest how stakeholder theory needs to be seen as a theory about how business actually does and can work. We make an explicit tie to the theory of entrepreneurship and outline the basics of the stakeholder mindset.

Stakeholder theory:[1] the basic mechanics

Many have argued that the business world of the twenty-first century has undergone dramatic change. The rise of globalization, the dominance of information technology, the liberalization of states, especially the demise of centralized state planning and ownership of industry, and increased societal awareness of the impact of business on communities and nations have all been suggested as reasons to revise our understanding of business.

The dominant way of understanding business and management theory was developed during a time when there was much less concern with turbulence. Weber's ideas about bureaucracy still dominate the managerial landscape, and

[1] In Chapter 3 we explain how we ground our approach to "stakeholder theory" in a philosophical pragmatism.

the economists' idea of an orderly march towards equilibrium still dominates most of the business economics area.[2] Corporations are seen as the property of their owners – shareholders in public corporations – and as limited in their liability for their effects upon others. In a world where concerns are primarily domestic, such models may be appropriate, since governments may well be able to abrogate any adverse effects in a way that is fair to all. There is no such world today.

Stakeholder theory has been developed over the last thirty years to counter this dominant mindset. In particular, it has been developed to solve or at least reconceptualize several specific problems. The first might be given the following title:

The problem of value creation and trade. How can we understand business in a world where there is a great deal of change in business relationships, and where these relationships shift depending on the national, industry, and societal context? How is value creation and trade possible in such a world?

As outlined originally in Freeman (1984), stakeholder theory was concerned with the problem of value creation and trade. From its early articulation at the Stanford Research Institute, through the various theorists at Wharton such as Ackoff, Trist, Emshoff, Mitroff and Mason, and Perlmutter, these thinkers were concerned to explain how business could be understood against this backdrop of environmental turbulence to which they saw no end.[3]

It quickly became obvious that trying to solve this problem using the existing fundamental assumptions was fruitless. Most ideas about business assumed the dominance of a kind of economics that assumed that questions of values and ethics were at best "extra-theoretic" if not downright irrelevant. Yet in the real world people were becoming ever more aware of the effects of capitalism on all parts of their lives, so that the second problem may be called:

The problem of the ethics of capitalism. As capitalism became the dominant means of organizing value creation and trade, it became clear that restricting attention to its "economic" effects yields a damaging partial view. An increasing number of thinkers have begun to ask questions about the relationship between capitalism and the other institutions in society. Such questions include: (i) How can we understand capitalism so that all its effects can be taken into account by decision makers, rather than externalized on

[2] This dependence on a Weberian view of the firm and its underlying ideas about equilibrium may well have been appropriate for understanding a more stable and localized business environment, though Austrians such as von Hayek would still raise many logical questions. However, we believe that in today's world the usefulness of equilibrium-based models is much more limited.

[3] We offer a more comprehensive history of the idea from multiple perspectives in Chapter 2.

society? (ii) Can we continue to divide the world into the "business realm" and the "ethical realm"? (iii) Is it possible for business executives to "do the right thing," all things considered, no matter how complicated the world is? And (iv) how can we understand both "business" and "ethics" so that we can put them together conceptually and practically?

These questions are relevant to every executive and business thinker today. Given the recent turbulence in financial markets, they have begun to take center stage in the public policy discussions about the reregulation of business. Indeed, the forces of globalization have become stronger, and as information technology has led to more calls for transparency, openness, and responsibility, we have seen an increased interest in understanding how capitalism, ethics, sustainability, and social responsibility can be forged into new ways of thinking about business.

It has become easy to see that solving the problem of value creation and trade only by looking narrowly at the economics of value creation and trade creates the problem of the ethics of capitalism. When the two are combined we find a third, very practical problem. Almost all stakeholder theorists have been engaged in training managers, executives, and MBAs, and have encountered the obvious problem of what to teach.

The problem of managerial mindset also raises a number of questions. (i) How can we utilize and redefine economic theory so that it becomes useful in a turbulent world full of ethical challenges? (ii) How can managers adopt a mindset that puts business and ethics together to make decisions on a routine basis? (iii) How can dealing with turbulence, globalization, and ethics become a routine part of how we understand the manager's job? (iv) What should be taught in business schools?

These questions are relevant to managers who are wondering how to develop their people so that they can be successful in the twenty-first century, and they are relevant to business schools. Business thinkers as diverse as Sumantra Ghoshal and Jeffrey Pfeffer have suggested that current mindsets about business are just not appropriate for the turbulent business environment of today. Since the theories that we teach become "enacted" in the real world, this is much more than an academic issue.[4]

Stakeholder theory suggests that if we adopt as a unit of analysis the relationship between a business and the groups and individuals who can affect or are affected by it, then we have a better chance to deal with these three

[4] In Chapter 3 we attempt to explain why we agree with Sumantra Ghoshal that we enact our theories.

problems (and surely there are others, or other ways to conceptualize these).[5] Stripped down to its bare essentials, stakeholder theory emerges out of the following four ideas: the separation fallacy, the open question argument, the integration thesis, and the responsibility principle.

Freeman (1994) suggests that most theories of business rely on separating "business" decisions from "ethical" decisions. Indeed, this is the genesis of the problem of the ethics of capitalism, and is seen most clearly in the popular joke about "business ethics as an oxymoron." More formally, we might suggest that we define:

The separation fallacy

It is useful to believe that sentences such as "x is a business decision" have no ethical content or any implicit ethical point of view. And it is useful to believe that sentences such as "x is an ethical decision, the best thing to do, all things considered" have no content or implicit view about value creation and trade (business).

Wicks (1996) and others have shown how deeply this fallacy runs in our understanding of business as well as in other areas in society.[6] There are two implications of rejecting the separation fallacy. The first is that almost any business decision has some ethical content (Harris and Freeman, 2008). To see that this is true one need only ask whether the following questions make sense for virtually any business decision.[7]

[5] Many will object here that we need to be clearer about whether we are talking about normative stakeholder theory, descriptive stakeholder theory, or instrumental stakeholder theory, as Donaldson and Preston divide the literature (1995). We believe that for some purposes these distinctions are useful, but for others they are not. In particular, we believe that stakeholder theory is inherently managerial. It is about how we do and can understand how we create value and trade with each other. Donaldson and Preston seem to recognize this in their important paper (1995), but it is a point lost on many business school scholars who see research in a narrower vein. See Freeman and Newkirk (2008a, 2008b) for a different view of research in business schools. For a more detailed idea of our pragmatist philosophical views see Wicks and Freeman (1998), as well as Chapter 3.

[6] For a recent discussion of the separation thesis, or separation fallacy, see Joakim Sandberg (2008a); the ensuing discussion, Jared D. Harris and R. Edward Freeman (2008); Ben Wempe (2008); John Dienhart (2008); and Joakim Sandberg (2008b). Sandberg's thesis seems to be that by not accepting the fact–value distinction, we somehow make a philosophical mistake. Harris and Freeman argue that the pragmatist view of language that undergirds this distinction is rooted in the philosophical traditions of Wittgenstein, Quine, Dewey, Rorty, and others.

[7] The original open question argument is due to G. E. Moore in *Principia Ethica*, and was meant to show that "good" and words like that were "supervenient properties." We believe that our current use of the argument is meant to show an openness to most business decisions or, more precisely, theories which may explain business decisions. Thus it is meant to establish that "ethical questions are always there" rather than argue for any particular view of ethics or ethical language.

The open question argument

(1) If this decision is made, for whom is value created and destroyed?

(2) Who is harmed and/or benefited by this decision?

(3) Whose rights are enabled and whose values are realized by this decision (and whose are not)?

Since these questions are always open for most business decisions, it is reasonable to give up the separation fallacy. We need a theory about business that builds in answers to the "open question argument."

One such answer would be, "Only value to shareholders counts," but such an answer would have to be enmeshed in the language of ethics as well as business.[8] In short, we need a theory that has as its basis what we might call:

The integration thesis I

Most business decisions or statements about business have some ethical content or an implicit ethical view. Most ethical decisions or statements about ethics have some business content or an implicit view about business.

Yet another way to articulate this idea is:

The integration thesis II

(1) It makes no sense to talk about business without talking about ethics.

(2) It makes no sense to talk about ethics without talking about business.

(3) It makes no sense to talk about either business or ethics without talking about human beings.

One of the most pressing challenges facing business scholars is to tell compelling narratives that have the integration thesis at its heart. This is essentially the task that those scholars, called "stakeholder theorists," have begun over the last thirty years. Statement (1) challenges much work done in the name of "value-free economics and science"; (2) challenges much work done by philosophers who have little knowledge of either economics or business; and (3) challenges much work done in all the business disciplines that ignores "the human sciences" or "humanities" or, more concretely, the fact that most human beings are pretty complex (Donaldson and Freeman 1994; Freeman and Newkirk 2008a, 2008b). Stakeholder theory has developed primarily around

[8] We shall see later that Friedman, unlike most of his expositors, actually gives such a morally rich answer.

(1); its future development and usefulness depends largely on how it deals with (2) and (3).[9]

To begin to address (1) we need to go to the very basics of ethics and we suggest that something like the following principle is implicit in most reasonably comprehensive moral views.

The responsibility principle[10]

Most people, most of the time, want to, and do, accept responsibility for the effects of their actions on others.

Clearly the responsibility principle is incompatible with the separation fallacy. If business is separated from ethics, there is no question of moral responsibility for business decisions, hence the joke is that business ethics is an oxymoron. More clearly still, without something like "the responsibility principle" it is difficult to see how ethics gets off the ground. "Responsibility" may well be a difficult and multifaceted idea; there are surely many different ways to understand it. But if we are not willing to accept responsibility for our own actions (as limited as that may be due to complicated issues of causality and the like), then ethics understood as how we reason together so that we can all flourish is likely an exercise in bad faith.[11]

One response to the responsibility principle is that some people in fact do not want to be responsible or ethical. They simply want to get away with as much as possible at the expense of others. People sometimes act "opportunistically and with guile." While there is some truth in this view, the question is one of starting points. Start with the responsibility principle and one has to design in how to deal with opportunism. Start with opportunism and one is likely to leave out important ideas such as human dignity, cooperative endeavors, and the creative spirit, all of which, we suggest, are the cornerstones of capitalism. We need a more thorough understanding of the responsibility principle, its origins, and implications, on account of each of these.

[9] We make some suggestions along these lines in Chapters 9 and 10.

[10] "Responsibility" is a difficult concept. There is a burgeoning philosophical literature on it from the time of Plato. We do not intend that the responsibility principle sets forth any particular view of responsibility. Instead, we intend it as "whatever you think about responsibility, something like this principle is necessary." Of course, portions of it could be modified depending on how responsible you believe people actually are, or on difficult claims about joint causality, institutional roles, and the like.

[11] We might call our overall view on ethics something like "ethics as conversation." It is about trying to work out how we can simultaneously be what Harold Bloom calls "strong poets" and build communities that support human solidarity and flourishing.

It is now easy to see that the genesis of "stakeholder theory" is simply the integration thesis plus the responsibility principle. Give up the separation fallacy, in part because of the open question argument, and there is not much alternative. People engaged in value creation and trade are responsible precisely to "those groups and individuals who can affect or be affected by their actions" – that is, stakeholders. For most businesses, as we currently understand it today, this means paying attention at least to customers, employees, suppliers, communities, and financiers.[12]

"Stakeholder theory" does not mean that representatives of these groups must sit on governing boards of the firm, nor does it mean that shareholders (we prefer "financiers" as a more inclusive term) have no rights. It does imply that the interests of these groups are joint and that to create value, one must focus on how value gets created for each and every stakeholder.[13] How value gets created for stakeholders is just how each is affected by the actions of others as well as managers.

"Stakeholder theory" is fundamentally a theory about how business works at its best, and how it could work. It is descriptive, prescriptive, and instrumental at the same time, and, as Donaldson and Preston (1995) have argued, it is managerial. Stakeholder theory is about value creation and trade and how to manage a business effectively. "Effective" can be seen as "create as much value as possible." If stakeholder theory is to solve the problem of value creation and trade, it must show how business can in fact be described through stakeholder relationships. If it is to solve the problem of the ethics of capitalism, it must show how a business could be managed to take full account of its effects on and responsibilities towards stakeholders. And if it is to solve the problem of managerial mindset, it must adopt a practical way of putting business and ethics together that is implementable in the real world.

For the most part writers on stakeholder theory have taken an approach that looks at reasonably large existing businesses. They have tried to use the idea to address issues such as "corporate social responsibility," "corporate

[12] For some purposes it might make sense to pay such attention to others as well. In Chapter 7 we explain why we eschew the line of thought that tries to define all stakeholders for all firms. The business world is simply too diverse.

[13] If there is a jointness, or partial jointness to stakeholder interests, perhaps the insights of Thomas Schelling will be applicable. Schelling (1965) imagined a number of coordination games whereby actors had to coordinate their joint interests. Of course, stakeholder interests may also be in partial conflict, but if the possibility of innovation and the redefinition of interests is always present, then we can more profitably focus on the jointness of interests rather than on the conflict. We believe that the firm could be conceptualized as a "Schelling focal point" that preserves the possibility of innovation through time. We do no more than suggest this idea for others to explore.

legitimacy," "theory of the firm," and even macro-societal issues such as "building the good society." With rare exceptions little thought has been given to a host of important issues that have concrete practical significance: how are we to understand value creation and trade at the simplest level? How do entrepreneurs create and sustain value? How does value creation and trade take place within and among multiple state regimes? While at first glance these questions may seem intractable, we want to suggest that we can take a stakeholder approach to them to yield some interesting insights, and to highlight some assumptions about business which we may wish to make optional.

There are a number of competing "standard accounts" of value creation and trade. They all revolve around the idea that shareholders or owners or investors are entitled to the residual gains that accrue from value creation and trade. Stakeholder theory suggests that matters are more complicated – that is, that stakeholder relationships are involved, and that human beings are more complex than the standard accounts assume. We shall look, in turn, at the views of four influential theorists, Milton Friedman, Michael Jensen, Michael Porter, and Oliver Williamson. We shall argue that if we see these standard accounts in the proper light they are all compatible with stakeholder theory, but they are not terribly useful for the purposes of solving our three problems. We follow these analyses with a return to the very basics of business – entrepreneurship – and we anchor the basics of stakeholder theory in this realm.

The Friedman problem: business as markets and maximizing shareholder value

Since the first formal articulation of stakeholder theory over twenty-five years ago, there has been much debate about the difference between the views of business that are centered on stockholders and those that are centered on stakeholders. Milton Friedman's article (1970) has long been juxtaposed against stakeholder theory, and the ensuing debates have revealed few new or useful insights. In an attempt to move beyond the narrow, supposed stakeholder/stockholder dichotomy, we spell out our reading of Friedman's controversial article, which we believe to be compatible with stakeholder theory – in fact we see Friedman as an early stakeholder theorist.

Friedman writes, "It may be in the long-run interest of a corporation that is a major employer in a small community to devote resources to providing amenities to that community or to improving its government"; he goes on to say that it is wrong to call this social responsibility because "they [the actions] are entirely justified in its [the corporation's] self interest" (Friedman 1962: 132).

For Friedman, supporting stakeholder interests is not about social responsibility; it is about capitalism. According to Friedman the purpose of business is to "use its resources and engage in activities designed to increase its profits so long as it stays within the rules of the game, which is to say, engages in open and free competition, without deception or fraud" (Friedman 1962: 133).

All this sounds well and good to us. A key difference between our view and Friedman's is what makes business successful. Friedman believes that it is maximizing profits. We believe that in order to maximize profits, companies need great products and services that customers want, solid relationships with suppliers that keep operations on the cutting edge, inspired employees who stand for the company mission and push the company to become better, and supportive communities that allow businesses to flourish. So in our view Friedman could have written the above quotation as:

> Business is about making sure that products and services actually do what you say they are going to do, doing business with suppliers who want to make you better, having employees who are engaged in their work, and being good citizens in the community, all of which may well be in the long-run (or even possibly the short-run) interest of a corporation. Stakeholder management is just good management and will lead to maximizing profits.

Under this reading Friedman is at least an instrumental stakeholder theorist.[14] He may also believe that individuals have a responsibility not to destroy the basis of capitalism – freedom, in his view. In his book *Capitalism and Freedom* he spells out that one of the virtues of the market economy is that it protects individuals from social conformity and abuse of political power. For Friedman, power must be checked and used responsibly. Since in his view economic freedom is a large subset of political freedom, we may deduce that he would agree that economic powers are also subject to responsible use. Friedman may come to something like stakeholder theory out of more than just instrumentalism; he could see it, as we do, as the very basis of capitalism.[15]

There may also be a difference in the theories about the way the world works. Friedman may actually believe that if you try to maximize profits you will do so. We believe that trying to maximize profits is counterproductive, because it takes attention away from the fundamental drivers of value – stakeholder relationships. There has been considerable research

[14] Instrumental stakeholder theorists believe that creating value for nonshareholder stakeholders actually creates the most value for shareholders. See Jones (1995), Donaldson and Preston (1995), and Jones and Wicks (1999).

[15] We explain how stakeholder theory can be the basis for a new capitalism in Chapter 9.

that shows that profitable firms have a purpose and values beyond profit maximization.[16] Profit maximization may be better thought of as a result or outcome.

Both we and Friedman agree that business and capitalism are not about social responsibility. We contend that stakeholder theory is about business and value creation and, as we said above, it is managerial. Economics may not fundamentally be about value creation in real business. At its best it may be an idealized and abstract view of markets built around the goals of prediction, not around the way that actual business works. It is clearly useful for many purposes, but perhaps not for solving the problems of understanding business in the twenty-first century.

Despite these differences, we believe that Friedman's maximizing shareholder value view is compatible with stakeholder theory. After all, the only way to maximize value sustainably is to satisfy stakeholder interests.

The Jensen move: business as agency

Michael Jensen, in a paper titled "Maximization, stakeholder theory, and the corporate objective," argues that stakeholder theory needs an objective function, namely value maximization. He says,

> Value maximization states that managers should make all decisions so as to increase the total long-run market value of the firm. Total value is the sum of the values of all financial claims on the firm – including equity, debt, preferred stock, and warrants. (Jensen 2002: 236)

Jensen argues that stakeholder theory is incomplete because it does not offer answers to the questions, how do we keep score? and how do we want the firms in our economy to measure better versus worse? His argument is built on two major premises.

First, Jensen states that purposeful corporate behavior requires a single value objective function. He gives the example of a manager who is forced to choose between maximizing profit or market share – given that every incremental increase in market share comes at higher cost. Here he believes that managers are forced to choose between the two goals and that value maximization offers them an objective principle for making the trade-off. He continues,

[16] We review this literature in Chapters 4 and 8. Of particular note is the work of Collins and Porras (1997) and Graves and Waddock (1994).

A firm can resolve this ambiguity by specifying the tradeoffs among the various dimensions, and doing so amounts to specifying an overall objective function such as V=f(x,y, ...) that explicitly incorporates the effects of decisions on all the goods or bads (denoted by (x,y, ...)) affecting the firm (such as cash flow, risk, and so on). (Jensen 2002: 238)

We do not believe that the complexity of management can be made so simple. Primarily, the variety of metrics used in a firm can not be folded so easily into a single overall objective function. Firms and people do not simply arrange values and preferences in hierarchical and easily understandable decision trees. Jensen's view ignores lexicographical orderings, or dictionary orderings. Additionally, to create a final score or objective measure of the kind that Jensen wants, different metrics must be weighted. The process of choosing weights for these metrics requires some other notion of purpose or mission – it requires firms to answer the questions, who are we? and who do we want to be? These questions go beyond objective value maximization.

Second, Jenson claims that total firm value maximization makes society better off. He also admits that for this to be true some special conditions must be in place. He says,

When monopolies or externalities exist, the value maximizing criterion does not maximize social welfare. By externalities I mean situations in which the decision-maker does not bear the full cost or benefit consequences of his or her choices; water and air pollution are classic examples. (Jensen 2002: 239)

For Jensen, Ronald Coase provides the solution to these issues by reassigning property rights to avoid a second-best solution. But Coase's ideas of rights assignment come from a utilitarian perspective for which there are few arguments. Jensen, and Coase, simply ride roughshod over the idea of rights, assuming as Charles Fried (1981) has argued, that everything is alienable, even our right to bargain at all. Fried suggests, and we agree, that such a view is at best incoherent.[17] So, Jensen's faith that total firm value maximization makes society better off is dependent on a number of further arguments. While these arguments may be interesting to economists and philosophers, they do not serve much purpose in understanding how value gets created.

Jensen as much as acknowledges this point as he comes to see stakeholder theory as the primary vehicle for understanding how value creation and trade takes place. He says,

[17] This issue is addressed in more detail in Freeman and Evan (1990).

> We can learn from the stakeholder theorists how to lead managers and participants in an organization to think more generally and creatively about how the organization's policies treat all important constituencies of the firm. This includes not just financial markets, but employees, customers, suppliers, the community in which the organization exists, and so on. (Jensen 2002: 245)

Jensen refers to the coupling of the objective function and stakeholder theory as enlightened value maximization. Like Friedman, Jensen can be seen as an instrumental stakeholder theorist. He believes that managers need to make trade-offs and that they should be guided by the principle of enlightened value maximization. For a second time we see that if we interpret stakeholder theory as a theory about how value gets created, we have little difference with economists like Friedman and Jensen.[18]

Porter's strategy: business as competitive strategy

Since 1980 Michael Porter has explicated a way to think about business that takes the metaphor of "competitive strategy" as a central one. Porter (1980) situates the theory of business squarely in the "structure–conduct–performance" paradigm of industrial economics. The general idea is that effective strategy (conduct) is a function of the structure of an industry, and that a particular performance results. Porter's second major book (1985) added a description of five forces that determine the nature and level of competition in an industry, as well as suggestions for how to use this information to develop competitive advantage. He provided a value chain that described a firm's primary resource transformation processes and the activities that support those processes. By comparing a firm's value chain to that of competitors, managers could devise ways to develop competitive advantage. More recently Porter and Kramer (2006) have suggested that companies can add thinking about corporate social responsibility and sustainability to their strategic arsenals to gain advantage.

Business is, according to this view, a struggle for advantage. Companies compete with each other to find an advantage that will last – that is, sustainable competitive advantage. The search for advantage is to be found primarily in industry structure and the company's contribution to the value that gets

[18] Similarly we argue in Chapter 4 that the recent theory of incomplete contracting in economics lays down yet another economic keystone for a stakeholder theory of business. See especially the recent work of Joe Mahoney (2005), Russ Coff (1999), and other strategic management theorists who ground stakeholder theory in this approach. More fundamentally see Oliver Hart (1995).

created in the industry. External issues such as corporate responsibility and environmental sustainability can lead to advantage, especially if companies find innovative ways to approach these challenges that are better than those of industry rivals.

While Porter puts more emphasis on "industry" and "competitive strategy" than he does on stakeholder theory, there is much compatibility between the two approaches. To begin with, if we take a somewhat broader view of "value chain," we can easily see that it is just the stakeholders who are a part of this chain. Porter recognizes this fact in making "bargaining power of customers and suppliers" a critical force. But, just as clearly, the bargaining power of employees, the ability of a community to approve regulations or legislation that affects the value chain, and the emergence of other value chain actors such as nongovernmental organizations (NGOs) that call for responsibility and sustainability, are all sources of "advantage." Indeed, the latest Porter work, on corporate social responsibility (CSR), seems to acknowledge this fact.

One might easily develop a Porter-like stakeholder theory along the following lines of a "stakeholder – conduct – performance" paradigm. At any point in time a company exists in a network of stakeholder relationships, a subset of which we might designate as "industry" if we are so inclined. Businesses then try to craft a value proposition that meets the needs or expectations of a certain group of these stakeholders.[19]

Implicit in the Porter account is the idea that the interests of stakeholders can conflict. While this is indeed true, such an account underestimates the extent to which the interests of customers, suppliers, employees, financiers, and communities go together. Without a jointness to their interests, there will be no deal among them. If these interests can be kept "going in the same direction," then the deal can be sustainable. We could describe such a deal as "competitive advantage," or alternatively we could describe it as a "system of cooperation."[20] In the view of most economists like Porter, business and capitalism are to be seen as systems of competition for resources. It only takes a very slight twist to see this same system as one of social cooperation and value creation. Stakeholder theory focuses on the jointness of stakeholder interests rather than solely on the trade-offs that sometimes have to be made. It does not deny that such trade-offs are necessary, but suggests that they also represent opportunities to think beyond trade-offs to a question of value

[19] In Freeman (1984) we find several ways to connect stakeholder theory with Porter's view.

[20] This seems to be the major intuition behind the so-called "resource-based view" of the firm. See Barney and Arikan (2001).

creation. Stakeholder theory solves the value creation question by asking how we could redefine, redescribe, or reinterpret stakeholder interests so that we can figure out a way to satisfy both, or to create more value for both. Porter's view, like that of Friedman, Jensen, and others, offers a good building block from which to ask the value creation question.

The Williamson result: business as transaction cost economizing

In a pathbreaking paper, Ronald Coase (1937) questioned the economic orthodoxy of the time, and wondered why some transactions seem to be organized by markets as economic theory demands, while others seem to be organized by hierarchical arrangements, such as firms. Coase's answer was that most of the time there is a cost to using the pricing mechanism, and that when these "transactions costs" are sufficiently high, someone will organize the transaction via a hierarchy or firm, as opposed to a market. The literature on "transactions costs" or "markets and hierarchies" is now a well-established area of social science.

Indeed, Oliver Williamson (1984a), one of Coase's main modern disciples, has suggested that we can understand transactions cost theory in terms of contracts, and that the standard account of firms as a nexus of contracts follows. Shareholders still bear the residual risk, while other stakeholders have arranged bilateral contracts with built-in safeguards, so that shareholders are entitled to the returns. There is no need to give a "stakeholder account" of transactions cost theory on this interpretation of Williamson's view.[21]

The first point to make here is that, like the standard account of Friedman, this view does not offer much practical insight into how to create value and trade. The best it can do is to exhort us to "understand the structure of transaction costs." While this may not seem much, recent work on e-business, supply chain management, and other issues resulting from the application of information technology offer much insight into the actual practice of value creation and trade. However, on closer examination of these issues, each appears to be simply a detailed analysis of particular stakeholder relationships. After all, how can one see supply chain management as anything other than integrating the supplier–firm–customer chain of interests? So it may be that to turn transactions cost theory towards the practical understanding of value creation and trade, one needs to overlay a stakeholder network.

[21] There is a burgeoning literature on transaction cost economics in the economics and strategic management disciplines.

Second, Freeman and Evan (1990) have questioned Williamson's analysis here by introducing the idea that if contracts have safeguards, then the question of who pays the cost of the safeguards is relevant. For instance, if management and labor contract against a backdrop of the liberal state, complete with safeguards for labor such as labor boards, processes that must be followed under penalty of law, and so on, then both parties have successfully exported the costs of the safeguards of their contract to society as a whole. Indeed, we suggest that a distinction between exogenous safeguards (where the costs are externalized to society or other stakeholders) and endogenous safeguards (where the parties to the contract pay the cost of contracting including safeguards) is crucial for seeing the necessity for a stakeholder approach to markets and hierarchies.

In a more recent paper, Williamson and Bercovitz (1996) seem partly to accept this idea. They suggest that shareholder boards be seen as endogenous safeguards. They even suggest that stakeholder-oriented "boards of overseers" may well be a good idea to get more stakeholder input into the value creation process, of which stakeholders are clearly a part. But they fail to deal adequately with the criticism that safeguards have costs. The implication of such a view is that the contractual arrangements that we observe will be a function of how parties to the contract have been able either to accept or to offload the costs of safeguards. This process is not necessarily a transaction cost economizing process, but rather a political one. If the parties to the contract can externalize the costs of safeguards to others, such as taxpayers, then we would expect to see them use their own power in the political process to realize such gains. In fact, we are appealing to nothing more than the strict "opportunism" assumption in transactions cost theory.[22] In Williamson's well-known diagram, slightly revised, it would be difficult to tell whether a particular governance mechanism appeared at node B or at node D (see Figure 1.1).

In summary the argument is this. Assume a version of the modern state, the rule of law, and a set of institutions that makes contracting viable. One can then understand the creation of value and trade against this backdrop of background institutions. In a world in which these institutions emerge so

[22] The only way to explain voluntary interactions with stakeholders or endogenous safeguards would be to appeal to either a lack of political power, or something like the responsibility principle and subsequent stakeholder theory. The recent financial crisis is a textbook case study of how destructive exogenous safeguards can be.

Williamson's Original Diagram

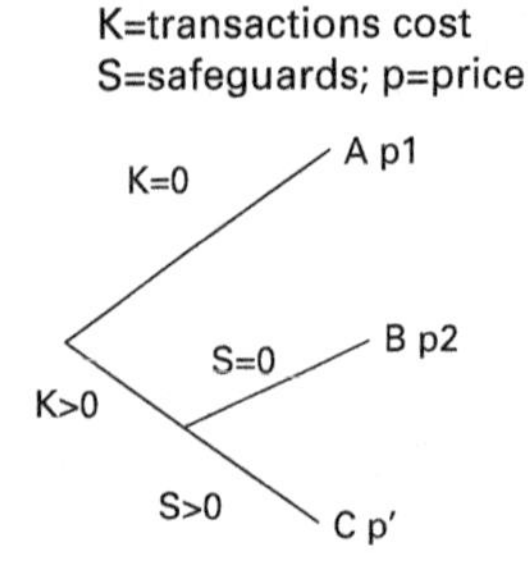

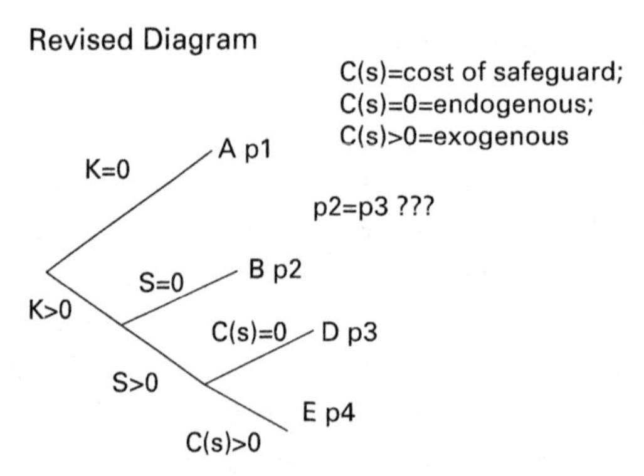

Figure 1.1. Transactions cost theory

that financiers have the right to the residuals of the firm, something like the standard story emerges. Absent these institutions we are left wondering who pays or should pay for whose safeguards. If this is in fact an open question, then a series of other questions is relevant. Could it be interesting to imagine a world where there are only endogenous safeguards? A world in which there are no background institutions, or where there is only the presumption that value creation and trade will continue over time? A world in which there are many conflicting and competing background institutions and there is the desire for value creation and trade to continue over time?

We want to suggest that these last questions must take us substantially beyond what has been done so far in the transactions cost literature, and must put us firmly in the middle of stakeholder theory. Transaction costs economics (TCE) simply focuses too heavily on one sort of governance mechanism – traditional boards of directors. And TCE is too concerned with yielding the traditional view of economics. However, we have suggested that one can use TCE reasoning to see that if the cost of safeguards were assigned differently, then other arrangements may well be possible. We do not see those arrangements because of the way in which we currently think about safeguards as "primarily the government's job."

However, TCE's idea of stakeholder boards of overseers is actually quite interesting. Suppose such a board's task were (i) to reduce information asymmetry among key stakeholders so that management could more easily create even more value; (ii) to view the interest of financiers, customers, suppliers, communities, and employees as joint; and (iii) assume the continuation of the corporation through time. It may well turn out that such a board becomes a very effective "governance mechanism" to help managers create as much value as possible for stakeholders.

Business as entrepreneurial opportunity: basic ideas of stakeholder theory

In a path-breaking set of articles that both summarizes and extends the entrepreneurship literature, Sankaran Venkataraman has suggested that understanding entrepreneurship can fill the gap left by the standard accounts of business activity. He suggests that

> In most societies, most markets are inefficient most of the time, thus providing opportunities for enterprising individuals to enhance wealth by exploiting these inefficiencies (the Weak Premise of Entrepreneurship).

and, alternatively, that

> Even if some markets approach a state of equilibrium, the human condition of enterprise, combined with the lure of profits and advancing knowledge and technology, will destroy the equilibrium sooner or later (the Strong Premise of Entrepreneurship). (Venkataraman 1997: 121)

Venkataraman explicitly connects entrepreneurship with the stakeholder literature by claiming that

> The essence of the corporation is the competitive claims made on it by diverse stakeholders. It is a fact of business life that different stakeholders have different and often conflicting expectations of a corporation. Indeed, the firm itself can be said to be an invention to allow such conflict to be discovered, surfaced, and

resolved, because conflicting claims have to be discovered and methods for resolution executed ... This inherent conflict is a feature not only of the established giant corporation, but also of the very act of creation of the productive enterprise. Entrepreneurship involves joint production where several different stakeholders have to be brought together to create the new product or service. (Venkataraman 2002: 46)

According to this view, the existence of entrepreneurial activity in a society acts as an equilibrating force. It offers an alternative to stakeholders whose needs are not being met by the current arrangement.[23] There is both a weak and strong equilibrating process.

The weak equilibrating process holds that whenever a stakeholder justifiably believes that the value supplied by him or her to a firm is more than the value received, the entrepreneurial process will redeploy the resources of the "victimized" stakeholder to a use where value supplied and received will be equilibrated. The strong equilibrating process holds that if the redeployment of individual stakeholders does not work freely and efficiently and serious value anomalies accumulate within firms and societies, the entrepreneurial process will destroy the value anomalies by fundamental rearrangements in how resources and stakeholders are combined.[24]

The very processes of entrepreneurial activity, whereby entrepreneurs find or create opportunities because they have knowledge or experience that others do not, depend on understanding how stakeholder interests have been or cannot be satisfied. In the following paragraphs we want to unpack these processes in more practical terms to see how value creation and trade can actually come about.

Suppose that Smith has a particularly good recipe for bread. He finds that friends and relatives are always taking second and third helpings of bread at dinner, asking for the recipe, and cornering Smith for tips on how to bake such good bread. Smith reasons that if the bread is so good, there must be people who are willing to pay for the bread, and after all who can't use the extra cash? So, Smith starts to sell his bread to others. Perhaps he delivers it to steady customers or even "contracts" with the local grocer to sell the bread in her store. Smith has become an entrepreneur. And perhaps the standard account can explain Smith's success or failure.

[23] This is the reason behind the insight that "behind every disgruntled stakeholder and critic of a company lies a business opportunity."

[24] Venkataraman (2002), at 50.

On the standard account we would expect the growth and development of Smith Bread Company to be a function of the market for bread. We would try to understand the structure of that market, for instance the number of buyers and sellers, the product ranges of each, the price points of the offerings, and so on. If Smith Bread Company succeeds, it would be because Smith is able to offer a similar product at perhaps a lower price, or perhaps with another feature that buyers of bread want. If Smith Bread Company fails, it would be because others offered the same product at a lower price. In fact, the strict neoclassical view of the standard account would suggest that all the information regarding features and product performance is reflected in the price of the product. A "second best" version of this view, à la Michael Porter's view of strategy, argues that in most real markets it would be slightly more complex, and Smith could position the company to take advantage of those complexities or not. In short, Smith's success or failure is a matter of the market for bread. Understand that market and you'll understand all you need to know about Smith Bread Company.

None of this gives much advice to Smith or explains how Smith Bread Company really came about. This view of markets – as consisting of buyers and sellers – is interesting only to the extent that the question, "how does this market work?" is an interesting question. Understanding the Dutch flower market, the Chicago futures market, the coffee exchange in Uganda, and others is a set of interesting questions but ultimately they are questions about the distribution of value in very specialized situations, rather than its creation.[25]

Let us go further and suppose further that Smith's bread is a big hit with all who try it. Soon Smith must quit his full-time job (perhaps Smith is professor of economics and moral philosophy at Edinburgh) and devote all day to baking bread. He quickly realizes that the kitchen oven is being monopolized by the bread baking, so he invests money in another oven and fixes up the spare room to do nothing but bake bread. But even this is not enough. The demand for Smith's bread is so great that he decides to invest his savings and perhaps talk to his local banker about a loan. Smith builds a bread factory, hires workers to bake the bread in the ovens. Smith spends his time directing the baking and selling of bread.

The transaction cost view is relevant here. It would suggest that Smith Bread Company is successful simply because Smith is correct that he can

[25] Amartya Sen's *On Ethics and Economics* (1987) diagnoses what has gone wrong with economics as a discipline. Also see Julie Nelson (2006) for an insightful critique.

organize some of the transactions internally via the authority relationship, such as hiring workers to bake the bread, rather than buying bread in the market for bread and reselling it. Indeed, this view might tell us that if it could be done more cheaply, it may well be in Smith's interest to begin to grow his own wheat. The success of Smith's venture will not only be a function of the market for bread, but also a function of the markets for the factors of production, such as the labor market and the market for ingredients such as wheat and yeast.

While this view is a more fine-grained analysis of what is happening to Smith Bread Company, it gives little practical advice, for how is Smith to know whether the costs of organizing transactions inside the firm are actually lower than using the market mechanism?[26]

Now let us take a more fine-grained view of Smith's enterprise. What must Smith do to be successful? He must buy raw materials from suppliers such that he can be assured they are of good quality. He must have employees who will make the bread as Smith would, and this is easier when these employees come to want to make the bread as Smith would. He must find customers who want and enjoy his bread so much that they want to buy it again and again.[27] To the extent that he has extended his financial resources to include the bank, relatives, or even shareholders, Smith must make a return for these other financiers, as well as profits (in some form) for himself. And, perhaps more subtly, Smith must be a good citizen in the community. At a minimum Smith must not use his property to harm others. Suppose, for instance, that Smith's new bakery emitted noxious fumes, smelled by other members in the community. Smith would come under pressure to do something about it, and if Smith lived in a relatively free society, community members could claim that Smith has damaged them, and sue for relief, either through the courts, or via legislation.

Venkataraman has suggested that the conflicts that exist between actors in the factor markets will ultimately be sorted out by the entrepreneurial process (the strong or weak force). But, alternatively, we can look at these conflicts from the standpoint of Smith and the stakeholders in Smith Bread Company. From Smith's point of view, his job is to try and resolve these conflicts in a way that is good for the "joint enterprise" that is Smith Bread

[26] Paradoxically, this knowledge itself is a transaction cost.

[27] Strictly speaking, this premise is not necessary. There are some businesses that rely on one-time purchases. But, in the real world, managers and entrepreneurs think of customers as wanting to buy again and again. This is the whole reason for brands.

Company. When customers have complaints, he wants to resolve these complaints so that they don't stop buying bread. Now, there will be limits to what Smith is able to do, and against these limits the entrepreneurial forces will operate. When employees become disgruntled so that they do not put forth their best effort or even think about leaving, Smith wants to find a way to keep creating a sufficient level of value for them to stay. Smith always asks the value creation question. Again, there will be limits, but, practically speaking, Smith always seeks to test these limits by creating as much value as possible for all stakeholders.

As a practical solution to this problem, Smith needs to see the interests of stakeholders as moving roughly in the same direction. And he needs to see that the interests of one stakeholder may well be enhanced in the presence of others.[28] Many stakeholder theorists have focused on the inherent conflict between stakeholder interests and, in doing so, they have forgotten that stakeholder interests are also joint. Many other theorists have asserted that stakeholder theory claims that all stakeholders are equally important. Again, they have forgotten the real world beginnings of the theory.[29] All are not equally important at all points of time, but all have the equal right to bargain over whatever their interests are. (We take this to be a simple statement of some notion of classical liberalism.) And all interests have roughly to go together over time, otherwise, in a relatively free society, stakeholders will turn to the state for restitution.

In short, when Smith successfully, over time, satisfies customers, financiers, suppliers, employees, and the community, then Smith Bread Company flourishes. Notice that the success of Smith Bread Company is still dependent on the market for bread, and the various factor markets, but Smith now has some tangible advice about how to create value and sustain it. Figure 1.2 gives the standard picture of value creation and trade among stakeholder theorists.[30] Smith creates value for stakeholders.

[28] A simple example of what we have in mind here is the fact that our interests are better served when we are on the same faculty as Venkataraman where we can easily work together.

[29] These are especially problematic interpretations for the so-called "normative" disciplines. See Chapters 7 and 8.

[30] Of course, this is only one of many possible pictures. Clearly, the corporation is not the center of the universe, though for some purposes it is useful to see the world from the corporation at the center point of view. For other purposes it is useful to diagram stakeholders as being at the center. The Danish company, Novo Nordisk puts "people with diabetes" at the center of its stakeholder map. See Freeman, Harrison, and Wicks (2007) for more suggestions about stakeholder maps. Fassin (2008) contains several useful depictions of the stakeholder idea. Figure 1.2 is due in large part to conversations with Robert Phillips. See in particular Phillips (2003).

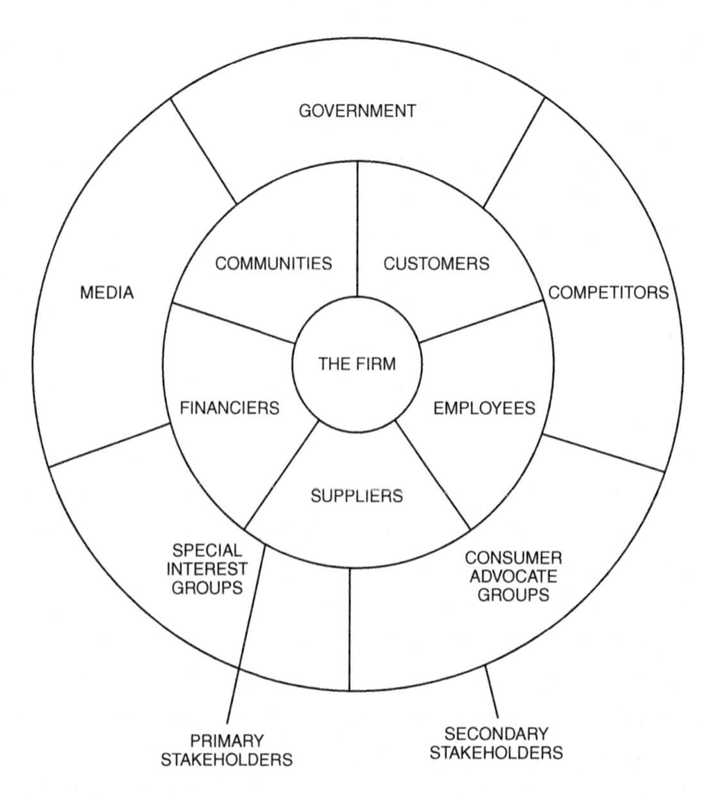

Figure 1.2. Creating value for stakeholders
Source: R. Edward Freeman, Jeffrey S. Harrison, and Andrew C. Wicks 2007. *Managing for Stakeholders: Survival, Reputation, and Success.* New Haven: Yale University Press. Originally from a conversation with Robert Phillips.

The stakeholder mindset

The basic idea of creating value for stakeholders is quite simple. Business can be understood as a set of relationships among groups which have a stake in the activities that make up the business. Business is about how customers, suppliers, employees, financiers (stockholders, bondholders, banks, etc.), communities, and managers interact and create value. To understand a business is to know how these relationships work. And the executive's or entrepreneur's job is to manage and shape these relationships.

Owners or financiers (a better term) clearly have a financial stake in the business in the form of stocks, bonds, and so on, and they expect some kind of financial return from them. Of course, the stakes of financiers will differ by type of owner, preferences for money, moral preferences, and so on, as well as by type of firm. The shareholders of Google may well want returns as well as be supportive of Google's articulated purpose of "do no evil." To the extent that it makes sense to talk about the financiers "owning the firm," they have a concomitant responsibility for the uses of their property.

Employees have their jobs and usually their livelihood at stake; they often have specialized skills for which there is usually no perfectly elastic market. In return for their labor, they expect security, wages, benefits, and meaningful work. Often, employees are expected to participate in the decision making of the organization, and if the employees are management or senior executives, we see them as shouldering a great deal of responsibility for the conduct of the organization as a whole. Employees are sometimes financiers as well, since many companies have stock ownership plans, and loyal employees who believe in the future of their companies often voluntarily invest. One way to think about the employee relationship is in terms of contracts.

Customers and suppliers exchange resources for the products and services of the firm, and in return receive the benefits of the products and services. As with financiers and employees, the customer and supplier relationships are enmeshed in ethics. Companies make promises to customers via their advertising and when products or services do not deliver on these promises, then management has a responsibility to rectify the situation. It is also important to have suppliers who are committed to making a company better. If suppliers find a better, faster, and cheaper way of making critical parts or services, then both supplier and company can win. Of course, some suppliers simply compete on price, but, even so, there is a moral element of fairness and transparency to the supplier relationship.

Finally, the local community grants the firm the right to build facilities and, in turn, it benefits from the tax base and economic and social contributions of the firm. Companies have a real impact on communities, and being located in a welcoming community helps a company create value for its other stakeholders. In return for the provision of local services, companies are expected to be good citizens, as is any individual person. It should not expose the community to unreasonable hazards in the form of pollution, toxic waste, and so on. It should keep whatever commitments it makes to the community, and operate in a transparent manner as far as possible. Of course, companies do not have perfect knowledge, but when management discovers some danger or runs afoul of new competition, it is expected to inform and work with local communities to mitigate any negative effects as far as possible.

While any business must consist of financiers, customers, suppliers, employees, and communities, it is possible to think about other stakeholders as well. We can define "stakeholder" in a number of ways. First of all, we could define the term fairly narrowly to capture the idea that any business, large or small, is about creating value for "those groups without whose support, the business would cease to be viable." The inner circle of Figure 1.2 depicts this view. Almost every business is concerned at some level with relationships between financiers, customers, suppliers, employees, and communities. We might call these groups "primary" or "definitional." However, it should be noted that as a business starts up, sometimes one particular stakeholder is more important than another. In a new business start-up, there are sometimes no suppliers, and paying a lot of attention to one or two key customers, as well as to the venture capitalist (financier), is the right approach.

There is also a somewhat broader definition that captures the idea that if a group or individual can affect a business, then the executives must take that group into consideration in thinking about how to create value. Or, a stakeholder is any group or individual that can affect or be affected by the realization of an organization's purpose. At a minimum some groups affect primary stakeholders, and we might see these as stakeholders in the outer ring of Figure 1.2 and call them "secondary" or "instrumental."

There are other definitions that have emerged during the last thirty years, some based on risks and rewards, some based on mutuality of interests. And the debate over finding the one "true definition" of "stakeholder" is not likely to end.[31] We prefer a more pragmatic approach of being clear of the purpose of using any of the proposed definitions. Business is a fascinating field of study. There are very few principles and definitions that apply to all businesses all over the world. Furthermore, there are many different ways to run a successful business or, if you like, many different flavors of creating value for stakeholders. We see limited usefulness in trying to define one model of business, based on either the shareholder or stakeholder view, which works for all businesses everywhere. We see much value to be gained in examining how the stakes work in the value creation process, and the role of the executive.

Executives play a special role in the activity of the business enterprise. On the one hand, they have a stake like every other employee in terms of an actual or implied employment contract. And that stake is linked to the stakes of financiers, customers, suppliers, communities, and other employees. In addition, executives are expected to look after the health of the overall enterprise,

[31] We examine this debate in Chapters 7 and 8.

to keep the varied stakes moving in roughly the same direction, and to keep them in harmony.[32]

No stakeholder stands alone in the process of value creation. The stakes of each stakeholder group are multifaceted, and inherently connected to each other. How could a bondholder recognize any returns without management paying attention to the stakes of customers or employees? How could customers get the products and services they need without employees and suppliers? How could employees have a decent place to live without communities? Many thinkers see the dominant problem of stakeholder theory as how to solve the priority problem, or "which stakeholders are more important?" or "how do we make trade-offs among stakeholders?" We see this as a secondary issue.[33]

First and foremost we need to see stakeholder interests as joint, as inherently tied together. Seeing stakeholder interests as "joint" rather than opposed is difficult. It is not always easy to find a way to accommodate all stakeholder interests. It is easier to trade off one against another. Why not delay spending on new products for customers in order to keep earnings a bit higher? Why not cut employee medical benefits in order to invest in a new inventory control system?

Stakeholder theory suggests that executives try to reframe the questions. How can we invest in new products and create higher earnings? How can we be sure that our employees are healthy and happy and are able to work creatively so that we can capture the benefits of new information technology such as inventory control systems? In a recent book reflecting on his experience as CEO of Medtronic, Bill George (2003) summarized the stakeholder mindset:

> Serving all your stakeholders is the best way to produce long term results and create a growing, prosperous company ... Let me be very clear about this: there is no conflict between serving all your stakeholders and providing excellent returns for shareholders. In the long term it is impossible to have one without the other. However, serving all these stakeholder groups requires discipline, vision, and committed leadership.

[32] In earlier versions of this argument we suggested that the notion of a fiduciary duty to stockholders be extended to "fiduciary duty to stakeholders." We believe that such a move cannot be defended without doing damage to the notion of "fiduciary." The idea of having a special duty to either one or a few stakeholders is not helpful. See Phillips, Freeman, and Wicks (2003) for the arguments. We have also put the point in other places as the need to "balance" the interests of stakeholders. We prefer the metaphor of thinking about keeping stakeholder interests in "harmony." "Harmony" depicts a "jointness" to the interests that is perhaps the major contribution of a stakeholder approach to business. The notes are different but they must blend together.

[33] See especially Mitchell, Agle, and Wood (1997) for an example. We discuss this paper in Chapter 8.

Even the well-known takeover artist Henry Kravis has climbed aboard the stakeholder approach to business. Speaking at the Super Return Conference in Dubai in 2008, the KKR chief said:

> All of us need to accept responsibility for the damage done to the free-market system ... We've moved too slowly to replace management in some situations ... We wait too long hoping they'll improve, but they never do ... You have to focus on all the stakeholders. It's a new thing for us and something we're really hammering. Long-term value is only achieved if growth benefits all stakeholders in a company, from owners to employees, communities and even governments. We are also conscious we are fiduciaries to millions of hard-working men and women and university endowments ... Trust must be earned over the long haul and maintained constantly. We have not always adequately explained what we do to the man on the street. Even some of our investors, although happy with the returns we deliver, don't fully understand what we do and why they should invest with us.[34]

The primary responsibility of the executive is to create as much value as possible for stakeholders. Where stakeholder interests conflict, the executive must find a way to rethink the problems so that these interests can go together, so that even more value can be created for each. If trade-offs have to be made, as often happens in the real world, then the executive must figure out how to make the trade-offs, and immediately begin improving the trade-offs for all sides. **A stakeholder approach to business is about creating as much value as possible for stakeholders, without resorting to trade-offs.**

We believe that this task is more easily accomplished when a business has a sense of purpose. Furthermore, there are few limits on the kinds of purpose that can drive a business. Wal-Mart may stand for "everyday low price." Merck can stand for "alleviating human suffering." The point is that if an entrepreneur or an executive can find a purpose that speaks to the hearts and minds of key stakeholders, it is more likely that there will be sustained success.

Purpose is complex and inspirational. The Grameen Bank wants to eliminate poverty. Tastings (a local restaurant) wants to bring the taste of really good food and wine to lots of people in the community. And all of these organizations have to generate profits, or else they cannot pursue their purposes. Capitalism works because we can pursue our purpose with others. When we coalesce around a big idea, or a joint purpose evolves from our day-to-day activities with each other, then great things can happen.

[34] We are grateful to Michael O'Brien and several other students for bringing this quotation to our attention. The source is Dan Primack (2008).

To create value for stakeholders, executives must understand that business is fully situated in the realm of humanity. Businesses are human institutions populated by real live complex human beings. Stakeholders have names and faces and children. They are not mere placeholders for social roles. As such, matters of ethics are routine when one takes a "managing for stakeholders" approach. In the words of one CEO, "The only assets I manage go up and down the elevators every day."

Conclusion

Stakeholder theory has evolved to address the problems of (i) understanding and managing a business in the world of the twenty-first century (the problem of value creation and trade); (ii) putting together thinking about questions of ethics, responsibility, and sustainability with the usual economic view of capitalism (the problem of the ethics of capitalism); and (iii) understanding what to teach managers and students about what it takes to be successful in the current business world (the problem of managerial mindset).

By focusing on the basic mechanics of stakeholder theory we argue that we can understand capitalism as a set of relationships between customers, suppliers, communities, employees, and financiers (and possibly others), all of whom consist of human beings fully situated in the realm of both business and ethics. This approach is consistent with the main ways in which we understand capitalism. In particular we have argued that it is consistent with the market-based approach of Milton Friedman, the agency theory approach of Michael Jensen, the strategic management approach of Michael Porter, and the transactions cost theory of Oliver Williamson. However, we believe that a more useful theory can be built by understanding the "distinctive domain of entrepreneurship" and entrepreneurial theory. By focusing on the jointness of the stakes of stakeholders, and the entrepreneurial dictum to create as much value as possible, we have suggested several features of the stakeholder mindset.

2 The development of stakeholder theory: a brief history

The purpose of this chapter is to trace the development of what has come to be known as "stakeholder theory." We intend to accomplish this in what is perhaps an unusual manner. To begin we go back to Freeman's original book and retell the story, told there, of the origins of the idea of stakeholders. We then suggest a number of additions and revisions that have been made to this history in the literature of the last twenty-five years. We move to what could be called "autobiographical" or "idiosyncratic" accounts of the development of stakeholder theory, mostly from the point of view of one of the authors, Freeman. We do this because we want to illustrate a philosophical point about the general issue of "theory development" and the importance of a role for "the author." There are many different versions of "stakeholder theory" and we do not wish to try to synthesize all of them into something approximating "the correct version."[1] A viable social science has an important place for what we might call "the author." To claim that "the author" has such a role in the development of management theory is neither to promote the self-importance of particular individuals nor to deny the role of intersubjective agreement that is so vital in science. Rather it is to claim that contextual factors and serendipity can be crucial in the process of theory development. Finally, we give an assessment of Freeman's 1984 book. Fortunately Jim Walsh had begun this process in a number of recent papers and presentations; we add our voices to Walsh's assessment.

The development of stakeholder theory

The literature story in Freeman[2]

The actual word "stakeholder" first appeared in the management literature in an internal memorandum at the Stanford Research Institute (now SRI International,

[1] See Chapter 3 for the reasons why we resist finding a "correct" version.

[2] We have changed the tense from the original present tense in Freeman (1984) to the past tense for consistency and readability. We have made a number of additions and revisions to the strategy literature,

Inc.) in 1963.[3] The term was meant to generalize the notion of stockholder as the only group to whom management need be responsive. Thus the concept of the stakeholder was originally defined as "those groups without whose support the organization would cease to exist." The list of stakeholders originally included shareowners, employees, customers, suppliers, lenders, and society. Stemming from the work of Igor Ansoff and Robert Stewart in the planning department at Lockheed, and later Marion Doscher and Stewart at SRI, the original approach served an important information function in the SRI corporate planning process.[4] The SRI researchers argued that unless executives understood the needs and concerns of these stakeholder groups, they could not formulate corporate objectives which would receive the necessary support for the continued survival of the firm.[5] From the original work at SRI, the historical trail diverges in a number of directions: (i) the strategy literature; (ii) the work of Russell Ackoff, C. West Churchman and systems theorists; (iii) the literature on corporate social responsibility; and (iv) the work of Eric Rhenman and other organization theorists.

The strategy literature[6]

In his now classic book, *Corporate Strategy* (1965), Ansoff argued for a rejection of the stakeholder theory, which he explicated in the following passage:

but it should be emphasized that the next section of this chapter, "The development of stakeholder theory: additions and revisions" is the history of the idea as it appeared in the 1980s, albeit a more complete version. Subsequent sections will offer some caveats and revisions.

[3] Harrison has found an even earlier use of "stakeholder" in Silbert (1952). Slinger (1998) locates it as an eighteenth-century idea of the person who holds stakes of betters in a gamble, and cites *Merriam-Webster's Dictionary*. The *Oxford English Dictionary* concurs.

[4] The precise origins of "stakeholder" were surprisingly difficult to track down in 1982. Ackoff (1974) credits Ansoff (1965) and quotes the references in Ansoff's book to Abrams (1951) and Cyert and March (1963). Mason and Mitroff (1982) attribute the term to Rhenman (1968). An anonymous referee for *Applications of Management Science* pointed out to Freeman that the concept had originated at SRI, which he duly acknowledged in Emshoff and Freeman (1981). Soon thereafter Dr. William Royce, of SRI International, in private correspondence, recounted the story of Ansoff, Robert Stewart, and Mario N. Doscher at Lockheed and SRI in the early 1960s. Professor Kirk Hanson of Stanford then pointed out that Rhenman was visiting at Stanford while he was writing *Industrial Democracy and Industrial Management* (1968). A trip to SRI International in summer 1980 and a talk with Dr. Royce and Dr. Arnold Mitchell clarified a number of historical issues. They were gracious enough to share some original files from that period of time. In a private correspondence dated July 26, 1996, Rebecca Profit of the Centre for Strategic Business Studies notes that a letter in *Management Consultancy* (UK, March 1996) cites Robert F. Stewart and Dr. Otis J. Benepe from Lockheed Aircraft Co. as coining the "stakeholders concept" in the 1950s and developing it at Stanford Research Institute in the early 1960s. Gamble and Kelly attribute the idea to Stewart, Benepe, and Rhenman (2001: 44). We have been unable to verify this claim about Benepe from additional sources, although Stewart's and Rhenman's roles have been well known. In fact Giles Slinger credits Marion Doscher, a technical writer, with coining the term.

[5] Again, Slinger substantially revises this account, as we set out later in the chapter.

[6] Chapter 4 is an up-to-date review and assessment from 1984 to the present of the role of stakeholder theory in the strategy literature.

While as we shall see later, "responsibilities" and "objectives" are not synonymous, they have been made one in a "stakeholder theory" of objectives. This theory maintains that the objectives of the firm should be derived balancing the conflicting claims of the various "stakeholders" in the firm: managers, workers, stockholders, suppliers, vendors. (Ansoff 1965: 34)

Ansoff credited Abrams (1954) and Cyert and March (1963) with a similar view, but went on to reject the theory in favor of a view which separated objectives into "economic" and "social," the latter being a secondary, modifying and constraining influence on the former.[7] The passage quoted above clearly indicates that Ansoff has the "dominant coalition" view of organizations in mind when he explicates the stakeholder view. The point of the SRI definition is, however, somewhat different.[8] The issue is simple: survival. Without the support of these key groups the firm does not survive, by definition of what we mean by "stakeholder." Of course, whether SRI has the right groups is a different issue. Are lenders necessary for the survival of a debt-free firm? Is "society" (however that loose term may be defined) necessary for the survival of a privately owned specialty steel firm? Conversely, isn't government necessary for the survival of public utilities?

The thrust of Ansoff's criticism is to point out that the stakeholders whose support is necessary for survival are a contingent phenomenon, dependent on a number of situational variables. Ansoff rejected such a theory in favor of one which searches for a universal objective function, where stakeholders serve as constraints on the level of the objective which is obtainable at a point in time. Such a search for the real objective of the firm was to occupy a substantial part of the corporate planning literature during the subsequent years.

By the 1970s the stakeholder concept began to surface in a number of places in the strategic planning literature. In a review article on the state of the art of corporate strategy, Bernard Taylor (1971) claimed that the importance of

[7] Thus Ansoff directly appeals to what we called in Chapter 1 "the separation fallacy." The necessity of analyzing social and political issues together with economic and technological ones is argued in Ansoff (1979), Hayes and Abernathy (1980), and Charan and Freeman (1980), as well as numerous other places. The split between "economic" and "social" analysis has always been conceptually arbitrary, or at least since the beginnings of modern utility theory as a foundation for economics (von Neumann and Morgenstern 1946). Rational agents have preferences over many kinds of things, only some of which are measured in dollar terms. The concept of rationality is much broader than some business theorists pretend. See for instance Schelling (1960, 1978), Tullock and Buchanan (1962), and the work of many other "decision theorists."

[8] A word of caution about the role that definitions play in theories is appropriate here. Quine (1960) claims that "sentences do not confront the tribunal of experience alone." Austin (1962), Wisdom (1957), and Wittgenstein (1953), and the resulting literature in philosophy of language, give quite complex and sophisticated analyses of the role that definitions play in languages.

stockholders would diminish. He thought that business would eventually be run for the benefit of stakeholders (Taylor 1971). Haselhoff (1976) explored the implications for the formulation of organizational goals. King and Cleland, in their text *Strategic Planning and Policy* (1978), gave a method for analyzing "clientele groups," "claimants," or "stakeholders," which grew out of their earlier work on project management. Taylor (1977) summarized the latest SRI approach. Rothschild (1976) used the concept to explain a planning process developed at General Electric. Hussey and Langham (1978) presented a model of the organization and its environment with stakeholders being differentiated from the firm and consumers, and used it to analyze the role that management plays in effective corporate planning processes. Derkinderen and Crum (1979) used the stakeholder notion in their analysis of project set strategies, and the idea plays a central role in Heenan and Perlmutter's analysis of organization development for multinational corporations (1979). Specific applications of the concept in managerial processes in the strategic planning literature include Davis and Freeman's (1978) method for technology assessment and Mitroff and Emshoff's (1979) method for strategy formulation called "strategic assumptions analysis." This technique was later developed by Emshoff (1980) and Mason and Mitroff (1982), and Rowe, Mason, and Dickel (1985) as a method for dealing with ill-structured organizational problems. This line of inquiry suggested that managers often held divergent assumptions about their stakeholders, and suggested that deliberate analysis of a broad group of stakeholders could improve organizational decision making:

> In contrast to stockholder analysis, stakeholder analysis asks a manager to consider *all* the parties who will be affected by or who affect an important decision. It asks the manager to list as many parties or interest groups as he or she can who have a *stake* in the policy under consideration. This list of parties is typically much broader than the single category "stockholders." While important, the stockholders are only one of many contending groups having an impact on and a stake in a corporation. (Mitroff, Emshoff, and Kilmann 1979: 586, emphasis added)

Their technique was applied to the case of an industrial materials business (Emshoff and Finnel 1979), and further improvements were made to it in Mitroff and Mason (1980), Emshoff (1980), and Mason and Mitroff (1982).

In a groundbreaking article published in *Long Range Planning* in 1975, William R. Dill outlined three challenges for companies that want to be known for their "strategic prowess." Organizations need (i) to evaluate the changing environment, and (ii) to ensure an appropriate organizational response.

The third and, according to Dill, least well understood challenge is "coping with an active intrusive environment which is made up of individuals and organizations which seek to influence the strategic decisions of the enterprise" (Dill 1975: 57). Dill's work was important in developing the stakeholder concept for the strategy literature, because he defined stakeholder relationships in terms of both influences and responsibilities. He described these factors in both directions: the firm towards its stakeholders and stakeholders towards the firm. He also addressed the difficult challenge of deciding whom a firm should include as relevant stakeholders when making decisions.

In addition, Dill examined the various types of relationship that exist between a stakeholder and a firm, including owner/investor, customer/client, competitor, employee, supplier, dependent on services, circumstantial consumer of by-products, conserver, taxpayer, or student/analyst/researcher, as well as some of the ways in which stakeholders intervene in firm processes, such as through protest, balloting or ratifying, or regulating. He concluded by outlining ways in which a firm can deal more effectively with stakeholders, with an emphasis on open communications and increased interactions. Perhaps his most important insight, from the perspective of where the field of strategic management is now, is that stakeholders can be used as active participants in strategic decisions:

> For a long time, we have assumed that the views and initiatives of stakeholders could be dealt with as externalities to the strategic planning and management process: as data to help management shape decisions, or as legal and social constraints to limit them. We have been reluctant, though, to admit the idea that some of these outside stakeholders might seek and earn active roles with management to make decisions. The move today is from *stakeholder influence* toward *stakeholder participation*. (Dill 1975: 58, emphasis added)

Dill's "stakeholder participation" foreshadowed the increasing importance of interorganizational relationships such as joint ventures and strategic alliances in strategic management (Barringer and Harrison 2000).

At around the same time the stakeholder concept was also applied to strategic planning at the international level. After a thorough summary of the many strong international forces and changes that have made management more difficult, Ringbakk advises,

> The key to progress does not lie in formal planning systems or in the use of sophisticated management technology. The key is developing international managers with more environmental sensitivity and understanding – with empathy for the aspirations and demands by the multinational stakeholders MNCs [multinational corporations] in the future must serve. (Ringbakk 1976: 10)

A stakeholder approach is also evident in Heenan and Perlmutter's analysis of organizational development for multinational corporations (1979).

By the late 1970s the stakeholder concept found its way into the planning processes of some corporations. For example, Rothschild (1976) described these processes at General Electric, a pioneer in strategic planning. Stakeholder-based approaches were also included in a variety of strategic planning texts (Taylor and Sparkes 1977; Hussey and Langham 1978; King and Cleland 1978). The stakeholder concept was being introduced into many planning contexts. For example, Raymond and Greyser (1978) argued that arts organizations need good management as much as for-profit companies do, and suggested that many patrons of the arts consider themselves stakeholders of the organizations they patronize. Also, O'Toole (1979) criticized the way in which business–government relations were being handled in the United States, since stakeholders were put in the difficult position of having to take extreme and unproductive positions on issues in order to be heard.

Wommack (1979), in describing the responsibilities of the board of directors, suggested that an organization should create value for both society and the corporation and that corporate objectives should be established that satisfy the expectations of stakeholders. Puccini and Marley-Clarke examined the competing interests of stakeholders in offshore resource management zones in the United States. They proposed a model that would maximize equity among those competing interests. They also suggested that "the governments of coastal states should play the arbiter's role in attempting to rationalize the trade-offs affecting stakeholders" (Puccini and Marley-Clarke 1979: 13).

Keeley applied the stakeholder concept to performance evaluation. He defined stakeholders as groups that provide resources to the organization and examined the difficulties associated with satisfying multiple, conflicting demands. He stated directly that subordinates should be evaluated on the basis of how well they satisfy the stakeholders that are assigned to them, and placed responsibility squarely on the shoulders of firm administrators:

> It is the function of the organizational administrator to translate the demands of stakeholder groups into organizational objectives and procedures which result in consequences (output) required to sustain their contributions. Obviously, if the demands of these groups are well-defined, relatively modest, stable over time, and compatible with one another, the administrator's task is rather uncomplicated. Under such conditions, the task environment is non-ambiguous or "certain." But if organizational stakeholders press vague demands which are inconsistent over time and incompatible in the aggregate, the organizational administrator may have great

difficulty in translating these demands into objectives and procedures for subordinates. Rather, he or she may mediate these demands by holding organizational units directly accountable to stakeholders (or to other internal units which, in turn, are so accountable). (Keeley 1978: 433)

In 1980, Slatter declared,

The idea of stakeholder analysis – the process by which the expectations of various groups with which the company interacts are analysed – has tended to go out of fashion as business planning has focused on developing and maintaining sustainable competitive advantages on a product market segment or strategic business unit (SBU) basis. This development in business planning has undoubtedly been correct as it has helped firms focus on the critical economic issues facing their businesses. While some firms have paid lip service to the idea of stakeholder analysis put forward in the late 1960s and early 1970s, few firms took stakeholder analysis very seriously – largely because of the difficulty of identifying practical economic pay-offs from the analysis. (Slatter 1980: 58)

Slatter's notion that the emphasis on pure economics was "correct" is questionable. In fact, Slatter explained later in the article that the stakeholder perspective should be re-evaluated as a public relations tool because "All the firm's stakeholder groups provide the firm with both threats and opportunities" (58).

At the same time, Burton and Naylor made an early and deliberate attempt to tie economics and corporate planning together. They noted that "one finds a dearth of explicit application of microeconomics to corporate planning" (Burton and Naylor 1980: 249). Instead of rejecting the stakeholder perspective in favor of pure economics, they developed a microeconomic theory of strategic search that identifies key stakeholders and acknowledges their conflicting objectives.

Several articles in the early 1980s recognized the increasing complexity of modern corporations, the increasing intensity of stakeholder claims on those organizations, and the usefulness of stakeholder-oriented planning processes in dealing with these issues (Armstrong 1982; Carroll 1983; Charan and Freeman 1980; Fombrun and Astley 1983; MacMillan 1982, 1983; Mendelow 1983; Ruffat 1983). In addition, Mahon and Murray (1981) applied stakeholder theory to strategic planning in regulated companies. They argued that managers in those companies should expend considerable resources in wooing their external stakeholders. They also suggested that strategies based on the integration of economic, political, and social goals are more likely to be successful.

The stakeholder approach was also applied directly to the development of mission statements. Pearce (1982) argued that managers should acknowledge the legitimate claims of both internal and external stakeholders when developing a mission statement. He suggested a procedure whereby claims are identified, prioritized, and coordinated with other elements of the mission.

According to Pearce,

> Each of these interest groups has justifiable reasons to expect, and often to demand, that the company act in a responsible manner toward the satisfaction of its claims. In general, stockholders claim appropriate returns on their investments; employees seek broadly defined job satisfaction; customers want what they pay for; suppliers seek dependable buyers; governments want adherence to legislated regulations; unions seek benefits for members in proportion to their contributions to company success; competitors want fair competition; local communities want companies that are responsible "citizens"; and the general public seeks some assurance that the quality of life will be improved as a result of the firm's existence. (Pearce 1982: 22)

Although there were many definitions of "strategy," "policy," "planning," and so on at the time, the basic idea was that strategy was concerned with the configuration of an organization's resources in relation to its external environment.[9] The concept of strategy was and is inherently connected with setting some direction for the organization, based on an analysis of organizational capabilities and environmental opportunities and threats. Thus adequate information about the environment, past and future changes, and emerging strategic issues and problems is vital to an effective strategy and strategy-making process. As the literature moved from reactive policy making to proactive strategy formulation, the need for "environmental scanning" increased.

SRI's original use of stakeholder analysis was precisely in this area. By developing "measures of satisfaction" of those groups whose support was necessary for the continued survival of the organization, an important input into the planning process was made. Information systems could be developed to scan and track the responses of key stakeholder groups to changes in corporate strategy. Adjustments could be made if stakeholder expectations became far enough out of line to warrant withdrawal of their support. Stakeholder behavior was taken as given, or as a constraint on strategy, in Ansoff's terms. Strategy was formulated against this static environment,

[9] Our arguments in Chapter 3 and in earlier footnotes about "what is stakeholder theory?" also apply to "what is strategic management?" For an early attempt to deal with these issues, see Freeman and Lorange (1985).

which was forecastable in principle in the long run. This use of the stakeholder concept was as an intelligence-gathering mechanism to predict more accurately environmental opportunities and threats.

A second feature of this use of "stakeholder" is that stakeholders were identified at a generic level as customers, suppliers, owners, public, society, and so on, and analysis was performed at that level of generality. Hence public-attitude surveys, stockholder interviews, and the like were the available analytical techniques. Since the major concern was with forecasting the future environment and not with changing specific stakeholder behavior, there was no need to go beyond this generic stakeholder analysis.

The concern with future forecasts of stakeholder behavior so that the corporation can plan its "best reply" assumed that there would be no radical shifts in a stakeholder's actions. Because the stakeholder environment was taken as static, and because only generic analysis was necessary, adversarial groups were not considered as stakeholders.[10] Particular "special interest groups" interested in negotiation have no place. One negotiates with Ralph Nader, not with "special interest groups" as a generic entity. Therefore the early strategic uses of stakeholder theory were really another way of getting more useable information on "friendly" groups. The use of the stakeholder concept was to provide information to strategists at a generic level about traditional "relatives" of stockholders such as employees, managers, suppliers, consumers, and the public. In the 1950s, 1960s, and early 1970s the business environment of most US firms was quite stable and few strategic surprises occurred, making this interpretation of the stakeholder concept adequate.[11]

The systems theory literature

In the mid-1970s researchers in systems theory, led by Russell Ackoff and C. West Churchman, "rediscovered" stakeholder analysis, or at least took Ansoff's admonition more seriously.[12] Stemming from their joint work in applying Jungian psychology to develop a personality theory that could be

[10] This was not true for Dill's ideas of kibitzers (Dill 1975).

[11] The mainstream of research into strategy followed quite different lines, with uses of the stakeholder concept being the exception rather than the rule. We lay out the history of strategic management as a field in Chapter 4.

[12] The precise origins of systems theory are hard to determine. Certainly Barnard (1938) is a candidate for founder. However, the systems perspective on problem solving goes much further back. Descartes (c. 1628) argued that both analysis (breaking things down into its component parts) and synthesis (building things up by seeing what they were a part of) went together in his oft-derided "rational method." See Churchman (1971) for an attempt to relate the systems approach to traditional philosophy.

useful for business problem solving (Churchman, Ackoff, and Wax 1947), they were instrumental in developing systems theory into a powerful tool for addressing a number of issues in social science (Churchman 1968; Ackoff 1970). Ackoff (1974) rehashed Ansoff's argument and defined a method for stakeholder analysis of organizational systems. Propounding essentially an "open systems" view of organizations first put forward by Barnard (1938), Ackoff argued that many societal problems could be solved by the redesign of fundamental institutions with the support and interaction of the stakeholders in the system.

This notion of "stakeholders in a system" differed from the use of the concept in the strategy literature. To be concerned with the organizational level of analysis was a mistake, on the systems view. Problems should not be defined by focusing or analysis, but by enlarging or synthesis. For example, a problem of low earnings, which affected stockholders, would first of all be understood in terms of the entire stakeholder system, which formed the context of the problem. The concerns of other stakeholders as they relate to the problem of low earnings would first be explicated. Ackoff argued that system design could only be accomplished by stakeholder participation, and thereby argued for the inclusion of stakeholder groups in solving system-wide problems.[13] Ackoff (1974) contains case studies of how to use this methodology in designing large-scale projects.

The concept of corporate or organizational strategy, on this systems view, seemed to give way to that of collective strategy, a now popular concept in organization theory.[14] It would be a mistake, in systems terms, to take the point of view of planning for one organization in the system, for such a plan might optimize a sub-system and destroy larger system goals and objectives. Organizational planning should be done only so far as it is relevant to system goals.

There are two variants of this position which are important to consider. The first might be called "the co-optation" view, where an organization and its stakeholders plan together for the future of the organization. Larger system goals are ignored or postponed as the organization and its stakeholders try to reach agreements (hopefully mutually beneficial ones, as "co-optation" may imply "cooperation") on how the organization is to proceed. The second variant involves the collaboration of a subset of stakeholders planning for

[13] Ackoff here is clearly influenced by Trist, the Tavistock group, and others, at least according to Slinger (1998).

[14] See Fombrun and Astley (1983).

the future of each. This idea is best exemplified by labor-management planning of quality of work life experiments, and Trist's (1981) work on socio-technical systems.

Each of these variants tries to overcome the general problem with the systems view that there is not a starting point, or entry point, from which collaboration towards "the systems view point," which is necessarily "god-like," can proceed. Thus a utility might sit down with its "consumer advocate" stakeholder and try to plan how it should proceed with a rate increase proposal. But to create the future of the stakeholder system which includes the utility, consumer group, and other stakeholders is a much more difficult, if not impossible, task. The systems model of stakeholders, by emphasizing participation, is a far-reaching view of the nature of organizations and society. It continues to be quite useful in problem formulation, and represents an ongoing stream of research using the stakeholder concept. It is not, however, focused on solving strategic management problems which are narrower than total system design.

The corporate social responsibility literature

Another trail from the original work at SRI on the stakeholder concept was the concern of a number of researchers with the social responsibility of business organizations. The corporate social responsibility literature is too diverse to catalogue here.[15] It has spawned many ideas, concepts, and techniques and brought about both real and ephemeral change in organizations. Suffice it to say that the social movements of the sixties and seventies concerning civil rights, anti-war efforts, consumerism, environmentalism, and women's rights served as a catalyst for rethinking the role of the business enterprise in society.

The distinguishing feature of the literature on corporate social responsibility is that it can be viewed as applying the stakeholder concept to non-traditional stakeholder groups that are usually thought of as having an adversarial relationship with the firm. In particular, less emphasis is put on satisfying owners and comparatively more emphasis is put on the public, the community, or the employees.

During this period two major groups of researchers emerged to form a sub-discipline in management, variously called "business and society" or "social issues in management." In the School of Management at Berkeley a number of scholars began to address a broad range of issues. Votaw (1964) studied

[15] We undertake a partial review of this literature in Chapter 8.

corporate power in Europe. Epstein (1969) conducted a classic study of business and the political arena in the USA. Sethi (1970) analyzed the role of minorities in the firm. During roughly the same period, the Harvard Business School undertook a project on corporate social responsibility. The output of the project was voluminous, and of particular importance was the development of a pragmatic model of social responsibility called "the corporate social responsiveness model." Essentially it addressed Dill's challenge with respect to social issues, namely, how can the corporation respond proactively to the increased pressure for positive social change? By concentrating on "responsiveness" instead of "responsibility" the Harvard researchers were able to link the analysis of social issues with the traditional areas of strategy and organization (Ackerman 1975; Ackerman and Bauer 1976; Murray 1976).[16] And they avoided the clearly moral notion of "responsibility," so that the separation fallacy continued to work.

For the most part stakeholders were analyzed at a generic level, even though Ackerman and Bauer analyzed how to integrate social objectives with traditional business objectives and thus return to Ansoff's original argument. Hargreaves and Dauman (1975) coined the phrase "stakeholder audit" as a part of the more generic "corporate social audit" (Bauer and Fenn 1972). The purpose of the social audit and the resulting literature on social performance was to rethink the traditional scorecard for business. The social audit attempted to construct a social "balance sheet," and to analyze the actions of a firm in terms of social costs and benefits. Methodological problems, however, have made the search for the social analog of the balance sheet and income statement an elusive one.

In addition to these concepts that analyzed the social responsibility of business, there is a much older body of literature on which scholars in business and society have drawn. Historians, political scientists, economists (especially the more recent public-choice economists), and political philosophers have been concerned with the relationship between the corporation and government. Epstein (1969) has analyzed the literature on the role of the corporation in US politics and concluded that "at the present time, corporations should not be subject to special restrictions limiting the nature and extent of their political involvement," going on to argue that "associational political participants" should be governed by requirements on disclosure and lobbying. Epstein (1969, 1980) pointed out that there was an amazing scarcity of scholarship on corporate political activity. While kindred concepts in the

[16] For a recent update and more complete history see Frederick (2006).

political science literature, such as "constituency" (see Mitnick 1980 for a review), "interest group," "publics," and "the public interest," have been around for some time, there were few besides the "institutional economists" such as John R. Commons who recognized and dealt with the complex situation in which the modern corporation found itself.

While there were many criticisms of the research into corporate social responsibility, perhaps the most troubling aspect was the very nature of "corporate social responsibility," as if the concept were needed to augment the study of business policy. Corporate social responsibility was often looked at as an "add-on" to "business as usual," and the observation often heard from executives was that "corporate social responsibility is fine, if you can afford it." This conceptual split between the "profit-making" aspect of business and the "profit-spending" or "socially responsible" part was and continues to be mirrored in the academic world, where the Academy of Management has a division concerned with "social issues in management" and one concerned with "business policy and strategy."[17]

Given the turbulence that business organizations faced and the very nature of the external environment, consisting of economic and socio-political forces, there was a need for conceptual schemata which analyzed these forces in an integrative fashion. Isolating "social issues" as separate from the economic impact which they had, and conversely isolating economic issues as if they had no social effect, missed the mark both managerially and intellectually.

While the corporate social responsibility literature was important in bringing to the foreground in organizational research a concern with social and political issues, it failed to indicate ways of integrating these concerns into the strategic systems of the corporation in a non-ad hoc fashion.

The organization theory literature

While most organization theorists did not specifically use the term "stakeholder," their work remains a constant source of insight. In Sweden, Eric Rhenman (1968) explicitly used the stakeholder concept in his work on industrial democracy.[18] Rhenman argued,

[17] While too much cannot be made of the way in which professional organizations choose to organize themselves, it should be noted that such an organizational principle could tend to reinforce the split between "business" and "social" issues from an intellectual standpoint.

[18] Mason and Mitroff (1982) mistakenly give Rhenman credit for developing the stakeholder concept. Professor Kirk Hanson, now of Santa Clara University, was instrumental in tracking down the influence of Rhenman on the development of the stakeholder concept. According to Hanson, in private conversation, Rhenman spent time at Stanford as a visiting scholar while he was writing *Industrial Democracy and Industrial Management* (1968). Curiously enough, the stakeholder concept does not play a role in Rhenman (1973).

We shall be using the term "stakeholders" to designate the individuals or groups which depend on the company for the realization of their personal goals and on whom the company is dependent. In that sense employees, owners, customers, suppliers, creditors as well as many other groups can all be regarded as stakeholders in the company. (Rhenman 1968, cited in Freeman 1984: 45)

While similar to the SRI concept, Rhenman's definition was narrower, including any group that placed demands on the company and on whom the company had claims, rather than any group whose support was necessary for the survival of the firm. Rhenman went on to argue that a "stakeholder" conception of the firm could lead to a theory of industrial democracy. Rhenman's use of the stakeholder concept paralleled its use at SRI. Again, he was interested in stakeholders at the generic level or as categories of particular groups. His narrow construal of the concept, using "and" to denote the fact that the company and stakeholder must have mutual claims, could rule out important groups, most notably government and adversarial groups, who were dependent on the firm, but on whom the firm did not depend.

During the same period several other organization theorists were concerned with exploring the relationship between organization and environment. In the early 1960s William Evan began to develop the concept of "organization-set" which analyzes the interactions of an organization with "the network of organizations in its environment." Evan (1966) postulated several concepts and hypotheses which could be used to study interorganizational phenomena, arguing that the majority of organizational research had concentrated instead on intra-organizational relationships. Evan's work led to a host of subsequent research on interorganizational relationships, both conceptual and empirical. During roughly the same period important conceptual models were developed by Katz and Kahn (1966), calling for an "open-systems" approach to the study of organizations, which focused on defining the organization relative to the larger system of which it is a part, and by Emery and Trist (1965), exploring the second-order environments of organizations – the connections which occur among environmental elements which affect the organization. Lawrence and Lorsch (1967) proposed a model of "differentiation and integration," whereby organizations segmented themselves into smaller units to deal with specific parts of the external environment. Van de Ven, Emmett, and Koenig (1975) reviewed the organization–environment literature and proposed several meta-conceptual schemes for understanding the burgeoning research. Nystrom and Starbuck (1981) contained essays which assessed the state of the art in understanding the organization–environment relationship. Of particular importance in this volume was the work of Aldrich and Whetten on the concept of "populations" of organizations and their evolution, and network analysis which claimed to "go beyond" the concept of the "organization set" and the attention to stakeholders. Pennings analyzed the concept of "strategically interdependent organizations," and proposed a set of strategies which organizations could use to cope with the uncertainty that comes with interdependence. Other essays in this volume, as well as in two additional volumes of essays by Katz, Kahn and Adams (1980) and Van de Ven and Joyce (1981), were rich sources of ideas for the development of the stakeholder concept as it applied to strategic management.

James Thompson's (1967) classic study of organizations resurrected the notion of "clientele" as a way to designate outside groups, and used Dill's notion of the "task environment" of the organization. Thompson put the notion quite simply: "We are now working with those organizations in the environment which make a difference to the organization in question" (Dill 1958: 28).

It is precisely this notion of "those groups which make a difference" which was the foundation of the stakeholder concept. This is especially true from a strategic standpoint, since the main concern should be the management of the relationships of those groups which "make a difference." Mahon (1982) argued explicitly that Thompson, when his views on the social responsibilities of organizations were taken into account, anticipated the stakeholder notion.

Pfeffer and Salancik (1978) reviewed the literature and constructed a model of organization–environment interaction which depended on an analysis of the resources of the organization and the relative dependence of the organization on environmental actors to provide those resources. While they did not explicitly define "stakeholders," they did claim that

> Our position is that organizations survive to the extent that they are effective. Their effectiveness derives from the management of demands, particularly the demands of interest groups upon which the organizations depend for resources and support. (Pfeffer and Salancik 1978: 2)

They went on to argue for a "radical" external view of organizations, where theorists would look to the environment for most of the explanatory force in organization theory. They argued that while many had claimed the need to look at the external environment, few theorists had developed concepts which allowed the environment to enter into the organizational equation. Their definition of interest groups in terms of dependence and resources was quite similar to the SRI concept of stakeholders, even though there were no references to a reasonable body of work on stakeholder theory in the strategy literature. And there did seem to be a wall separating the work in organization theory from the work in strategy. As a result, the literature of organization theory stopped short of producing a framework for setting and implementing direction in organizations. There was little explicit "fit" between the organization theory literature and the strategy literature, as well as the systems theory and corporate social responsibility literatures. While these four literature streams provided a rich set of ideas for the construction of a stakeholder approach to solving the problems of value creation and trade, ethics, and mindsets, little effort was made in this direction.

The development of stakeholder theory: additions and revisions

There have been a number of additions and revisions to this now standard story of the development of the stakeholder idea. First of all, Giles Slinger has told a slightly different, but important, story about the development at SRI. Second, Juha Näsi has told a different story about the use of the idea in Scandinavia and the work of Eric Rhenman. Finally, a number of people, such as Lee Preston, Melissa Schilling, and others, have pointed out that the intellectual history of the main ideas of stakeholder theory is much richer than the relatively recent work at SRI. We shall deal with each of these in turn.

Slinger's revision of the SRI story

Giles Slinger's doctoral thesis at Cambridge retraced the original history of the stakeholder idea. Slinger began with the history as set forth in Freeman (1984), then made several important additions and reinterpretations. First of all, he re-contacted the same people at SRI as had Freeman, but Slinger obtained more detail about the origins of the stakeholder idea, as he was able to examine more of the original documents at SRI, which were unavailable to Freeman. We quote here a fascinating footnote in Slinger's dissertation which tells the story of how the word evolved.[19]

[19] Slinger's entire dissertation, "Essays on stakeholding," is worth reading, yet it has never been published as a whole. He has published several papers, but none are as inclusive about the history of the stakeholder

Bill Royce, in an unpublished paper written in January 1998, says,

"I asked Bob Stewart. His version was that in late 1962, the team that was writing *The Strategic Plan* were discussing the question of who should have an influence on the determination of 'corporate purpose' (or mission) – considered by most people the keystone on which any strategy or strategic plan must be built. They listed the various persons or groups who contributed to the success of a business and whose needs or demands must be heeded, at least to some extent, by management.

"Other authors with Stewart were J. Knight Allen, J. Morse Cavender, both senior industrial economists on the SRI staff. Marion Doscher was a staff writer with the TAPP group ... I recall her as well-educated, an excellent editor and writer. She was only at SRI a few years.

"According to Stewart, it was during this discussion that Marion Doscher broke in with the assertion that:

'You mean they are all "stakeholders," because they all have a stake in the business!'

"Doscher went on to describe the term as being old Scottish, referring to those who have a legitimate claim on something of value.

"Others in the TAPP (Theory and Practice of Planning) group immediately accepted the term and the definition and it quickly became gospel around SRI. The description was included in the *Strategic Plan* report, with an illustration of a simple method of analyzing stakeholder expectations."

Second, Slinger connects the early development of the stakeholder idea with the human relations approach developed at the Tavistock Institute in London and the National Training Laboratories in Bethel, Maine, in the USA. Bion's work on the role of participation and inclusion in group work, Emery and Trist's work on self-organizing work groups in coal mining, and other mostly clinical (and sometimes psychoanalytic) studies informed most of the early development by the stakeholder theorists in the 1960s.

The Tavistock connection is an important addition to the story in Freeman (1984). Eric Trist was at the Wharton School of the University of Pennsylvania during the 1980s and was a participant in an early Wharton seminar that

idea as the first chapter of the dissertation. The question that remains is the exact connection of Rhenman with SRI. Freeman (1984) is based on a private conversation between Freeman and Professor Kirk Hanson, then of Stanford, now of Santa Clara University. Hanson told Freeman that Rhenman had been a visitor at Stanford at around the same time as the stakeholder idea was being developed at SRI. Stymne (2004) says that it was customary for Swedish doctoral students to spend a year in the USA; he does not mention where Rhenman chose to study. Stymne himself chose to go to the Institute for Social Research (ISR), University of Michigan, which at the time was still under the influence of Kurt Lewin. Hence there is a nice connection to Slinger's claim about the importance of the Tavistock Institute and the human relations view of the stakeholder idea. For purposes of full disclosure it should be noted that Freeman was the external examiner for Slinger's dissertation at Cambridge.

Freeman (2005) believed was so important to the development of the theory. Indeed, the entire approach of the researchers at Wharton – Ackoff, Emshoff, Mitroff, Freeman, and others – was a clinical one. To try to find statistical relationships between stakeholders and to "prove" that managing for stakeholders creates economic value constitute a relatively recent phenomenon. The appropriate background disciplines for stakeholder theory were, according to Slinger, psychoanalysis and social psychology, especially the theory of groups, and their allied disciplines. Business disciplines were important, but they contained built-in assumptions about why stakeholders could be ignored, and why relationships were not the basis of business.[20]

Slinger claims that the result of missing the Tavistock connection is that Freeman's definition of stakeholders relies on a later version of the idea that emerged from SRI, rather than the original definition, which he claims is as follows:

> Determination of corporate purpose requires comprehensive information about the expectations of the firm's "stakeholders." (These are all groups – such as owners, employees, and suppliers – who have something directly at stake in the company's progress.) [21]

The original idea was not a matter of firm survival but rather a way to understand how a firm could meet the expectations of groups in its environment. Thus the original intention of the stakeholder idea was less to redefine business in stakeholder terms, and more to make it responsive to external demands. In short, it looks as if the original insight is more in keeping with Barnard's (1938) and March and Simon's (1958) idea of inducements and contributions.[22]

Näsi's revision of the Scandinavian story

The late Juha Näsi (1995) recounted a slightly different history of the idea as it was brought to Scandinavia, in particular to Finland and Sweden. Näsi rightly

[20] We seek to rectify this situation in this book by showing how the stakeholder idea is relevant to the disciplines of business. However, we also believe that we need much stronger connection with the foundational disciplines such as psychoanalysis, social psychology, philosophy, history, literature, and the creative arts.

[21] Slinger at p. 49 note 146 gives the reference as Stewart, Allen, and Cavender (1963): 1.

[22] There is one difficulty here in reconciling all the parts of Slinger's view. If we go to Emery and Trist's idea of turbulent social fields, as it emerged from their Tavistock work, it does seem as if the two definitions become a matter of degree, depending on the amount of turbulence. But perhaps it is better to see the idea of stakeholders as necessary for survival as more appropriate for the more economic views of the firm that are influential in business today. What we could mean by a "behavioral stakeholder theory" is an interesting open question. We are indebted to Professor Jared Harris for this insight.

credits with the main impulses of the idea Barnard (1938), Dill (1958), March and Simon (1958), Cyert and March (1963), and Thompson (1967), though others have gone even farther back, as we shall see later. He claims that while the stakeholder idea may have been marginal in the USA and most of the rest of the world, it had a large impact in Scandinavia. Näsi locates the idea in the thinking of Eric Rhenman (1964) and in Rhenman and Stymne's book (1965), in which they "explicitly outlined the stakeholder approach or, as they themselves put it, the stakeholder theory" (Näsi 1995: 20). Rhenman in 1964 defined "stakeholder" as follows:

> Stakeholders in an organization are the individuals and groups who are depending on the firm in order to achieve their personal goals and on whom the firm is depending for its existence. (Rhenman, quoted in Näsi 1995: 22)

Interestingly enough, this original definition could be seen as including both Freeman's wide sense of stakeholders, since there are many groups on whom one's personal success depends, as well as the narrow sense, in terms of firm survival.

Näsi suggests that for these early Scandinavian theorists the concept of the transaction plays a more central role than that of overall "interests" or "stake." Näsi writes,

> The Scandinavians preferred to talk about the contributions made by the stakeholders to the company and about the rewards which the stakeholders demand from it. Both contributions and rewards can take many forms, such as money, goods, information, status, power, prestige and so on.[23] (23)

This view is corroborated in a recent autobiographical essay by Bengt Stymne (2004). Stymne tells of being a doctoral student sequestered in the attic of the Stockholm School of Economics, studying administration in the late 1950s and early 1960s. He and others such as Eric Rhenman, a fellow doctoral student, began to look at the firm from the outside in, rather than from the perspective of a set of internally defined goals. He writes that during this period they began to see that

> [G]oals are a product of the exchange process among the various stakeholders that make up the firm. What one stakeholder contributes will serve as a reward for another. Through mutual adjustments, an unstable balance between contributions and rewards is temporarily created. Like a drunk on his way from the pub, the firm is

[23] Näsi cites Rhenman (1964), Rhenman and Stymne (1965), Ahlstedt and Jahnukainen (1971), and Näsi (1979, 1982) as the key sources here.

stumbling along to regain the balance it is constantly on the verge of losing. The goal of the firm which could be imputed from this perspective, if any, is not one set by management or the owner but rather is to obtain an unstable balance so as to survive. (Stymne 2004: 39)

This passage locates the idea of stakeholders in the work of the Carnegie School and their idea of inducements and contributions. However, the idea of the "unstable balance" is quite interesting, since it leads to the idea, discussed in Chapter 1, of the equilibrating, entrepreneurial forces. Friction among stakeholders becomes the source of organizational innovation, and in fact saves the modern corporation from the bureaucratic fate envisioned by Schumpeter.

Indeed, in *Administrative Behavior* in 1947,[24] Simon identifies customers, employees, suppliers, and entrepreneurs as organizational participants in the inducement–contribution model that forms the foundation of the behavioral theory. Organizational goals are a function of these several groups, rather than of one. March and Simon's (1958) view of organizations, and Cyert and March's (1963) work on behavioral theory are important precursors of stakeholder theory. Of course these thinkers owe much, as they acknowledge, to Barnard (1938). It is Barnard, rather than his Carnegie School followers, who seems to understand more explicitly the centrality of morality – what we have called the problem of the ethics of capitalism – at least to the role of the executive. He writes, foreshadowing the development of modern views of business ethics that are grounded in stakeholder theory,

Executive positions (a) imply a complex morality, and (b) require a high capacity of responsibility, (c) under conditions of activity, necessitating (d) commensurate general and specific technical abilities as a moral factor … In addition there is required (e) the faculty of creating morals for others …

For the morality that underlies enduring cooperation is multi-dimensional. It comes from and may expand to all the world; it is rooted deeply in the past, it faces toward the endless future. As it expands, it must become more complex, its conflicts must be more numerous and deeper, its call for abilities must be higher, its failures of ideal attainment must be perhaps more tragic; but the quality of leadership, the persistence of its influence, the durability of its related organizations, the power of the coordination it incites, all express the height of moral aspirations, the breadth of moral foundations. (Barnard 1938: 272, 284)

[24] See Simon (1947). The fourth edition, which was consulted here, was published in 1997. See especially 141 ff.

Barnard here articulates the problems of value creation and trade, the ethics of capitalism, and managerial mindsets. In our view it is really Barnard who set the stage for the development of modern stakeholder theory.

Additional underlying ideas

A number of scholars have suggested that in addition to those already suggested there were many who could be seen as early stakeholder theorists. In particular, Preston and Sapienza (1990) have traced the origins of the underlying idea of stakeholders further back from SRI and Rhenman to some early documents at both Johnson and Johnson and at Sears. They write,

> The truth, however, is that the substance of the stakeholder concept, if not the term itself, has been reflected in the speeches and writings of thoughtful analysts and executives for many decades. The classic formal statement by Harvard law professor E. Merrick Dodd appeared in 1932. Dodd (1932) quoted with approval the views of General Electric executives and others who identified four major stakeholder groups: shareholders, employees, customers, and the general public. (Dodd's famous piece appeared in the course of a debate with Yale law professor A. A. Berle, who at that time defended conventional views. More than twenty years later, Berle (1954) acknowledged that Dodd had been right all along; see also Rostow (1959).) Robert Wood Johnson's list of "strictly business" stakeholders – customers, employees, managers, and shareholders (the managers were a new and subsequently significant addition) – first appeared in print in 1947 (Johnson (1947)), and ultimately evolved into the well-known Johnson and Johnson "Credo" (Buchholz (1989) at 230). In 1950, General Robert E. Wood, CEO of Sears, listed the "four parties to any business" (in, he said, "the order of their importance") as "customers, employees, community, and stockholders." (quoted in Worthy 1984: 64)

In a remarkable article in the 1956 *Dartmouth Alumni Magazine*, J. Irwin Miller, chairman of the Cummins Engine Company, articulates the responsibilities of the executive along similar lines. He claims that the power of the manager must be used responsibly towards shareholders, customers, suppliers, employees, government, community, and society. It is perhaps the clearest articulation of the modern stakeholder theory without using the term.[25]

[25] J. Irwin Miller, "The responsibilities of management," *Dartmouth Alumni Magazine* (March 1956). We are grateful to his son, Will Miller, CEO of Irwin Financial, for this reference and a conversation about the way in which the Miller family has always tried to run its companies along stakeholder lines. We discuss this version of leadership and use Will Miller as an example in Freeman, Harrison, and Wicks (2007), Chapter 6.

Slinger takes the idea even further back. He locates the concept partly in the view of business as a social institution put forward by Robert Owen, John Ruskin, and others. However, he differentiates this idea from what he calls the distinctiveness of the modern idea of stakeholders by its emphasis on "inclusiveness." He argues that the Christian communities of the 1930s focused on the company as not being the property of shareholders. He singles out the work of George Goyder and Samuel Courtauld. In a newsletter he finds as evidence: "'Shareholders are merely one of several groups of people who, each in their different ways, go to make up a company.'"[26] Goyder goes on to propose the concepts of social audit and responsible company at around the same time as Harold Bowen, who is generally seen as one of the originators of the idea of corporate social responsibility.[27]

Slinger, Freeman (1984), and most others simply ignore the work of Mary Parker Follet. In an important paper Melissa Schilling (2000) has convincingly argued that while the role of Barnard and the subsequent Carnegie School has been well documented in the stakeholder theory literature, theorists have overlooked Follet's ideas. Her relational view of both the self and organization is a far better starting point than Barnard's view of the role of the executive. In fact Follet can also be seen as a founder of the human relations school, which gave rise to the work of theorists such as Bion, Lewin, and others.

Finally, in a recent article Shah and Bhaskar (2008) have suggested that the basic idea of the modern stakeholder concept can be traced to ancient Indian scriptures.[28] They make a cogent argument that the very nature of business activity, what we have called "value creation and trade," can be understood in stakeholder terms. We shall return to this theme in Chapter 9.

While Freeman has often suggested that his role in the development of stakeholder theory has been to show how the concept was developed by others, and to take it seriously as a management principle, the evolution of the modern idea is often traced to his 1984 book. We believe that it is therefore instructive to look at how that book came to be written. In particular, we believe that the role of "the author"[29] and the serendipity which governs forms of life have not been thoroughly investigated. This is especially important given the diffuse nature of the development of ideas like stakeholder theory.

[26] *Christian News-Letter*, Supplement to No. 242 (1943–5), 9. This note is due to Slinger.

[27] This fascinating story is told in Chapter 1 of Slinger (1998).

[28] We are grateful to Dr. Harish Srivatsava for helpful conversations on this issue and for pointing out to us the work of Professor N. Balasubramanian, "Corporate governance in India: traditional and scriptural perspectives," *Executive Chartered Secretary* (March 2005), 279–282.

[29] In the sense of "any author," not Freeman per se.

We argue that the actual lineage of an idea is relatively unimportant relative to its usefulness. However, we do need to understand more thoroughly how ideas accidentally get developed. Hence we tell the following personal and idiosyncratic story.

The development of stakeholder theory: Freeman's personal story

After studying philosophy and mathematics at Duke University and graduate study in philosophy at Washington University in St. Louis, Freeman accepted an appointment on the research staff at the Wharton School, University of Pennsylvania, with a group called the Busch Center, run by Russell Ackoff, acknowledged as a pioneer in operations research and systems theory.[30] After working at the Busch Center on several projects for a few months Freeman moved to a new splinter group started by James R. Emshoff, a former student under Ackoff. This new group was called "the Wharton Applied Research Center," and its mission was to serve as "Wharton's window to the world," a kind of real-world consulting arm that would combine research staff, students, and the Wharton faculty. This new center was organized much like a traditional consulting firm, by projects and by "development areas," which were conceptual spaces where the center wanted to develop both expertise and new clients to try out ideas.[31]

The stakeholder concept was very much in the air at the Busch Center. Ackoff had written about the idea, extensively in *Redesigning the Future* (1974).[32] And the idea was at the center of several projects under way at the Center. In particular, the Scientific Communication and Technology Transfer project funded by the National Science Foundation, as a kind of Library of the Future design project, used the idea of getting stakeholder input into radical

[30] To illustrate what we said earlier about the role of serendipity, Freeman would never have accepted an appointment at Wharton – indeed, he did not even know what or where Wharton was – but for the fact that his girlfriend, Maureen Wellen, now his wife of more than thirty years, was studying fine arts at graduate school at Pennsylvania.

[31] The center never got much traction with the traditional Wharton faculty, and was eventually privatized; it exists today in Philadelphia as the Applied Research Center under the leadership of Dr. Lynn Oppenheim, a psychologist.

[32] To expand on the story begun in note 30, Freeman originally got an interview at Wharton because Professor Richard Rudner's son, an anthropology student at Penn, knew people at the Busch Center, and Rudner knew that Ackoff had a philosophy degree. (Rudner was on Freeman's dissertation committee.) What no one knew was that Ackoff was in a period of reasonable hostility towards academic philosophers. But none of this mattered since he was out of the country when Freeman interviewed, and left these hiring decisions to others.

system redesign. More relevant to business, the idea had been used in assessing the strategic direction of a large Mexican brewer which was dealing with its government and other key stakeholders. However, the use of the idea at that time was mainly as a way of organizing thinking about the external environment, or in thinking about system design.

At around the same time Ian Mitroff was visiting at the Busch Center, and he and Emshoff and Richard Mason were working on strategic assumptions analysis, a project in which the stakeholder idea was used to organize the assumptions that executives made about their external environment. This use of the stakeholder idea as an organizing concept was consistent with the original use at Stanford Research Institute.

There was little in the way of a "management approach" that could help executives actually make decisions, other than at a very high level.[33] At around this same time Emshoff and Ackoff organized a "faculty seminar" around "what are we to make of this 'stakeholder' idea?" Eric Trist, Howard Perlmutter (management), Alan Shapiro (finance), and a few others attended. Freeman was a very junior person, without even a faculty appointment at the lowest level. He listened intently to these senior people discussing how they interpreted the stakeholder idea. There seemed to him to be a common thread in the seminar, and that was the reluctance of any of these management thinkers to talk about issues of values, ethics, or justice. At almost every meeting someone would draw a stakeholder "wheel and spoke" map on the board, throwing their hands up in the air and claiming, "Well, that's a normative problem of distributive justice, and we can't say anything about that." As a philosopher, Freeman was fairly naive, and had not yet experienced the fanatical concern with "method" and "positive" and "empirical" that so defines most business school intellectuals. He remembers thinking, "Well, I can certainly say something about normative and justice issues."

Emshoff encouraged Freeman to begin exploring these ideas and writing about them and, together, they prepared a working paper, entitled "Stakeholder management," that was sent out to a mailing list of companies and people. At some point in 1977, some executives from the Human Resources Department at AT&T came to the Applied Research Center to discuss developing a portion of a four-week seminar for their "leaders of the future." They had done a survey of their Bell System officers, and "how to manage the external environment" ranked high on the list of skills needed by the leaders of the future.

[33] And the idea of using stakeholder theory for "sense making" or "framing" simply had not occurred to anyone as far as we know.

While Emshoff and Freeman were novices at executive education, they believed that they had something to offer on the basis of thinking about how the stakeholder idea could anchor an approach to managerial decision making. Ram Charan, at the time from Northwestern, Fred Sturdivant from Ohio State, and Mel Horwitch from Harvard were also working with AT&T on this project, and they designed a one-week course that was aimed at sensitizing managers to the need to deal with stakeholders, giving them some tools and techniques for tasks like prioritizing stakeholders, and putting them into a decision-making simulation where they had to confront live strategic issues of importance to the company. The design involved a number of real stakeholders in the training and, over time, the team created a very successful experience.[34]

These ideas were developed in two papers. The first was a conceptual paper laying out the argument for why managers needed an active managerial approach for thinking about stakeholders. "Stakeholder" was defined in a broad strategic sense as "any group or individual that can affect or is affected by the achievement of a corporation's purpose." While this definition has been the subject of much debate in the ensuing years, the basic idea was quite simple. Freeman and Emshoff were taking the viewpoint of the executive, and the claim was that if a group or individual could affect the firm (or be affected by it, and reciprocate), then executives should worry about that group in the sense that it needed an explicit strategy for dealing with that particular stakeholder.

Emshoff and Freeman (1981) developed some of the techniques of "stakeholder management," as they began to call it, in a paper for a volume of applications of management science. In "Stakeholder management: A case study of the US brewers and the container issue," they looked at the Center's ongoing work with the United States Brewers Association and their struggle over what to do about taxes, recycling, and regulation of beverage containers. At that time Freeman and Emshoff were enamored of the promise of applying management science techniques to allocating resources among stakeholders more accurately, a view which Freeman now believes to be deeply wrongheaded and mistaken. But they did develop a useful way of thinking about stakeholder behavior in terms of thinking through actual behavior, cooperative potential, and competitive threat for each stakeholder group.[35]

[34] At least by the measure of the number of managers who were "trained," it was successful. Freeman recalls that over a period of something over six years, more than a thousand managers were trained in the one-week seminars. Literally thousands more were given a one-day version of the course.

[35] For a modern version of these techniques see Freeman, Harrison, and Wicks (2007), Chapter 5, and Harrison and St. John (1998).

During the same time they developed a managerial version of the same material published in the *Wharton Magazine*, entitled pretentiously, "Who's butting into your business?" (Freeman and Emshoff 1979).[36] This was an attempt to show managers that stakeholders had at least "managerial legitimacy" – that is, from a strategic standpoint executives needed to put explicit strategies into place. They drew from their clinical experiences with the Bell companies, since they had begun to carry out many consulting/applied research projects after the successful seminars in the late 1970s. And Ram Charan and Freeman published a paper, "Negotiating with stakeholders" (1980), in a magazine put out by AMACOM, that focused on what they had learned about the negotiation process with a variety of stakeholder groups.

The questions which Freeman had during this time were pretty straightforward: (i) Could one develop a method for executives to strategically manage stakeholder relationships as a routine ongoing part of their day-to-day activities? (ii) Could strategic management as a discipline be recast along stakeholder lines rather than as the six tasks of Schendel and Hofer? And (iii) why was any of this thinking controversial, since it seemed to be complete "common sense" to Freeman?[37]

While he was not completely ignorant of management theory, Freeman had no systematic knowledge of any of the subfields. He began to read widely in strategy, organization theory, management history, systems theory, and a burgeoning literature on corporate social responsibility. It was here that he encountered what he knew to be philosophically outdated ideas of "theory," "evidence," the "normative–prescriptive" distinction, the "fact–value" distinction, and a whole host of ideas around methodology that was based on the positivist philosophy of the 1920s.[38]

[36] The article was published in the short-lived *Wharton Magazine* after being rejected by the *Harvard Business Review* after multiple revisions. In the words of one of the editors at the time, "I couldn't get the others to agree." There is some irony in the paper's rejection for essentially stakeholder management reasons.

[37] In 1980 serendipity again entered the equation. Freeman's brother was killed in a car accident, and like many when faced with such a personal loss, he was "forced" to think about what he really wanted to do with his life. Did he want to continue consulting (with teaching being a part-time assignment), or did he want to commit to actually trying to answer these questions, and trying to live a more scholarly life? He chose the academic route and was fortunate to be offered a position as assistant professor in the Management Department at Wharton. Freeman set himself the rather clear tasks of working out the stakeholder approach to strategy in a book, and of writing as many scholarly articles as he could to develop the ideas. It was really at this point that Freeman entered the academic world of management theory.

[38] And these ideas still drive most of the research in the business disciplines. See Chapter 3 for an outline of a different view based on philosophical pragmatism.

Essentially he ignored all these "rules and methods for research." He knew that he was dealing with a real problem, "how can executives make better decisions in a world with multiple stakeholder demands?" – what we have earlier called the problem of value creation and trade. And he knew that he was getting the clinical experience through consulting projects with real executives dealing with this real problem, what we have earlier called the problem of managerial mindsets. So Freeman decided to build from his experiences by developing more general ideas about how to systematize the stakeholder approach.

For instance, when he worked with companies whose executives were trying to deal with critical stakeholders by changing their entire points of view about the company, the idea arose that perhaps it would be more fruitful to work on small behavioral changes rather than large attitude changes. When a company expert guaranteed that he knew what a particular stakeholder group wanted from the company, and it turned out to be wrong, Freeman began to question the idea that structuring a team of stakeholder experts was necessarily the best way to run a strategic planning process. The clinical lessons were countless. Unfortunately (but maybe fortunately), Freeman knew nothing about qualitative research or grounded theory or some of the other ways to dress up intelligent observation in scientific clothes. He was stuck with such models as Graham Allison's *Essence of Decision* (1971), Selznick's book on the TVA (Selznick 1966), Freud's clinical studies, and other more classic works of "social science."

Freeman also began to get involved in the management academic community through the Academy of Management. Jim Post of Boston University invited him to give a talk to the Social Issues in Management Division in 1980 in Detroit. Even though he knew little about this group, he agreed because he had read Post's book with Lee Preston (Preston and Post 1975), and knew that it was important. In Detroit, Freeman gave a paper on the idea of stakeholder management, which argued that this was a better unit of analysis than an "issue." There was a lot of heated discussion, although Freeman himself was unsure why anything he had said was controversial.

During this time Freeman began to work with Professor William Evan, a distinguished sociologist at Penn. Evan saw collaborating with Freeman on stakeholder theory as a way to democratize the large corporation. Even though Evan was an impeccable empirical researcher, he immediately saw the normative implications of coming to see business as "serving stakeholders." Evan and Freeman began to meet weekly and talk about how to do the "next project" after *Strategic Management: A Stakeholder Approach*, even though that project was not yet finished. Indeed, they began an empirical study aimed at seeing how chief executive officers made trade-offs among stakeholders. They planned a book that would deal with the normative implications of re-conceptualizing the corporate governance debate in stakeholder terms. They offered a seminar to University of Pennsylvania students on "stakeholder management" around the 1982 academic year. While the book was never finished, they did complete a number of essays, one of which was reprinted countless times in business ethics textbooks. Freeman claims that Evan gave him the courage to tackle the normative dimension in an intellectual atmosphere – the modern, twentieth-century business school – that disdained such analysis. Freeman credits Evan for the inspiration necessary to tackle what we have called the problem of the ethics of capitalism.

In summary, Freeman spent most of his time from 1978 until 1983 teaching executives and working with them to develop very practical ways of understanding how they could be more effective in the relationship with key stakeholders. In the summer of 1982 he sat down at his home in Princeton Junction, New Jersey, and drafted the initial manuscript of *Strategic Management: A Stakeholder Approach.*[39] The purpose was to set forth a method or set of methods or techniques for executives to use to better understand how to manage key stakeholder relationships. In addition, Freeman tried to track down the origins of the stakeholder idea and give credit to its originators and the people whose work he had found so useful.

Strategic management: an assessment of the stakeholder approach

In a recent article in the *Academy of Management Review*, Jim Walsh of the University of Michigan assesses the impact of Freeman's *Strategic Management: A Stakeholder Approach* (1984). Walsh suggests that more people have cited the book than have actually read it.[40] He claims that the

[39] Bill Roberts was starting Pitman Publishing Inc. in the USA, as a subsidiary of Pitman UK. Edwin Epstein, of the University of California, Berkeley, was the editor of a new series, and had encouraged Freeman to work on these ideas. The book was published in 1983 with a 1984 copyright. During late 1982 and early 1983, Freeman made extensive revisions based on notes and conversations with Gordon Sollars, now a professor at Fairleigh Dickenson University, and Edwin Hartman, now a professor at New York University, as well as Roberts and Epstein. Of particular importance during this time was a conversation that Freeman had with William Frederick of the University of Pittsburgh, who encouraged Freeman to write the book he wanted to write, to "say what you have to say."

[40] This is surely borne out in fact. The original and only print run of the book was only 2,500. A recent check of Google Scholar suggests roughly 4,000 citations.

book is a practice-based companion to Pfeffer and Salancik's *The External Control of Organizations*, and that

Many readers may be surprised to learn that the father of stakeholder theory draws such a clear distinction between "real" strategic issues and social responsibility issues, and between the important and the small, insignificant, non-important stakeholders. Readers may cheer his recommendation to create "stakeholder managers" (p. 233) but then chafe when he talks about how they are to be used in a firm: "Stakeholder experts would ideally operate as a profit center within the corporation, selling their services to SBU managers" (p. 236). Of course, the idea of a stakeholder manager running a profit center is perfectly consistent with the business orientation of the book, but the idea of a stakeholder manager justifying her existence on the basis of a positive cash flow is not at all consistent with how so many have reconstructed this book over the past twenty years. This intensely business-first, manager-friendly, strategic management text has somehow left a generation of scholars with the idea that Freeman offered a stakeholder theory to compete with what might be called stockholder theory. (Walsh 2005: 429)

Walsh wonders how the stakeholder idea became a rallying point for issues such as corporate social responsibility when Freeman (1984) explicitly rejects them. Walsh's close reading finds two places in the text where it seems to admit the possibility of something like a stakeholder theory of the firm, but he claims these come "out of the blue." He does not see that part of the point of stakeholder theory was to integrate ethical and social issues directly into strategy, thereby enlarging the field of strategy. Freeman (1984) is not very clear on this issue and it is only articulated later in *Corporate Strategy and the Search for Ethics* (Freeman and Gilbert 1988).[41]

Walsh's conclusion about the usefulness of stakeholder theory[42] is one with which we are in agreement. He writes:

Freeman, Wicks, and Parmar (2004b) recently articulated what they called the core of stakeholder management; it captures this point very nicely: "Managers must develop relationships, inspire their stakeholders, and create communities where everyone strives to give their best to deliver the value the firm promises" (p. 364). Neo-classical economists sometimes overlook the importance of the verb "to manage," along with such attendant verbs as "to develop," "to inspire," and "to create." Stakeholder theory brings these ideas and practices to the fore. (Walsh 2005: 437)

[41] It is worth noting that Freeman thought that this book was an important sequel to Freeman (1984). However, it was not very widely read; Google Scholar lists only 235 citations.

[42] Walsh's review includes the work of Post, Preston, and Sachs (2002a, 2002b) and Phillips (2003).

Our conclusions about this work are quite similar. *Strategic Management* contained an underlying narrative about how to be a more effective executive. The "evidence" for this approach was the conversations that Freeman had had with literally thousands of executives over the previous seven years, plus the countless stories in the business press about good and bad stakeholder management, clinical experiences at Wharton with a number of clients and companies, and a small literature on the stakeholder idea. And, it was fundamentally about business – about solving what we have called here the problem of value creation and trade.

The point of the book was clear to us – in what way could executives and academics think about strategy or strategic management if they took the stakeholder concept seriously, or as the basic unit of analysis of whatever framework they applied?[43] The basic insight was to suggest that a more useful unit of analysis for thinking about strategy was the stakeholder relationship, rather than the tasks of "formulating, implementing, evaluating, etc." or the idea of "industry," or the other myriad ideas of the times. Freeman took this to be a matter of common sense and practicality, rather than some deep academic insight. Executives found thinking about stakeholder relationships very helpful for dealing with the kinds of change that were confronting their corporations. It seemed to bring some clarity to what we have called the problem of value creation and trade.

[43] Freeman (2005: 423) claims: "The approach of the book was modeled after what I took to be some of the best writing I had encountered that tried to interweave clinical cases and facts with the development of insights and ideas. So, I relied on the 'clinical cases' I had worked on with a number of companies over these years, as well as my reading of the business press, case studies written by others, and my conversations with other people (experts) worried about the same phenomena. Again I was trained as a philosopher, so what was important to me was the overall logic of the argument. I found the insistence of some colleagues on empirical methods and an obsession with 'methodology' to be highly amusing and full of logic mistakes. Surely the insights of thinkers like Freud or Harry Levinson in management, or Graham Allison in politics, did not become questionable because of their methods, but because of their logic. The obsession with what Richard Rorty has called 'methodolatry' continues even in this world of critical studies, post-modernism, pragmatism, and other assorted post-positivist justifications of intellectual activity. I confess to paying no attention to methods. Perhaps if I had kept careful notes, interview transcripts, had a panel of experts sort all of the 'data,' I could have gained even more insight into the phenomena of businesses trying to deal with stakeholder relationships. However, I thought that all of this stuff was just silly window dressing. I never had interest in the question, 'Are you doing something that is descriptive of the way companies act, or are you prescribing how they should act, or are you suggesting that if they act in this way it will lead to these results?' Donaldson and Preston (1995) have suggested that stakeholder theory can be separated into descriptive, prescriptive, and instrumental categories. I thought I was doing all three and that any good theory or narrative ought to do all three. In short the stakeholder approach has always been what Donaldson and Preston have called 'managerial.' There is more than adequate philosophical justification for such an approach and Andy Wicks and I (1998) have tried to set forth such a pragmatist 'methodology.'"

We would summarize *Strategic Management: A Stakeholder Approach* in the following logical schemata:

1. No matter what you stand for, no matter what your ultimate purpose may be, you must take into account the effects of your actions on others, as well as their potential effects on you.
2. Doing so means that you have to understand stakeholder behaviors, values, and backgrounds or contexts, including the societal context. To be successful over time it will be better to have a clear answer to the question, "what do we stand for?"
3. There are a few well-defined ways to think about stakeholder management, or focal points, that can serve as answers to the question, "what do we stand for?" or enterprise strategy.[44]
4. We need to understand how stakeholder relationships work at three levels of analysis: the rational, or "organization as a whole"; the process, or standard operating procedures; and the transactional, or day-to-day bargaining.[45]
5. We can apply these ideas to think through new structures, processes, and business functions, and we can especially rethink how the strategic planning process works to take stakeholders into account.
6. Stakeholder interests need to be balanced over time.

This argument has a number of implications. If it is correct, then the idea of "corporate social responsibility" is probably superfluous. Since stakeholders are defined widely and their concerns are integrated into the business processes, there is simply no need for a separate CSR approach. Social issues management or the "issue" is simply the wrong unit of analysis. Groups and individuals behave, not issues. Issues emerge through the behavior and interaction of stakeholders, therefore "stakeholder" is a more fundamental and useful unit of analysis. Finally, the major implication of this argument, which cannot be overemphasized today, given the development of stakeholder theory, is that "stakeholders are about the business, and the business is about the stakeholders."[46]

There are several obvious weaknesses of the book.[47] First of all, much of the language of the book was couched in the idiom of strategic planning in

[44] The book laid out a typology which no one ever took seriously, and the typology is updated in Freeman, Harrison, and Wicks (2007).

[45] These levels are just the three levels in Graham Allison's *Essence of Decision: Explaining the Cuban Missile Crisis* (1971).

[46] We are indebted to Professor John Kay for the phrasing of the issue at a conference of the European Association of Business in Society, held in Ghent in 2005.

[47] During the ensuing twenty years Freeman has continued to try and work out the implications of this basic argument, concentrating on more of the ethical and normative aspects of the stakeholder approach, while steadfastly maintaining that the normative–descriptive distinction is not hard and fast. In 1983 he

general, and Lorange's (1983) version of strategic planning in particular.[48] Therefore there was far too much "process-speak" and far too much "consultant-speak," both of which served as a barrier to understanding the basic idea. Second, the book was overly analytical. One can get the view that if we draw the stakeholder maps accurately enough – model and predict their behavior – then we can cast out uncertainty from the strategic thinking process. Obviously there are limits to our ability to analyze, and just as obviously we can use analysis to hide behind, rather than going out and actively creating capabilities for dealing with, stakeholders. Again, part of this weakness came from relying on the strategic planning literature of the time. Third, there was a tension in the writing of the book between "managerial thinking" and "academic thinking." Chapter 2 was interesting only to academics, by whom it was widely read and cited. Alternatively, almost no one read Chapters 5 and 6, which were interesting only to executives who were trying actually to manage for stakeholders. This tension served neither audience very well. Fourth, the book underestimated the value of questions of purpose, values, ethics, and other elements per Walsh's criticism. While it did crudely follow Drucker (1980) and Schendel and Hofer (1979), in articulating "enterprise strategy," these issues are far more important in the day-to-day management of the enterprise than the book gave credit. Strategic management as a field universally ignored these issues for years, and many scholars continue to do so today.[49] Fifth, there was a missing level of analysis, and so

moved to the University of Minnesota with the explicit understanding that he would be teaching more Ph.D. students, and more ethics. At Wharton Freeman taught primarily business policy and principles of management. At Minnesota he had the opportunity to immerse himself in the business ethics literature, and to try and contribute to it. On reflection, given the split or separation between "business" and "ethics," this may have been a mistake, as it led to many misinterpretations of the basic argument. Once again serendipity played a large part in the decision. Freeman's wife was working for a consulting firm and traveling extensively. They were commuting three hours a day (when everything worked), and the chance for both to have jobs in Minneapolis meant that they could actually spend a lot of time together. As a result of that decision, "stakeholder theory" became more embedded in "business ethics" than it did in strategic management. In 1986 the family, now including their nine-month-old son, decided to move to Virginia and the Darden School. Freeman's charge at Darden was to help build the research capability of the school and the Olsson Center for Applied Ethics, which had been founded in 1967. Again, this personal move can be seen as helping to influence the interpretation of "stakeholder theory" as belonging more to ethics than to management. For the last twenty-three years Freeman has worked with many colleagues at Darden in an environment that is much more like the one at the Wharton Applied Research Center. Darden is very "business oriented," and the basic argument of "stakeholder theory" – that it is about helping executives make better decisions – has found a friendlier home.

[48] Lorange was at Wharton at the time and Freeman was heavily influenced by his ideas.

[49] Once Freeman came to see this as perhaps the most important flaw in the book, he undertook to write what he hoped was a sequel with Daniel R. Gilbert, Jr., entitled *Corporate Strategy and the Search for Ethics* (1988); unfortunately almost no one reads or refers to that book today. Again the role of serendipity emerged. While he was at Minnesota, Dan Gilbert was a doctoral student. Freeman sat in on one of Gilbert's classes to assess his teaching, and the class he chose was one in which Gilbert was

virtually nothing about how business or capitalism would look if we began to understand it as consisting of "creating value for stakeholders." Sixth, there is too much concern with structure in the book. While some of the insights about corporate governance may be interesting, the chapters on recasting the functions of business along stakeholder lines were misguided. The underlying issue is the separation of business and ethics in the foundational disciplines of business, not the practical organization and working of these disciplines.

This book is an attempt to correct some of these inadequacies and resulting misinterpretations in stakeholder theory as it has developed. Like any useful idea, the development of stakeholder theory has been haphazard. There is a tendency to attribute too much intentionality to its developers. We have suggested that there are usually more idiosyncratic explanations about how knowledge evolves. In these first two chapters we have made a number of claims about how theory works, but we have failed to distinguish theories along some more usual lines, such as normative and descriptive. It is time for us to be clearer about our underlying approach and method.

using *Strategic Management: A Stakeholder Approach*, and arguing to the students that Freeman was a utilitarian. An ardent Rawlsian at the time, Freeman was appalled, and determined to fix this inadequacy in the book, so he and Gilbert began to work on *Corporate Strategy and the Search for Ethics*. There are many classes Freeman could have picked to sit in on, and many other topics were covered by the class.

3 Stakeholder theory, pragmatism, and method

Many of the arguments in this book will seem unusual to those scholars who are accustomed to reading the traditional management journals, such as *Academy of Management Review*, *Academy of Management Journal*, and *Administrative Sciences Quarterly*. Indeed, traditional philosophers who teach business ethics and read the *Journal of Business Ethics* and *Business Ethics Quarterly* may also not recognize the kind of arguments that we use here. Each of the intellectual communities of which these journals are a part has fairly well-defined ideas about the use of such terms as "theory," "method," "hypothesis," "proposition," and other philosophical concepts. While we respect, reference, and quote the bodies of literature that are contained in these and many other management and philosophy journals in the succeeding chapters, our approach is somewhat different. Consequently, we want to be as clear as possible that we are philosophical pragmatists about most issues around theory and method. In this short chapter we shall try to say what our view is about this pragmatism and why we believe that it can serve as a set of unifying ideas around a body of literature that has begun to change the underlying narrative about business.

There has been a great deal of discussion about what kind of entity "stakeholder theory" really is. Some have argued that it is not a "theory," because theories are connected sets of testable propositions. Others have suggested that there is just too much ambiguity in the definition of the central term for it ever to be admitted to the status of theory. Still others have suggested that it is an alternative "theory of the firm," contra the shareholder theory of the firm. As philosophical pragmatists we do not have much to say about these debates. We see "stakeholder theory" as a "framework," a set of ideas from which a number of theories[1] can be derived. And we often use "stakeholder theory" to refer to the rather substantial body of scholarship which depends on the centrality of the stakeholder idea or framework. For

[1] In this narrower, accepted sense of "theory" as producing a connected and established set of propositions.

some purposes it is surely advantageous to use the term in very specific ways (e.g. to facilitate certain kinds of theory development and empirical testing), but for others it is not. Think of stakeholder theory as a genre of management theory. That is, rather than being a specific theory used for one purpose (e.g. resource dependence theory in management), seeing stakeholder theory as a "genre" is to recognize the value of the variety of uses one can make of this set of ideas. There is enough commonality across these uses to see them as part of the same genre, but enough diversity to allow them to function in an array of settings and serve different purposes. In the following brief sections we shall try to clarify our pragmatist approach. We begin with an analysis of several recent critiques of business schools in general to set the context for what we hope to offer as an alternative approach. We then describe the pragmatist alternative, focusing on the recent work of philosopher Richard Rorty. Finally we summarize an argument showing how such a pragmatism can serve as a more useful way to think about business and management theory in particular.

The critique of business schools

The dominant narrative of business schools – that management is a science, and can usefully be researched, taught, and practiced in those terms – has a real grip on the hearts and minds of business school professors and administrators. A number of recent critiques have begun the process of self-examination with regard to this assumption.

Pfeffer and Fong (2002) have suggested that the whole idea of the MBA is suspect. They argue that it is neither necessary nor sufficient for business success and, further, that grades earned during this two-year period are not correlated with a flourishing career. The subtext is that much of what MBAs learn is of limited usefulness, that business school research is of limited influence, and that true "evidence-based" management is a rare species. Pfeffer and Fong suggest that most business school researchers get "good science" wrong and that the resulting MBA is overrated and does not much matter. We take Pfeffer and Fong to be arguing that business schools and business school research do not adequately address what we called the problem of value creation and trade because, according to them, researchers get "good science" wrong.

In a recent book, management theorist Henry Mintzberg (2004) has delivered a blistering critique of business education. He suggests that for the most part MBA programs have the wrong students, that students in their mid- to late 20s are simply neither ready for nor capable of learning management. Mintzberg sees management differently from Pfeffer and Fong, as a craft rather than a science. Crafts are built around "knowing how to" rather than the "knowing that" of science.[2] Hence according to Mintzberg studying management is a waste of time. One needs to be engaged in the "doing" rather than the "talking about doing." There is simply too much emphasis on both the disciplines of business and the traditional modes of teaching and learning in business schools. Consequently, MBAs have become exploiters rather than explorers and innovators. In addition, Mintzberg holds the managerial class, defined by MBAs, as responsible for what we have called the problem of the ethics of capitalism, resulting in a lot of economic misery in society. Mintzberg rightly traces much of the problem back to research and the emergence of a "cult of methodology," whereby the worthiness of a particular piece of research is based neither on its usefulness nor how it allows us to live, but on the "validity" of the methodology by which it has been executed. In short, Mintzberg suggests that we get "management" wrong and the resulting MBAs do real and lasting damage in the world.

In an influential article entitled "Bad management theories are destroying good management practices," the late Sumantra Ghoshal (2005) argued that the dominant narratives that have taken hold in business schools are the real culprits. In particular, Ghoshal singles out both the ideologues who, concentrating on the economic or financial aspects of business, propose that the only legitimate purpose of a business is to maximize shareholder value and those who propose to understand business as a complex agency problem where managers are seen as agents of shareholders. Ghoshal invokes Nobel laureate Friedrich August von Hayek's idea of "the pretense of knowledge" to suggest that we misunderstand the nature of social science. Social science theories become known – "ideas in good currency," as Trist would say – and students and business people begin to act as if these ideas are true. They enact the dominant narrative. In doing so, they implicitly enshrine the opportunistic mindset that makes ethics and "value creation for stakeholders" a drag on good business. Ghoshal writes:

> In courses on corporate governance grounded in agency theory, we have taught our students that managers cannot be trusted to do their jobs – which, of course, is to maximize shareholder value … In courses on organization design, grounded in transaction cost economics, we have preached the need for tight monitoring and

[2] A useful set of distinctions around knowledge can be found in William Dray (1964).

control of people to prevent "opportunistic behavior." In strategy courses, we have presented the "five forces" framework to suggest that companies must compete not only with their competitors but also with their suppliers, customers, employees and regulators. (Ghoshal 2005: 75)

Ghoshal's view is that theories of business shape business itself – that is, that there is not a set of stable underlying phenomena. Business school researchers have simply misused scientific methods by pretending that business is like the physical sciences, with fixed rules and repeatable phenomena. The result is not the useless and noninfluential theory of Pfeffer and Fong, but the potentially highly destructive theory that Mintzberg's MBAs are inflicting on the world.

In an enlightening passage, Ghoshal suggests that the answer might lie in a closer connection between the great thinkers of the sciences and humanities, adopting a method of "common sense." He writes:

In describing himself and his work, Sigmund Freud wrote: "[Y]ou often estimate me too highly. I am not really a man of science, not an experimenter, and not a thinker. I am nothing but by temperament a conquistador – an adventurer, if you want to translate the term – with the curiosity, the boldness, and the tenacity that belong to that type of being." (Ghoshal 2005: 81–82, quoted in Jones 1964: 171)

Freud's inductive and iterative approach to sense making, often criticized for being ad hoc and unscientific, was scholarship of common sense. So indeed was Darwin's, who too practiced a model of research as the work of a detective, not of an experimenter, who was driven by the passions of an adventurer, not those of a mathematician. Scholarship of common sense is the epistemology of disciplined imagination, as advocated by Karl Weick (1989a), and not the epistemology of formalized falsification that was the doctrine of Karl Popper (1968).

To protect the pretense of knowledge, we have created conditions under which this kind of scholarship can no longer flourish in our community. This is true of all social science disciplines but curiously, perhaps it is most intensely true in business schools where, in our desire for respect from scholars in other fields, we have become even more intolerant of the scholarship of common sense than those whose respect we seek. (Bailey and Ford 1996)

In short, Ghoshal suggests that we get theory wrong, management wrong, and social science wrong and we should not be surprised at the resulting moral decline of business. We should not be surprised by what we have called the problem of managerial mindsets.

The upshot of these critiques can be diagnosed into the three interconnected problems we suggested in Chapter 1. Freeman and Newkirk (2008) add to this diagnosis by suggesting that what the critics themselves miss is that most of the time we get "business" wrong. Business is not an independent, repeatable phenomenon, an "economic clockwork" subject to its own, discoverable rules. In fact business is a deeply human institution and to see it as anything less misses the mark. We continue that line of thought here as we try and diagnose a further level of detail in these three problems. Our three problems[3] come from both external turbulence in the business world and from the dominant narratives about business, which do not, for the most part, see it as a fundamentally human enterprise.

The result is that a kind of early twentieth-century positivism has overtaken business schools. This became clear to us after many years of writing letters for promotion and tenure for colleagues at many business schools around the world, and serving on the tenure and promotion committees at the various institutions where we have worked. Positivism, in this context, leads to a view, roughly, that research is to be modeled on the physical sciences. Only measurable, repeatable phenomena are "real." Knowledge, on this view, results from empirical investigation. Theory is important only to the extent that it leads to testable propositions and measurable hypotheses. The results of this view are to treat method and data with a kind of reverence that ultimately leads to what Hambrick (2007) has argued is a fetishism for theory: theory that makes sense out of the data, out of what can be measured, regardless of its causal relevance.

In his Nobel lecture von Hayek has summarized the problem of applying "scientific" scholarship to human activities quite nicely:

> Unlike the position that exists in the physical sciences, in economics and other disciplines that deal with essentially complex phenomena, the aspects of the events to be accounted for about which we can get quantitative data are necessarily limited and may not include the important ones. While in the physical sciences it is generally assumed, probably with good reason, that any important factor which determines the observed events will itself be directly observable and measurable, in the study of such complex phenomena as the market, which depend on the actions of many individuals, all the circumstances which will determine the outcome of a process, for reasons which I shall explain later, will hardly ever be fully known or measurable. And while in the physical sciences the investigator will be able to measure what, on the basis of a prima facie theory, he thinks important, in the social sciences often that is treated as important which happens to be accessible to measurement. This is sometimes carried to the point where it is demanded that our theories must be formulated in such terms that they refer only to measurable magnitudes. (Hayek, 1974: 180)

[3] The three problems are the problem of value creation and trade, the problem of the ethics of capitalism, and the problem of managerial mindsets. See Chapter 1.

This is precisely the problem in business research. Simply add "organization" to Hayek's idea of the complexity of markets, and one begins to see the folly of such a view. Add the idea that business is a human institution, one that is fully situated in the real world of human complexity, morality, and human hopes and aspirations, and most importantly, one where theory shapes behavior, and the quantitative techniques of modern empirical scholarship, when they are left to their own devices, begin to seem feeble.

We are not arguing that data-driven research offers no interesting insights. And we are not arguing that empirical investigations into business phenomena do not yield interesting insights. In fact, we want to argue that when those investigations are grounded in the practice of business they can lead to quite interesting and useful results. However, we are suggesting that the kind of positivism that has overtaken business research has run its course. It is surely not the only way to understand business phenomena, and it is based on an untenable distinction between "normative" and "positive."

We argued in Chapter 1 that the separation fallacy undergirded much of the current narratives about business, and it is easy to see how the problem of the ethics of capitalism arose, especially in business schools which adopted this new positivism. As Sandberg (2008b: 230) notes, values are "embedded in social contexts from which they cannot be removed." We cannot single out particular "facts" from their underlying narratives.[4] As Searle pointed out, the "inclination to accept a rigid distinction between 'is' and 'ought,' between descriptive and evaluative, rests on a certain picture of the way words relate to the world" that ignores contextual notions such as "commitment, responsibility, and obligation" (Searle 1964: 52, 54). In other words, statements about the external world do not "face the tribunal of sense experience" alone (Quine 1951: 38). James and Dewey, Putnam and Rawls, Rorty and Goodman have all put forward similar arguments. Philosophers of science such as Kuhn (1962) and Feyerabend (1975) have highlighted the challenge this poses to the very concept of scientific inquiry as being solely descriptive and objective.

Similarly, in *The Collapse of the Fact–Value Dichotomy*, Hilary Putnam (2002: 27, 61–62) suggests that facts and values are deeply "entangled" and, as a result, "the picture of our language in which nothing can be *both* a fact *and* value-laden is wholly inadequate." As an illustration, Putnam's analysis of the word "cruel" as being both descriptive and value-laden illustrates how a great deal of language works, and demonstrates the limitation of employing a sterile, objectivist view of language and meaning. Putnam then analyzes

[4] This section draws heavily on Jared Harris and R. Edward Freeman (2008).

Amartya Sen's *On Ethics and Economics*, in which Sen (1987) specifically suggests that we have forgotten that economics is inherently entangled with matters of ethics, and argues that the false dichotomization of the two has impoverished discipline-based analysis in both economics and ethics.

Yet the entanglement of facts and values has implications beyond our mere conception of "business" language as being both normative and descriptive. Such entangled concepts apply directly to actual practices, which always embody both facts ("business" considerations) and values ("ethical" considerations). Consider, for example, the arrangement by which a business firm provides employment to a particular individual. Has the corporation provided economic value, or moral value? How can such things be disentangled?[5] Along these lines, any economic assertion is ultimately both descriptive and value-laden. Furthermore – and ironically – any *explicit* contention that commerce and morals involve mutually exclusive considerations (e.g. Friedman 1970; Jensen 2002) is *also* both descriptive and value laden.

Finally we argued that the problem of managerial mindset arises in part because the first two problems make what we teach managers more problematic. This is precisely the point of the critiques of business schools, that a false sense of knowledge pervades them. We teach and act as if we have created complete, or near-complete, causal theories about business. We act on, and teach students to act on, "the pretense of knowledge." And there is a self-reinforcing cycle to this knowledge which makes it particularly troublesome.

For instance, if we teach that business decisions and ethical decisions have nothing to do with each other, then we have created a generation of business leaders who look for business and ethics to conflict. Open questions are answered with "this is business," or "this is a business decision," or "I've got to do this for the good of the business." Thus Ghoshal (2005) and others (e.g. Ferraro, Pfeffer, and Sutton 2005; Frank, Gilovich, and Regan 1993), in showing that we enact the very theories of social science that we propose – and therefore demonstrating that the moral consequences are indistinguishable from the theories themselves – highlight the danger of *attempting* to separate business from ethics. When theorists suggest and managers enact an approach that views "business" decisions as if there are no moral consequences to them (e.g. describing unfettered profit maximization as the "single objective function" of business firms), this inculcates a societal narrative about business and ethics in which ethical considerations are no less real, but merely devalued and

[5] And if they cannot be disentangled, what are the implications for ideas such as "corporate social responsibility" and "triple bottom line," or even "economic value"?

denatured. If we treat the world of business as discovered, not created, we absolve managers of their responsibility for its structure. Is the view that owners of firms and their employees are one-dimensional maximizers of self-interest with convex utility functions for monetary wealth simply a matter of fact? Is the assumption that incentives effectively ameliorate agency conflicts unassailable? While some research (e.g. Frank 1988; Harris and Bromiley 2007) calls into question the prima facie descriptive accuracy of such assertions, important implications also arise from the assumptions about morality that are embedded *within* such statements, and their reifying influence on managerial behavior and social norms. That business decisions have moral content is inescapable; pretending that the two are divisible at best obscures important considerations and at worst paradoxically encourages a particular set of ethical norms that may be unintended.

The pragmatist alternative

In the philosophical literature pragmatism is usually credited to its "founders" or "pioneers" such as Charles Peirce, William James, and John Dewey.[6] For our purposes we rely on the more recent work of the philosopher Richard Rorty and those who have become known as "the new pragmatists."

Analytic philosophy was dominant in most American philosophy departments during the twentieth century and took as its wellspring the idea that the philosopher's job was to serve as the clarifier of conceptual schemes, a so-called "handmaiden to the sciences," an analyzer of language and logic. The mantra was "if it can be said, it can be said clearly." Philosophers worried about "meaning" rather than Socrates' question, "How should we live?" Ethics itself was turned into meta-ethics or the analysis of the meanings of words such as "good" and "right." Rorty was part of the center of this analytic mainstream as a full professor at Princeton University, one of the top American philosophy departments. His main insight, which he credits to Dewey and others, but which was really crystallized in *Philosophy and the Mirror of Nature* (Rorty 1979), was that most of this way of doing philosophy rested on a set of distinctions we inherited from the Greeks and a view of language as representing the world. He argued that the idea of representation made no sense, that it was based on taking vision as a foundational sense, and

[6] See Rosenthal and Buchholz (2000); Gutting (1999); Westbrook (1991); and Rorty (1982) for a complete history.

that, at least since Wittgenstein (1953), we should know that language does not work that way. Rather, language is a tool, not a representation. There simply is no other way to deal with the world other than through language. To assume otherwise is to invoke the "appearance versus reality" distinction common to philosophers since Plato and crystallized in Kant. According to Rorty, we needed to return to Dewey and see the intellectual's task as producing social hope and of always trying to figure out how we could live better. In short, Rorty turns us back to Socrates, focused on how we should live.[7]

The controversial way in which Rorty often explains what he is up to is to claim that we need to replace the idea of "truth" as the goal of inquiry with the goals of "hope" and "freedom." Intellectual life matters precisely because we can offer descriptions and re-descriptions of what we humans do that allows us to live better. Rorty claims that we should adopt Dewey's goal for inquiry as "increasingly free societies and increasingly diverse individuals within them" (Rorty 1999: 49). He argues,

> Pragmatists ... treat inquiry in both physics and ethics as the search for adjustment ... [Pragmatists ask] the practical question, "Are our ways of describing things, of relating them to other things as to make them fulfill our needs more adequately, as good as possible? Or, can we do better? Can our future be made better than our present?" (Rorty 1999: 72)

In short, it is up to us to figure out which projects to pursue, which descriptions and re-descriptions might serve us better, and there are no guarantees that we shall be successful.

Pragmatists like Rorty believe that there are only two interesting projects for us to engage. The first is ever more useful descriptions and re-descriptions of "self"; the second is ever more useful descriptions and re-descriptions of "community." Indeed, some have suggested that these twin pragmatist projects are just two sides of the same coin, since "selves exist in communities" and since communities without "individuals" are pretty uninteresting.[8]

Rorty's view of humanity is a thoroughly Darwinian one in which we are a species of "souped-up" chimpanzees or bonobos who can cleverly adjust what we do in collaboration with each other through language. He recommends that

> [W]e see ourselves as having the beliefs and emotions we do including our (potentially) "specifically moral" beliefs and emotions because of some very particular

[7] Rorty has a nuanced view here. "How should we live?" is not a question that admits of an answer true for all time. Rather, we are constantly trying to find better ways to live; we struggle for adjustment.

[8] See Freeman (1998). Rorty makes his first foray into business ethics in the same volume, replying to a former student, Cornell West.

> idiosyncratic things that have happened in the history of the race, and to ourselves in the course of growing up … It [pragmatism] lets one see oneself as a Rube Goldberg machine that requires much tinkering, rather than as a substance with a precious essence to be discovered and cherished. (Rorty 1986: 9)

Rorty claims that rather than trendy postmodern theorizing, we need to reread Nietzsche and Emerson on how we can undertake the project of self-creation. Indeed, he quotes (1989: 29) literary theorist Harold Bloom on the existence of strong poets who are horrified at "finding oneself to be only a copy or replica." We want to make more of ourselves than a copy of someone else. Equally, we need to read Whitman and Dewey, who emphasize that we must have solidarity with others for the individual to be able to accomplish any of her projects, implying that we are constantly trying to remake our communication.

This positivist view of management theory, decried by at least Ghoshal and Mintzberg, simply eschews individual difference. We search to find the theory, even a contingency theory, about how every organization has to work, how every employee is motivated, how all top teams work together or do not. Rorty is suggesting that a more fruitful course would be to produce some fine-grained narratives that focus on how we could live together better. Management theorists should be in the thick of this re-description, not at its periphery.

A Rortian and Deweyan vision of inquiry is quite far from where we find "management science." Management thinkers seem to debate tirelessly the "empirical vs. normative" distinction, and they argue endlessly and with obvious delight about definition and "proper method." While this is not the occasion to address all these issues, one suggestion is to simply give up such distinctions as "theory" and "practice," or "empirical" and "normative." We would need to develop criteria by which we judge the usefulness of work, but it would be connected to, rather than divorced from, how value actually gets created for stakeholders. That is a long story, but one that needs telling, and the current volume is offered in this spirit.

Pragmatism for stakeholder theorists

Wicks and Freeman (1998) outline a new approach to research in organization studies research, using pragmatism as a way of reshaping research to create a viable presence of ethics. Their pragmatism highlights the moral dimensions of organizing and helps to discredit embedded assumptions that make research less useful and less capable of creating a viable role for ethics.

Positivism is their prime target, since it enshrines critical assumptions that delude researchers into believing that they can conduct value-free scientific inquiry that advances knowledge without directly examining the presuppositions or implications of their work from a moral point of view. Wicks and Freeman argue that positivism in effect leads researchers – because they do not address the subject and try to remain value-neutral – to do ethics badly. At the same time, researchers who have come to reject the core assumptions of positivism and instead embrace "anti-positivism" as the basis for their research have not addressed the core problems raised by positivism. Indeed, rather than solving the problem, they have merely inverted problematic views and created new difficulties (e.g. moral relativism). While some researchers argue that future research can find a viable place for ethics if we simply "split the difference" between positivism and anti-positivism (e.g. Zald 1993), Wicks and Freeman argue that we have to move beyond the assumptions of both views as well as develop conceptual innovations that create a more intentional and substantive place for ethics.

The approach they offer is Rorty's "pragmatic experimentation." The focus of pragmatic experimentation is away from methodology and the devotion to science as a special and privileged form of inquiry and towards a focus on research as a tool that can help us lead better lives (1998: 124). It is "experimental" in that researchers should continually be looking for newer and better ways of organizing that advance human flourishing and employ a wide array of methods (quantitative and qualitative) that can be of help.

In their critique of positivism, Wicks and Freeman isolate a range of problematic assumptions related to the core belief that science is the only method of generating knowledge. More specifically, positivism enshrines sharp distinctions between finding (the world is given and science simply objectively reveals that truth without any influence from perspective, culture, or language) and making (all human inquiry, even science, is shaped by human perspective, culture, or language); descriptive (simply talking about something as it is) and prescriptive (talking about something as it should be); and science (knowledge creation done using the methods of scientific inquiry) and nonscience (any other inquiry that does not use the methods of science). In contrast to positivists, pragmatists do not draw sharp distinctions between these categories, and instead maintain four ideas central to their vision of "epistemology": "the world is 'out there' but not 'objective'" (there is no method of getting outside human experience to describe reality); "facts and sentences are intertwined" (any "facts" are embedded within language, culture, human artifact); "all inquiry is fundamentally interpretive or narrative" (science is part of the "narrative" tradition, not categorically separate from it); "science as a language game" (there are predetermined ground rules that shape all inquiry and its "progress").

In short, science is simply one more tool that can provide us with a set of narratives that can be incredibly useful as we sort out how to live well. Science becomes, on this view, a fully moral endeavor, as Rudner (1953) laid out many years ago. Ethics and science are grounded in the world, in the human institutions we have created. Ethics and other (nonscience) disciplines are not categorically below (or above) science as a method of inquiry to help generate knowledge of the world. Science is especially helpful in testing existing beliefs and allowing us to discern reasons to come up with better explanations. However, it is not a privileged form of discourse; it is part of our efforts to make sense of the world (like other non-science disciplines), and it cannot address the important questions for us (i.e. "What shall we do and how shall we live?" as expressed by Tolstoy). Another way of expressing this is to say that we need to dissolve the distinction between science and ethics, keeping what is best and most useful about each.[9]

Anti-positivism provides a well-intentioned alternative to positivism, particularly in highlighting the subjectivity of all scientific inquiry and the impossibility of true "objectivity." However, the problem with anti-positivism is twofold: first, it retains the problematic assumptions and categories of positivism even as it inverts them (i.e. towards subjectivity and away from objectivity); second, in its emphasis on the subjectivity and particularity of all knowledge, anti-positivism fosters a relativism that is both problematic and counter-productive. Rather than generating "liberation" and unleashing human creativity, anti-positivism pushes us to simply create as many views as possible without offering any method for deciding which are preferred or best (see, e.g., Astley 1985; Morgan 1986). One narrative is as good as the next – leaving us as unable to ask directly and systematically whether or how research advances human purposes as we were able to with positivism. Anti-positivists elevate the human-ness of all inquiry, even that based in science, but it undercuts our ability to tackle questions of values and meaning by making all points of view equally valid and any effort to establish a "better" or "best" narrative little more than a power grab. It throws out the intersubjective agreement that is so important to any form of inquiry, especially science, for the sake of human purpose.

[9] We realize that there is much more to be said about these issues.

In this context pragmatism is offered as a way of shifting the conversation. Rather than seeing research as being about the generation of objective knowledge, or the proliferation of competing narratives (all of which are as valid as the others), pragmatists see the goal of inquiry as generating insights that help us to lead better lives. If an insight or method is "useful" in this sense (i.e. this is not a simple form of utilitarianism), then the pragmatist would embrace it, but there is a strong desire to get beyond a focus on strong assumptions, categories, and methods as the starting point for inquiry. Instead, the pragmatist would push us to address front and center the larger purposes of inquiry and the importance of values to the study of organizations. In thinking about usefulness, the pragmatism of Wicks and Freeman encompasses two dimensions simultaneously: the epistemological (is it useful in terms of providing credible, reliable information on the subjects at issue?) and the normative (is it useful in making our lives better?). It is the criterion of usefulness that allows the pragmatist to make judgments about inquiry where the positivist and anti-positivist could not. Research becomes a vehicle to express human hope and push people to think about their larger purposes, how they want to live, and how they can cooperate with others to make us all better off. It is decidedly "experimental," in getting past existing constraints on research, in pushing us to ask new questions about whether and how particular research helps us live better, and in looking for insights that are better for us (rather than just more efficient, moving us further down the path of an existing paradigm).

In thinking about pragmatism and how it might move the conversation forward in a different direction, Wicks and Freeman highlight some of its core features. One central challenge is how to address the emphasis on purpose that is characteristic of ethics, without crippling inquiry or leading research down the relativist path laid out by anti-positivism. Pragmatism puts a priority on the "political," in the sense that conversations around purpose should be focused primarily on the tasks at hand (e.g. terms for our cooperation in getting a particular job or task done at a company), rather than on trying to get agreement on larger issues such as epistemology, the meaning of life, or religious belief. Especially in a pluralistic society there will be widespread disagreement about such matters. Instead of getting caught up in endless debates about whether Protestantism or Catholicism provides a more compelling case for endorsing capitalism, people should focus on the terms for their cooperation – whether it be on the ground rules for their economy, a corporation, or getting along with their team – and specific processes that allow them to reach agreement. Such an approach makes the task of researchers more akin to how we get along in life in other domains, and while the questions may be hard and generate intense disagreements, resolving them in constructive ways is critical if our efforts are going to help us live better.

Beyond this broad perspective on pragmatism, Wicks and Freeman also try to lay out some other details to help envision how research might proceed differently. They emphasize the work of Karl Weick (1979, 1989b, 1993) and some of the major themes within his work, refined by the authors' emphasis on pragmatism.

One key concept is equivocality, the notion that phenomena admit of multiple interpretations and that there is no one underlying "truth." Another core concept is to see "organizations as social," which is an extension of the equivocality idea. If experience of phenomena is equivocal, then a key issue for researchers is how individuals share and create meaning out of their experiences – that is, the social aspect of organizations becomes central rather than the search for ahistorical underlying laws and structures. A third notion is enactment. For Weick, reality is enacted rather than discovered. People make choices and impose meaning on their experiences rather than having meaning determined for them by nonhuman forces. This puts emphasis on human choice, language, and agency within the larger context of a community, culture, and patterns of discourse – all things that are central to pragmatism.

A final element of Weick's work that is helpful is justification – that is, the efforts to create new forms of sense-making do not come from an "anything goes" attitude (à la anti-positivism). Rather, sense-making occurs within existing social structures and practices, such that any new efforts need to be understood and evaluated in terms of what already is. It is only on that basis that the community can determine whether the new meanings are an improvement or a regression. At bottom, all these innovations put an emphasis on narrative, on particular human beings and human communities, and on the choices individuals make – factors that highlight the centrality of ethics.

In looking at the broader domain of organization studies and how they can be reshaped, pragmatism provides guidance as well. Several key insights shape a pragmatist view of the "macro"-level changes needed for research:

A pragmatic understanding of multiple interpretations

Researchers need to be cognizant of the multiple concepts and classificatory schemes that can be brought to bear on a given phenomenon. Rather than begin with the idea that one provides a privileged perspective, researchers need to consider the merits of multiple perspectives and to evaluate them in terms of their usefulness.

The importance of conceptual framing or categorization

Pragmatism puts emphasis on the choice of words and categories in terms of what we see and find. Being critical of language and aware of key assumptions is essential for inquiry to bear fruit, and also puts ethics at the center of research (what are good assumptions? what are the value implications of these choices?) – something that is especially true in terms of the behavioral assumptions and core concepts we attribute to business.

Strengthen the theory–practice link

Pragmatism does not take sides in debates between theory and practice, seeing instead that both are important touchstones in sorting out how we live better. Practice reminds us of the importance of what can be done, while theory pushes us to explore beyond existing horizons and consider more radical possibilities. Each becomes stagnant without the other.

Multiple methods and forms of evidence

Rather than focusing strictly either on particular methods as privileged or on claiming that all methods are as good as each other, pragmatism puts an emphasis on asking good questions and allowing the mode of inquiry to emerge from that, recognizing that there is room for both qualitative and quantitative methods. It is essential to maintain strong standards for research inquiry that are appropriate to the methods used, but this should not be used to confuse us regarding the limited nature of all research inquiry and the role that a variety of perspectives and methods play in any robust research agenda.

Direct linkage of ethics and mainstream management literature

The pragmatic criterion of value provides the impetus to bring together both the ethics and management literatures. Management scholars cannot escape the fundamentally moral quality of their work, both in terms of their assumptions and the implications. At the same time, ethicists need the insights and resources of management scholars to deepen their understanding of business and the practice of management – to make their inquiry more relevant and useful to real managers and real companies. Linkages across the normative and empirical divide, and the importance that both play in discerning useful practices, underscores the need for cooperation and collaboration across domains of research.

Pragmatism creates a context for thinking about how organization studies might move forward in a way that makes ethics, science, and other disciplines central and essential players.

To take advantage of the pluralism that is a part of pragmatic experimentalism we must avoid the temptation of hubris. No one mode, and no single discipline, has a monopoly on insight. An analysis of markets tells us a lot about business, but it does not give us the whole story. An understanding of creativity and its sources may help us to develop leaders, but it will not speak to the purpose of business. Similarly, deep insights into the human condition and how we make joint meaning gives much insight into how business works, but again, it is not the whole story. Indeed, we would surmise that there never is "the whole story." Each mode of research and their combinations are always subject to revision and the generation of new insights. In fact, by applying to another the methods and thinking of one mode we can sometimes generate useful ideas. By being explicit about the underlying narratives in the empirical mode, we can generate new narratives and, perhaps, new testable propositions.

We must keep Ghoshal's warning about the self-reinforcing nature of social science in mind. No theory is without impact, and no powerful idea leaves the observed phenomenon unchanged. In fact, we believe that any piece of research always leaves a certain set of questions open. And we suggest that these open questions begin to be explicitly acknowledged and answered. We want to build on the ideas of Michael Gonin (2007), and suggest that the following set of questions become routine ones:

(1) Does this work answer the question(s) it proposes?
(2) Was the question meaningful and appropriate?
(3) Are there alternative modes of research that could lend insight into the question(s)?
(4) What are the direct consequences of this research?
(5) If we teach this insight to managers and students, what might be the result if they act on it?
(6) What is the background narrative(s) of this research?
(7) How will we begin to see ourselves and others if we act on this work?
(8) How will this work shape the context in which value creation and trade takes place?

Modeled after questions in the field of technology assessment (Davis and Freeman 1978), these become a kind of "research assessment." We are not suggesting that every piece of research must actually answer these questions, but instead that we open up a line of research that is devoted to asking and answering these questions. It is problematic that such a critical line of inquiry does not exist in many business disciplines. Most simply stop after the first two questions on the list, which are devoted to the efficiency and effectiveness of research, but leave unaddressed the subsequent questions on its assumptions and impact.

We see these changes as implications of pragmatism, developed with an eye to seeing the role of ethics in human affairs, for all domains of research on organizations. While this includes stakeholder theory, we want to mention a few items specific to stakeholder theory, some of which will be developed later in this volume. First, it is a mistake to see stakeholder theory as a specific theory with a single purpose. Researchers would do well to see stakeholder theory as a set of shared ideas that can serve a range of purposes within different disciplines and address different questions. Second, stakeholder theory provides a powerful vehicle for the pragmatists' injunction to put questions regarding priorities and purpose front and center for organizations. Rather than starting with a clear and predetermined sense of why they exist, stakeholder theory echoes the idea that people need jointly to seek and create meaning within organizations. Third, in seeing the plurality of theories that emerge under the umbrella of stakeholder theory, researchers need to adopt the pragmatist mindset of asking good questions as the starting point of inquiry and letting methods play a supporting role in shaping a research agenda, rather than vice versa. Fourth, the pragmatist mindset suggests that stakeholder theorists need to bring a large portion of humility to their craft. Rather than celebrating or privileging the inquiry of the academy, pragmatism reminds us that the perspective of the manager matters and should be an important touchstone for helping to define what counts as a good question. Research needs to be "useful," even if it is not always directly applicable to a manager operating in an organizational context.

Part II

Stakeholder theory and the traditional disciplines of business

4 Stakeholder theory and strategic management

Stakeholder theory has much to say about strategic management. The stakeholder perspective offers an alternative that can enhance the economic perspectives of modern strategic management. We have already argued in Chapter 1 that the idea of stakeholder theory is consistent with strategy theories such as Michael Porter's industrial economics and Oliver Williamson's transactions cost theory. The body of work that we have called "stakeholder theory" was developed during approximately the same time frame as the economic approaches that are more mainstream today.

Although the stakeholder approach to strategic management has influenced thinking in the field, there are numerous interpretations of it, the results of which are that it sometimes still struggles for acceptance among mainstream strategic management scholars.[1] For example, Michael Hitt (2005), a widely acknowledged expert in the field, reviewed the development of the strategic management discipline and highlighted important areas for future research and discussion. His review suggested that the most important theoretical perspectives include industrial organization economics, corporate strategy and diversification, transaction cost economics, evolutionary economics, resource dependence, and the behavioral theory of the firm. Within these perspectives, he mentioned dozens of individual topics such as agency theory, corporate governance, mergers and acquisitions, international strategy, and the resource-based view. Not once did he mention the stakeholder perspective, although he did refer to the closely related concept of network strategies (Dyer and Singh 1998; Gulati and Singh 1998; Ireland, Hitt, and Vaidyanath 2002). His omission did not come from lack of awareness of the

[1] One probable cause of this reluctance is that many stakeholder theorists, including the authors of this book, have refused to accept the "purely scientific" approach that affects much of strategic management. In the zeal to be as rigorous as economics, which has a similar zeal to be as rigorous as physics, it is often forgotten that the human sciences may be developed along multiple lines. We are not arguing that the "scientific" approach to strategic management, largely developed by a group of scholars around the *Strategic Management Journal*, is not useful but, rather, that it is not the only useful approach. See Chapter 3.

topic (Hitt, Harrison, and Ireland 2001; Hitt, Freeman, and Harrison, 2001), but more likely from the view of many strategic management scholars that stakeholder theory is a part of the social responsibility literature and not central to strategic management theory.[2] Recently this has changed, as strategic management scholars have "rediscovered" stakeholder theory. This renewed interest has been led by scholars who have been able to see that a stakeholder approach to value creation is consistent with economic theories and may provide a more robust foundation for strategic management.

This chapter will trace the influence of the stakeholder concept in the strategic management discipline. We begin with a brief history of the emergence of the strategic management concept up to 1984, to augment what we have said about the history of the stakeholder idea in Chapter 2. The history is not intended to be exhaustive, but rather to provide a context, so that readers can understand how the stakeholder perspective was received and how it related to the major ideas in the field at the time. We shall examine the key themes in the strategic management literature as they relate to stakeholder theory, including how practitioners have made use of the stakeholder concept. Finally, we shall offer an overall assessment and suggest some future research directions.

The rise of modern strategic management

Surprisingly, strategic management as an academic discipline has its roots in a business school course. Fairly early in the twentieth century, many business schools began offering a course called "business policy." Based on a study of business school curricula sponsored by the Ford Foundation, Gordon and Howell (1959) suggested that

> [The] capstone of the core curriculum should be a course in "business policy" which will give the students the opportunity to pull together what they have learned in the separate business fields and utilize this knowledge in the analysis of business problems. Without the responsibility of having to transmit some specific body of knowledge, the business policy course can concentrate on the integrating of what has already been acquired and on developing further the student's skill in using that knowledge. (Gordon and Howell 1959: 206)

[2] Strategic management as a field of inquiry is built on the separation fallacy, as we discussed in Chapters 1 and 2.

Standard E of the American Assembly of Collegiate Schools of Business made the business policy course a requirement for accreditation. Also, the Academy of Management formed a Business Policy and Planning Division to support academic pursuits in this area.

The business policy approach

The business policy course, as it was usually taught, focused on developing policies that would solve business problems through an integrated, multi-functional approach. As the quotation from Gordon and Howell suggests, there were no widely accepted models for developing these policies. Rather, the course gave students experience, through business cases, in dealing with business issues from a number of perspectives simultaneously. As late as 1972, Schendel and Hatten noted that business policy was still thought of as a course rather than a field of study or an academic discipline (Schendel and Hatten 1972).

The standard business policy approach did not provide sufficient training to help executives deal with the complex and dynamic management problems that became evident in the post-World War II era (Schendel and Hofer 1979). This era has been filled with dramatic advances in technology, especially in communications and transportation, as well as increasing national and global competition. Rapid social, political, and economic changes have created a turbulent business environment, making effective management very difficult. In addition, the sheer size and complexity of modern business firms has made them difficult to manage. Scholars, in concert with large consulting firms such as the Boston Consulting Group, recognized the need for development of theory to support business policy as a separate discipline. Specifically, there was an acknowledgement that organizational success was dependent on successfully navigating an increasingly difficult external environment.

Definitions of strategy

Chandler's work was among the most influential in guiding early business policy scholarship. A business historian, Chandler defined strategy as "determination of the basic long-term goals and objectives of an enterprise, and the adoption of courses of action and the allocation of resources necessary for carrying out these goals" (Chandler 1962: 16). This definition embraced the notion that a firm should establish goals, strategies to achieve them, and an implementation (allocation) plan, but it did not address the essential role strategy plays in linking the firm to its environment. Shortly thereafter, Ansoff discussed strategy in terms of product/market scope, growth vector, competitive advantage, and synergy (Ansoff 1965). With its emphasis on market factors, Ansoff's definition is more oriented towards the external environment. Ansoff rejected the core of stakeholder theory by establishing a typology of objectives as "economic" or "social," with the social objectives playing the less important role of constraining or modifying economic objectives.[3]

Around the same time, Learned, Christensen, Andrews, and Guth defined strategy as "the pattern of objectives, purposes, or goals and major policies and plans for achieving these goals, stated in such a way as to define what business the company is in or is to be in and the kind of company it is or is to be" (Learned, Christensen, Andrews, and Guth 1965: 17). They also identified four components of strategy: "(1) market opportunity, (2) corporate competences and resources, (3) personal values and aspirations, and (4) acknowledged obligations to segments of society other than stockholders" (21). This treatment of the strategy concept was well ahead of its time, in that it foreshadowed the importance of a resource-based perspective (Barney 1991), acknowledged external obligations beyond those owed to stockholders, and suggested the importance of values and purpose.

Political strategy formulation, organizational learning, and resource dependence

Also important to the early strategy literature was recognition that strategy formulation contains both rational-deductive and political processes (Thompson, 1967; MacMillan 1974, 1978; Katz and Kahn, 1978). MacMillan (1978) drew from this literature to create a practical set of tools that managers could use to devise a political strategy. He argued that organizations should not concentrate exclusively on customers, markets, and products when they are formulating strategy, but should also include analysis of "symbionts" such as shareholders, employee groups and unions, competitors, and suppliers. He defined symbionts as "those elements of the environment on which the organization is dependent for inputs" (MacMillan 1978: 66). His perspective, like stakeholder theory, viewed organizations as systems that are dependent on external stakeholders for survival (Ackoff 1974; Barnard 1938; March and Simon 1958). "Thus, all organizations are dependent upon the environment for the provision of certain inputs; which the organization then

[3] See Chapter 2.

transforms into outputs; which it, in turn, uses to get more inputs" (MacMillan 1978: 66).

MacMillan (1978) defined the steps in political strategy formulation as (i) systems analysis to identify key actors; (ii) analysis of the power, influence, and negotiating base of the firm; (iii) selection and analysis of allies and negotiation with them; (iv) analysis of political systems of opponents; (v) formulation of offensive and defensive strategies; (vi) anticipation of resistance from opponents and negotiation with them; and (vii) monitoring of results. MacMillan's model, like stakeholder theory, was very deliberate with regard to assessing stakeholders and working with them to achieve organizational goals. However, he took "no specific ethical stance" (MacMillan 1978: 5). He acknowledged that his political strategies could be used for unethical or ethical purposes. Stakeholder theory, in contrast, joins ethics and economics in a deliberate fashion. Furthermore, MacMillan admonished, "It cannot be stressed too strongly that the fundamental basis of long-run survival lies in a sound economic strategy, which strategy is the reason for the firm's very existence in society. So the purpose of political strategy is to enhance and complement the economic strategy" (MacMillan 1978: 110). On the other hand, stakeholder theory is intended to be the central organizing paradigm for strategic management and not a supplemental theory. So although MacMillan's work established the importance of developing deliberate strategies for dealing with a broad group of stakeholders, its premises were fundamentally different from those found in stakeholder theory.

Mintzberg's work also had a significant impact on early scholarship in business policy (Mintzberg 1971, 1978). He challenged the assumption that strategies are always the result of deliberate plans conceived in advance of particular organizational decisions. Instead, he advanced the perspective that organizations learn what works through a process of trial and error. In his view, strategy is "a pattern in a stream of decisions" (Mintzberg 1978: 934). His organizational learning approach is consistent with the stakeholder-based argument that firms can learn from their external stakeholders. Some of Mintzberg's earlier work is also stakeholder-friendly. Based on week-long observations of five CEOs in different industries, he identified ten work roles (Mintzberg 1971). Half of the roles he identified dealt directly with managing external stakeholders. For example, he discovered that CEOs serve as liaisons with external stakeholders in an effort to bring favors to the organization and spokespersons that transmit company information to outsiders. They also negotiate with stakeholders and serve as figureheads in receiving visitors from outside the organization, signing contracts, and presiding at ceremonial events. In addition, they collect and evaluate information from the external environment. The other roles focused on managing internal stakeholders and resources. Mintzberg's work helped to establish that CEOs, the primary architects of firm strategy, are basically stakeholder managers.[4]

Also important is agency theory (Jensen and Meckling 1976), based on the idea that managers serve as agents for the owners or shareholders. If managers take actions that are in their own best interests rather than the shareholders, an agency problem is said to exist. In the strictest interpretation of this theory, managers are considered irresponsible if they take any substantive action that is in the best interests of anyone other than the shareholders. The popularity of agency theory seemed to motivate strategic management scholars to stay focused on the shareholder as the principal beneficiary of managerial action. Several years later, Jensen would admit that satisfying multiple stakeholders is essential to maximizing the objective function of wealth maximization for shareholders (Jensen 2001).

"Strategic management" is born

In the 1960s and 1970s, scholars who were teaching and doing research in the business policy area began to meet and share their ideas. Around this time the term "strategic management" began to replace "business policy." Strategic management is a broader term that implies that simply establishing business policies to integrate functional strategies was not an adequate solution to the problems executives and their organizations were facing (Schendel and Hofer 1979). An important meeting of these scholars occurred in May 1977 at the University of Pittsburgh. Experts in fourteen topic areas associated with strategic management gathered to share their work and discuss ideas. This meeting set the stage for what we now think of as strategic management. It is interesting to note that the Pittsburgh meeting did not include papers specifically on social responsibility. According to the conference organizers, there simply was not space on the program (Schendel and Hofer 1979: viii).

[4] Unfortunately, Mintzberg has always had a stylized view of stakeholder theory. He continuously identifies stakeholder theory with an overly control-oriented view of the importance of planning and forecasting. While there is some evidence for this view in, for instance, Emshoff and Freeman (1978) and even in Freeman (1984), there is much more to the theory. Surely Freeman and Gilbert (1987) made this clear, as did Wicks, Gilbert, and Freeman (1994), as did many of the other developers of stakeholder theory. Mintzberg is simply laboring under a misapprehension here.

In Pittsburgh Schendel and Hofer presented a model containing the basic activities in the strategic management process that, with some variations, continues to be used today (Schendel and Hofer 1979). The activities included organizational goal formulation, environmental analysis, strategy formulation, strategy evaluation, strategy implementation and strategic control. Environmental analysis, as they defined it, included an evaluation of a firm's competitive and "more general environments," with the intention of determining opportunities and threats facing the firm (Hofer and Schendel 1978). External stakeholder groups would presumably fall into these more general environments. The general premise underlying their formulation process was that the most effective firm strategies were those that best "fit" the environment. In other words, a firm should adapt to its environment because that environment determines the most appropriate strategies to pursue (for excellent analyses of this issue and its weaknesses, see Bourgeois 1984; Hrebiniak and Joyce 1985).

The deterministic perspective of strategy formulation was challenged by Bourgeois, who stated,

> [T]he strategy of a firm cannot be predicted, nor is it predestined; the strategic decisions made by managers cannot be assumed to be the product of deterministic forces in their environments ... On the contrary, the very nature of the concept of strategy assumes a human agent who is able to take actions that attempt to distinguish one's firm from the competitors. (Bourgeois 1984: 589)[5]

These early arguments regarding environmental determinism were important to the relationship between business policy and stakeholder theory because they reinforced the idea that although firms are dependent on their environment for success, they still chart their own course and, in large part, determine their own destiny. The careful balance between allowing external influences (stakeholders) to determine completely organizational strategies and totally ignoring them is at the heart of modern stakeholder theory.

Also at the Pittsburgh meeting, Newman (1979) presented what amounts to a stakeholder map, although he never mentioned the word "stakeholder" (see Figure 4.1). He identified several external groups that the company needs, including customers, suppliers, stockholders, unions, and tax officials. He suggested that a key to successful management is obtaining a mutually acceptable relationship with these groups and that doing so is a "never-ending task." Commenting on Figure 4.1, he stated,

[5] See also Hrebiniak and Joyce (1985).

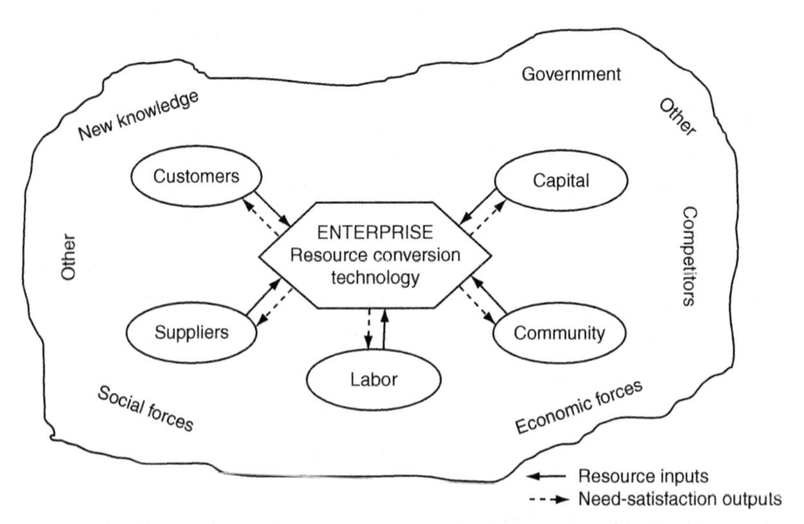

Figure 4.1. Generalized contributor group interaction between the firm and its environment
Source: W. H. Newman 1979. Commentary. In D. E. Schendel and C. W. Hofer, *Strategic Management: A New View of Business Policy and Planning.* Boston: Little, Brown. 45.

Strategy deals in large part, but not entirely, with a configuration of relationships between the company and such external "contributors." They may be called resources, or interest groups, or in systems jargon, "inputs." Since the company benefits from, and is dependent upon, a continuing cooperative exchange relationship with each contributor group, wise strategy formulation and implementation is vital to the company's existence. (Newman 1979: 45)

Economics and strategy

In the early 1980s Porter's work captured a lot of attention from strategic management scholars and practitioners. His influential book (1980) combined the emerging competitive strategy literature with industrial organization economics. "Competitive strategy is an area of primary concern to managers, depending on a subtle understanding of industries and competitors. Yet the strategy field has offered few analytical techniques for gaining this understanding, and those that have emerged lack breadth and comprehensiveness" (Porter 1980: ix). To fill the void, Porter (1980) articulated three "generic" competitive strategies – low-cost leadership, differentiation, and focus – and provided detailed tools based on competitive intelligence gathering to guide managers in determining which strategies are most appropriate in a variety of industry contexts.

Porter's work had the effect of reinforcing the economic theory upon which much of the field of strategic management was already based (e.g. Andrews 1980; Christensen, Andrews, and Bower 1980; Schendel and Hofer 1979). The primary, and to some scholars the only, important dependent variable was economic performance, typically measured in terms of profitability or shareholder returns. Studies were conducted to determine how high economic performance was achieved. This perspective is important to understanding why the stakeholder approach has struggled for broad acceptance in the field of strategic management. The only way to convince many strategy scholars of the importance of stakeholder theory is to demonstrate a strong positive link between following its precepts and economic performance, measured in traditional terms. As we shall demonstrate in the discussion that follows, supporters of the stakeholder approach have spent much of their intellectual time trying to establish that link in theory and in empirical tests.

Freeman (1984) offered an alternative approach to strategic management that addressed many of the concerns the field had identified as important. The stakeholder approach (i) embraced external analysis as a way to help firms deal with an increasingly turbulent environment (Schendel and Hofer 1979); (ii) "acknowledged obligations to segments of society other than stockholders" (Learned et al. 1965: 17); (iii) integrated economic with political strategy-making processes (MacMillan 1978); (iv) was consistent with Newman's (1979) "contributor group" approach; (v) contained elements of both adaptation and enactment (Bourgeois 1984); (vi) was consistent with what managers actually do (Mintzberg 1971); (vii) incorporated an organizational learning perspective (Mintzberg 1978); and (viii) included the concept of resource dependence (Pfeffer and Salancik 1978). In his final paragraph, Freeman summarizes,

> The business environment of the 1980s and beyond is complex, to say the least. If the corporation is to successfully meet the challenges posed by this environment, it must begin to adapt integrative strategic management processes which focus the attention of management externally as a matter of routine. (Freeman 1984: 249)

So far we have traced the emergence of modern strategic management up to the early 1980s and of the stakeholder concept in that emerging field during the same time frame. We have found that most of the mainstream strategic management writers did not use the term "stakeholder," but that many of their ideas were friendly to the stakeholder approach. Simultaneously, a literature was growing that included stakeholder concepts directly.

Freeman's book (1984) summarized and extended the early work on stakeholder theory. It offered a viable approach to the strategic management process that was very different from the economics-based approaches popular at the time.

In the same year Carroll and Hoy (1984) developed a model that integrated corporate social policy into the strategic management process. They acknowledged the responsibility of an organization to generate profits for its shareholders, but also suggested that managers should ask, "What responsibilities do we have to consumers, environmentalists, minorities, government, employees, and other stakeholders while we pursue profits?" (Carroll and Hoy 1984: 53). According to Carroll and Hoy, social policy should be established simultaneously with other corporate policies. Their work addressed the prevailing practice in strategic management at the time in which separate social policies were established (Hofer, Murray, Charan, and Pitts 1980), possibly a continuation of the idea that social objectives should act only as constraints on economic objectives (Ansoff, 1965). In contrast, stakeholder relationships are the central organizing framework for Freeman's (1984) strategic management approach.

Astley (1984) further elaborated on the concept of collective strategy as a tool for managing organization–environment relations. He identified the most common approaches to managing these relations as responding to environmental opportunities and threats, negotiating resource interdependencies with external stakeholders, and competitive maneuvering. He offered an alternative approach that consisted of jointly formulating and implementing strategies with external stakeholders, which he called "interorganizational collectivities" (Astley 1984: 526). Collective strategies are an important aspect of the stakeholder-based approach to strategic management.

Finally, MacMillan and Jones (1984), citing a statistic that 90 percent of American corporations had been unsuccessful in formulating and implementing strategies (Kiechel 1979), attributed the very high failure rate to implementation problems. Their solution involved a series of questions that organizations should ask when designing a competitive strategy. Stakeholders played a key role in their process. Specifically, stakeholder impact was to be identified and managed. Their process also involved deliberate management of internal and external stakeholder support and specific strategies for dealing with both positive and negative reactions.

The rest of the 1980s did not see many significant advances in the stakeholder concept in the mainstream strategy literature. Several things seem to have caused this void. First, Porter's (1985) highly successful second book further established the importance of the economic approach to strategic management. Second, while Freeman (1984) had both summarized and advanced the stakeholder approach to strategic management, the best we could say is that the field was evaluating what he said rather than trying to add to it. Third, a lot of attention was focused on social responsibility and whether firms that are good corporate citizens also have high financial performance (e.g. Aupperle, Carroll and Hatfield 1985; McGuire, Sundgren, and Schneeweis 1988; O'Neill 1989; Ullman 1985; Wokutch and Spencer 1987).

The results of the early empirical studies of the relationship between social and financial performance were mixed and inconclusive. This seemed to have a double effect on strategy scholars. First, they started to equate stakeholder theory with social responsibility and, as a consequence of the poor empirical results, they began to be skeptical about whether the stakeholder approach was economically viable and therefore worthwhile. Of course, the social responsibility literature tends to focus on the environment, special interest groups, social causes, community, and employee interests. In contrast, Freeman's approach considers the needs of these stakeholders as well as shareholders, customers, suppliers, and any other group "who can affect or is affected by the organization's purpose" (1984: 52). Consequently, the concerns of strategic management scholars were based on faulty assumptions, yet these concerns continue to persist in the minds of many scholars today.

Chakravarthy (1986) suggested measures of strategic performance that go beyond traditional profitability measures. Specifically, he suggested that firms might measure performance in terms of their ability to satisfy all their relevant stakeholders rather than just the stockholders. Along these lines, Malekzadeh and Nahavandi (1987) examined outcomes from corporate takeovers in terms of their influence on multiple stakeholders. Similarly, Vincent (1988) suggested that the key to realizing strategic advantage is to balance stakeholder interests so that all parties benefit.

As the Chakravarthy article suggests, the stockholders vs. stakeholders debate was ongoing during this time (Freeman and Reed 1983; Jensen 1989), stemming from the belief held by some that the social responsibility of a business is to increase profits (Friedman 1962). Efforts and resources directed at doing anything other than increasing profits limit the ability of the firm to be competitive in the market. According to Jensen, if the advocates of the stakeholder approach "argue for spending corporate funds on constituencies without any expectation of long-term benefit to the company, then they're advocating the waste of corporate resources" (Jensen 1989: 187). He goes on to explain that resources should be allocated to increase social benefits only if the benefits to the organization exceed the costs, but that there is no system in place to ensure that managers will allocate resources in this manner. He does acknowledge that shareholder needs cannot be met without satisfying, to some degree, the needs of other stakeholders such as customers, suppliers, financiers, and government regulators, a point that he would later reaffirm (Jensen 2001). Jensen's arguments bring us back to the importance to many strategic management scholars of providing an economic rationale for the stakeholder approach.

One other development during this period is worthy of discussion. Jansen and Von Glinow (1985) carefully examined the values conflicts that may emerge between a firm and its stakeholders. They defined ethical ambivalence as a situation "in which (a) the behaviors, attitudes, and norms that are shaped and maintained by the organizational reward system conflict with (b) the behaviors, attitudes, and norms congruent with the ethical values and judgments of organizational stakeholders" (Jansen and Von Glinow 1985: 814). Ethical ambivalence occurs "when the espoused values behind dominant norms conflict with reward system practices" (817). For example, stakeholders need honest and open reporting, yet organizational rewards systems may encourage behaviors such as falsification of data. Effective stakeholder management requires that managers be very deliberate in addressing value conflicts with stakeholders. Jansen and Von Glinow (1985) focus attention on rewards systems as a tool for addressing these conflicts.

The resource-based view of strategic management

During the mid- to late 1980s the resource-based view was gaining a lot of attention in the strategic management literature (Barney, 1986; Dierickx and Cool 1989; Wernerfelt 1984). The perspective assumes that firms are heterogeneous in their resources, that those resources cannot be transferred from firm to firm without cost, and that their characteristics determine, in part, firm outcomes such as performance (Barney 1991; Penrose 1959). Consequently, a primary task of managers is to acquire, develop, and manage firm resources. With regard to firm performance, Barney (1991) argued that resources that have market value, are scarce and nonsubstitutable, and are difficult to imitate have the potential to lead to a sustainable competitive advantage. These ideas, often referred to as "resource-based theory," led to an abundance of research on the nature of resources that lead to superior firm performance (Barney and Arikan 2001).

The resource-based and stakeholder perspectives are complementary rather than competing. Firm competitiveness requires effective management of both organizational resources and stakeholder relationships. Furthermore, a firm is dependent on its stakeholder network for most of the resources it acquires. Consequently, resource dependence theory (Pfeffer and Salancik 1978) provides a bridge between the two theories. However, the theoretical links between stakeholder theory and the resource-based view have not been adequately established in the minds of many strategic management scholars. As the resource-based view became a driving force in the strategic management literature, stakeholder theory was pushed to the side as a tangential theory associated with social responsibility and business ethics. Nevertheless, a relatively smaller group of scholars continued to advance the stakeholder concept in the strategy literature.

Key themes relating stakeholder theory to strategic management

We have examined the birth of modern strategic management and its concepts as they relate to stakeholder theory. While this history is ongoing, we shall switch to an examination of themes that relate stakeholder theory to strategic management. We shall begin with a discussion of the economic justification for a stakeholder approach to strategic management.

Economic justification for a stakeholder approach

The resource-based approach, with its emphasis on developing competitive advantage to enhance the creation of economic rents, reinforced the field's obsession with economic performance as the most important dependent variable. To gain wide acceptance in the strategic management field as it is currently situated, the stakeholder theory probably has to be justified in economic terms (Clarke 1998). Fortunately, many reasons exist to explain why stakeholder management should be associated with higher financial performance (Jones 1995). As Post, Preston, and Sachs argued, "Mutually beneficial stakeholder relationships can enhance the wealth-creating capacity of the corporation" (Post, Preston, and Sachs 2002a: 36), while "failure to establish and maintain productive relationships with all of the firm's stakeholders is a failure to effectively manage the organization's capacity to generate future wealth" (53).

Some researchers have argued that responsible stakeholder treatment can help a firm to avoid value-destroying outcomes associated with stakeholder actions such as legal suits, adverse regulation, consumer boycotts, strikes, walkouts, and bad press (Cornell and Shapiro 1987; Harrison and St. John 1996; Shane and Spicer 1983; Spicer 1978; Steadman, Zimmerer, and Green 1995). Avoiding negative outcomes reduces expenses as well as reducing the risks associated with variations in returns. Risk reduction enhances the value of a firm's securities because investors consider both future cash flows and risk simultaneously when assessing the value of a security (Fama 1970; Graves and Waddock 1994). Also, to the extent that firms are able to manage risk effectively, stakeholders may be more inclined to invest in the organization, whether these investments involve the efforts expended by employees, purchases by customers, sales from suppliers, or capital provided by market participants (Wang, Barney, and Reuer 2003). All other things being equal, stakeholders prefer to conduct business with stable organizations.

Based on the perspective that firms are collections of multilateral contracts over time, Freeman and Evan (1990) demonstrated how effective stakeholder management puts firms in a stronger position to adapt to external demands. The firm enjoys greater efficiency through an enhanced ability not only to create and satisfy individual contracts, but also to coordinate multiple contracts simultaneously. As Post, Preston, and Sachs explain, "The long-term survival and success of a firm is determined by its ability to establish and maintain relationships within its entire network of stakeholders" (Post, Preston, and Sachs 2002a: 7). Excellent relationships and effective management of the entire network can enhance organizational flexibility (Harrison and St. John 1996). Along similar lines, Hill and Jones (1992) extended agency theory (Jensen and Meckling 1976) by suggesting that managers have a responsibility to act as trustworthy agents to multiple stakeholders rather than just the stockholders. In their view, managers have the responsibility to draw together stakeholders to accomplish tasks in an efficient manner. Explicit and implicit negotiating processes serve as monitoring and enforcement devices that motivate managers to stay focused on financial objectives.

An excellent reputation in the marketplace can be a source of competitive advantage and increased economic value (Fischer and Reuber 2007; Fombrun 2001; Fombrun and Shanley 1990; Jones 1995; Puncheva 2008). One reason is that firms that have reputations as good citizens across a broad group of stakeholders are more attractive business partners and associates (Hosmer 1994). For example, customers may be more likely to shop at a store with an excellent reputation or suppliers may offer greater discounts to a firm that is known to be responsible in its treatment of stakeholders. Similarly, the best potential employees may be drawn to firms with reputations for excellent employee treatment (Moskowitz 1972; Turban and Greening 1996). It also seems probable that firms with excellent customer relationships should be able to tap those relationships such that their new product success rates will be higher (Harrison and St. John 1996).

In addition, responsible corporate behavior can facilitate the formation of alliances, long-term contracts and joint ventures (Barringer and Harrison 2000; Harrison and St. John 1996). A trustworthy reputation becomes a source of competitive advantage as the firm is presented with a larger number of better business opportunities from which to select. It seems likely also that increased trust leads to fewer transactions costs (Williamson 1975), by reducing the resources needed to create and enforce contracts and by eliminating the need for elaborate safeguards and contingencies that require detailed monitoring (Post, Preston, and Sachs 2002a).

The resource-based view also supports the relationship between responsible stakeholder management and firm performance. Intangible assets such as a reputation for trustworthiness and efficient contracting increase the ability of a firm to acquire and develop valuable resources (Sussland 2001). These assets provide a source of sustainable competitive advantage for the firm because they appear to satisfy Barney's (1991) conditions of market value, uniqueness, nonsubstitutability, and inimitability (Post, Preston, and Sachs 2002). The market value of a strong reputation and the ability to acquire resources efficiently is evident. In addition, no two reputations are the same, nor can a firm substitute something else for its reputation or precisely copy the reputation of another firm. However, the advantages accruing to the firm through efficient resource acquisition are not as clear-cut. Competing firms may be able to use other means such as technology to enhance their own processes, in essence substituting technology for strong relationships to achieve a similar level of efficiency in resource acquisition. To the extent that the technologies they employ are easy to imitate, whereas strong relationships with stakeholders are not, it is still arguable that relationships provide a more sustainable source of advantage. Consequently, if a firm has a greater capacity to acquire valuable resources due to its reputation and the strength of its stakeholder network, then it should have a greater capacity to develop a competitive advantage, leading to higher financial performance (Barringer and Harrison 2000; Lorca and Garcia-Diez 2004; Ruf, Muralidhar, Brown, Janney, and Paul 2001).

Along these lines, Bosse, Phillips, and Harrison (2009) challenged the widely held assumption in strategic management theory that economic actors are exclusively self-interested utility maximizers. Instead, they drew on research from numerous disciplines to argue that people tend to assess fairness in their interactions with others and reciprocate by rewarding those they deem fair. They used this assumption of "bounded self interest" to explain why firms that exhibit patterns of distributional, procedural, and interactional justice are likely to have higher financial performance. Bosse, Phillips, and Harrison (2009) also developed a model that explains that stakeholders are more likely to reveal a nuanced understanding of their own utility functions to trustworthy firms that exhibit these types of justice. This knowledge can then be used by the firm to envision actions it can take to create value, thus enhancing firm performance. In other words, nuanced knowledge of stakeholder utility functions can unlock the potential for product and/or process innovation and the creation of new interorganizational relationships (Barringer and Harrison 2000).

The resource-based view would also suggest that firms with an ability to develop unique stakeholder-satisfying resources internally can also enjoy competitive advantages (Russo and Fouts 1997). Stakeholders make firm-specific investments that are essential to the competitiveness of the firm (Blair 1998; Wang, Barney, and Reuer 2003; Wheeler and Sillanpää 1998). To the extent that a firm can motivate its stakeholders to invest more in the firm, it can enhance its competitive strength.

The empirical evidence

A clear definition of stakeholder management is essential to understanding the empirical evidence that does or does not provide support for the idea that managing for stakeholders is related to financial performance. As one would expect, there are multiple interpretations of stakeholder management in the empirical literature. For the purposes of this section, we shall take our starting definition from what is probably the first effort to validate empirically the basic concepts found in Freeman (1984). Preston and Sapienza defined stakeholder management as "the proposition that business corporations can and should serve the interests of multiple stakeholders" (Preston and Sapienza 1990: 361). They also identified a "related notion that corporate management involves the balancing of multiple (and at least partially conflicting) stakeholder interests" (362). They suggested that this notion was a key to organizational success and had not really been tested previously.

Preston and Sapienza used data collected by *Fortune* magazine, based on a survey of senior executives, directors, and analysts. These experts rate the ten largest companies in their own industries on a scale of 1 to 10 for eight attributes of reputation. The model that they developed and tested was based on variables they created from the data, which represented four stakeholder groups: shareholders, employees, customers, and the community. As expected, Preston and Sapienza (1990) found positive correlations between ten-year rates of return and each of the other stakeholder variables, as well as among the stakeholder variables themselves. They also found that pursuit of the interests of shareholders, employees, and customers was positively related to sales growth. They concluded that their results offered evidence in support of stakeholder management.

Two other studies published around the same time made use of *Fortune*'s reputation system and substantiated the results of Preston and Sapienza. Riahi-Belkaoui (1991) argued that organizational effectiveness and social performance are conceptually similar. He measured organizational effectiveness using a combined scale that included all eight of the factors that *Fortune*'s reputation survey measures. He also tested a model that used only the social performance part of the reputation index. His conclusions were the same for both models. He found that both organizational effectiveness and social performance were positively related to size and profitability and negatively related to risk, measured as the beta of the stock. Fombrun and Shanley (1990) also provided strong evidence in support of the idea that the eight different dimensions of *Fortune*'s survey are highly related. They used factor analysis and extracted a single factor with an eigenvalue of 6.68 that accounted for 84 percent of the variance. They concluded that the eight attributes were components of a single factor of reputation.

The *Fortune* data have been criticized in the social responsibility literature because of the possibility of a "halo" effect (Fombrun and Shanley 1990; Brown and Perry 1995; Baucus 1995). The high correlation between the individual attribute representing social responsibility and the other attributes has been interpreted by some to mean that it is more a function of the overall perception of the firm than the socially desirable behavior of the firm (Fryxell and Wang 1994). However, this issue is not a problem for stakeholder theory as Freeman (1984) conceptualized it, because the theory specifically predicts that there will be a positive relationship between the variables. Another concern with the *Fortune* measures is that they are subjective in both their measurement and assessment criteria (Cochran and Wood 1984; McGuire, Sundgren, and Schneeweis 1988). However, Brown and Perry (1995) argued that their subjectivity may be a source of strength rather than weakness. Experts are more familiar with the specific situations of a firm and its industry. Consequently, they may be better able to adjust for those situations in their ratings, as opposed to a purely objective measure.

Several other empirical studies have added support for the idea that stakeholder management leads to higher levels of organizational performance. Greenley and Foxall (1997) surveyed top executives of British companies to test the idea that a multiple stakeholder managerial orientation would be positively associated with company performance. Specifically, they measured the importance of formal research for understanding the interests of each stakeholder group, the importance of manager understanding of stakeholder interests, the extent of planned strategies for addressing stakeholder interests, the extent of managerial discussions about each stakeholder group, and the relative importance of each stakeholder group in the corporate missions of their firms. They used cluster analysis to form groups based on their stakeholder orientations.

In tests carried out on the clusters, Greenley and Foxall (1997) discovered that the cluster of companies with the highest multiple stakeholder orientations had a larger proportion of high-performing firms and the smallest proportion of low performers for sales growth, market share, and new product success, but not return on investment. Furthermore, these differences were statistically significant when compared with the cluster containing firms that were low on the multiple stakeholder orientation dimension. Differences between the other clusters were not statistically significant. These results are not overwhelming, but the methods may have contributed to weak findings. Cluster analysis is probably better suited to descriptive research than the testing of hypotheses. Furthermore, examining proportions of high- and low-performing firms within the clusters reduces test precision by eliminating the continuous properties of the original performance data.

Kotter and Heskett (1992) found that the managers of a small number of highly performing companies tended to consider the interests of all major stakeholders in their important business decisions. Along these same lines, Mitchell, Agle, and Wood (1997) identified three attributes that give particular stakeholders salience in the eyes of managers: power, legitimacy, and urgency. A model was tested using the three salience attributes for five stakeholder groups: shareholders, employees, customers, government, and communities (Agle, Mitchell, and Sonnenfeld 1999). They also looked at resulting performance outcomes.

To measure salience, the research team asked CEOs to respond to statements based on their firm's interactions with each stakeholder during the previous month. They included measures of corporate performance along dimensions related to each of the stakeholders: industry-adjusted financial performance to represent shareholder interests, and a set of stakeholder measures based on data collected by Kinder, Lydenberg, Domini and Co. (KLD).[6] CEO values were assessed and used as a moderating variable, although this variable did not turn out to be important to the model. They found strong support for the hypothesis that the stakeholder attributes of power, legitimacy, and urgency were related to stakeholder salience, but little support for the link between salience and social or financial performance. The only exception was a significant positive relationship between community salience and community performance.

Over a decade earlier, Aupperle, Carroll, and Hatfield (1985) were similarly disappointed to find no relationship between social orientation and performance. This earlier citation is relevant because of methodological similarities between the studies in the way they collected social orientation data. Specifically, Aupperle et al. also carried out a survey of CEOs to determine their orientations towards a number of social issues. The social issues do not correspond exactly with the salience items of Agle et al. (1999); however, there are enough similarities to raise the issue of whether CEO orientation is really an accurate reflection of the stakeholder orientation of the whole firm. Other measures of stakeholder orientation are needed to sort out this situation, since the Aupperle et al. (1985) and Agle et al. (1999) results are inconsistent with Kotter and Heskett (1992) and with the rest of the empirical literature, which seems to indicate that firms that pay attention to a broad group of stakeholder interests have higher performance. For example, measures based on actual corporate behaviors would be a step in the right direction.

Ogden and Watson (1999) took advantage of the privatization of the water industry in the United Kingdom, using the event as a case study to determine whether water companies were able to balance competing interests. They used government information on levels of customer service as well as accounting and market performance data to study the issue. Their results indicated that

[6] Kinder, Lydenberg, Domini and Co. (KLD) conducts regular audits of the social performance of companies on the basis of several attributes. They include community relations, employee relations, environmental issues, product issues, treatment of women and minorities, military contracts, and involvement in nuclear power or other socially undesirable activities. KLD makes its ratings on the basis of consistent and objective screening criteria (Graves and Waddock 1994). They use publicly available information as well as follow-up contacts with firms to establish the rankings. Beginning in the mid-1990s, much of the research on the relationship between stakeholder management and performance has made use of these measures. They also have widespread use in social responsibility research. Ultimately, these data rest on the separation fallacy. But this line of research is surely useful for particular purposes.

higher levels of customer service had a detrimental effect on accounting-based performance over the short term due to the costs involved. However, share prices increased as a result of improved customer service, an indication that investors could anticipate the longer-term economic consequences. Ogden and Watson (1999) concluded that the water companies were able to balance the interests of customers and shareholders, in spite of the associated short-term costs.

Berman, Wicks, Kotha, and Jones (1999) explored the validity of two different models of the relationship between firms' concern for stakeholders and their financial performance. The strategic stakeholder model suggests that firms address stakeholder concerns when they believe that doing so will enhance financial performance. On the other hand, intrinsic stakeholder commitment suggests that firms address stakeholder concerns because it is morally correct to do so. Furthermore, in the intrinsic model, this commitment should drive strategic decision making. Berman et al. used KLD data to measure stakeholder relationships with employees, customers (product safety/quality), special interests (diversity), society (natural environment), and the community. Return on assets was the dependent variable for performance. Four variables were used to reflect the business strategy of each firm: selling intensity, capital expenditures, efficiency, and capital intensity. These variables are indicative of whether a firm has more of a cost leadership or differentiation orientation. They also controlled for environmental variables (dynamism, munificence, and power). The initial sample was the top 100 firms listed on the *Fortune* 500 for 1996. Six years of data were collected for each firm. Missing data reduced the sample to eighty-one firms.

Berman et al. (1999) found that two of the five KLD variables – employees and product safety/quality – were significant predictors of financial performance in a direct test. However, in secondary tests, all five stakeholder variables moderated the relationship between strategy and performance. They concluded that the moderated regression result offered support for the strategic stakeholder management perspective. They also applied a mediation model to the data and found no support for the intrinsic stakeholder commitment view.

Berman and his colleagues were disappointed that not all five of the stakeholder variables were significant in their direct test. However, the environmental variable may not have worked out because the importance of environmental programs varies a lot by industry, which may have created error in their model. In addition, diversity, while important, may have had a negligible effect on overall firm performance. Of the three nonsignificant stakeholder variables, community is the hardest to understand in the stakeholder context. Nonetheless, the stakeholder variables representing employees and customers were significantly positive. Furthermore, the most important contribution of the study was probably the finding that stakeholder relationships serve as moderators between business strategy and performance.

Hillman and Keim (2001) decided to separate stakeholder management attributes from social issue attributes in the KLD data. They hypothesized that attending to employees, customers, the community, and suppliers would likely have a positive effect on shareholder value creation, while paying attention to social issues by avoiding investments in particular industries (e.g. alcohol, gambling, military weapons, nuclear power) or particular countries (e.g. Burma, Mexico), or providing very low compensation to top management would not influence shareholder value. Using market value-added (MVA) as the performance variable (market value minus invested capital), they found that stakeholder management was positively associated with value creation while social issue participation had a negative effect.

In this chapter we have deliberately avoided studies that focus only on social responsibility and performance, except as they have added clarity to our discussion. Social responsibility will be treated in depth in Chapter 8. Instead, our focus has been on models that incorporate multiple stakeholders and test the proposition that addressing a broad group of stakeholder interests simultaneously enhances financial performance. However, we would like to point out that much of the social responsibility literature is closely tied to the proposition (Ruf, Muralidhar, Brown, Janney, and Paul 2001). Few strategic management scholars would dispute the idea that firms must treat customers, suppliers, and employees well if they want to prosper. On the other hand, issues associated with social responsibility, such as community and the environment, lead to criticism of the stakeholder management approach. From this perspective, we would like to add that the social responsibility empirical literature is generally but not completely supportive of the idea that firms that are strong in social performance are also high performers (Orlitzky, Schmidt, and Rynes 2003; Orlitzky and Benjamin 2001). An interesting advancement in this literature came from Barnett (2007), who developed a compelling argument that the relationship between social and financial performance is not direct; rather, social performance influences the nature of stakeholder relationships, which, in turn, influences financial performance. He uses this argument to explain why empirical results regarding social performance and financial performance can be inconsistent.

In addition to the social performance studies, we should acknowledge some recent work from marketing scholars that provides fairly convincing evidence that stakeholder management is associated with higher firm performance (Sisodia, Wolfe, and Sheth 2007). Their work is reviewed in Chapter 5.

In conclusion, some fairly strong theoretical and empirical support exists for the notion that business organizations "can and should serve the interests of multiple stakeholders" (Preston and Sapienza 1990: 361), and that such service is associated with higher financial performance. The empirical literature on social responsibility and performance adds support to this notion. However, there is also evidence that measuring the salience given by top management to particular stakeholder groups may not be the best way to capture the phenomenon (Agle et al. 1999). Instead, the phenomenon is best measured through actual corporate behaviors such as strategies for addressing the interests of stakeholders (Greenley and Foxall 1997). As a final caveat, there is some evidence that CEOs of the largest corporations may not receive higher financial rewards for satisfying the needs of a broad group of stakeholders (Coombs and Gilley 2005). However, this issue requires further study.

The influence of stakeholder theory on the strategic management process

Many of the early stakeholder theorists provided stakeholder-based strategic management tools. Freeman's (1984) model of the strategic management process began with evaluation of stakeholders, continued with a set of tools for managing stakeholders to facilitate the accomplishment of organizational objectives, and ended with measuring stakeholder satisfaction with organizational outcomes. Harrison and St. John (1994) provided further development of this approach by integrating stakeholder-based perspectives with a variety of other strategic perspectives, based on the theories of industrial organization economics, the resource-based view, cognitive theory, institutional theory, organization theory, transactions cost economics, and agency theory. They used the stakeholder approach as an overarching framework within which traditional approaches operated as strategic tools. According to Harrison and St. John, who used dozens of company examples in their book, it was not a difficult integration process:

> The process of integrating the traditional theory of strategic management with stakeholder analysis and management was as natural as applying Porter's Five Forces to the study of industry competition. Everything fits. In fact, we discovered

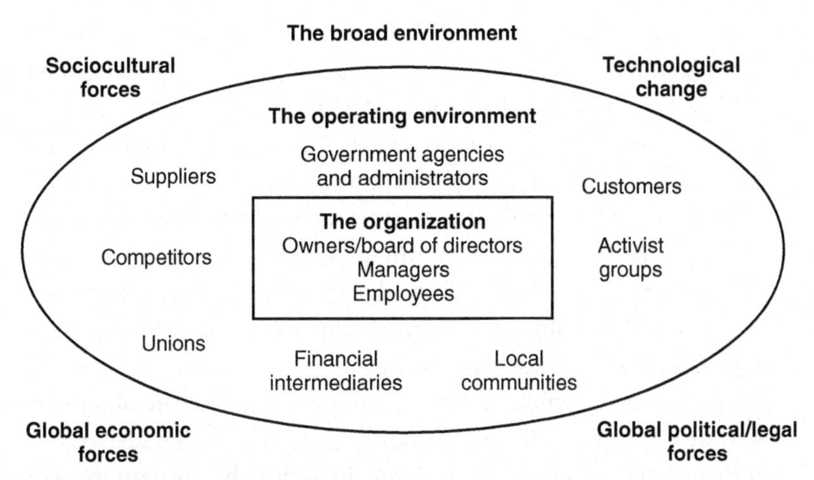

Figure 4.2. The organization and its primary stakeholders
Source: J. S. Harrison and C. H. St. John 1998. *Strategic Management of Organizations and Stakeholders: Concepts and Cases.* Cincinnati, OH: Southwestern College Publishing. 8.

that many of the best-run organizations have already integrated comprehensive stakeholder analysis and management processes into their organizational planning. (Harrison and St. John 1994: xiii)

Harrison and St. John (1994, 1998) divided the stakeholder environment into three regions (see Figure 4.2). The broad environment (society, technology, economy, and political/legal) forms the context in which the firm and its operating environment exist. The firm has little or no influence over components of the broad environment. The operating environment consists of external stakeholders that influence the firm and over which the firm has some influence. Finally, the internal organization is made up of stakeholders with formal ties to the firm. In Harrison and St. John's strategic management process model, the resource-based view is a tool to help managers determine how internal stakeholders may be used to create competitive advantage. Porter's (1985) five forces are integrated into an analysis of external stakeholders, and traditional economic approaches are used to analyze the remote environment (Harrison and St. John 1994, 1998). As might be expected, their chapter on strategic direction is infused with the stakeholder-friendly concepts associated with enterprise strategy, or the joining of ethics with strategy (Freeman and Gilbert 1988). Later, Post et al. (2002a) would refer to the three regions identified by Harrison and St. John as the social political arena, the industry structure, and the organizational resource base.

Harrison and St. John (1994) also applied organization theory and industrial organization economics to the task of prioritizing and managing stakeholders as a part of the strategic management process. They argued that priority should be given to external stakeholders based on their ability to influence the environmental uncertainty facing the firm and its managers, which is a function of their economic and political power, as well as strategic choice. Furthermore, they outlined the two basic postures for managing stakeholders: buffering and bridging (Daft 1992). Buffering is a low-interaction stakeholder management approach with the purpose of containing the effects of stakeholders on the firm. It involves monitoring activities such as market research, public relations, and planning. On the other hand, bridging is more appropriate for high-priority stakeholders because of their potential influence on uncertainty. Bridging includes the formation of longer-term interorganizational relationships such as joint ventures, alliances, and strategic partnerships (Barringer and Harrison 2000). This approach recognizes common goals, lowers organizational barriers, and builds on interdependencies among stakeholders.

The establishment of strategic direction, as evidenced by a firm's mission and vision statements, is probably the component of the strategic management process that is most closely linked to the stakeholder perspective (Copulsky 1991; Campbell and Yeung 1991; Klemm, Sanderson, and Luffman 1991). It would be hard to define a mission without including statements about how a firm treats several stakeholder groups. Even a firm that claims in its mission statement that its purpose is to maximize shareholder returns is, by default, suggesting that the claims of other stakeholders are not given as much weight. However, mission statements with a single shareholder focus are no longer fashionable. Firms typically include broad goals dealing with customers and employees, and may also discuss community, suppliers, other stakeholders, or the environment. One of the ways to envision a firm's broad purpose is through its enterprise strategy, which joins ethical and strategic thinking (Freeman and Gilbert 1988; Hosmer 1994; Schendel and Hofer 1979). Enterprise strategy provides the organization with the best possible reason for its existence by stating how the firm will satisfy the interests of a broad group of stakeholders.

Another development in the strategic management process related to the stakeholder perspective is scenario planning (Schoemaker 1993, 1995; Wack 1985; Huss 1988). Building from the well-understood idea that uncertainties in the environment make strategic planning difficult, Schoemaker (1995) proposed that developing scenarios based on basic trends and uncertainties can help decision makers avoid "tunnel vision" and therefore reduce the number of poor decisions they make. Scenario planning is viewed as collective learning and therefore incorporates many stakeholder-based processes. For example, early in the process the key stakeholders and their positions are identified. Later in the process their positions are used as a tool to determine consistency in and plausibility of the scenarios. Potential stakeholder reactions to the actions of the firm are also forecast. More recently, Strand (2008) proposed that firms develop what he called a "stakeholder dashboard" to track stakeholder perceptions about the firm as a way to enhance firm decisions.

Finally, the processes associated with the generation of strategic alternatives have benefited greatly from the stakeholder perspective. Nutt (2004) suggested that strategic decision makers can expand the number of alternatives they consider, thus reducing their rush to judgment, by identifying key stakeholders and examining their concerns and claims. Hart and Sharma argued that even fringe stakeholders can be used to increase the number of strategic options available to the firm. They proposed a concept referred to as radical transactiveness to help organizations deal with the volatile business environment:

> Moreover, the knowledge needed to generate competitive imagination and to manage disruptive change increasingly lies outside the organization, at the periphery of firms' established stakeholder networks. Unfortunately, most companies still tend to focus management attention only on known, salient, or powerful actors to protect their advantages in existing businesses. In recognition of these challenges, we develop the concept of Radical Transactiveness (RT). RT is a dynamic capability which seeks to systematically identify, explore, and integrate the views of stakeholders on the "fringe" – the poor, weak, isolated, non-legitimate, and even non-human – for the express purpose of managing disruptive change and building imagination about future competitive business models. (Hart and Sharma 2004: 7)

Related to these process issues, some strategists have engaged in a discussion about "nonmarket" strategies as a source of competitive advantage (Baron 1995; Shaffer, Quasney, and Grimm 2000; Jones and Kunz 2005). These strategies encompass how a firm deals with government, interest groups, activists, and the public. In reality, nonmarket strategies are just strategies for dealing with corporate social responsibility, which has its own literature (reviewed elsewhere in this volume). One possible advantage of the different label could be that it will increase the interest of some strategic management scholars and practitioners. However, the exclusive focus on nonmarket stakeholders could also solidify the incorrect impression that this is what stakeholder theory advocates. Of course, stakeholder theory is much more comprehensive in its scope, including both market and nonmarket stakeholders.

Stakeholder theory and the relational view

Dyer and Singh offer "a relational view of competitive advantage that focuses on dyad/network routines and processes as an important unit of analysis for understanding competitive advantage" (Dyer and Singh 1998: 661). In a footnote attached to that sentence they explain, "For the convenience of exposition, we use two firms, rather than multiple firms, as the unit of analysis." They argue that interorganizational competitive advantage comes from relationship-specific assets, knowledge sharing, effective governance, and complementary resources and capabilities. Lavie (2006), using the resource-based view as a guide, further develops this view by distinguishing shared from nonshared resources and examining how various firm-, relation-, and partner-specific factors determine the rents that may be extracted from collaborative relationships. He concludes that the nature of relationships is more important than the nature of the resources. In support of this idea, Hardy, Phillips, and Lawrence (2003) find that embeddedness and involvement facilitate knowledge transfer across networks.

Dyer and Singh provide evidence in support of their relational view (Dyer and Nobeoka 2000; Kale, Dyer, and Singh 2001; Dyer and Hatch 2004). However, there is a very real question regarding whether the view is unique or whether it is simply an application of stakeholder theory with a different set of labels. Some management scholars seem to believe that the stakeholder perspective is an extension of Dyer and Singh's work. For example, in Mattingly's review of Post et al. (2002a), he states:

> Fundamentally, the SHV (stakeholder view) is partly an extension of the relational view of the firm (Dyer and Singh 1998) to sociopolitical stakeholders – especially local communities and governmental and regulatory agencies, as well as private organizations such as citizen interest groups. The relational view suggests that the interfirm relationships a firm develops – particularly among participants in its supply chain – provide a potentially sustainable source of competitive advantage. (Mattingly 2004: 520)

In reality, although Dyer and Singh do not acknowledge it, this concept has always been at the heart of stakeholder theory. Many scholars have directly applied stakeholder theory to the study of interorganizational relationships in a similar fashion (e.g. Barringer and Harrison 2000; Kochan and Rubenstein

2000; Kanter 1994; Lorange, Roos, and Bronn 1992; Mills and Chen 1996). Also, the stakeholder perspective has always included customers and suppliers, the focal stakeholders in Dyer and Singh's article (1998). The development and increasing popularity of the relational view in the strategic management literature may be evidence that the field is reaching for stakeholder theory without even knowing it, believing instead that stakeholder theory deals largely with noneconomic stakeholders.

Stakeholder influence on firm strategies

From its inception, the stakeholder perspective has envisioned the firm and its stakeholders in two-way relationships. While much of the attention in the literature has been directed towards a firm's management of its stakeholders, some scholars have focused specifically on the influence stakeholders have on the firm and its strategies. Clearly, the influence of external stakeholders on a firm's strategies has increased dramatically in recent years (Scholes and Clutterbuck 1998; Sharma and Henriques 2005; Rodgers and Gago 2004; Wright and Ferris 1997).

Early stakeholder theorists such as Dill (1975) and Freeman and Reed (1983) examined the ability of stakeholders to influence the firm in terms of the nature of their stakes and the source of their power. Harrison and St. John (1996) added stakeholder influence on environmental uncertainty, which is partly a function of power. Mitchell, Agle, and Wood (1997) identified urgency, power, and legitimacy as factors that determine how much attention management will give to various stakeholders. Rowley (1997) further developed the idea that multiple stakeholders influence the firm simultaneously. Using social network analysis (Granovetter 1985; Wasserman and Glaskiewicz 1994) and institutional and resource dependence theories (Oliver 1991), he argued that the density of a firm's stakeholder network (number of ties among stakeholders) and the firm's network centrality influence its level of resistance to stakeholder demands.

Frooman (1999) uses resource dependence theory (Pfeffer and Salancik 1978) to identify four types of stakeholder influence strategies: withholding, usage, direct, and indirect. Withholding strategies give stakeholders influence only if their threat of withdrawal is credible. Usage strategies involve attaching conditions to supply contracts. Direct influence strategies are defined as those in which stakeholders directly manipulate the flow of resources, whereas indirect strategies involve influence on resource flows by third parties. Frooman also develops theory to predict which strategy stakeholders will use, based on the two-way dependence relationships that exist between the firm and its stakeholders. Along this same line of reasoning, Coff (1999) examines the extent to which stakeholders are able to extract economic rents from the firm. According to Coff, "bargaining power is highest when stakeholders (1) are capable of acting in a unified manner, (2) have access to key information, (3) have a very high replacement cost to the firm, and (4) face low costs if they move to another firm" (Coff 1999: 122).

Murillo-Luna, Garcés-Ayerbe, and Rivera-Torres (2008) added additional empirical evidence regarding the ability of stakeholders to influence firm decisions. Specifically, they analyzed the influence of stakeholders or "pressure agents" on the strategies adopted by 240 industrial firms as they responded to environmental requirements. They classified response patterns based on the level of proactivity of firms, as indicated by the scope of their environmental objectives and their allocation of internal resources. Their results demonstrated that stakeholders had an impact on which of four response patterns the firms adopted. A related study found that aspects of the general business environment moderated the relationship between the stakeholder integration capability of 134 service firms in the ski industry and their environmental strategies (Rueda-Manzanares, Aragón-Correa, and Sharma 2008).

Corporate governance from a stakeholder perspective

Interest in the topic of corporate governance has blossomed in recent years (Chatterjee and Harrison 2001), possibly due to the increasing number of large corporate scandals that have been plaguing the business community. Because of the vastness of the strategy literature on corporate governance, we shall pare down our discussion by focusing specifically on the intersection between governance and stakeholder theory, and shall leave the legal implications for Chapter 6.

From a strategic management perspective, corporate governance deals with the forces that influence how firms and their managers behave in the execution of their responsibilities. Some of these forces are completely external to the firm. For example, the market for corporate control, as manifested in attempted or completed takeovers, is considered a governance mechanism. From this perspective, incumbent managers of poorly performing public corporations are motivated by a potential takeover to improve the performance of their firms, because they fear that after the acquisition they will lose their jobs (Chatterjee, Harrison, and Bergh 2003; Denis, Denis, and Sarin 1997). Large block stockholders, bond rating agencies, and even government regulators are other examples of external governance forces.

Governance may also be internally derived, as in a board of directors. Although board members also provide resources and advice, most scholars believe that the most important function of board members is to monitor top managers to make sure that they are acting responsibly with respect to the interests of the stockholders who elected them. Managers are perceived as agents for the shareholders, and agency problems exist to the extent that they act in their own interests rather than the interests of the shareholders (Jensen and Meckling 1976; Williamson 1984a; Fama and Jensen 1983; Vilanova 2007). When these situations become extreme, the governance system is examined to determine why the inappropriate behavior was not corrected.

Governance gains much of its importance through the separation of ownership from control in modern corporations, where individual shareholders typically have little influence over the decisions of managers (Berle and Means 1932). Close scrutiny of managers would be costly for the shareholders relative to the size of their investments in the firm. Consequently, they are compelled in most cases to trust that the directors will ensure that agency problems are not serious. Williamson (1985) argues that shareholders occupy a unique position with managers because their entire investment is at risk, they have no formal contracts that offer protection or safeguards, as do suppliers or creditors, and their contracts do not come up for renewal so that they do not have the opportunity to renegotiate terms.

Hill and Jones argue that nonshareholder stakeholders also deserve representation by managers:

> Whatever the magnitude of their stake, each stakeholder is a part of the nexus of implicit and explicit contracts that constitutes the firm. However, as a group, managers are unique in this respect because of their position at the centre of the nexus of contracts. Managers are the only group of stakeholders who enter into a contractual relationship with all other stakeholders. Managers are also the only group of stakeholders with *direct* control over the decision-making apparatus of the firm (although some stakeholders, and particularly the suppliers of capital, have indirect control). Therefore it is incumbent upon managers to make strategic decisions and allocate resources in the manner most consistent with the claims of the other stakeholder groups. (Hill and Jones 1992: 134)

Hill and Jones (1992) base this argument on the idea that a power differential exists between the firm and its stakeholders. Agency theory is based on the assumption that efficient markets adjust rapidly when conditions change (Barney and Ouchi 1986). If actors in a firm's nexus of contracts can easily enter into or withdraw from contracts with the firm, then they are able to exit a relationship if they are not satisfied with the way they are treated. However, lack of other business opportunities for stakeholders, combined with sources of friction such as organizational inertia and entry and exit barriers, make the market inefficient by reducing the ability of a stakeholder to exit a relationship. It is interesting to note that shareholders may actually be in the strongest position to exit from a relationship with the firm, since they have very low switching costs and many other favorable options for investment.

With regard to Williamson's (1985) concern that shareholder contracts never come up for renewal, it is arguable that their contracts come up for renewal on a daily basis and that shareholders renew their contracts each time they decide to retain their shares.[7] They also have voting rights not enjoyed by other stakeholders (Boatright 1994). In addition, Marens and Wicks (1999) argue that the fiduciary duties owed to shareholders do not prevent managers from being sensitive to and generous with other stakeholders. They point out that managers have a wide range of legal responsibilities to other stakeholder groups. Consequently, both legal and intellectual arguments support the idea that managers should care for the needs of all of their stakeholders. Along these lines, Lubatkin (2007) developed a revised framework for corporate governance that includes all an organization's stakeholders.

Boards that consist largely of independent (nonemployee) directors are expected to be better monitors of executive actions (Bainbridge 1993; Baysinger and Butler 1985). In stakeholder terms, these directors could be external stakeholders. In theory, independence should lead managers to be more responsible as agents for the firm, which should lead to higher firm performance. However, Dalton, Daily, Ellstrand, and Johnson (1998), in a meta-analysis, found little evidence to support this relationship. On the other hand, there is some evidence that governance characteristics such as board independence matter more in time of organizational stress than during good times (Chatterjee and Harrison 2001; Daily 1996; Daily and Dalton 1994, 1995).

The other, less studied, function of a board of directors is to provide the firm with resources such as links to other organizations, advice, and legitimacy (Hillman and Dalziel 2003; Chatterjee and Harrison 2001; Pfeffer and Salancik 1978). For this function, stakeholder theory would advocate appointing external stakeholders to the board. Research evidence supports this proposition. For example, appointing representatives from financial institutions can facilitate capital acquisition (Johnson, Daily, and Ellstrand 1996; Stearns

[7] See Chapter 1.

and Mizruchi 1993). Entrepreneurial firms have far fewer resources and may especially benefit from such appointments (Johnson, Daily, and Ellstrand 1996).

The influence of the stakeholder perspective on management practice

Given the practical orientation of the stakeholder approach to strategic management, it is no surprise that stakeholder terms and concepts have been embraced fairly broadly by practicing managers and management consultants. As developed societies around the world have become increasingly sensitive to issues such as corporate wrongdoing, environmentalism and sustainability, and the treatment of workers, the stakeholder perspective has gained popularity. In this regard, the social responsibility movement has been a two-edged sword. As we mentioned previously in this chapter, it may have distracted strategic management scholars away from a more comprehensive approach to the theory as they came to believe that the stakeholder theory was all about social responsibility. On the other hand, the popularity of the theory in the corporate world is at least partly a result of this belief, coupled with the reality that the application of stakeholder theory really does lead to better results from a societal perspective. Consequently, many business organizations throughout the world directly address the needs of multiple stakeholders during their strategic management processes. The publicly available artifacts of these processes are found on many websites as statements of "stakeholder goals" or "corporate sustainability principles" or "corporate purpose."

Stakeholder-themed books targeted at managers have also influenced business practitioners. While many practitioner books since Freeman (1984) have included stakeholder concepts and terminology, four are focused mainly on the stakeholder management approach to business. Freeman and Gilbert (1988) further developed the notion of an enterprise strategy as a statement of corporate purpose, seen through the lenses of multiple stakeholder groups. Nearly a decade later Wheeler and Sillanpää (1997) examined numerous case studies of successful businesses that embraced stakeholder-inclusive management as a central philosophy. Chief among the companies highlighted in their book is the Body Shop (UK). Both Wheeler and Sillanpää had been involved in a number of independently verified audits of the Body Shop's social and environmental performance. The book also includes a practical management system for both auditing and improving relationships with a variety of stakeholders. Post et al. (2002a) also use cases to drive home points about the importance of taking care of the needs of a broad group of stakeholders as a prerequisite for both business success and survival. They examine Cummins, Shell, and Motorola in some depth to demonstrate that firms can use their productive relationships with stakeholders to enhance wealth both by creating new opportunities and by avoiding, reducing, and controlling costs. Finally, Graham Kenny (2001) presents an entire management system around what he refers to as "strategic factors." Strategic factors are the things an organization has to get right in order to succeed with its key stakeholders. Managers look at the organization from the outside in. They ask how their stakeholders evaluate firm performance and what they look for from the firm. In Kenny's view, strategic factors provide a logical link between strategic planning and performance measurement.

These and other practitioner books have been accompanied by countless articles directed at managers both in the popular business press and in the practitioner-oriented academic literature in strategic management. In 1998, *Long Range Planning* devoted an entire issue to the "stakeholder corporation" (Clarke 1998). The *Harvard Business Review* has published articles dealing with how effective management of stakeholders and stakeholder networks can lead to the creation of value (Florida and Goodnight 2005; Ibarra and Hunter 2007). The *California Management Review* (e.g. Freeman and Reed 1983; Post, Preston, and Sachs 2002b) and the *MIT Sloan Management Review* (e.g. Atkinson, Waterhouse, and Wells 1997; Hall and Vredenburg 2005; Pirson and Malhotra 2008) have also published articles that contribute to the practitioner literature on stakeholder management.

Organizational interest in the principles of stakeholder management has prompted the consulting industry to provide guidance in how to develop, monitor, and manage relationships with a broad group of stakeholders. CoreRelation Consulting[8] focuses specifically on stakeholder strategy development and stakeholder engagement. They have developed what they call a "co-creative engagement model" that is network-focused as opposed to organization-centric (Svendsen and Laberge, 2006). As another example, Walker Information,[9] a research and consulting firm, has a vision that they "will continue to be recognized as the global authority in stakeholder measurement and management." Many other consulting firms have incorporated stakeholder concepts and tools into the services they provide. The point of this section is not to provide a comprehensive review of the influence of the stakeholder concept on business. Rather, we would like to reinforce the idea

[8] http://www.corerelation.com. [9] http://www.walkerinfo.com.

that the stakeholder approach to management has been found to be quite useful by real managers, regardless of the theoretical verdict.

Critical evaluation and future directions

From the inception of what we now call strategic management, scholars have been interested in stakeholder concepts. However, writers of the mainstream literature have tended to develop their own models and terminology to deal with the idea that organizations are at the center of a network of constituencies that require attention. In the early development of the field, we saw discussions of configurations of relationships, with stakeholders being called external contributors, resources, interest groups, or inputs. Environmental analysis included many stakeholder groups. Even Porter's (1985) five forces model, from a stakeholder perspective, is an evaluation of the power of three critical stakeholders: customers, suppliers, and competitors. Most recently, the relational approach has emerged (Dyer and Singh 1998). With some very notable and important exceptions, the strategic management discipline has tended to view stakeholder theory as the domain of business ethics and social responsibility, and efforts to apply stakeholder theory to strategic management have been undercut by the widely held belief that there is a conflict between serving shareholders and serving a broad group of stakeholders (Argenti 1997), as well as a misconception that stakeholder theory advocates equal treatment of all stakeholders (Gioia 1999).

What is most interesting in this debate is that the field of strategic management now seems to be moving towards stakeholder theory in a more deliberate way, possibly out of necessity. Corporate scandals have created more interest in the problem of the ethics of capitalism and "ethical management processes." Also, the sheer complexity and volatility of the business environment – what we have called the problem of value creation and trade – calls for newer and more comprehensive models (Lowendahl and Revang 1998; Hitt, Keats, and DeMarie 1998). External stakeholders have become much more proactive in exerting pressure on organizations, and scholars are struggling to find ways to incorporate these multiple influences into their theories and planning models. Of course, it is also obvious that companies are not likely to survive unless they deliver value to a fairly broad group of stakeholders (Campbell 1997). Finally, stakeholder management concepts have found their way into the planning processes of many, or perhaps the most highly visible, business organizations in the USA and many other countries. In spite of all this, stakeholder theory still seems to have to prove its economic efficiency in the minds of many strategy theorists before it will be perceived as a completely viable set of ideas.

This chapter has provided substantial evidence in support of the concept that serving the needs of a broad group of stakeholders can and does enhance economic performance. Several forces are moving the field towards stakeholder theory and an important part of this process will be the direct integration of stakeholder theory into other mainstream theories. The highly popular resource-based view of the firm holds particular promise in this regard.

While resource-based theory has been pervasive in its influence on strategic management and other disciplines, it has been criticized for not providing much guidance with regard to *how* firms should manage resources to achieve competitive advantage (Priem and Butler 2001). Another limitation of resource-based theory is that it does little to help researchers understand how resulting economic rents are or should be distributed once they are created (Barney and Arikan 2001: 175). Stakeholder theory can help to enhance resource-based thinking by addressing these limitations. It provides a reasoned perspective of how firms should manage their stakeholders to facilitate the development of competitive resources. The stakeholder perspective also explains how a firm's stakeholder network can itself be a source of sustainable competitive advantage (Harrison, Bosse, and Phillips 2009). In addition, stakeholder-based reasoning provides a practical motivation for firms to act responsibly with regard to stakeholder interests, including fair distribution of economic rents (Harrison, Bosse, and Phillips 2009). Specifically, fair treatment and reasonable compensation of stakeholders helps to ensure their continued cooperation. Compensation is viewed as a multidimensional construct that includes economic rents as well as accommodating behavior (i.e. behavior that is desirable from the perspective of specific stakeholders).

The resource-based and stakeholder views are complementary rather than competing. The resource-based view envisions firms as bundles of resources, while the stakeholder perspective views firms as networks of stakeholders. In reality, firm competitiveness requires effective management of both organizational resources and stakeholder relationships. Furthermore, a firm is dependent on its stakeholder network for most of the resources it acquires. Consequently, resource dependence theory (Pfeffer and Salancik 1978) provides a natural bridge between the two theories. Basically, the resource-based view *needs* stakeholder theory to be complete. Furthermore, because the resource-based view has economic performance as its dependent variable, integrating the two theories will enhance the position of stakeholder theory in the minds of many scholars.

Also important to advancing the economic expediency of the stakeholder approach will be the application of longer-term methods. Current evidence comes largely from case histories or cross-sectional studies. Even if the studies include multiple years of data, the relationships are tested such that each year is an observation, with multiple years representing multiple observations within the same companies. For example, a study may include a measure of community responsiveness, with a corresponding economic variable for each year. The assumption is that community responsiveness will have an immediate positive effect on performance. At most, researchers may apply a lag of a year or two, forward or backward, in their tests. However, effective stakeholder management may take years to pay off in economic terms.

There is also a need in the field to develop better models for managing stakeholder relationships. Stakeholder management means that organizations serve a broad range of stakeholders, but does not specify what is meant by this service. We have suggested in Chapter 1 that trying to create as much value as possible without resorting to trade-offs is a starting point. However, we need more fine-grained conceptual models of this idea. Bosse, Phillips, and Harrison (2009) moved in this direction by defining stakeholder treatment in terms of distributive, procedural, and interactional justice. Also, Jones, Felps, and Bigley (2007) developed a scheme for classifying firm cultures based on how they treat stakeholders. They explain that the cultures lie on a continuum from individually self-interested (agency culture) at one end to other-regarding (altruist culture) at the other.

Competitors present a point of confusion for strategists interested in stakeholder theory. Most models of the stakeholder perspective envision competitors alongside other types of stakeholder (e.g. Freeman 1984; Harrison and St. John 1994, 1998). A more useful conceptualization would have competing networks of stakeholders, where one competitor's network is in competition with the others (see Figure 4.3). This conceptualization also addresses the economic efficiency issue, since the economic performance of competing networks of stakeholders could be directly compared. Of course, competitors can still play other roles, such as supplier, customer, or joint venture partner, but working out these multiplicities would just enrich the competitive models. For example, Lado, Boyd, and Hanlon (1997) have conceptualized competition and cooperation as interrelated dimensions and developed a typology of rent-seeking strategic behaviors.

The notion of sustainability also seems to hold the potential to engage more strategists in stakeholder-based thinking. Sustainability is a multidimensional construct that involves all of the key stakeholders, as well as the environment and society at large.

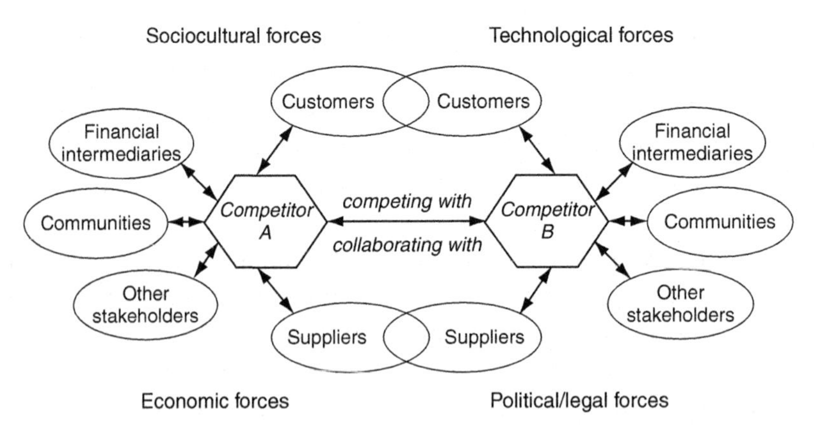

Figure 4.3. Competing stakeholder networks
Note: The overlapping ovals are an indication that competitors are likely to share some of the same customers and suppliers. We acknowledge that overlaps may also occur with other types of stakeholders as well.

According to Stead and Stead,

> The economic dimension of sustainability also involves the need to create for posterity an ecologically balanced and socially just economic system that provides humans with the goods, services, economic justice, and meaningful employment necessary for a high quality of life ... the rapid entropy associated with high economic growth rates is not sustainable over the long run. (Stead and Stead 2004: 22)

Sustainability has already received a considerable amount of attention in the strategic management literature (e.g. Boutilier 2007; Frost and Mensik 1991; Bansal 2005; Sharma and Henriques 2005; Kolk and Pinkse 2007). Buysse and Verbeke (2003) directly integrated environmental strategy with stakeholder management in an empirical test. Based on a sample of 197 firms operating in Belgium, they found that more proactive environmental strategies are associated with a deeper and broader coverage of stakeholders. Nevertheless, the sustainability literature also carries the risk of further reinforcing the idea that stakeholder theory deals only with social responsibility. In this regard, the one important difference between the social responsibility and sustainability literatures seems to be that sustainability puts more emphasis on the economic dimension of firm performance as an essential element of the theory. Perhaps, then, the sustainability literature is not as risky as was the social responsibility literature with regard to sidetracking stakeholder theory.

This chapter has emphasized the economic implications of stakeholder management because economic performance is the most important dependent variable in the strategic management literature. However, as Donaldson and Preston point out, "the notion that stakeholder management contributes to economic performance ... is insufficient to stand alone as a basis for the stakeholder theory" (Donaldson and Preston 1995: 87). The alternative approach, an exclusive focus on shareholder interests, makes no sense from an instrumental perspective because the cooperation of a broad group of stakeholders is required in order to achieve high shareholder returns (Jensen 2001). In addition, such a perspective is morally untenable (Donaldson and Preston 1995). Stakeholder theory is in a strong position relative to other strategic management theories, because it deliberately addresses ethics and values (Phillips, Freeman, and Wicks 2003).

An obvious solution to the field's obsession with purely economic performance measures is to build a strong case for measuring performance along multiple stakeholder dimensions simultaneously, or maximizing total value creation in the system (Atkinson, Waterhouse, and Wells, 1997; Chakravarthy 1986; Freeman 1984; Greenhalgh 2001; Vincent 1988; Cameron 1980). For example, the study we mentioned previously, by Malekzadeh and Nahavandi (1987), looked at multiple stakeholder outcomes from corporate takeovers. Also, Mills and Chen (1996) measured joint venture outcomes across multiple stakeholder dimensions. Such an approach can be used in determining general corporate performance or it can be applied to other organizational changes such as implementation of particular strategies. The key is to use several measures simultaneously in the same study so that the strengths and weaknesses of the phenomenon, as well as any trade-offs, may be understood.

The case for including multiple stakeholder dimensions can be built on the basis of solving the problem of value creation and trade. From a realistic perspective, managers face simultaneous pressure from multiple stakeholders. It is also a better way to understand longer-term implications of firm actions, since ignoring or harming any of a firm's key stakeholders can lead to negative implications for the firm in the future. For example, a corporate restructuring that hurts trust between employees and management could lead to cost savings in the short term, but to serious problems with employee turnover and productivity in the future. As broadly-based performance measures are developed, it will be important to avoid the assumption that they are all treated equally (Phillips, Freeman, and Wicks 2003). Instead, evaluation of a firm based on multiple stakeholder dimensions might be accompanied by an analysis of their respective contributions, costs, and risks.

We began this journey through the stakeholder-based strategic management literature by suggesting that some strategic management scholars do not see stakeholder theory as central to the strategic management literature (Hitt 2005). We have demonstrated that some of the most common tenets of stakeholder theory have been a part of mainstream strategy literature since its inception, although sometimes disguised with other labels. Going forward, the theory is well poised to address some of the most important issues in strategic management. In fact, Ireland and Hitt suggest that ethical, stakeholder-based practices will be essential to strategic leadership in the future. They argue,

> An understanding of the interests of all legitimate stakeholders will come only through analysis of and sensitivity to cultural diversity. A strategic leader's commitment to serve stakeholders' legitimate claims will contribute to the establishment and continuation of an ethical organizational culture. (Ireland and Hitt 2005: 72)

5 Stakeholder theory in finance, accounting, management, and marketing

Stakeholder theory is beginning to have a greater reach in the academic literature on business. The purpose of this chapter is to examine how it has been applied in the four major business disciplines – finance, accounting, management, and marketing (economics was addressed earlier, in Chapter 1, and strategic management in Chapter 4). This chapter suggests that researchers have selected those portions of the theory that are most applicable to the questions they are trying to answer. Integration of stakeholder concepts with the theories of their own discipline has occurred; however, this integration has not, unfortunately, contributed much to the core stakeholder literature. In other words, stakeholder theory has informed the business disciplines, but the disciplines have done little to inform stakeholder theory. Perhaps another way to say this is that stakeholder theorists have not paid adequate attention to the disciplines. We offer the ideas in this chapter as a beginning to bridging this disciplinary gap. There are opportunities for scholars in all the business disciplines to advance both stakeholder theory and practice.

In the next section we shall briefly discuss the emergence of the primary business disciplines. We shall also explain how we have defined the content of each discipline for the purposes of this analysis. Each of the four disciplines has a subsequent section devoted to it. We begin each of these sections with some introductory thoughts about the role of stakeholder theory in the discipline, followed by a discussion of some of the primary applications of the theory. We conclude each section with a critique of the literature and recommendations regarding fruitful paths scholars might take in the future.

The rise of the business disciplines

In 1881 the first business school housed in a university environment was established at the University of Pennsylvania (Sass 1982; Wharton School 2000). The Wharton School was the brainchild of successful entrepreneur Joseph

Wharton, who wrote a letter to the university asking it to create a school to prepare young men to be leaders in an increasingly complex commercial environment. During the ensuing years Wharton devoted not only his energy but a sizable amount of his own fortune to helping the school fulfill its charter. The first five degrees awarded were in the area of finance. In 1904 Wharton began instruction in marketing. Around the same time, other disciplines were added, including accounting, industrial management, transportation, and insurance. On another front, the first graduate business school was established at Dartmouth College in 1900 (Broehl 1999). A little over a decade later, in 1911, Dartmouth's Amos Tuck School of Administration and Finance held a major conference on scientific management. The conference was attended by 300 leading industrialists, including Frederick W. Taylor and Lillian Gilbreath. The conference helped to establish business as a field of scientific study. Academic associations around particular disciplines also aided their development (Sweetser and Petry 1972).

Following the leadership of the Wharton School and on the foundation of increased science-based knowledge, the business disciplines continued to develop even as the number of university-based business schools expanded. In 1920 there were 1,576 bachelor's degrees and 110 master's degrees awarded in business (Gordon and Howell 1959). By the late 1950s over 50,000 degrees were awarded each year, including approximately 100 doctorates. In the middle of the last century, Gordon and Howell (1959) conducted a study of higher education for business. They examined the knowledge and skills needed by business, using deductive reasoning and observation as well as surveys of executives. They used this research as a foundation for assessing the curricula of business schools. They concluded that a broad-based business curriculum was needed, with a large core of required courses including accounting, statistics, economics, organization and administration, marketing, finance, the social, legal, and political environment, and a capstone course in business policy (Gordon and Howell 1959: 134). Their findings were consistent with the requirement instituted in 1949 by the American Assembly of Collegiate Schools of Business (AACSB) regarding a core of courses to which all member schools would be held.

Work in stakeholder theory has influenced the business disciplines of finance, accounting, marketing, and management (Buchheit, Collins, and Reitenga 2002). Theories and methods associated with the four business areas tend to overlap (Biehl, Kim, and Wade 2006). This is especially evident in the fields of accounting and finance, where many journals publish work from both disciplines. Nevertheless, for our purposes we shall define the accounting discipline as primarily associated with issues regarding measuring and reporting information on firms, both internally and externally. Finance will include topics related to financing the firm efficiently and maximizing financial returns.

Management is an even more ambiguously defined discipline. Gordon and Howell (1959) identified the "theory of administration" as an important topic for study, which they defined as the "scientific study of human behavior in organizations" (180). In modern parlance, this would include organizational behavior, organizational theory, and human resources management (previously called personnel). Traditionally, scientific management would include what is now called operations management, manufacturing management, or, more broadly, management science. These courses are frequently taught within management departments in modern business schools. Although they tend to be much more quantitative than other management topics, they still deal with the efficient deployment of people and other organizational resources within a firm. Consequently, we shall include a discussion of these topics within the management section.

Marketing is cross-disciplinary in nature, both drawing from and contributing to the other disciplines. However, the traditional emphasis tends to be on the relationship between a firm and its customers (Lorigan 2006/2007), with the intention of providing high returns for shareholders. For the marketing section we shall review the work published in marketing journals and books published by marketing scholars, regardless of their potential application to other disciplines.

Information technology (also called information systems or management information systems) is emerging as a separate discipline. However, information technology is often applied to the other disciplines. In this chapter, work related to information technology will be found in the section on the discipline to which it pertains rather than trying to break it into a separate section. In addition, much of this work on information technology falls into the management science side of management.

Before we begin, we should explain how we selected studies for inclusion in this review and how we shall examine them. We have a fairly broad notion of what we mean when we speak of stakeholder theory.[1] No doubt our perspective has crept into many parts of this book. However, there are a variety of other interpretations of the theory found in the business literature, and our intention is to be inclusive in our review of this literature. Consequently, we

[1] See Chapter 3 above.

have included articles and books as long as the authors used the term "stakeholder" *and* have included arguments, theories, or models that advanced the core idea that a firm is responsible to multiple stakeholders and/or multiple stakeholders influence the firm.

Stakeholder theory in the finance literature

This section will argue that the field of finance has come to appreciate a practical view of the stakeholder perspective, while not fully embracing the core concept of balancing the competing interests of a broad group of stakeholders. Although finance scholars traditionally ignore the moral foundation of stakeholder theory (except as it relates to the obligation of a firm to its shareholders and other financiers), most now recognize the importance of stakeholders in providing high financial returns consistent with an instrumental stakeholder perspective (Jones 1995). We shall begin with a review of work that establishes the place of stakeholder theory in the finance literature. We shall then review the debate concerning shareholder wealth vs. stakeholder welfare from the finance perspective. Finally, we shall review a few scattered applications of stakeholder theory in finance.

A foundation for stakeholder theory in finance

One of the earliest significant uses of the stakeholder perspective in the finance literature was by Cornell and Shapiro (1987),[2] whose work led them to receive a first prize from the Financial Management Association for distinguished applied research in financial management. Building from the fundamental insight of Coase (1937) – that firms exist because they are less expensive than alternative structures for transactions between parties – Cornell and Shapiro (1987) carefully examined how implicit claims differ from explicit contracts with stakeholders and how both types of claims influence financial policy. Explicit claims come from legally binding contracts with stakeholders, whereas implicit claims come from expectations of stakeholders that result from vague promises or past experiences with the firm. According to Cornell and Shapiro,

[2] Alan Shapiro was a participant in the original seminar at Wharton during the late 1970s, as we mentioned in Chapter 2.

> The distinguishing feature of implicit claims, as we define them, is that they are too nebulous and state contingent to reduce to writing at a reasonable cost. For this reason implicit claims have little legal standing. Typically, the firm can default on its implicit promises without going bankrupt or liquidating. (Cornell and Shapiro 1987: 6)

Cornell and Shapiro (1987) explained that stakeholders (such as customers or suppliers) will have very little influence on the financial policy of a firm if its managers only consider explicit contracts, because their claims typically are senior to those of the stockholders and debt holders. If bankruptcy risk is low, then the explicit claims of stakeholders are nearly risk-free. On the other hand, the implicit claims of stakeholders are highly uncertain. Therefore the value of implicit stakeholder claims is highly sensitive to information about the firm's financial condition. Since a firm's implicit claims are an embedded feature of the firm (i.e. cannot be separated and sold independently of the firm), the market value of the firm is dependent on how information provided to the market influences the value of both its implicit and explicit claims.

Another interesting implication from the perspective advanced by Cornell and Shapiro (1987) is that if a firm intends to make large payoffs on implicit claims in the future, it should "bond" those claims in the present. For instance, a firm might make an announcement regarding a new product it intends to release in two years. In addition to the announcement, it would establish a financial structure that is supportive of the claim, which might entail holding excess cash on the balance sheet. This sort of bonding allows the firm to gain maximum value now for its implicit claims in the future. For instance, it can allow the firm to "sell" the implicit part of its value at a higher price when engaging in contracts that are associated with the new product. This analysis also suggests that financial distress is likely to have a much greater impact on the firm than just the cash drain, because stakeholders will begin to lose confidence in the ability of the firm to honor its implicit claims. This conclusion is supported by Subrahmanyam and Titman (2001), who describe how relatively small changes in stock prices result in substantial changes in asset values. These events, which they call "cascades," result from complementarities across stakeholders. Nonfinancial stakeholders, such as customers, employees, and suppliers, make decisions contingent, in part, on information revealed by the price of the stock.

Over a decade after Cornell and Shapiro (1987) published their foundational paper, Zingales (2000) provided another strong rationale for a stakeholder perspective in finance research. He argued that corporate finance theory is deeply rooted in the theory of the firm and that the firm that existed when the financial theory was being developed is no longer typical in today's economy. The firm of the past was very asset-intensive and highly vertically integrated, with tight control over its employees and stable organizational boundaries. He suggests that most of the big conglomerates have been broken up and the vertically integrated firms have relinquished direct control of their suppliers in favor of looser forms of cooperation. The boundaries of the firm are constantly changing, physical assets have become commoditized, and human capital has become the most valuable asset.

Zingales (2000) suggests that some of the basic questions that need to be addressed by corporate finance, given the nature of contemporary firms, include: (i) how can a firm without unique assets succeed in acquiring power in ways that are different from typical market contracting? (ii) how can such power be obtained, increased, or lost? (iii) how can this power be used in ways that go beyond simple market transactions? and (iv) how can the surplus that is generated be allocated among the stakeholders that created it?

A new theory of the firm might help finance scholars address some of these questions. One such theory describes the firm as a web of specific investments built around a valuable resource, which may be a physical or alienable asset or even human capital (Zingales 2000). The entrepreneur uses this critical resource to draw participants to the firm. These participants make firm-specific investments based on the expectation of increased rewards from participation with the firm and access to its resources. The entrepreneur structures relationships around the critical resource so as to create a nexus of specific investments that can produce more value than a competing entrepreneur with the same critical resource starting from scratch. This theory of the firm is consistent with the fundamental ideas of stakeholder theory.[3]

Some of the research in finance supports the positions advanced by Zingales (2000) and Cornell and Shapiro (1987). For instance, finance scholars have found that nonfinancial stakeholders influence the debt structure of firms (Istaitieh and Rodriquez-Fernandez 2006). Titman (1984) found evidence that firms that produce durable or unique goods are more likely to have low debt levels because their customers may not be willing to do business with a

[3] It is noteworthy that although Zingales's (2000) paper is perfectly consistent with stakeholder theory and, in fact, uses many of the same arguments and citations found in core stakeholder theory, he only uses the term "stakeholder" once in his article, and does so in a somewhat disparaging way (his quotation is reproduced in the next section of this chapter). It is not unusual for scholars in finance or other business disciplines to describe stakeholder concepts while not acknowledging them as such (i.e. the relational view [Dyer and Singh 1998]). Some of this neglect may be a result of ignorance, while it is also apparent that some scholars deliberately avoid the term because, in their minds, it carries with it the incorrect notion that stakeholder theory is exclusively about advancing societal interests, even at the expense of shareholders.

firm that appears likely to experience financial problems, thus cutting off supply of a needed product. In contrast, firms that produce nondurable goods or services that are widely available can have high debt levels and still be attractive as suppliers, because if they go out of business the firms they are supplying should still be able to get what they need from another source (see also Barton, Hill, and Sundaram 1989; Maksimovic and Titman 1991; Kale and Shahrur 2008).

These findings regarding the influence of nonfinancial stakeholders on financial structure also address one of the central tenets of stakeholder theory – that stakeholders vary in the strength of their bargaining power and thus their ability to influence firms. Sarig (1998) treated this issue directly. Specifically, he argued that the bargaining power of skilled employees increases as a function of firm leverage, because highly leveraged firms are more vulnerable to damage caused by employees who leave the firm. Of course, the leverage effect is not limited to negotiations with employees, but can also affect negotiations with the supplier of any firm-specific factors of production. Similarly, Holder, Langrehr, and Hexter (1998) discovered that firms with highly influential noninvestor stakeholders have lower dividend payout ratios, presumably an indication of the ability of those firms to make good on the implicit claims of their stakeholders.

Sperling (2006) examined the reciprocal influence of various stakeholders in the health-care sector, including private-sector employers, insurance companies, governments, and consumers. Also, Wood and Ross (2006) conducted a decision-making experiment and found that financial managers were more responsive to stakeholder opinion than government subsidization, cost, or any other factor when making decisions about environmental social controls.

Although moral considerations do not tend to be a primary driver of research in finance, scholars in the field have recognized the practical considerations associated with moral constraints. For example, Long and Rao (1995) found evidence that persistently negative, abnormal stock returns were associated with announcements of unethical business conduct. They explained this phenomenon in terms of increased monitoring costs and risks to stakeholders in the firm. Their conclusion was that unethical business behavior is not compatible with shareholder wealth maximization. On the positive side, Hausman (2002) examined the benefits associated with being trustworthy, such as an excellent reputation and uncertainty reduction. He concluded that "in certain environments firms may serve the interest of their stakeholders by placing moral constraints on their actions" (Hausman 2002: 1767). Related to the idea that moral behavior is consistent with higher financial returns is the core stakeholder argument that managing for a broad group of stakeholders actually improves firm performance and longevity.

We find evidence in these studies that there is a foundation for stakeholder theory in the finance literature. A central issue in this literature is whether managing for stakeholders improves profits (Allen 2003; Smith 2003). The debate is frequently examined in terms of shareholders vs. stakeholders, based on the assumption that satisfying a broad group of stakeholders is inconsistent with the idea of shareholder wealth maximization.

Shareholders vs. stakeholders from a finance perspective

Financial economists tend to give shareholder interests a preeminent position over the interests of other firm stakeholders. From the finance perspective, the primary responsibility of managers is to maximize shareholder value (Rappaport 1986; Wallace 2003). The oft-cited quotation from Milton Friedman provides the essential argument: "There is one and only one social responsibility of business – to use its resources and engage in activities designed to increase its profits so long as it … engages in open and free competition, without deception or fraud" (Friedman 1962: 133).[4] Agency theory reinforces this idea by envisioning managers primarily as agents for the shareholders, with the responsibility of looking after their interests (Jensen and Meckling 1976; Fama 1980). Earlier work by Dodd paved the way for agency theory:

> The legal recognition that there are other interests than those of the stockholders to be protected does not, as we have seen, necessarily give corporate managers the right to consider those interests, as it is possible to regard the managers as representatives of the stockholding interest only. (Dodd 1932: 1162)

As we discussed in Chapter 1, Michael Jensen is a vocal champion of the shareholder wealth maximization perspective. According to Jensen, wealth maximization does not mean that firms should completely neglect stakeholders:

> Several writers imply that running the corporation in the interests of shareholders means ignoring the interests of other corporate stakeholders. A corporation managed so as to maximize the value of its stock, they suggest, will ignore (or even harm) employees, suppliers, customers, and the communities in which it operates. This perspective simply makes no economic sense. A shareholder-driven company doesn't ignore its stakeholders. What it does is invest resources to benefit each of these

[4] See Chapter 1 above for our view of this statement.

constituencies to a point where the additional benefits to the company … exceed the additional cost. (Jensen 1989: 186)

However, in the same article Jensen warns against allowing managers too much discretion with regard to allocating resources to satisfy a broad group of stakeholders. His admonition stems from a mistrust of managers and their propensity to allocate resources according to their own desires at the expense of efficiency. This position is, of course, consistent with agency theory (Jensen and Meckling 1976). Jensen also argues that shareholders should be given the most importance in managerial decisions because they "are the only constituency of the corporation with a long-term interest in its survival" (Jensen 1989: 187). It is easy to see the fallacy of this latter argument, as shareholders can easily sell their stock at any time and reinvest in another company. In contrast, employees would find it relatively more difficult to change employers, customers could lose an essential source of supply, and certainly local communities are hurt if an organization ceases to exist. Furthermore, Cloninger pointed out that "In the presence of asymmetric information, the avid pursuit of share price maximization may lead managers to violate certain stakeholder interests and employ business practices that are unethical, immoral, or illegal" (Cloninger 1995: 50).

Many attempts have been made to reconcile shareholder wealth maximization with stakeholder perspectives. Some of these are found in the finance literature and some in other literatures (e.g. law, ethics, management). As noted in Chapter 4, Hill and Jones (1992) extended agency theory by arguing that managers have a responsibility to act as trustworthy agents to multiple stakeholders rather than just the stockholders. This view is consistent with the "nexus-of-contracts" perspective of the firm (Macey 1999), which suggests that a corporation can be described as a "complex set of explicit and implicit contracts" (Macey 1999: 1266) with stakeholders. There are also parallels with the earlier work of Coase (1937) and Cornell and Shapiro (1987). Similarly, Boatright (2002) pointed out that the concept of contracting applies as much to nonshareholders as it does to shareholders, and that both types of stakeholders face risks associated with their relationships with the firm (see also Boatright 1994). Zingales, drawing from the perspective that a firm is a nexus or formal and informal contracts, argued:

Once we recognize the existence of implicit contracts, then there are other residual claimants besides equity holders who may need to be protected (the famous stakeholders, often mentioned in the public policy debate). It then becomes unclear whether control should reside in the hands of shareholders, because the pursuit of shareholders' value maximization may lead to inefficient actions, such as the breach of valuable implicit contracts. (Zingales 2000: 1634)

In 2001 Jensen revised his arguments regarding the conflict between value maximization and stakeholder theory. He once again asserts that a firm should not ignore its stakeholders. However, he also argues that stakeholder theory does not specify how to make the necessary trade-offs among the competing interests of stakeholders. Basically, there is no clear way to measure corporate success or failure. "With no way to keep score, stakeholder theory makes managers unaccountable for their actions. It seems clear that such a theory can be attractive to the self interest of managers and directors" (Jensen 2001: 297). The underlying premise is that managers cannot be trusted and that they will allocate resources according to their own interests unless they have to justify allocations against the metric of firm value maximization, measured in financial terms. We argued in Chapter 1 that the later thinking of Jensen around the idea of "enlightened value maximization" begins to make his theory more consistent with the insights of stakeholder theory.

Not all finance scholars agree with Jensen's sole objective of financial value maximization. Previously, Cloninger (1997) had argued that the appropriate goal should be maximizing stakeholder value and that such a goal "reduces the incentive of agents to favor one group of stakeholders at the expense of others while doing no disservice to traditional financial techniques or analysis" (Cloninger 1997: 82).

Although the bulk of the empirical research regarding the relationship between financial and stakeholder performance is found in the management and business ethics literatures, there are some exceptions. Wallace (2003) linked various measures of nonfinancial stakeholder satisfaction to financial performance, and found that higher levels of value creation are directly connected to a firm's reputation for treating stakeholders well. He concluded that "it pays for companies to spend an additional dollar on stakeholder relationships as long as the present value of the expected (long-run) return is at least a dollar" (Wallace 2003: 120). These findings are, of course, consistent with studies from nonfinance disciplines, which we have reviewed elsewhere (e.g. Preston and Sapienza, 1990; Greenley and Foxall 1997; Kotter and Heskett 1992; Berman, Wicks, Kotha, and Jones 1999; Hillman and Keim 2001; Orlitzky, Schmidt, and Rynes 2003).

In addition, some work in progress also suggests the superiority of a stakeholder management perspective. Allen, Carletti, and Marquez (2007) applied a mathematical model to the question and conclude that stakeholder-oriented firms have lower relative output but higher prices, which can lead to higher firm value. They also found that firms may voluntarily select a stakeholder orientation in an effort to increase their value and that consumer preferences for the products of these types of firm can lead to a larger number of them. The one downside they observed is that consumers pay higher prices for products and services from stakeholder-oriented firms. These finance researchers expressed surprise at their findings.

Other applications of stakeholder theory in finance

Stakeholder theory has been used in a variety of other contexts in the finance literature. One of the most interesting recent applications is enterprise risk management (ERM), which "seeks to strategically consider the interactive effects of various risk events with the goal of balancing an enterprise's entire portfolio of risks to be within the stakeholders' appetite or tolerance for risk" (Beasley, Chen, Nunez, and Wright 2006: 49). According to Beasley and Frigo (2007), the approach differs from a traditional "silo" approach, which seeks to manage risks in isolation. Beasley et al. (2006) integrated the concept of ERM into the balanced scorecard approach, providing a useful way for top managers to manage their firms' total risk.

Lim and Wang (2007) also used a stakeholder-based view of risk management, arguing that financial hedging reduces a firm's systematic risk and thus encourages firm-specific investments by stakeholders. On the other hand, too much firm-specific investment will load too much idiosyncratic risk on to stakeholders, thus making firm diversification more attractive. Their arguments are important to the finance literature because hedging and diversification have traditionally been viewed as substitute rather than complementary means of risk management. Baele, De Jonge, and Vander Vennet (2007) also examined the risk effects of diversification from a multiple stakeholder perspective.

In addition to risk management, the stakeholder perspective has been used to examine takeovers, financial distress, and leveraged buy-outs. With regard to takeovers, Chemla (2005) argued that because takeovers tend to transfer value to target owners and away from other stakeholders, the threat of a takeover can reduce stakeholder investment in the firm. The key to understanding this phenomenon, according to Chemla, is that stakeholders' bargaining power increases their incentive to invest in the firm. Consequently, anything that reduces that bargaining power acts as a disincentive to future investments. Yehning, Weston, and Altman (1995) examined the recontracting arrangements with a variety of stakeholders of firms in financial distress. Ippolito and James (1992) argued that going-private transactions are motivated by the desire to transfer wealth to equity holders from the firm's other stakeholders. These three studies are similar in that they all examine stakeholder bargaining power.

Discussion and future directions for stakeholder theory in finance

One of the most confining assumptions found in the finance literature on stakeholder theory is that stakeholder relationships are a "zero-sum game" (Smith 2003). In other words, a firm that allocates resources to one stakeholder group is taking those resources away from another. In the immediate term, and from a purely mathematical perspective (consistent with financial theory), this may be easy to demonstrate. However, over any term longer than the immediate term, the reasoning becomes more suspect. A more useful perspective, and one that could unlock the potential of stakeholder theory to explain financial phenomena, is that stakeholder relationships are a mutually reinforcing, interactive network (Post, Preston, and Sachs 2002a, 2002b). If financial theorists accept this alternative view, then they could devote energy to determining how to maximize total network value. The question is, what is the total value created for the network from a particular firm tactic or decision? Once the long-term value of a particular tactic or decision is determined, then the firm's share of that value can likewise be determined.

Some of the possibilities and difficulties associated with such an approach can be demonstrated using a simple example. Suppose that a firm decides to work cooperatively with community leaders to enhance the local business environment where its primary manufacturing facility is located. Consequently, the firm provides both financial and human resources to the community to achieve this purpose. The immediate result is a short-term drain on the firm's resources. However, the business community is enhanced, which brings value to the firm and many of its stakeholders as well as to other firms, which may include competitors. To examine the attractiveness of such a strategy in financial terms, measurement issues will need to be addressed. Specifically, the firm must estimate the total potential value to the system and then estimate the firm's portion of that value. While measurement issues might make such an analysis very difficult, it should be possible to model such a decision by making reasonable assumptions based on observations of real phenomena. Furthermore, the measurement and modeling issues are not particularly more problematic than others found in the financial economics literature. Work has already begun on addressing one measurement issue. McHale (2006) defined the concept of relationship capital and described how a strength relationship index was used by an Australian firm.

Options analysis could also add credence to this discussion. An option gives a firm the right, but not the obligation, to take a particular course of action in the future (Trigeorgis 1993, 1997). Options analysis provides a firm with the opportunity to reduce its downside risk while also assessing the upside potential from a particular course of action (Reuer and Leiblein 2001). Such an analysis could be supportive of the notion that serving the interests of a broad group of stakeholders can lead to higher value because frequently an investment in a particular stakeholder provides future opportunities. Basically, the concept of an option opens the door to evaluating more fully the longer-term implications from short-term actions that result from balancing stakeholder interests.

The international dimension could also be very interesting to finance scholars and practitioners. Bradley (2003) examined governance issues in the Anglo-American and European markets from a stakeholder perspective. Specifically, he found that Anglo-American markets are more liquid and governance issues are focused on financial stakeholders. In contrast, European markets are less liquid and governance is more likely to be extended to a broader group of stakeholders. Previously, Grinyer, Sinclair, and Ibrahim (1999) found evidence that would seem to corroborate his analysis. They found that corporations in the United Kingdom do not seek stockholder wealth maximization as a primary goal. Another interesting finding suggests that Australian initial public offerings (IPOs) are not increasing stakeholder representation on their boards of directors, which runs counter to trends in other countries. Differences in the priority given to a broad group of stakeholders from one country to another are likely to have huge implications with regard to financial management for the firms in those countries. Comparative studies would be in order, as would studies that try to determine the most efficient financial management policies for a variety of economic and political/legal situations.

Finance scholars have barely tapped the potential of the stakeholder perspective in improving financial decisions. Financial market participants clearly are not the only stakeholders that influence financial outcomes. A broadened perspective of stakeholder influences could help finance researchers better explain such phenomena as why some initial public offerings are more successful than others, why two firms with a very similar financial structure get a different interest rate from the same bank, or how residual returns are influenced by stakeholder bargaining power. While it seems unlikely that finance scholars will soon abandon their singular obsession with maximizing the financial value of the firm in favor of a broader perspective on firm performance, the stakeholder dialogue is increasing and researchers are beginning to apply a stakeholder perspective to a fairly wide range of finance-related questions.

Stakeholder theory in the accounting literature

The accounting discipline has grown considerably in the past half century due to recognition of its importance and the increasing demand for its graduates (Fogarty and Markarian 2007). Research in the discipline has also grown in both volume and importance. Stakeholder theory has contributed to this literature, but until recently this contribution was fairly minimal.

In 1984, Schreuder and Ramanathan argued that markets and monitoring systems leave corporate managers with little discretion to work in the interests of any other stakeholders except the shareholders. In fact, market failures and incomplete contracting are just as applicable to other stakeholders as they are to shareholders. Another relatively early contribution to the accounting literature came from Dermer (1990), who described the organization as an ecosystem in order to demonstrate the significance of accounting to strategy. In his view, organizations are held together by a desire to survive, and stakeholders compete for control of firm strategy. In this context, accounting data and accounting systems take on unanticipated roles. For instance, accounting becomes a tool used by stakeholders to construct reality.

Neither of these early contributions seemed to have a strong influence on the literature in accounting. However, another article describing a corporate reporting practice foreshadowed what has become in the accounting literature an important stream of research that has made ample use of stakeholder theory. In 1988, Meek and Gray discussed issues surrounding the inclusion of a value added statement in the annual reports of US corporations. The purpose of a value added statement is to demonstrate the wealth created for a diverse group of stakeholders, including all the firm's suppliers of capital, as well as government and employees. Meek and Gray (1988) argued that these statements are useful in focusing attention on a wider group of stakeholders while still allowing the firm to maintain its primary orientation on shareholders. Rahman (1990) also argued that multinational firms should provide local value added statements in host country financial reports. These reports would provide useful decision-making information for dominant stakeholders in the host countries. Discussion of social reporting was not new to the accounting literature. However, these are two of the first studies to discuss corporate social reporting using stakeholder terminology.

We shall begin this section with a discussion of the influence of stakeholder theory on corporate social reporting, as found in the accounting literature. We shall then examine the influence of stakeholders on other accounting practices such as earnings reports and accounting methods. We shall continue the discussion by reviewing a few miscellaneous applications of the stakeholder concept in the accounting literature. Finally, we shall provide an analysis of use of stakeholder theory in the accounting literature and provide some recommendations for future research.

Stakeholder theory and accounting for firm influence on stakeholders and society

Just as business ethics scholars have used stakeholder concepts to support their theories about corporate social responsibility, so accountants have made ample use of stakeholder logic to develop ideas about the reporting of social responsibility practices and outcomes. Accountants had been debating issues surrounding social reporting since at least the 1970s (Gray, Kouhy, and Lavers 1995).

In 1992 Roberts used stakeholder theory to predict levels of corporate social disclosure. Specifically, he discovered that stakeholder power, strategic posture, and economic performance are all related to the amount of disclosure. Around the same time, Rubenstein (1992) advocated the creation of a natural asset account that would help a firm to determine whether its practices are sustainable from an environmental perspective. His arguments focused on firms' social contracts with the stakeholders to whom they are accountable. Ilinitch, Soderstrom, and Thomas (1998) followed similar logic as they developed both theoretical and empirical approaches to defining corporate environmental performance. They explained that such information is necessary in order to provide important stakeholders with information upon which to base strategic decisions. Furthermore, they argued that the accounting domain is the appropriate place to develop metrics regarding environmental performance.

Since Roberts (1992), several accounting scholars have examined factors that influence social disclosure. In recent studies, Campbell, Moore, and Shrives (2006) found that community disclosures are a function of the information needs of stakeholders, and Boesso and Kumar (2007) demonstrated that social disclosure in general is influenced by the information needs of investors, the emphasis in the company on stakeholder management, and the relevance of intangible assets and market complexity. Wood and Ross (2006) found that stakeholder opinion is more influential in influencing manager attitude towards environmental social controls than subsidization, regulatory cost, or mandatory disclosure. Also, Magness (2006) discovered that companies that keep themselves in the public eye subsequent to a major disaster in the industry are more likely to divulge more information. While this conclusion seems obvious, of more interest is her finding that financial performance seems to have no influence on the amount of disclosure in these situations.

In a case study, Moerman and van der Laan (2005) examined the influence of the World Health Organization on social reporting in a major international tobacco company. The study is significant because it explores the influence of a worldwide stakeholder for many organizations on the reporting behavior of an individual company. Another case study found that stakeholder groups put pressure on the clothing industry in Bangladesh and on one large company in particular (Islam and Deegan 2008). The researchers linked this pressure to changes to social and environmental disclosure practices.

One factor that complicates the research into stakeholder influence on social disclosure is that it tends to vary considerably from one country to another, a result of the influence of societal norms, political and economic systems, and government regulations. Information on social reporting practices across the European Union can be found in Freedman and Stagliano (1992), while other studies have examined these practices in the United Kingdom (Freedman and Stagliano 1992; Gray, Kouhy, and Lavers 1995), Spain (Moneva and Llena 2000), and Ireland (O'Dwyer, Unerman, and Hession 2005; O'Dwyer 2005; O'Dwyer, Unerman, and Bradley 2005). Smith, Adhikari, and Tondkar (2005) compare Norway and Denmark with the USA and conclude that the way in which a society defines the relationship between a firm and its stakeholders is a primary influence on the level and type of social disclosure. Boesso and Kumar (2007) compare companies in the USA and Italy.

There is also speculation regarding whether firms act responsibly with regard to their stakeholders as they report social information. An in-depth longitudinal case study discovered that data from two sources that were external to the firm painted a very different picture from what the firm had actually reported with regard to ethics, society, and the environment (Adams 2004). Another study based on interviews with corporate managers, auditors, and consultants concluded that social and ethical accounting, auditing, and reporting practices amounted to little more than "corporate spin" (Owen,

Swift, and Hunt 2001). Even those firms that might be considered the best in reporting to stakeholders may not be as good as they appear. A study of European companies that were given formal recognition for their sustainability reporting discovered reluctance on the part of management to address statements to specific constituencies or to include stakeholders in assurance processes (O'Dwyer 2005).

One of the conclusions that can be drawn from the literature on stakeholder influence on social reporting is that reporting is a function of multiple influences and that these influences are interconnected. Furthermore, there are different types of reporting and these different types are also interconnected. Bhimani and Soonawalla (2005) discussed the tensions that exist based on stakeholder and other influences with regard to corporate financial reporting, corporate governance reporting, corporate social responsibility reporting, and stakeholder value creation reporting. They argued that these different types of reporting should be integrated into a spectrum of corporate disclosure responsibility. The advantage of an integrated approach is that issues regarding both conformance and performance reporting can be comprehensively addressed in an interlinked manner rather than separately.

Stakeholder influence on other accounting practices

Social reporting is not the only accounting area that is influenced by stakeholder theory. In this section we shall examine some of the other accounting phenomena that researchers have speculated might be subject to stakeholder influence.

Some studies have investigated how stakeholders influence reporting of financial information. For instance, Bowen, Johnson, Shevlin, and Shores (1992) used stakeholder theory to explain the timing of earnings announcements. They argued that timing of such announcements can influence the perceptions of stakeholders who do not find it cost-effective actively to monitor the firm. They found evidence to support the idea that managers attempt to influence the perceptions of their stakeholders regarding firm performance. Richardson (2000) added the notion of information asymmetry to this argument. When asymmetry between a firm and its stakeholders is high, they do not have adequate resources to monitor manager behavior, which can lead the manager to practice earnings management. His results support a relationship between earnings management and the level of information asymmetry.

Another example of the influence of stakeholders on financial reporting is found in a study by Scott, McKinnon, and Harrison (2003), who used stakeholder theory to examine the influence of various stakeholders on the method of financial reporting in two New South Wales hospitals over a period of more than a century. Also, Shah (1995) examined stakeholder and non-stakeholder influences on decisions made by UK companies with regard to "creative accounting," especially abuse of goodwill provisions. In addition, Burgstahler and Dichev (1997) explained earnings management practices of firms in terms of information-processing heuristics applied by various stakeholders. Finally, Adler and Chaston (2002) studied information that stakeholders use to predict whether an organization will decline.

Reporting is not the only accounting phenomenon that has been linked to stakeholder influence. Winston and Sharp (2005) studied the influence of four stakeholder groups – users (i.e. shareholders, employees, creditors), preparers, accountants, and regulators – on the setting of international accounting standards. They concluded that none of the groups had absolute power in determining standards, although some stakeholders exhibited a higher level of influence. Previously, Nobes (1992) identified five stakeholders – users, auditors, managers, government, and the International Accounting Standards Committee (IASC) – that influenced the creation of the goodwill standard in the UK. In another example, Baskerville-Morley (2004) applied the Mitchell, Agle, and Wood (1997) stakeholder salience model to examine how professional associations responded to a significant transgression in their industry. Her study identified an unusually high level of activity among the associations' stakeholder groups and also provided a useful framework for understanding the responses of these associations. Finally, Ashbaugh and Warfield (2003) found that multiple stakeholders influence the selection of a firm auditor, and Chen, Carson, and Simnett (2007) found that particular stakeholder characteristics influence the voluntary dissemination of interim financial information.

Accounting researchers have also examined the influence of different international contexts in terms of whether they support a pure stakeholder or multi-stakeholder orientation (Ball, Kothari, and Robin 2000; Bartov, Goldberg, and Kim 2005; Ely and Pownall 2002; Hilary 2003). The assumption underlying this work is that the US financial system is oriented almost exclusively towards shareholders, so that its accounting regulations and requirements are focused on providing shareholders with the information they require. In contrast, other countries support a culture in which the needs of a broader group of stakeholders are taken into consideration. Germany (Bartov et al. 2005) and Japan (Ely and Pownall 2002) have both been used as examples of countries with more of a stakeholder orientation than the USA.

Market observers, researchers, and regulators tend to believe that the shareholder model provides better financial information. In support of this idea, Ely and Pownall (2002) found that earnings and book values are more closely associated with market value in the USA (shareholder-oriented) compared with Japan (stakeholder-oriented). Bartov et al. (2005) found limited supporting evidence in a comparison of US and German companies, but their results were sensitive to self-selection bias and whether the firms were profitable.

Other stakeholder applications in accounting

Stakeholder concepts and ideas are also used in a variety of other contexts in the accounting literature. One of these contexts is governance (Ghonkrokta and Lather 2007; Keasey and Wright 1993). We have examined the contribution of stakeholder theory to the broader governance literature elsewhere in this volume. However, some of that discussion has found its way into accounting. For example, Baker and Owsen (2002) presented a stakeholder-based perspective on the role of auditing in corporate governance. Similarly, Seal (2006) developed a stakeholder-based institutional framework for understanding how management accounting is related to corporate governance (see also Collier 2008). Joseph (2007) extended ideas found in the corporate governance literature to corporate reporting practices, and developed a "normative stakeholder view of corporate reporting" based on responsibility to multiple stakeholders. In doing so, he hoped to

> reveal moral blind spots within the prevailing accounting worldview that fails to acknowledge the impact of the corporation on multiple stakeholders and thereby harness the intellectual and creative potential contained in accounting to address the larger issues that affect the public interest. (Joseph 2007: 51)

CEO compensation, which is tied to the governance literature, has also been addressed. Arora and Alam (2005) found that changes in CEO compensation are significantly tied to the interests of diverse stakeholder groups, including customers, suppliers, and employees. Similarly, Coombs and Gilley (2005) discovered that stakeholder management influences CEO salaries, bonuses, stock options, and total compensation.

Independence is another topic found in the governance literature. Although independence refers to whether a particular director has a close tie with the organization or CEO in that literature, a similar concept has been applied to auditors. Schneider, Church, and Ely (2006) examined auditor independence in light of the nonaudit services that are provided to firms. They organized their analysis around the decisions and judgments of three stakeholder groups – financial statement users, auditors, and managers.

The impact of the Internet on accounting has only recently begun to be investigated. The Internet is considered significant because stakeholder dialogue is important to corporate social and environmental governance and accountability. Gowthorpe and Amat (1999) examined the websites of Spanish companies and discussed the potential of the Internet as a way of establishing a corporate dialogue. Similarly, Unerman and Bennett (2004) examined the potential of an Internet-based communications platform to identify and reach a wider range of stakeholders as well as determining their expectations. They evaluated this potential on the basis of an ideal speech situation. Shankar, Urban, and Sultan (2002) proposed a stakeholder theory of online trust that will help information systems professionals better understand the perspectives of multiple stakeholders. Because the Internet is such a powerful communications tool and much of accounting deals with communicating with stakeholders, it seems likely that this area will attract much accounting research in the future.

Discussion and future directions for stakeholder theory in accounting

A quick perusal of the literature we have just reviewed demonstrates that much of the application of the stakeholder perspective in the accounting literature has occurred since 2002. It is probably not a coincidence that this date coincides with passage of the Sarbanes-Oxley Act, which extended the regulatory powers of the US Securities and Exchange Commission (SEC) regarding corporate governance procedures. The act provides new requirements to ensure the independence of auditors, restricts firms that provide accounting services from either auditing or consulting services, creates rules requiring the creation and disclosure of effective financial controls, requires that business records be retained for at least five years, and requires that financial reports be personally certified by the CEO and the chief financial officer (Kane 2004; Osheroff 2006). In general, this legislation is considered to be stakeholder-friendly in that it increases the accountability of an organization to a broader group of stakeholders (although shareholders are still the primary beneficiary). Of course, Sarbanes-Oxley was a direct response to several highly visible scandals, some of which implicated accounting firms. Those scandals have, by themselves, created a higher level of interest in ethics and responsibility to stakeholders.

There is, of course, some question as to whether the accounting profession is genuinely interested in increasing its responsibility to a wider range of stakeholders. Reports commissioned in the USA and the UK in the 1970s to identify the needs of users of financial statements still resulted in a focus on shareholders. Another study in the 1980s resulted in the publication of the international conceptual framework (IASC 1989). Although the framework is considered to be a stakeholder model, it had little impact on the amount of stakeholder disclosure (Friedman and Miles 2006).

Even if the accounting profession as a whole becomes more stakeholder-friendly, it may be difficult to change the behavior of auditors because of the difficulty in measuring phenomena that are important to stakeholders. One study demonstrated that auditors spend a relatively long time and devote considerable energy to things that can be satisfactorily verified, but not to other things that they knew were important to stakeholders (Ohman, Hackner, Jansson, and Tschudi 2006). We have already mentioned a study by Owen, Swift, and Hunt (2001) that concluded that social reporting tends to be focused on impression management rather than reality. A report on the World Bank's effectiveness in developing countries demonstrates the inadequacy of conventional accounting in helping to balance competing stakeholder interests (Saravanamuthu 2004). Consequently, it appears that one important direction accounting researchers could take is the development of reporting practices and standards that are genuinely stakeholder-friendly.

Another indication of the interest of accountants in stakeholder theory is use of the stakeholder perspective in accounting education. Stout and West (2004) reported on a stakeholder-based approach to substantially revising an accounting program. However, stakeholder theory is inadequately covered in accounting textbooks. Specifically, an analysis of twenty-one introductory accounting textbooks demonstrated that the interests of shareholders are predominant and that other theoretical perspectives are given scant attention (Ferguson, Collison, Power, and Stevenson 2005). Similarly, a survey of accounting educators found that too much emphasis is put on the shareholder perspective in accounting textbooks (Ferguson, Collison, Power, and Stevenson 2007). If the accounting profession really intends to put more emphasis on reporting information that is useful to multiple stakeholders, it needs to begin the process of change as it trains educators. Legislation and regulation alone are likely to be insufficient to effect such a change in perspective.

The accounting discipline might also be able to take advantage of an opportunity in the area of decision-making support. Wooldridge and Weistroffer (2004) argued, based on the existing decision-making research, that revenue planning could be improved by including the viewpoints of a diverse group of stakeholders. They developed a two-step model that used a decision support system and a Delphi-type approach and applied it in a mid-sized city. Development of multi-stakeholder decision support models seems to fit nicely into the accounting domain.

Finally, there are great opportunities for accounting researchers who would like to tackle some of the most difficult issues associated with stakeholder accounting. These are, of course, measurement issues. As we have suggested in the first part of this section, social reporting is problematic because of inconsistent and otherwise inadequate performance measures. However, the stakeholder theory extends well beyond traditional corporate social responsibility. Better measures need to be developed to gauge the performance of organizations relative to the implicit and explicit claims of employees, managers, communities, suppliers, and customers, for a start. Quagli (1995) was well ahead of his time in suggesting that intangible assets should include much more than just those assets derived from financial transactions with external parties. He argued that intangibles, at their core, stem from the competencies and knowledge of humans who are affiliated with the firm.

Stakeholder theory in the management literature

Much of the stakeholder-based work found in management journals is either central to the stakeholder discussion or pertains to the intersection of stakeholder theory and strategic management as discussed in Chapter 4. However, management also includes behavioral areas such as organizational behavior, organizational theory, and human resource management. Traditionally, management has also included management science, manufacturing, and operations management. We now examine contributions in each of these areas, including a critique and suggestions for future research.

The stakeholder perspective in the "soft" side of management

One of the earliest applications of the stakeholder perspective in the management literature was by Sturdivant (1979). His article is based on work conducted by the Wharton Applied Research Center, which has been discussed in Chapter 2. He examined the attitude gaps that exist between managers and activist group members. He also advanced the idea that managers should seek cooperation from among their entire system of stakeholders. Sturdivant's article clearly was management focused, although it did not generate much of a response from main stream management researchers at the time.[5]

Mitroff (1983a) also was a pioneer in the study of management issues through a stakeholder lens. He synthesized phenomenological, ethnomethodological, and social action theory to examine the complex ways in which humans develop images of themselves, their organizations, and their environments. His analysis led to the conclusion that the "deeper symbolic aspects of human systems can be understood in terms of a special set of stakeholder entities" (387), which he called archetypes. Mitroff developed these ideas further in a book called *Stakeholders of the Organizational Mind* (1983b). He used the stakeholder concept in an analysis of corporate policy making, examined the influence of external stakeholders on managers and the manager's personality as a stakeholder, and advocated new ways of looking at organizations in the social sciences.

Since Mitroff's early contribution, the organizational behavior topic that has been influenced most by stakeholder theory is probably leadership. In the 1990s, several scholars included stakeholder themes in their discussions of effective leadership. For instance, Taylor (1995) advocated a broad stakeholder perspective in managing radical changes in a turbulent environment. Friedman and Olk (1995) studied executive succession processes from a stakeholder perspective and discovered that the way in which stakeholders respond to a succession process influences the new CEO's leadership effectiveness. In addition, Nwankwo and Richardson (1996) developed a stakeholder-based framework for developing leadership skills. It included assessment of the power bases and formulation of political bargaining strategies. Heller (1997) also examined leadership and power sharing from a stakeholder perspective. Heller's study is especially interesting because of his findings that continental countries take a broader stakeholder perspective than do Anglo-American countries. He also studied differences in the abilities of stakeholders to share power with organizational leaders. Legal and formal structures facilitate power sharing with employees, but customer influence tends to be limited to primarily market mechanisms.

Recently some organizational scholars applied an even more direct and comprehensive stakeholder approach to leadership. This effort began with Schneider (2002), who developed a stakeholder model of leadership based on an organization–environment co-evolution framework. Stakeholder theory

[5] Indeed, it was a footnote in this paper that led Freeman to attempt to discover the history of the stakeholder idea as explained in Chapter 2.

was found to provide an appropriate basis for the model because of its flexibility in accommodating various leadership relationships in the context of increasingly "fuzzy" organizational boundaries, flatter hierarchies, and greater use of subcontracting. Other applications to leadership found in the behavioral management literature include leadership development strategy (Andreadis 2002), leader accountability (Hall, Blass, Ferris, and Massengale 2004), ethical leadership (Thomas, Schermerhorn, and Dienhart 2004), post-merger leadership (Fubini, Price, and Zollo 2006), and a systems model of leadership (Sternberg 2007). The practitioner-oriented leadership literature has also been strongly influenced by stakeholder theory, as evidenced in an article by Clement (2005) and a popular book by Covey and Merrill (2006).

In addition to leadership applications, a stakeholder approach has also been used to help assess organizational effectiveness. Cameron (1980, 1984) described four different ways of assessing effectiveness. One of his approaches, the strategic constituencies approach, is based on at least minimally satisfying the demands and expectations of key stakeholders. An important step in this approach is the stakeholder audit, which helps a firm to identify all the constituencies that are impacted by the organization's performance (Roberts and King 1989). This procedure is well described by Kreitner and Kinicki (2008). Daft and Marcic (2001), on the other hand, used a stakeholder approach to integrate goal, resource-based, and internal process approaches to measuring organizational effectiveness. They argued that the approach is broad enough to incorporate multiple perspectives (see also Gibson, Ivancevich, Donnelly, and Konopaske 2003; Tsui 1990; Connolly, Conlon, and Deutsch 1980). Closely related to organizational effectiveness, goal setting also has made use of a stakeholder approach (Gregory and Keeney 1994; Kumar and Subramanian 1998; Hellriegel, Slocum, and Woodman 2001).

A few other contributions found in the organizational behavior literature indicate the flexibility of the stakeholder concept. Burke, Borucki, and Hurley (1992) studied the psychological climate among 18,457 sales personnel across hundreds of retail establishments. They discovered that work-climate perceptions could be described in terms of employee well-being and the well-being of other organizational stakeholders. They concluded that a multiple stakeholder perspective would help to advance research on the psychological climate. In a much less conventional study, Ostas (1995) used both stakeholder theory and social contract theory to develop arguments for why religious inquiry can and should be integrated into the practice of corporate relations. In a more recent study, Carter (2006) examined reputation management among Fortune

500 companies and discovered that firms direct their reputation management activities towards stakeholders that are more visible.

Human resource management has also been influenced by stakeholder theory. This influence is at least partly a result of the perspective that firms that practice effective and trustworthy stakeholder management are better able to attract a high-quality workforce (e.g. McNerney 1994; Albinger and Freeman 2000; Greening and Turban 2000). Of course, human resources scholars also recognize that human resources systems must be able to cope with the constant and ever-changing competing interests of organizational stakeholders (Vickers 2005). As early as 1984, Beer, Spector, Lawrence, Quinn Mills, and Walton suggested that stakeholder interests should be reflected in human resource management policies to ensure the longevity of an organization.

In a relatively early application of stakeholder theory to human resources research, Jansen and Von Glinow (1985) examined conflicts between the behaviors, attitudes, and norms that result from the organization's reward system and the behaviors, attitudes, and norms of organizational stakeholders. For example, they found that although stakeholders need honest and open reporting, the organizational reward system can encourage information falsification and nondisclosure. Olian and Rynes (1991) evaluated the efficacy of traditional organizational systems in implementing a total quality perspective within the firm. They concluded that these systems were inadequate and recommended several changes to organizational processes and measurement systems, along with changes in the values and behaviors of key organizational stakeholders.

More recently, Greenwood and Simmons (2004) observed that stakeholder theory has pervaded human resource management. They suggested that an organizational system needs to be viewed holistically through identification of the various stakeholder perspectives, the way they interact, and the way they influence the system. One of the advantages of the stakeholder perspective for human resource management, according to Greenwood and Simmons, is that it contains elements of organizational justice. They also demonstrated that stakeholder theory can help in the establishment of human resource standards. In a critique of the human resources (HR) literature, Dipboye was even stronger in asserting that "to bring HR research to the level of a successful science, programmatic, theory based research is needed in which there is a pursuit of important research questions and the use of diverse research methods. The needs of a variety of stakeholders must be considered in addition to corporate management" (Dipboye 2007: 96).

Stakeholder theory also has been applied directly to the development of human resources systems. For instance, Stewart (1984) used stakeholder theory in developing a technique for identifying constituencies and their concerns when selecting, developing, and evaluating personnel. In addition, Ulrich (1989) used a stakeholder perspective in developing practitioner guidelines for assessing human resource management effectiveness. Colakoglu, Lepak, and Hong (2006) made similar recommendations, but in a global context. Stakeholder theory has also proven helpful in creating strategic human resource development systems (Garavan 1995), in managing change (Hussain and Hafeez 2008; Kochan and Dyer 1993; Lamberg, Pajunen, Parvinen, and Savage 2008), in handling crises (Ulmer 2001), and in managing downsizing (Labib and Appelbaum 1993; Guild 2002; Tsai, Yeh, Wu, and Huang 2005).

The stakeholder perspective in the "hard" sciences of management

The "hard" sciences of management are so called because they tend to deal with physical processes and/or mathematical or computer-based management models. Although these processes and models obviously are not disconnected from people, they typically are not founded on a human behavior approach. Since stakeholder theory is about people and groups of people, it serves to integrate human elements into what might otherwise be pure quantitatively based management science models. For instance, in an early application of stakeholder theory in this literature, Nunamaker, Applegate, and Konsynski (1988) used stakeholder identification and assumption surfacing in the development of a group decision support system. Similarly, Keeney (1988) developed a problem-solving procedure to involve stakeholders constructively in analyzing problems of public interest. The central topics of this discussion include project management, manufacturing management, process improvement, problem solving, decision support, and information systems management.

Jones (1990) provided a relatively early application of the stakeholder concept in the project management literature. He examined the political context of project management from the perspective of chief executive officers of aerospace companies. He discovered that factors such as the degree of stakeholder representation in the structure of goals and the level of participation in decision making significantly influenced the level of internal politics. More recently a stakeholder approach to project management has become more common in the project management literature. For instance, Oral,

Kettani, and Cinar (2001) used a stakeholder approach to evaluate and select projects in an international context. In another example, McManus (2002) discussed the influence of multiple stakeholder values on project management. Along these same lines Karlsen (2002) developed a formal and systematic project stakeholder management process based, in part, on a survey of project managers in Norway. Also, Cleland and Ireland (2002) used a stakeholder conception of project management to tie different organizational stakeholders together. Olander (2007) applied stakeholder impact analysis to construction project management. Finally, Aaltonen, Kujala, and Oijala (2008) extended the concept of stakeholder management to global project management. Achterkamp and Vos (2008), after conducting a meta-analysis of the project management research, recognized that the importance of effective stakeholder management to project management success is commonly accepted in the field.

Stakeholder theory has been applied to manufacturing from two perspectives: the influence of manufacturing on stakeholders and the influence of stakeholders on manufacturing. Representing the former perspective, Steadman, Albright, and Dunn (1996) used stakeholder theory to explain the complex relationships between the firm and its various stakeholders in the context of the adoption of new manufacturing technologies such as flexible manufacturing systems or computer-integrated manufacturing. They included an impressively broad group of stakeholders in their analysis, including educators, trainers, line managers, auditors, suppliers, customers, human resource managers, stockholders, labor unions, the financial community, environmentalists, top managers, employees, government, local community organizations, directors, and bondholders. The influence of stakeholders on manufacturing is represented in studies by Foster and Jonker (2003) in the context of quality management, and Riis, Dukovska-Popovska, and Johansen (2006) for strategic manufacturing development.

Stakeholder theory has also been applied directly to improving manufacturing systems. As early as 1990, Maull, Hughes, Childe, Weston, Tranfield, and Smith developed a methodology for designing and implementing resilient computer-aided production manufacturing (CAPM) systems that began with developing an understanding of key organizational stakeholders. They argued that stakeholder analysis is essential to the provision of a strategic context for the specification of manufacturing systems and CAPM requirements. Sachdeva, Williams, and Quigley (2007) took a very different approach. Rather than focusing on the front end of the improvement process, they worked on implementation. Specifically, they argued that stakeholder resistance to changes arising from operational research in health-care organizations frequently led to poor implementation of results. They recommended active stakeholder participation during the operations research process.

From the perspective of improving environmental performance, Klassen (1993) discussed the influence of stakeholders on environmental issues. González-Benito and González-Benito (2006) examined the role of stakeholder pressure on the implementation of environmental logistics practices (see also Alvarez-Gil, Berrone, Husillos, and Lado 2007). Manring and Moore (2006) applied a virtual network learning model to integrate economic, ecological, and social dimensions of cleaner production. They demonstrated their model with a case found in the North Carolina textile wet-processing industry. Jørgensen, Remman, and Mellado (2006) argued that integrated manufacturing systems must be expanded to include all of a firm's stakeholders if they are to contribute to both competitive advantages and sustainable development. Sundkvist and Finnveden (2007) surveyed various stakeholders to develop recommendations regarding monitoring of integrated product policy (IPP) in Sweden. Similarly, Sandoval, Veiga, Hinton, and Sandner (2006) applied a multiple stakeholder approach to assess the applicability of sustainable development concepts in an alluvial mineral extraction project in Venezuela. Also, Lozano (2006) examined internal and external university stakeholder resistance to the incorporation of sustainable development principles into the university curricula. Finally, Moffat and Auer (2006) described a partnership-based Canadian government initiative designed to help increase innovation as well as environmental performance. These studies are only a few of many possible examples of the pervasive influence of the stakeholder concept in research on environmentally friendly manufacturing.

A stakeholder perspective has also found its way into research on new product and service development. McQuarter, Peters, Dale, Spring, Rogerson, and Rooney (1998) used a stakeholder approach to identify issues affecting the management of new product development. They characterized new product development problems as an illness where the symptoms are easy to detect but the causes are hard to determine. Stakeholder analysis became part of a five-part categorization scheme to determine the actual forces that lead to these types of problem. Similarly, Elias, Cavana, and Jackson (2002) used stakeholder analysis to improve research and development projects. Their methodology included rational, process, and transactional levels of analysis (Freeman 1984), combined with Mitchell, Agle, and Wood's (1997) approach to analyzing stakeholder dynamics. They applied the methodology to a road pricing project in New Zealand. Stakeholder theory was also applied to the development of new product service systems by Morelli (2006). In addition, Krucken and Meroni (2006) argued that building stakeholder networks is an important part of creating complex product-service systems. They applied their arguments to a research project funded by the European Commission.

This discussion has already demonstrated a wide range of applications of stakeholder theory in specific areas such as project management, manufacturing management, and process improvement. However, the stakeholder concept has also been used to develop tools that can be applied to a variety of problem-solving situations. For instance, Le Cardinal, Guyonnet, Pouzoullic, and Rigby (2001) developed a problem-solving framework to help organizations deal with the contradictions, antagonisms, and paradoxes that exist between stakeholders, each with a different strategy. The framework was developed based on the principle of trust and an in-depth analysis of the Prisoner's Dilemma. It is unique to the operations research literature because it describes the interpersonal interactions found in a complex situation in terms of fears, attractions, and temptations that the participants could feel as they interact. Other very interesting applications of stakeholder theory to problem solving include a collaborative simulation approach (den Hengst, de Vreede, and Maghnouji 2007), strategic option development and analysis (Hjortsø 2004), a risk-based approach to dealing with uncertainty (Carey, Beilin, Boxshall, Burgman, and Flander 2007), and an optimization-based approach to evaluating alternative strategies (Chang, Yeh, and Wang 2007).

Decision support is very closely related to problem solving in the operations research literatures and here also we found various applications of stakeholder theory. For example, Bryson and Mobolurin (1996) extended the analytic hierarchy process to accommodate ambiguous decision-making situations. They developed a multiple-criteria decision-making problem procedure to facilitate the understanding of key organizational stakeholders which, they argued, is critical to the successful implementation of the decision once it is made. Similarly, Firouzabadi, Henson, and Barnes (2008) combined the analytic hierarchy process with zero-one goal programming to create a decision support methodology when a single choice must be made in the presence of multiple stakeholders. Other examples of stakeholder concepts in multi-criteria decision models can be found in Chou, Chou, and Tzeng (2006), Henn and Patz (2007), Mohanty, Agarwal, Choudhury, and Tiwari (2005), Lewis, Young, Mathiassen, Rai, and Welke (2007), and Morgan and Matlock (2008).

The next logical step in this discussion is the information systems (IS) literature, since information systems support management decisions. Also, information technology can be used to understand stakeholders (Griffin

1998). A very early application of a stakeholder perspective, which predates any of the operations applications we found, is by Schonberger (1980). He applied a very broad perspective to the design of management information systems, arguing that in some cases the organization might find it appropriate to allow one of its stakeholders to take over the leadership role in a design project. This was a novel concept for its time. Schonberger defended his idea by citing Barnard's (1938) view that an organization consists of more than just its employees, but also includes customers, suppliers, the community, creditors, and other constituencies that have a stake in the organization. He also cited Ackoff's (1974) systems view of the organization as a justification.

Other, more recent applications of stakeholder theory can be found in the IS literature. Gupta (1995) argued that evaluation of the impact of an IS strategy must go beyond firm-level analysis to include a broader group of stakeholders. Along these lines, Coman and Ronen (1995) applied the theory of constraints to information technology management and used stakeholder analysis to identify the location of the constraints (see also Byrne and Polonsky 2001). In another application, Tesch and Klein (2003) developed a framework for identifying the skill requirements of IS specialists based on a multiple stakeholder perspective. Also, Córdoba and Midgley (2006) advanced an approach to IS planning based on what they called critical systems thinking. The approach involves analysis of stakeholders' perspectives prior to the selection and/or design of IS planning methods.

In addition to IS planning, the stakeholder concept has also been used in other planning contexts. Kent, Kaval, Berry, Retzlaff, Hormaechea, and Shields (2003) described efforts to link stakeholder objectives to planning processes in White River National Forest in Colorado. Walters (2005) took a multiple stakeholder approach to planning and control within virtual business structures. Chung, Chen, and Reid (2009) conducted an experiment in which business intelligence was gathered through classifying stakeholders on the Web. A stakeholder approach has also been applied to tourism research and management. Sauter and Leisen (1999) developed a tourism planning model based on what they called the relationship/transaction strategy continuum. It involves identifying and proactively considering both the transactions and relationships orientations of stakeholders. Congruency between perspectives increases the likelihood of stakeholder collaboration in service delivery. Another tourism-based study discusses sustained value creation from a stakeholder perspective (Ryan 2002).

There are a few additional applications in areas such as supply chain management, just-in-time management systems, crisis management, and environmental logistics. Also, it is not surprising that the stakeholder approach has been used to discuss ethical issues as they pertain to operations research and IS management (Acquier, Gand, and Szpirglas 2008; Kruchten, Woo, Monu, and Sotoodeh 2008; Gallo 2004; Keeney and McDaniels 1999; Al-Mudimigh, Zairi, and Ahmed 2004; Pagell, Krumwiede, and Sheu 2007; Peters and Austin 1995; Smith and Hasnas 1999).

Discussion and future directions for stakeholder theory in management

From the perspective of solving the problem of value creation and trade, stakeholder management *is* management. Consequently, this review, although useful for the purposes of analysis, may appear to some to create an artificial division between core stakeholder theory and other management theories. This is not our intent. On the contrary, we have intended to demonstrate that stakeholder theory can be applied easily to a wide variety of management topics.

Numerous opportunities exist for future scholarly activity. Institutional theory examines the influence of institutional environments on organizations, with an emphasis on organizational conformance due to social norms and expectations (DiMaggio and Powell 1983; Baum and Oliver 1991). In spite of the conceptual similarities of stakeholder theory to institutional theory, institutional theorists have practically ignored it. This neglect creates an opportunity for increased cross-fertilization and integration. Campbell's (2007) institutional theory of corporate social responsibility is a useful starting point, although stakeholder theory encompasses a much broader view of an organization's constituencies than just society. In fact, a logical next step would be for Campbell's work to include more stakeholders.

Dipboye's (2007) call for a more scientific approach to research in human resource management highlights another opportunity. He specifically mentioned that a multiple stakeholder perspective could help to strengthen the research. Opportunities exist to examine more fully the way human resource systems influence and are influenced by various stakeholder groups. Stakeholder theory might be used to better explain why some human resource management strategies work better than others. In addition, work has just begun on developing human resources systems that take advantage of relationships with external stakeholders and information obtained through those relationships (e.g. Guild 2002; Ulmer 2001). Increasing globalization also offers opportunities for human resources research using a stakeholder perspective (e.g. Tsai, Yeh, Wu, and Huang 2005).

Operations researchers and other management scientists may be in a good position to develop tools to measure inputs and outcomes associated with stakeholders. Some researchers have already taken first steps in this direction. For instance, Dey, Hariharan, and Clegg (2006) developed a performance measurement model that involves affected stakeholders. They applied their model in the intensive care units of three hospitals. Similarly, Frederiksen and Mathiassen (2005) involved stakeholders in the development of software metrics programs. On the soft side of management, Kaptein (2008) developed a stakeholder-based measure of unethical behavior in the workplace that is much more comprehensive than previous measures found in the management literature.

Laplume, Sonpar, and Litz (2008) made suggestions regarding research areas that may be fruitful for future study, based on a review of the management literature on stakeholder theory. They noted that there is very little research regarding stakeholder management practices in smaller firms, family firms, entrepreneurial firms, and not-for-profit organizations. There is also a need to understand better how stakeholder groups emerge and how those groups are influenced by leadership processes. They call for more fine-grained case studies that will facilitate a richer understanding of cognitive and managerial processes, as well as the motivations behind both stakeholder and firm behaviors (see Chinyio and Akintoye 2008 as an example of this kind of research). In addition, they recognize the need for the development of more practicable frameworks for studying how firms balance stakeholder interests.

Rapid advances in technology and increasing globalization have created highly complex decision-making environments that a multiple stakeholder approach can help to address (Liebl 2002). As Walker, Bourne, and Shelley (2008) point out, there are currently few tools available to managers who want to improve their stakeholder management skills. In addition, increasing ethical sensitivity must be addressed even in areas such as operations research (Theys and Kunsch 2004).

Stakeholder theory in the marketing literature

By definition the marketing discipline is focused primarily on the relationship between a firm and its customers, although there is also broad acknowledgement that firms have a primary responsibility to generate high returns for shareholders (Bhattacharya and Korschun 2008). In addition, marketing scholars examine human resource and management issues, especially as they pertain to a firm's ability to serve customers. Marketing also has much to say about the interface between society and the firm. Nevertheless, to recognize that the discipline examines relationships with multiple stakeholders is not to say that marketing scholars embrace stakeholder theory in its complete form. When marketing scholars do embrace a genuine stakeholder perspective, their ideas and models look a lot like management.

Frequently, applications of stakeholder theory in the marketing literature serve as a warning that too much emphasis on one or a very small set of stakeholders is no longer appropriate (e.g. Bhattacharya and Korschun 2008; Jackson 2001; Kotler 2003). For example, Philip Kotler, an acknowledged leader in marketing education, made the following statement:

> Companies can no longer operate as self-contained, fully capable units without dedicated partners ... Companies are becoming increasingly dependent on their employees, their suppliers, their distributors and dealers, and their advertising agency. This dependence involves some loss of company freedom of action, but it increases the prospect of higher productivity and profitability. The key is for the company to form close relationships with its stakeholders. The company needs to build a network of partners that all gain from their joint strategy and behavior. Mutual trust is the bond. Selecting good partners and motivating them is the key to stakeholder marketing. (Kotler 2003: 119)

Lest anyone should think that Kotler's admission is an indication that he has abandoned his marketing roots, we should also mention that in an earlier section of the same book, he chastens companies who do not put the customer first and then outlines ways to ensure that customers are given the highest priority in organizational activities and planning (21).

We shall begin with a discussion of some of the major works that have brought the general concept of a stakeholder approach into the marketing literature. We shall then present stakeholder-based marketing research that deals with ethics and with social and environmental responsibility. This will be followed by an examination of a few interesting studies that do not fall into one of the first two categories. We shall complete the section with an evaluation of the research and recommendations for future development of the stakeholder concept in marketing.

Core stakeholder concepts in marketing

As we suggested above, marketing tends to focus on a small number of stakeholders, which typically include customers, shareholders, and sometimes employees, to the extent that they help to satisfy customers. However, several marketing scholars have either advocated the inclusion of or have included in their research a broad group of stakeholders. In 1991, at the same time that Copulsky was suggesting that firms need to balance the needs of only two stakeholders (customers and shareholders), Miller and Lewis (1991) were taking a much broader approach. They introduced the stakeholder concept as a way to help identify all of the firm's important constituencies, both internal and external, and to evaluate their stakes in the firm. This approach, they argued, helps marketing managers to strategically manage the marketing function.

At around the same time, Christopher, Payne, and Ballantyne (1991) developed what is referred to as the "six markets" model to define relationships with traditional stakeholders (see also Christopher, Payne, and Ballantyne 2002). The six markets include customer markets (including intermediaries), referral markets (including existing customers who recommend the firm and other referral sources), supplier markets (including traditional suppliers and alliance partners), influencer markets (including financial analysts, shareholders, the business press, government, and consumer groups), employee markets, and internal markets (internal departments and staff). The model was later refined and tested in a variety of industry settings (Payne, Ballantyne, and Christopher 2005). Payne et al. (2005) found that stakeholder interactions in one market could impact another market. They also found that firms could identify and work with stakeholders in each of the six markets to create mutual value through new understandings that would develop over time.

A few years after Christopher et al. (1991) published their "six markets" model, Greenley and Foxall (1996) examined the attention that UK firms give to five different stakeholder groups – consumers, employees, competitors, unions, and shareholders. They found that the orientations of firms towards these groups were interrelated and that consumer orientation was a good predictor of a firm's attitudes towards both competitors and employees. Later they studied the relationship between these firms' attitudes towards their stakeholders and firm performance (Greenley and Foxall 1998), concluding that different types of stakeholder orientations are associated with specific measures of performance, and that these relationships are moderated by the external environment. Greenley, Hooley, Broderick, and Rudd (2004) also discovered that a firm's stakeholder orientation profile influences its approach to strategic planning.

Polonsky, Suchard, and Scott (1999) used stakeholder theory to directly challenge the deterministic view of the firm and its environment. They explained that marketing theory tends to view the external environment as an uncontrollable and fixed constraint. However, the firm and its environment are actually very interdependent, and many elements of the external environment are subject to firm influence. Given this situation, they argued that firms should use stakeholder theory to integrate a wider set of relationships into a model of marketing interactions, resulting in more options for the firm and thus greater opportunities to create value. Polonsky, Schuppisser, and Beldona (2002) later extended these concepts by distinguishing between the positive and negative side of stakeholder relationships. They also described the role of relational factors such as trust, learning, power, commitment, and reciprocity. While their perspective is useful for analyzing diverse stakeholder relationships, it is also helpful for firms that would like to change the nature of their relationships with specific stakeholders. Following the same logic, Polonsky and Scott (2005) developed what they called the "stakeholder strategy matrix." The matrix is based on stakeholder ability to cooperate with the firm on the one hand and to threaten organizational goals on the other. Based on a study of marketing managers who answered questions about a hypothetical new product development scenario, they determined that firms may be trying to influence stakeholders regardless of their true ability to influence them.

Podnar and Jancic (2006) also examined stakeholder groups based on their power in relation to a company, especially as that power relates to communications and transactions between firms and stakeholders. They surveyed employees in marketing and communications companies and discovered three levels of communication with stakeholders – inevitable, necessary, and desirous. Their work is conceptually tied to another stream in marketing that deals with managing relationships with stakeholders – called simply "relationship marketing." Zinkhan suggested that, at its simplest level, relationship marketing "prescribes that it is more effective to invest in long-term customer interactions than to rely on a series of potentially unrelated, one-time exchanges" (Zinkhan 2002: 5). Following from this logic, Palmer and Quinn (2005) examined stakeholder relationships in the context of international retailing. Also, Conway and Whitelock (2007) used a relationship marketing approach in an effort to determine keys to success in subsidized arts organizations.

Already in this review we have observed several core stakeholder concepts, such as inclusion of a broad group of stakeholders in analysis and planning, examination of power differences across stakeholder groups, and effectively managing stakeholder relationships. Marketing scholars have also made use of systems for measuring multiple stakeholder outcomes. For instance, Kotler (2003) advocated what he called a "stakeholder-performance scorecard," in which companies track the satisfaction of key stakeholders, including employees, suppliers, banks, stockholders, retailers, and distributors. Norms are set for each group and management takes action when one of these groups shows an increased level of dissatisfaction. Similarly, Murphy, Maguiness, Pescott, Wislang, Ma, and Wang (2005) developed a "holistic" method for measuring marketing performance, based on providing long-term economic, social, and environmental value to five key stakeholder groups in order to enhance sustainable financial performance. Key stakeholders included customers, suppliers, employees, the community, and shareholders.

Ethics and social and environmental responsibility

In addition to core applications of stakeholder theory in the marketing literature, we observed numerous applications of the stakeholder concept in the areas of ethics and social responsibility as they pertain to marketing. This is obviously a carryover effect from the influence of stakeholder theory on corporate social responsibility in general, which we have discussed in a previous chapter.

With regard to organizational ethics, Stearns, Walton, Crespy, and Bol (1996) developed a framework for analyzing the ethical component of marketing decisions. They based their framework on the premises that marketers need to identify and understand the obligations they have to key stakeholders and that those obligations will inevitably conflict. Resolution of the conflicts, they argued, depends on the ethical philosophies of the organization. More directly, Whysall (2000) addressed ethical issues in retailing from a stakeholder perspective. Also, Blodgett, Long-Chuan, Rose, and Vitell (2001) took a broad international perspective in studying the cultural effects of ethical sensitivity towards various stakeholders. In addition, Lindfelt and Törnroos (2006) compared from an ethical perspective business network and stakeholder approaches to value creation. Finally, Ferrell and Ferrell developed a macromarketing ethics framework, which deals with "the economic and social impact of the fair distribution of products and other resources through the marketing system" (Ferrell and Ferrell 2008: 24).

Another stream in this literature examines effects on stakeholders from various marketing actions. Fry and Polonsky (2004) argued that firms should evaluate their entire network of stakeholders to determine both the intended and unintended consequences from marketing activities (see also Polonsky,

Carlson, and Fry 2003). For instance, O'Sullivan and Murphy (1998) applied stakeholder theory in studying ethical issues surrounding "ambush marketing," which is the practice of holding a marketing event around a sponsored event without paying the sponsorship fee. Similarly, Arnold and Luthra (2000) applied a multiple stakeholder approach to studying the effects of opening large-format ("big box") retail locations in new markets. In addition, Hoek and Maubach (2005) examined stakeholder concerns associated with direct-to-consumer advertising of prescription medicines. The *Journal of Advertising* even devoted a special issue to the topic of responsible advertising, with articles such as "A multiple stakeholder perspective on responsibility in advertising" (Polonsky and Hyman 2007).

With regard to social responsibility in general, Carrigan (1995) outlined some of the major arguments in support of and against societal marketing; societal marketing pertains to looking out for the long-term interests of consumers. Carrigan explained that the essence of societal marketing is that "good deeds equal good business." Although the focus in societal marketing is still on the consumer, Carrigan (1995) applied the concept from multiple stakeholder perspectives. Furthermore, what is most interesting is that she applied the concept to the tobacco industry. She examined twenty-five different perspectives (e.g. people, promotion, product, strategy, techniques, implementation, tactics) around the question of whether societal marketing would be a good or bad idea in this industry. It is not surprising that she found both pros and cons across all twenty-five dimensions. For example, from a *people* perspective, she argued that most people would benefit from adoption of societal marketing in the tobacco industry (which would involve such things as honest and open advertising). However, she also argued that such an approach would disregard minority rights, attack free will, and be detrimental to some stakeholders' livelihoods. With regard to promotion, adoption of the societal marketing concept could encourage favorable publicity and enhance the tarnished images of tobacco companies. On the other hand, some stakeholders might respond to such promotion as manipulation.

In more recent work, Maignan, Ferrell, and Ferrell (2005) developed a multiple stakeholder framework to guide managers in integrating corporate social responsibility into marketing. The framework provides a step-by-step approach that can be applied across all organizations. Also, Neville, Bell, and Mengüc (2005) examined the influence of reputation on the relationship between corporate social responsibility and firm performance. Their arguments are interesting in light of the findings of Sen, Bhattacharya, and Korshun (2006), who found that stakeholders are not very aware of corporate social responsibility, which limits the returns to such behavior. However, Sen et al. discovered that stakeholders did react positively to corporate responsibility when they were aware of it, as long as they believed that the firm's efforts were genuine. Along these lines, Sweeney and Coughlan (2008) discovered a great deal of variance across industries with regard to how corporate responsibility is discussed in annual reports. Taken together, these studies suggest that firms should do a better job of building their reputations through promoting socially responsible actions to their stakeholders.

One of the most common applications of stakeholder theory in the marketing literature on corporate social responsibility is in the area of environmental responsibility. "Green marketing" is a very popular topic in the field. Davis (1992) integrated ethical perspectives into green marketing, arguing that as corporations have positioned their products to address the needs of environmentally conscious consumers, most of their claims are confused, misleading, or, in some cases, illegal. Although Davis included stakeholder concepts in his paper, Polonsky (1995) took an even more comprehensive approach in developing a method for designing an environmental marketing strategy. He and another scholar also argued for broad stakeholder participation in green new product development processes (Polonsky and Ottman 1998). Around the same time, Crane (1998) explored green marketing strategy through alliances with a variety of stakeholders. Later, Byrne and Polonsky (2001) used a systems-based approach to examine relationships between stakeholders with regard to impediments to consumer adoption of alternative fuel vehicles. Polonsky (2001) also studied alliances between firms and environmental groups. Clulow (2005) used stakeholder analysis to identify the perspectives of stakeholders on the sustainability of life in Australia in the future and Rivera-Camino (2007) demonstrated that stakeholders have an impact on green marketing strategy.

Other applications in marketing of the stakeholder perspective

There are other interesting applications of the stakeholder concept that do not fall into one of the previous categories. In the branding area (Balmer 2008), Roper and Davies (2007) argued that the emotional responses of all stakeholders towards the corporate brand should be considered, and not just the customer. They applied their arguments to a study of key stakeholder groups of a business school. They found significant gaps among the perspectives of staff, students, and employers of the school. These results are supported by a study that demonstrates that different stakeholder groups really are distinguishable target groups for corporate branding (Fiedler and Kirchgeorg 2007). Gregory (2007) observed that stakeholders are typically regarded as the targets of corporate branding rather than as partners. She then developed four practical communication strategies for involving stakeholders in corporate brand development. Stakeholder concepts have been applied to other marketing communications questions by Duncan and Moriarty (1998) and Whysall (2005).

A second application is in the marketing literature of the service sector. Jallat and Wood (2005) examined the interfaces between firms and stakeholders that are directly affected by the firm's service processes. They determined that the multiplicity and complexity of ties between firms and affected stakeholders make management difficult, but also provide opportunities for innovation and differentiation. Luk, Yau, Tse, Sin, and Chow (2005) studied the stakeholder orientations of 193 service companies in China, and discovered that interaction effects among the components that determine stakeholder orientations can, in part, determine business performance. Finally, Smith and Fishbacher (2005) conducted four qualitative, exploratory case studies in the public-health and financial sectors to explore new service development processes. They found that managers tend to select stakeholders for involvement in new service development based on how central they are to the process and how much power they have in influencing the final design. Surprisingly, they also found that customers were thought to lack the knowledge and experience needed to contribute in meaningful ways to the new service development process. They determined that involvement from multiple stakeholders puts pressure on managers due to the complexity of the development process.

Recent developments and future directions for stakeholder theory in marketing

Based on nominations from thousands of people all over the world (e.g. business professionals, marketing professors, students, consumers), Sisodia, Wolfe, and Sheth (2007) identified a list of companies that people "love." They then screened the companies based on how well they take care of their stakeholders and how their stakeholders feel about them. This led to a short list of sixty companies. They assigned teams of MBA students to each of the listed companies, asking them to gather information about how well they served their stakeholders, based on secondary data sources as well as interviews with executives, customers, employees, analysts, and others. Twenty-eight companies were selected as those with the highest levels of humanistic performance, which they called "firms of endearment" (FoEs). Examples of companies on their list of FoEs include Google, Honda, IKEA, Wegman's Food Markets, Southwest Airlines, and New Balance.

Sisodia et al. (2007) found that the publicly traded FoEs outperformed the Standard and Poor's 500 by a significant margin over several different time horizons. They explained that the performance of these companies surprised them, since they tend to pay above-normal salaries, spend a lot on their communities, and deliver great products at fair prices. However, as interesting as the performance results is their analysis of the marketing field in general. They argue that during the twentieth century marketing became increasingly sterile and mechanized, largely because of increased use of information technology to develop marketing strategies:

> That was when companies gained an unprecedented information advantage over consumers. Companies used information technology to reduce us all to dehumanized data sets. We were variously labeled by such sterile terms as *seats*, *eyeballs*, *lives*, and faceless *end users*. We were reduced to stimulus-response mechanisms virtually devoid of volition by predictive modeling programs that supposedly knew us better than we knew ourselves. (Sisodia et al. 2007: 103)

The solution they propose for reversing this dehumanizing process involves love and healing. While a complete exposition of the meaning of these words to Sisodia et al. (2007) is beyond the scope of this chapter, we should mention that they advocate the development of trusting relationships with stakeholders, in which firms satisfy both legal and emotional contracts. Emotional contracts are based on qualitative criteria that reflect the moral and ethical values of stakeholders. Of course, there is a great deal in the book about endearing stakeholders to the firm by listening to them, including them, and allocating resources to them in the form of payments (i.e. high salaries), and service.

Another promising new development is that a group of top marketing scholars formed the Stakeholder Marketing Consortium, supported by the Marketing Science Institute and in cooperation with Boston University and the Aspen Institute's Business and Society Program. The first meeting of the consortium took place in Aspen in 2007 and included scholars from numerous top universities and business consulting firms.

The theme of the first meeting was "Beyond the four Ps and the customer." Bhattacharya and Korschun (2008) reported on the discussion sessions. In the first session, the current firm-centric conceptualization of the marketing field was challenged: "It was suggested that both scholars and practitioners need to consider how marketing activity affects a firm's constituents from the unique perspective of each actor rather than relying exclusively on the myopic lens of a firm's financial performance" (113). The group also concluded that a firm's constituents are "embedded in interconnected networks of relationships through which the actions of a firm reverberate with both direct and indirect consequences" (113). Moving forward, participants recommended applying a systems-based approach and possibly ecosystems theory to study these interconnected networks. Over the course of the meeting they also discussed the need to identify not only connections between a firm and its stakeholders, but also the connections between the stakeholders themselves. In addition, they suggested that scholars need to develop new models of the relative merits and drawbacks of pursuing a stakeholder marketing perspective. They also recognized the need to develop "valid metrics that reflect the inherent complexity of the subject" (115). In the final session participants outlined a strategy for injecting more of a stakeholder perspective into the marketing field.

Marketing as a discipline tends to be more outwardly focused than the financial or behavioral management areas. Consequently, marketing is in a strong position to work on problems associated with monitoring and communicating with external stakeholders. Marketing scholars are well positioned to develop measures of stakeholder orientation. For instance, Yau, Chow, Sin, Tse, Luk, and Lee (2007) recently developed a scale that measures stakeholder orientation. They tested their scale using hundreds of companies in three important commercial cities in China.

Concluding thoughts on stakeholder theory in the disciplines

Stakeholder theory has been applied to a variety of topics in the business disciplines. However, discipline research has not contributed much to the core theory. Looking to the future, this analysis has identified meaningful opportunities for scholars in the business disciplines to contribute to stakeholder theory and practice, based on their own areas of expertise. As noted herein, finance researchers are best trained to deal with models that test notions associated with maximizing total firm value and with a firm's portion of that value. Accountants have tools to help deal with measurement issues and can also add value in terms of defining useful stakeholder communications platforms based on the Internet. Behavioral management scholars can contribute in meaningful ways regarding the psychological aspects of stakeholder relationships and how to manage them effectively. Operations researchers and other management scientists can help with the mathematical tools needed to measure stakeholder inputs and outcomes and to model relationships among them. With its natural focus on the external environment, marketing can contribute greatly to understanding, measuring, and modeling external influences associated with stakeholders.

There is also a place for integrative research across the disciplines. As one example, Chen and Sackett (2007) recently investigated an international marketing issue (return merchandise authorization) from a production research perspective. Their investigation included Asian-based high-technology companies that provide mass-market products to developed countries. They developed a stakeholder analysis methodology to help firms exploit global market opportunities and satisfy customers even in "ultra-fast-to-market" product segments. Because the stakeholder approach is inherently broad and applicable to a wide range of issues and environments, it provides excellent opportunities for cross-fertilization across the business disciplines.

6 Stakeholder theory in related disciplines

In this chapter we shall explore the footprint of stakeholder theory in some of the disciplines that are less frequently linked with business, but are nonetheless important to the study of organizations. The specific focus is on the use of stakeholder theory in the law, in public administration, in health care, and in environmental policy. As originally formulated, stakeholder theory is a theory about (business) organizations, so it is not surprising to see that stakeholder theory has had considerable influence on strategy, ethics, and other related disciplines. Other chapters of this book lay out in detail the considerable influence that stakeholder theory has had on research in these areas. What is more surprising, and a testament to the power and salience of stakeholder theory, is to see its influence in a range of other literatures that are partly inside and partly outside the domain of business.

Equally interesting are the ways in which stakeholder theory is interpreted and applied within these literatures. While there are some discussions of the normative dimensions of stakeholder theory, much of this literature focuses on instrumental use of the concept and specific methods for mapping out and engaging stakeholders. As was noted in Chapter 5, most of the work has involved the literatures under review here borrowing concepts from stakeholder theory rather than focusing on contributions to the core stakeholder literature, particularly as it relates to its normative dimensions. The primary exception to this overall characterization involves the debate within the law that addresses core questions of corporate governance and the primacy of stockholders vs. stakeholders – which parallels an ongoing debate within the business ethics literature. This work asks fundamental questions about the normative standing of stakeholders and explores the practical implications of how differing legal structures related to such standing affect the well-being of our society.

We shall provide an overview of the work in each area and then end with a discussion of how each area might deepen its connections with stakeholder theory in a way that both enriches the discipline in question and promises to enrich further work in stakeholder theory.

Stakeholder theory in the law literature

Though it has a limited influence within the legal literature, there is a significant body of work in the law that explicitly incorporates the stakeholder concept. Part of the migration of the stakeholder idea emerges from the fact that a number of authors writing in the area of business law are also active in the area of business ethics and strategy (e.g. Boatright 2000; Fort 1997; Jennings and Happel 2002–03; Orts 1992; Windsor 2000). However, part of this influence is due to the importance to legal theory of the theory of the firm, as well as the explicit pressure that has been placed on firms to specifically consider groups and interests beyond shareholders. This pressure has played itself out in a wide range of conversations within legal circles about whether, and to what extent, stakeholder theory requires changes within the law. Some theorists believe that stakeholder theory is a superior way of thinking about corporations and their obligations, so they ask what the law should look like if stakeholder theory is valid and sound. This puts a premium on our understanding of stakeholder theory and just how radical a departure it is from shareholder theory. Some stakeholder theorists see it as requiring fairly substantial and involved changes in the law, while others see the need for little or no change.

Corporate constituency statutes and corporate governance

One area where stakeholder theory has been used to make specific changes to the law is that of corporate constituency statutes. These statutes direct, or at least allow, managers to consider the interests of stakeholder groups beyond those of shareholders in making important decisions that materially affect the future of the corporation. Rather than covering all aspects of corporate activities, many of these statutes are specifically crafted for the context of corporate mergers and acquisitions, particularly as a measure that might provide a defense against takeover attempts. The list of groups most often provided includes employees, suppliers, customers, and the communities where corporations do business (Orts 1992, 1997). Though a majority of states in the United States have some form of corporate constituency statutes, not all states have them, and their wording and application have varied within the courts. A detailed analysis of individual statutes or a discussion of rulings in specific court cases is beyond the scope of this project.[1] However, we do wish to focus on trends in legal scholarship, particularly efforts to place discussion of these statutes in the larger context of corporate law and the purpose of the firm.

Timothy Fort offers a sustained discussion of stakeholder theory and its relevance to corporate governance, specifically in terms of corporate constituency statutes. Fort discusses stakeholder theory in its normative dimensions and considers the implications of taking this literature for the law, particularly how we are to look at corporations. In his mind, corporations are best seen as "mediating institutions," a form of community that socializes its members and mediates between the individual and society (Fort 1997: 175). Normative stakeholder theory, particularly emphasizing the Kantian dictum of treating individuals as ends (Evan and Freeman 1993) and the feminist notion of our interrelatedness (Wicks, Freeman, and Gilbert 1994), provides a useful heuristic through which to see the corporation as a mediating institution.

Fort also echoes Orts's insight that the legal literature has made either too little or too much of the creation of corporate constituency statutes and that their development represents only a modest shift from existing legal structures. He traces their origins back to several sources.

1. *The charter amendments of the 1970s.* A series of discussions in the 1970s that included the creation of a new "managerial creed," which stated that executives "should consciously make decisions that balance the often competing … claims of shareholders, employees, customers, and the general public" (Orts 1992: 71).
2. *Opposition to corporate takeovers in the 1980s.* In the wake of numerous takeovers and takeover attempts – which many argued disproportionately benefited some stakeholders (e.g. some shareholders and upper management) while hurting others (e.g. employees and local communities) – there was considerable public outcry in favor of changing the legal landscape and widening the focus of interests to be considered in such decisions.
3. *The Berle–Dodd debates of the 1930s.* A famous series of exchanges between these two leading intellectuals, who explored the implications of the separation of ownership and control, particularly for corporate governance and the duties of managers.

[1] And we should acknowledge that our analysis of the legal literature is based primarily on our rather limited understanding of the legal system in the United States. There are many more complexities in other domains, and an entire suite of issues around international law. These issues are crucial for understanding the problem of value creation and trade in a global business world, and they have received little attention in the business literature.

4. *Long-standing discussions about the purpose of the firm and the duties of directors.* Fort cites a source (Bamonte 1995) suggesting that the purpose of firms and duties of directors has long been a subject of conversation and that under the law there have been multiple legitimate approaches, only one of which is the primacy of shareholders.

Fort's primary focus is on using stakeholder theory and the corporate constituency statutes (CCSs) as a context for thinking about the firm as a mediating institution. Thus he spends less time delving into the specifics of the debates surrounding these statutes. However, he does take on three objections that should be noted.

1. *Too many masters.* Various critics, including Clark (1986), Van Wezel Stone (1991), and Hanks (1991), claim that CCSs create too many masters for a manager to serve coherently and fairly. The existence of other stakeholders as legitimate claimants on managerial attention and firm resources is draining, creates conflicts that may prove difficult or impossible to resolve, and allows managers to play stakeholders off against each other to enhance managerial discretion (and possibly self-dealing). Fort agrees with Jonathan Macey (1991–92) that these concerns are at least overblown. Even under a system with shareholder primacy as the objective, managers still have to deal with the demands and expectations of multiple stakeholders. Fort claims that without some means of reasonably limiting the stakeholders to whom management is responsible, the criticism becomes valid. However, if we limit the scope to value-chain stakeholders such as shareholders, employees, suppliers, customers, and local community, then the problems are tractable and not that different from the challenges managers already face (Fort 1997: 180–181).
2. *Slippery slope to socialism.* A second concern is that, by giving legal status to nonshareholder constituents, CCSs fundamentally alter the nature of the corporation and put us on the road to socialism. If the property of shareholders can be used to advance the interests of other groups, then the precedent would potentially open Pandora's box. Corporations would cease to be private entities and become public, the property of society at large. Fort cites Hayek (1979), who also claims that as long as managers are duty bound to consider only the interests of shareholders rather than other "public" or "social" interests, corporations will operate properly. However, once broader public interests are included as legitimate, then corporations will inevitably be subject to increasing public control. Fort makes three cogent replies to these objections. First, most of the CCSs only allow, rather than mandate, that other interests be considered. Second, even if CCSs

created mandates to include such things as board representation for employees, such changes would likely increase corporate autonomy rather than decrease it. That is, if firms provide a means to address the concerns of a core stakeholder internally, there is less need for the state to interfere directly in the affairs of the corporation. Third, Fort argues that even without CCSs there is the potential for stakeholders to use the power of the state to constrain managerial behavior through a variety of (non-CCS) mechanisms. Thus there is nothing special about these as a form of legal innovation that unduly raises the threat of socialism or places an undue burden on shareholder interests.

3. *Adjudicatory versus utilitarian rationality.* One critic, Biancalana, argues that corporations are distinctive in the form of utilitarian reasoning they employ to make decisions. Managers are to use a form of reasoning that maximizes preferences and is circumscribed by specific legal constraints and legal doctrines such as *ultra vires* actions (Biancalana 1990: 425, 434–436). He argues that the broader notions of utilitarian reasoning that include "adjudicatory rationality" and normative reasoning associated with notions such as "fairness" are simply out of place and undermine the fiduciary duties of management (425). Fort argues that this line of reasoning begs the question of the purpose of the firm – and he claims that stakeholder theory provides a compelling alternative view. Rather than creating a context that is unwieldy or ripe for abuse, stakeholder theory expands the set of relevant preferences in a way that is practical and sustainable.

For Fort, stakeholder theory provides an important theoretical contribution to the law of corporations and, in particular, to thinking about the role the corporations have as a mediating institution. Firms provide an important form of community between the individual and society. Stakeholder theory provides a lens for thinking about that relationship that should inform our view of the corporation, its purposes, and the legal structures that shape its function.

A complementary perspective on stakeholder theory and its role in corporate constituency statutes is provided by Eric Orts. Noting the intensity of conversations about this innovation in corporate law, he argues that

> Academic and professional responses to constituency statutes are often strident because the statutes strike, in plain terms, at core competing theories of the business corporation: (1) what is the corporation for? Shareholders alone or a "community of interests" or society at large? (2) to whom are directors accountable? To shareholders, a number of corporate interests, society as a whole, or nobody at all? The first question touches the greatest promise of constituency statutes. The second identifies their greatest danger. (Orts 1992: 123)

In his view, corporate constituency statutes do indeed reshape the law in significant ways – specifically by expanding the duty of care and business judgment rule – but he also notes that these changes are far from revolutionary in their intent or application. Indeed, they are better seen as acknowledgements of the more complex view of what it means to manage in the current era, when organizations and managers have to consider a wide array of groups in order to create value and remain profitable over the long term. Rather than taking sides in the stakeholder vs. stockholder debate, Orts argues that the statutes are best seen as providing explicit recognition that the law does not enshrine either view, but allows managers reasonable discretion to manage within the broad parameters of either view. Though they have had limited practical impact on corporate law, he argues that they remain an important part of the legal theory and the "real world of corporate governance" (Orts 1992: 41).

Orts takes on critics from both sides: critics like the American Bar Association (ABA) Committee on Corporate Laws, which see the statutes as dangerous and argue for interpretations of the statutes that are so narrow as to render them meaningless; and advocates like Millon (1991), who see a welcome revolutionary change embedded within the statutes, radically altering corporate law by mandating fiduciary duties to an array of nonshareholder stakeholders.

The ABA's Committee on Corporate Laws (along with other critics such as Hansen and Macey) sees the statutes as ripe for causing mischief and misdealing by management. Their argument is that the only legitimate way to view the statutes is according to the existing standards that mandate directors acting in the best interests of shareholders, in both the short and the long term (Orts 1992: 73) – a tactic that renders the considerations of these interests as superfluous and unnecessary. If consideration of stakeholder interests does, in fact, advance shareholder interests, then that is all to the good. However, we do not need constituency statutes to tell us this, since existing law already mandates such behavior. Interpreting the statutes to go beyond such a reading, to erode the interests of the shareholder to benefit other stakeholders, goes against the core of corporate law and provides leverage for management to self-deal and avoid accountability. Macey, in particular, argues that the statutes provide "hidden-implicit special interest" to groups beyond shareholders and that this goes against not only the sole claim of shareholders to fiduciary status, but also the public interest (Orts 1992: 77).

It is also worth noting the criticisms of other scholars, who, while not specifically linking their concerns to corporate constituency statutes, make points that are directly tied to this discussion. Authors such as Jennings and Happel (2002–03) argue that doctrines like stakeholder theory and corporate social responsibility are fatally flawed. These authors depict stakeholder theory and CSR as concepts that are not only similar, but stand in sharp contrast to "economics," given that they are grounded in the notion of "structured appeasement" (875). According to this view, stakeholder theory and CSR are nebulous concepts that risk infringing the freedoms that undergird capitalism; there is little empirical support for the idea that they promote economic benefits, they impinge on the dynamic interplay of the forces at the heart of shareholder capitalism which ensure both economic prosperity and attention to social concerns, and they invite the sort of managerial abuse and self-dealing found at Enron. In similar fashion there are a number of authors like Ribstein (2005–06), who claim that doctrines like stakeholder theory and corporate social responsibility not only are flawed ideas but produce more harm than good for society in terms of their consequences for corporate conduct (e.g. Minnow 1991–92; Macey 1991–92). Oswald (1998) provides a noteworthy twist to this conversation, claiming that constituency statutes "work a very real diminution in the shareholders' interests in the corporation," in that if managers can pursue interests that vary from those of the shareholders, their claim to residual earnings is weakened.

More radical advocates see similar implications, but welcome them as a more just way of structuring the corporation in US law. Scholars such as O'Connor, Van Wezel Stone, and Millon see the statutes as having broad application and considerable substance, a reading which suggests that they promise to fundamentally reshape corporate law (Orts 1992). Each of these advocates sees the statutes as creating some form of fiduciary duties to nonshareholder stakeholders. Millon is specific in claiming that management can defend as "rational" (i.e. in terms of the standard of rationality tied to the business judgment rule) decisions that trade off shareholder gain against nonshareholder benefit. According to Orts (1992), both Millon and Mitchell argue that the statutes provide nonshareholders with enforceable rights, including the potential for nonshareholders to have legal standing to sue for breach of the statutes.

In contrast to these views, Orts claims that when viewed in light of the breadth of the business judgment rule and the duty of care, the constituency statutes explicitly recognize the more complex reasoning that is currently commonly being used in corporations. Indeed, he cites a survey of directors and managers which finds that, when it comes to their own characterization of how they make decisions, the traditional view of shareholder primacy is not widely held. In this view the statutes are an acknowledgement of the legitimacy of such an "enlightened view" of management, whereby managers can incorporate explicit consideration of ethics, and see consideration of stakeholder interests as largely aligned with (long-term) shareholder interests. In accepting this more modest view of the statutes, Orts sees three important implications of the statutes for the day-to-day practice of management: (i) they provide legal validity for the practice of "stakeholder management"; (ii) they provide some measure of assurance that judicial opinions going forward will not work against such a stakeholder view; and (iii) that if challenged in court, management has explicit protection for "the practice of considering a wide spectrum of corporate interests beyond those of shareholders" (Orts 1992: 44).

Other applications of stakeholder theory in the law literature

There are some other notable uses of stakeholder theory in the legal literature. Some scholars argue that stakeholder theory may provide important resources for stakeholders in their quest to improve their situation. These take a variety of forms; Neugebauer (2003) claims that stakeholder theory may provide a useful strategy for indigenous peoples to protect their interests better. Rather than taking an oppositional stance towards companies who threaten to harm their way of life and relying on governmental intervention to protect them, Neugebauer claims that indigenous peoples would do well to reposition themselves as "stakeholders" who actively engage and cooperate with corporations. He argues, based on previous experiences (especially with petroleum companies), that firms will recognize the significance of these groups as stakeholders and understand why it is in their long-term interest to take their interests into account (1231).

Poindexter shows an admirable appreciation of the stakeholder literature, and sees stakeholder theory as providing a process for decision making that can be used to resolve conflicts over environmental issues. He argues, in examining "greenfield programs," that the merits of stakeholder theory are that "the decision maker considers the views of all constituents with a stake in the process, without giving priority to the interests of any particular constituency" (Poindexter 1995–96: 38). In this sense stakeholder theory offers "an ideal model for choosing among environmental equity, economic empowerment, and wider environmental goals" (38).

Fairfax (2006) argues that the stakeholder theory literature provides a powerful rhetorical device for corporations to reshape their image and provide a more humane veneer for their activities. She remains dubious as to whether such language matches reality, and argues that it is often invoked as window dressing to legitimate corporate behavior. Wheeler (1997) takes a similar view in the context of the UK and the controversy surrounding works councils, arguing that stakeholder theory is largely used as a tool to legitimate their activities while providing little real voice or control for stakeholders (e.g. employees).

Others, like Mason and Slack (1996–97), use stakeholder theory as a powerful device to scrutinize corporate behavior and argue for legal reform to rein in corporate behavior and more directly benefit nonshareholder stakeholders. In evaluating professional sports teams, the authors examine whether all the moves to relocate franchises benefit stakeholders or just the owners. They claim, based on their analysis of a range of relocation cases, that the current system of legal rules tends to favor owners disproportionately, at the expense of local communities, and may have other corrosive effects on the league and on public support for professional sports (1996–97: 399). Deakin and Slinger (1997) use stakeholder theory to assess corporate takeovers. They evaluate the empirical analysis to date and argue that takeovers have tended to benefit shareholders at the expense of the firm and other stakeholders. They use this analysis to help advocate a stakeholder view of the firm and provide implications for changes in the law and corporate governance that would move us towards that model.

Some in the legal literature, especially in the UK, argue for a "stakeholder economy" (Wheeler 1999). Though the precise details are not evident, such scholars believe that the principles of stakeholder theory can be extended to an entire economy and that it would be characterized by patterns of behavior that empower (and tend to benefit) all stakeholders, rather than primarily shareholders.

Discussion and future directions for stakeholder theory in law

In reviewing the use of stakeholder theory in the law literature, it is interesting to note the relatively limited use of this construct outside the debates about constituency statutes and corporate governance. In addition, there is considerable confusion about the practical meaning of "managing for stakeholders" and how it contrasts with a shareholder-dominated view. Critics of stakeholder theory, and of the constituency statutes, tend to see it as a radical and quasi-socialistic theory that explicitly undermines the status of shareholders by providing value to nonshareholders that should rightfully go to shareholders. It is interesting to note that one very useful facet of the conversation within the law is discussion of the practical implications of stakeholder theory as a critical dimension of its worth. However, there is intermittent attention to the stakeholder theory literature and minimal efforts explicitly to move forward the conversation about stakeholder theory.

Stakeholder theory in the health-care literature

The language of stakeholder theory has begun to influence the work of academics in health care and appears explicitly in a number of articles. Much of this work focuses on instrumental and descriptive work – using the language of stakeholder theory to analyze the forces at work within the health-care industry, and learning from them to improve organizational performance. A few articles delve into the normative dimensions of stakeholder theory and use it to ask more probing questions about how the health-care system should be structured, or to challenge certain practices and priorities within the health-care industry. One particular article that discusses the normative dimensions of stakeholder theory is by Ezekiel Emanuel (1999). The focus of the article is on the role of choice and representation, and Emanuel claims that the health-care system we currently have, driven by employers acting as representatives for employees, is riddled with conflicts of interest as long as the shareholder value-creation ethic dominates. The only way to get around the conflicts in the system would be for companies to adopt stakeholder theory and emphasize "total wealth creation," thinking of a range of stakeholders rather than just shareholders (135). Not only does Emanuel see this theory as not widely practiced, but as requiring significant changes in the law of corporations and widely accepted norms of business practice.

In a separate article Gilmartin and Freeman (2002) discuss stakeholder theory and its normative implications. They focus on how stakeholder theory is important for informing the underlying conception of business that drives our understanding of company strategy. The authors argue that "cowboy capitalism," understood as the "free-wheeling–anything-goes" approach to business associated with shareholder theory, is fundamentally problematic and leads to many of the concerns raised about business influencing health care. On this view, business and medicine conflict, and those concerned with patient well-being and a just health-care system would advocate insulating health care from the influence of "business." In contrast, stakeholder theory provides a way of creating value for all stakeholders, incorporating values into the core of organizational life, and realizing our core objectives for a just and robust health-care system. Thus, rather than needing to remove the influence of business and competition (as many in health care maintain), Gilmartin and Freeman argue that medicine needs more influence from capitalism – at least if it is informed by stakeholder capitalism and the six core principles they identify. Finally, Malvey, Fottler, and Slovensky (2002) make the case in their article for an evaluative step within the stakeholder evaluation process. While the substance of this work is within the stream focused on stakeholder analysis, the authors provide a fairly developed review of the literature within normative stakeholder theory, emphasize the nonfinancial dimensions of value creation, and incorporate these normative considerations into their evaluation method via a "report card."

However, the vast majority of the health-care literature offers few citations of the normative stakeholder literature in business ethics, though Freeman's 1984 book is a commonly cited work. A classic example of some of the work that could be characterized as "instrumental" is an article by Blair, Rock, Rotarius, Fottler, Bosse, and Driskill (1996). They argue that health care has evolved and that the executives within health-care organizations need to pay attention to who their key stakeholders are, especially since who is "key" has changed at an unprecedented rate and is likely to continue to do so. The rapid change in the way in which health care is delivered, and the evolution of groups that are integral to care delivery and cost containment, mean that managing in a health-care environment is incredibly complex. Blair et al. cite Shortell (1988) in arguing that the degree and the speed with which structural change has taken place in the industry are "unprecedented in postindustrial society" (Blair et al. 1996: 7). Given that backdrop, their focus is on correctly categorizing stakeholders and adopting the appropriate managerial strategy to deal with these stakeholders both to minimize threats and to maximize opportunities. The focus of the article is on testing and reexamining a typology developed earlier by Blair and Whitehead (1988) and Blair and Fottler (1990). They claim that executives should classify stakeholders in one of four categories – supportive, mixed blessing, nonsupportive, marginal – and that they should adopt generic strategies to manage them – involve, collaborate, defend, monitor. If executives correctly categorize stakeholders and utilize the appropriate strategy that is "matched" to it, then performance is enhanced. When there is miscategorization, or mismatching of strategy to stakeholder type (something other than the match of supportive/involve, mixed blessing/collaborate, nonsupportive/defend, marginal/monitor), performance suffers. In their empirical study the authors find that the core group of key stakeholders remained largely unchanged between 1984 and 1989 (one out of eight groups changed during that time). However, the claim that their results show mismatches persists, in particular that executives are too focused on cooperation with stakeholders and are not doing enough to protect their organizations against what they see as growing potential threats to health-care organizations.

Continuing in the vein of stakeholder theory as an analytical tool, Blair and Fottler (1990) define the process of stakeholder management as it is developed as a tool for strategic analysis. They identify six discrete stages: (1) stakeholder identification; (2) stakeholder assessment; (3) stakeholder diagnosis and classification; (4) stakeholder strategy formulation; (5) strategy implementation; and (6) evaluation of stakeholder management effectiveness. Dymond, Nix, Rotarius, and Savage (1995) build on Blair and Fottler's work (1990), emphasizing stakeholder assessment (stage 2) in their empirical study. They collect data and provide an assessment of four groups: integrated delivery systems/networks, managed care organizations, physicians, and hospitals. In thinking about their potential to be a "threat" or to cooperate, the authors focus on four key issues:

(1) the potential of each stakeholder to control the respondent's group practice;
(2) how likely each stakeholder is to form a coalition with the respondent's own group practice;
(3) the extent to which the stakeholder controls key group practice resources; and
(4) the relative power of each stakeholder in relation to the respondent's group practice (Dymond et al. 1995: 30).

Among the key findings of their study are that executives need to do a better job of creating a vision for how they will interact with their key stakeholders and to understand better the legal obligations they have to these groups (33).

In a follow-up article Blair and Buesseler (1998) examine a similar set of questions about managing stakeholders in terms of threats and opportunities in a changing environment, but this time the focus is on refining their analysis of the forces at play in the industry. They draw on the work of Michael Porter (1980, 1985), specifically his "five forces" model, and apply it to the context of a stakeholder level of analysis. While Porter's work highlights the role of power, Blair and Buesseler claim that collaboration is as important a factor as power in determining how stakeholders will behave (i.e. how they will act on the potential to either threaten, or cooperate with, the firm) (Blair and Buesseler 1998: 10). One wrinkle in this study is their claim that managers need to attend to specific issues and that stakeholder posture towards the focal organization changes as issues shift (e.g. an otherwise "cooperative stakeholder" can become nonsupportive on certain issues). Their focus continues to be on environmental scanning, stakeholder assessment, and classification matched with generic strategies that are "aligned," all under the umbrella of managing stakeholders to achieve predetermined organizational objectives. Blair, Savage, and Whitehead (1989) highlight the importance of negotiation within stakeholder theory, arguing that it provides a comprehensive approach to managing stakeholders from "strategy to process" (14). Improving on extant work within the negotiation literature that focuses on group or interpersonal negotiations, their work offers "an organizational level of analysis that meshes both of these micro and macro levels" which can cut across the entire array of firm–stakeholder relationships (22). They approach the topic in a way that links negotiation to the larger strategic dynamics and context of the hospital.

Other work also highlights the more traditional strategy posture of the executive trying to "manage" stakeholders for the benefit of the firm. Lim, Ahn, and Lee (2005: 831) develop a method for managing competing stakeholders within a health-care context that they describe as an "important weapon for strategic management." They claim that a central focus is on how to "exploit conflict stakeholders to maximize the firm's economies of scale," even as they acknowledge the importance of stakeholder relationships and concerns about corporate social responsibility (831). Their approach offers managers a way to deal with the complexity of modern health care and manage proactively. To aid managers in formulating strategy, they advocate going through a four-phase process – stakeholder analysis, strategy revival, strategy revision, and strategy implementation. This process is augmented by drawing on wisdom developed from previous similar cases and existing rules which may help inform the appropriate strategy for managers to use. Fottler, Blair, Whitehead, Laus, and Savage emphasize the comprehensive focus of stakeholder theory, claiming that it "integrates in a systematic way what managers often deal with separately – strategic management, marketing, human resource management, public relations, organizational politics, and social responsibility" (Fottler, Blair, Whitehead, Laus, and Savage 1989: 525). They claim that it is an important innovation in "middle-range theory," helping to direct hospital managers in how to understand and manage their key stakeholders. While much of the discussion in this article is consistent with other instrumental work discussed so far – emphasizing how to categorize stakeholders, assess their power, and "manage" them for the strategic benefit of the hospital – it is noteworthy that the authors draw attention to the values held by stakeholders and the degree of alignment across hospital groups. In particular, the survey results they collected reveal that 75 percent of the respondents felt that the values held by key stakeholders were "partly incompatible" with the values of hospitals.

Savage, Taylor, Rotarius, and Buesseler (1997) focus on the importance of networks and systems theory as a way of thinking about health care. They adopt the lens of stakeholder theory as a mechanism for understanding this complex dynamic operating in health care, and argue that "health care executives must learn to manage a portfolio of stakeholders" and comprehend their strategic implications (8). The deeper assumptions behind this work are that stakeholders exist as opportunities and threats, that managers need to move beyond their focus on managing individual stakeholders to thinking about multiple relationships, and that managers manage stakeholders for the benefit of the organization. An interesting aspect of this article, which emphasizes the governance challenges of integrated delivery systems networks and organizations, is that it examines both their financial performance and their "social responsibility" (18).

Discussion and future directions for stakeholder theory in health care

In an excellent review article, Brugha and Varvasovszky (2000) trace the influence of stakeholder theory both in health policy and the broader public policy literature. The authors identify some of the roots of stakeholder theory in the writings of public policy – describing it as "one approach to conducting policy analysis" (240) – making this piece a good transition point to a review of the public policy literature. We shall discuss more of the connections to public policy from this article in the next section. In terms of how the authors use the term within the health-care and health policy literature, they put emphasis on using the term "stakeholder analysis" with precision and differentiating it from other forms of analysis. As Phillips (2003a) raises concerns about how the term "stakeholder theory" is used, so these authors find evidence that many authors use the term "stakeholder analysis" quite loosely, often when all they have done is make reference to a particular stakeholder group or their interest. Brugha and Varvasovszky argue that much of the literature within health policy has emphasized "retrospective or concurrent analyses of the processes of health policy formulation in different contexts" (Brugha and Varvasovszky 2000: 240). In contrast, stakeholder analysis is more "prospective" (i.e. forward looking), systematic, and structured than other tools used by researchers in this domain. For them, the term "stakeholder analysis" should only be used when there is a "systematic analysis of stakeholders' roles, relationships, interest and influence in the decision-making process" (241).

Within these broad parameters, stakeholder analysis will differ depending on the purpose for which it is used: whether it is to try to attain advantage for the organization, put a policy into practice, or assess the development of particular policies or map out where they may evolve in the future. Further refinement of particular stakeholder analyses should be carried out with consideration of the cultural context and level of analysis to which the analysis is directed. The authors note that much of the extant stakeholder analysis work done to date has been conducted with the purpose of trying to attain advantage for the organization (e.g. Blair and Fottler 1990; Dymond, Nix, Rotarius, and Savage 1995; Topping and Fottler 1990). Analyses are done with the express purpose of determining how to develop the best strategy to manage each stakeholder (or group of stakeholders), with particular attention paid to things like whether stakeholders are "threats" or "opportunities," how much power they have, and what issues matter most to them. The authors note the importance of understanding the specific nature of stakeholder analysis and its appropriateness for the tasks sought by analysts, and applying it in cases where it appears to be the most useful tool – recognizing that there are other "tools" available to researchers which have some similar features.

Stakeholder theory in the public policy/administration literature

Though there are some sophisticated discussions of stakeholder theory in this literature, much of the extant work focuses on the techniques of analyzing and engaging stakeholders within predefined normative frameworks. Little time or space is devoted to exploring the normative terrain of stakeholder theory or pushing on its boundaries. Despite efforts to link the normative foundations of stakeholder theory to some foundational research in this domain, the subsequent discussions emphasize how the language and tools of stakeholder analysis can be useful within the public policy process.

Brugha and Varvasovszky identify a number of historical and conceptual foundations of stakeholder analysis that exist within the public policy literature. For them, "policy analysts have long been aware of the importance of interest groups in the policy process; and the need to characterize and categorize levels of interest and power which influence, and therefore impact on, particular policies" (Brugha and Varvasovszky 2000: 240). Thus, given this perspective, one can see how these authors see the origins of stakeholder analysis scattered throughout the policy literature – including writings on the structure of power (e.g. elitism, pluralism, Marxism, corporatism, professionalism, technocracy), policy network and community approaches (e.g. Kingdon 1984; Smith 1993), incrementalism (e.g. Lindblom 1959), and political mapping (e.g. Reich 1994). Within this literature context, stakeholder analysis becomes one of a series of potential tools for thinking about constituent groups, power, and engagement to accomplish objectives. The authors note that among the various related tools – whether political analysis, policy mapping and political mapping, or interest mapping – certain things stand out about stakeholder analysis, particularly its focus on groups within the policy-making process and its forward-looking orientation (i.e. trying to predict and shape the future). It is when such issues take on special importance that researchers should adopt this tool rather than the others.

Bryson (2004)[2] offers a sustained discussion of stakeholder theory and, in particular, detailed development of specific techniques of stakeholder analysis. He laments the relative lack of discussion of stakeholder theory and stakeholder analysis within the policy literature and encourages further attention to this construct and the development of its specific tools of analysis. Though it is not a developed part of the paper, Bryson mentions the importance of the way in which we define stakeholders and who is counted as a stakeholder, specifically for normative reasons that come from his concern with democracy and social justice. His own take is that stakeholder theory should not focus only on those with power or easily identified stakeholders, but that it should "urge consideration of a broader array of people, groups or organizations as stakeholders, including the nominally powerless" (Bryson 2004: 22). That said, he quickly moves into more conventional territory, discussing how stakeholder analysis is important for creating and sustaining "winning coalitions" and fostering organizational success over time. Bryson claims that key stakeholders "must be satisfied" at least minimally and that organizations need to "attend to the information and concerns of stakeholders" (23). He also keeps open the question of organizational mission within the public sector, but does talk about stakeholder analysis being conducted against the broad backdrop of "creat[ing] public value" by realizing its particular mission (23).

Bryson provides a range of ideas for thinking about the relevance of stakeholder analysis and the specific ways in which it is useful within the public-sector management process (Bryson 2004: 25, Figure 1). Special attention is given to several factors that make stakeholder analysis important: the need to determine the feasibility of certain objectives and to take measures to make

[2] It is worth noting as a historical note that Freeman and Bryson worked together at the University of Minnesota during the mid-1980s. See Bryson, Freeman, and Roering (1986).

them more likely to occur; the importance of keeping stakeholders satisfied (based on their own ideas of this); and the need to ensure that the managers have met the requirements of procedural justice, rationality, and legitimacy (26). Based on these insights, Bryson proposes that the systematic use of stakeholder analyses would be associated with more successful outcomes within the public sector. The remainder of the article is devoted to describing in detail a range of specific techniques that constitute "stakeholder analysis" – there are fifteen in all. Bryson emphasizes the importance of understanding the purpose of the analysis, monitoring how it may change over time, and adapting the specific techniques to ensure that they serve these larger purposes. Among the techniques described are a process for choosing participants, the basic stakeholder analysis technique, power versus interest grids, stakeholder influence diagrams, participation planning matrix, directions of interest diagrams, finding the common good and the structure of a winning argument, tapping individual stakeholder interests to pursue the common good, stakeholder–issue interrelationship diagrams, problem-frame stakeholder maps, ethical analysis grids, stakeholder support versus opposition grid, stakeholder role plays, policy analysis versus stakeholder capability grid, and policy implementation strategy development grid. Bryson ends by reminding the reader that policy analysis is an "art in which problems must be solvable" and that stakeholder analysis provides an indispensable set of tools for both understanding the problems that need to be solved and harnessing the means required to solve them (46).

Friedman and Mason (2005) discuss stakeholder analysis and stakeholder management and their usefulness as a lens for thinking through important public policy decisions such as the move of the Houston Oilers professional football team to Nashville, Tennessee. Their critical point of reference for analyzing the events of this case is the "interaction-based, constituent-centered approach central to stakeholder analysis" (95). They claim that their work in the paper underscores the importance of stakeholder analysis, its power to aid and enhance good policy management, and the need to incorporate it within the public arena. In assessing the literature within stakeholder theory, the authors deduce from Freeman's (1984) work that the use of stakeholder management principles will better satisfy constituent needs and claims, and, over the long term, help organizations achieve their objectives. In thinking through the challenge of balancing the various needs and claims of stakeholders, Friedman and Mason (2005) maintain that Freeman's work is not refined enough, and they draw on Mitchell, Agle, and Wood (1997) to prioritize. They then follow the four-step process outlined in a previous paper (Friedman and Mason 2004): first, a preliminary map is drawn of the core (thirteen) stakeholders; second, the map is adapted to fit Nashville's unique context and the particularities of the stakeholders involved; third, they conduct an event analysis to follow how the focal stakeholder (Phil Bredesen, the mayor of Nashville) sought to gain support and diminish opposition; fourth, key events and stakeholders are reassessed over time to reflect changed circumstances (Friedman and Mason 2005: 99). They then proceed to analyze the case by scouring various primary and secondary sources (e.g. 1,200 published articles, transcripts, election records, papers, and interviews) to go through their four-step process and to fit various stakeholders into the Mitchell, Agle, and Wood (1997) typology. Like Bryson (2004), these authors argue that their case study underscores the importance of a systematic use of stakeholder analysis for "more efficient and effective constituent management" (Friedman and Mason 2005: 112).

Provan and Milward (2001) bring stakeholder theory to bear in thinking about networks of public-sector organizations. The authors note how thinking about networks of organizations, and the multiple levels of analysis involved, poses significant challenges to researchers. At the same time they argue that cooperation within such networks is an important development in the public sector and deserves scholarly attention. Provan and Milward (2001) note several challenges, perhaps the most daunting of which is that network effectiveness can be understood through at least three levels of analysis: the community, the network, and the organizational participants (416). The authors adopt an agency theory perspective to inform their analysis of network constituent groups and inform their criteria for effectiveness at each level. They go through each level and discuss how to frame each of the three levels in terms of levels of analysis, key stakeholder groups, and effectiveness measures. In their assessment they note the difficulties of working across levels of analysis and the fact that things done to address major concerns at one level may prove either unproductive or counterproductive at another level. A particular challenge noted by the authors is that the perception and posture of "external" stakeholders changes from networks to individual organizations – that is, external stakeholders tend to focus their attention on the activities of individual organizations and often miss the connections to the larger network and its activities (422). Despite these difficulties, Provan and Milward (2001) argue that it is vital to undertake such analyses of network effectiveness.

Another interesting domain that has emerged in the public policy space that also generates interest in stakeholder theory is "e-government." In a brief article discussing the growth and change within e-government, Flak, Moe, and Sæbø (2003) discuss the importance of stakeholder theory for this domain. They claim that e-Government makes it especially important to not only identify key groups relevant to decisions and articulate their interests, but to also pay special attention to differences within groups (p. 140). In their view, e-Government increases concerns that traditional groupings and clusters of stakeholders may become re-configured, their interests may change, and greater diversity of interests within new groupings that emerge. Flak et al. (2003) see the "need for further elaboration of the stakeholders," of both who they are and what specific requirements they have.

One other noteworthy use of stakeholder theory is in terms of its role as a metaphor for a new political order within a democracy.[3] While Freeman, Phillips, and Wicks (2003) specifically argue that such a use is not what stakeholder theory was meant to address, Barnett (1997) follows the former UK prime minister Tony Blair and discusses the relevance of stakeholder theory as a way of thinking through how politics should operate in a democratic society, specifically within modern Britain in the wake of the influence of "Thatcherism." For Barnett, "stakeholding" (his version of what stakeholder theory means for individual citizens) provides a "fresh angle on democracy, that is to say on the way power can be distributed and exercised" in a British context (82). What sticks out about the relevance of stakeholder theory for political life is that opportunity is widely disbursed and no group or class is excluded (83); policy making can be a positive good and the true wealth of a society is more comprehensive than its stock market value (83–84); no one should be excluded from society and an underclass of "have-nots" should not be tolerated (89); new forms of voice and political involvement need to be devised to create a more inclusive society and political structure (90); and power should be widely shared (92).

Discussion of future directions for stakeholder theory in public policy/administration

Perhaps for more than any of the literatures reviewed in this chapter, it is surprising to not see more attention devoted to the normative dimensions of stakeholder theory. Given that public policy puts issues of purpose, and specifically what goals and whose interests should matter normatively, it is odd to see such questions either ignored or assumed to be resolved via a stakeholder participation model. While stakeholder participation, and

[3] We give our own view of this issue in Chapter 9.

methods of including stakeholder goals and values through such processes, may help, they do not replace the need for a more direct focus on normative issues that is clear and systematic. This appears to be a missed opportunity that future work would do well to address. As with health care, public policy research has focused predominantly on the analytical techniques that emerge from stakeholder theory and researchers have done an admirable job developing new methods that appear to work not only in a public policy context, but in a variety of other circumstances.

Stakeholder theory in the environmental policy literature

Because of the complexity and importance of environmental issues, combined with the array of interests involved, stakeholder theory has become popular in environmental policy. In Chapter 4 we suggested that a number of strategic management scholars such as Jean and Ed Stead had made substantial contributions to the stakeholder literature in strategic management via their analysis of environmental issues.[4] More specifically, dimensions of stakeholder theory have become widely used in developing environmental policies and managing conflicts over the proper use of environmentally sensitive areas. Many of the themes highlighted in this section will relate to previous discussions, particularly on public policy with its emphasis on combining a range of interests and techniques for analyzing and engaging stakeholders in the policy formation process. Several of the articles we shall discuss include references to specific natural resources and the experiences of managing these sites.

De Lopez (2001) provides a review of a "stakeholder management framework" in Ream National Park, Cambodia (47). Before getting to the specific five-step framework, the author makes a few key observations: (i) there are situations where there will be trade-offs between conservation and development; (ii) in the context of conservation projects, the participation of all the "stakeholders of conservation" is to be emphasized more than in traditional stakeholder theory, which focuses on management of stakeholders; (iii) the goal of managers within a conservation project is to "see that the objectives of

[4] See especially their fine book, *Management for a Small Planet* (Stead and Stead 1992). See also the work of Stuart Hart, Andrea Larson, Mark Starik, and many others in the Organizations and Natural Environment group of scholars at the Academy of Management, who have contributed to the development of stakeholder theory. These scholars are too numerous to name, and their work is of increased recognition and importance. On the more normative side a group of scholars gathered at the Ruffin Lectures in 1999. The resulting volume, *Environmental Challenges to Business*, is a snapshot of some of the philosophical issues.

the primary stakeholders are achieved and that other stakeholders, where possible, are also satisfied" (48); and (iv) any management of stakeholders should occur in ways that are both ethical and effective. The Ream National Park is somewhat unusual as a context for discussion, given the economic conditions of Cambodia. Tremendous pressures exist for developing and exploiting the natural resources of the country, and it took a royal decree in 1993 to create protected areas like Ream. The park is just over 100 miles southwest of Phnom Penh and is home to mangrove, lowland and evergreen forests, a freshwater river, beaches, and islands (48). The park is divided into four zones: one that has no resource use, a second that has limited use, a third that has some farming and degraded forest, and a fourth which is a community development zone with villages. The approach developed in the paper emerged out of a context of crisis, in which there were deep divisions about how to use this resource and attempts to engage all stakeholders failed to produce results. A smaller "stakeholder management team," comprising primarily UN Development Programme leaders and park officials, was developed to create a management approach. The five steps – stakeholder analysis, stakeholder mapping, generic strategies and development of a work plan, presentation of the work plan to park staff and local communities, and implementation – are familiar and, in themselves, are not particularly innovative. However, De Lopez notes the important role that stakeholder management provided in allowing room for creativity and creating strategic approaches to cut through conflicts and get to effective resolution. The five-step framework described in the paper helps managers to move beyond the focus on participation and conflict resolution that has characterized the conversation literature to date.

Jamal has discussed the role of stakeholder theory in environmental conflicts in the context of the Banff Bow Valley Round Table (BBVRT). Jamal and Eyre (2003) offer a detailed study of the multi-stakeholder process used to develop a new plan for this protected space in Canada. Banff National Park was named Canada's first national park in 1885. Over time, and as the park came to attract an array of different stakeholders, interests, and activities, conflicts between various groups (particularly between developers and environmentalists) led the federal government to intervene in 1994 and create a task force to search for a better way forward. The focus of the task force was to conduct a study to search for a way forward that would include such things as issue identification, public input and participation in shaping a coordinated strategy, developing a vision, and creating an action plan (421). The authors note that the engagement of a wide array of stakeholders in this process in a highly visible manner created considerable momentum to adopt the recommendations that emerged. Much of the paper is devoted to analyzing the conversations among the participants and the nature of their discourse. Jamal and Eyre (2003) use the work of Habermas (1978, 1989) to categorize the narratives at work in terms of three different cognitive interests: technical interests (i.e. instrumental/means–ends rationality; prediction and technical control; domain of empirical/analytical sciences); practical interests (domain of hermeneutics in the lifeworld; concern with intersubjective understanding; a role for shared norms and values, and socially defined ends and meanings); and emancipatory interest (emancipatory interest in self-reflection, apprehension, and rational action; focus on priority of different ends and how actions best realize those ends). Jamal and Eyre argue that in much of the conversation that took place the language of technical interests was allowed to dominate practical interests and, more specifically, instrumental considerations were allowed to override the normative considerations of environmentalists (and the wider community). In an ironic turn, the authors maintain that environmentalists were, themselves, caught up in this language and used scientific rationality to reinforce the focus on technical control and undercut the ability of nonanthropocentric environmental values (from the realm of practical interests) to have a meaningful role in the dialogue (Jamal and Eyre 2003: 423, 427). They develop four recommendations based on this study in order to improve the multi-stakeholder process in light of the concerns they raise: (i) guard against the domination of technical interests in nongovernmental organization (NGO) participation; (ii) pay careful attention to the role of scientists as experts and educators; (iii) be clear about the aim of the conflict process – distinguish meaning-making from strategy formulation; and (iv) improve decision making in park governance through an involved and active public sphere.

Jamal, Stein, and Harper (2002) delve more deeply into stakeholder dialogues and processes linked to planning in multi-stakeholder tourism–environmental conflicts. Reflecting once again on the experience at Banff National Park, the authors claim that entrenched philosophical assumptions, specifically essentialism and metaphysical realism, derailed the discourse. They provide numerous examples from the discourse over Banff National Park to support their claims (e.g. 170–173). Jamal et al. (2002) argue that in the context of tourism–environmental conflicts, participants need to adopt a neo-pragmatic approach, specifically drawing on the work of Rorty, Dewey, and Rawls (see parallels with Wicks and Freeman 1998). Such a shift in mindset allows people to move beyond seeing labels and concepts (e.g. "environmentalist" or "environmental integrity") as fixed and determined, and to see them as malleable and emergent from dialogue among stakeholders. Not only does this create dialogical space for people to develop their own understandings of such concepts that fit their concerns, it allows them the opportunity to craft a way of thinking about them that works with other values and priorities they may have (e.g. to enjoy a green space, to develop their economy, and to increase employment). The other important shift in adopting the neo-pragmatic approach is to move away from uncritical reliance on science as a primary authority in discussing environmental issues. The practical conclusions from their analysis are that not only should categories and labels be seen as emergent rather than settled and predetermined, but structuring participants into general interest categories during the early stages of dialogue can create barriers to identifying common interests and mutually advantageous agreements as well as foster conflict and mistrust (Jamal et al. 2002: 173, 176).

Research specific to fisheries management also notes trends that make stakeholder theory an important part of the dialogue. Noting the historic link between users and the management of fisheries, Mikalsen and Jentoft note that changes within public policy and fisheries have created pressure for managers to include an array of legitimate stakeholders:

> Management practices, of which user participation has been a key ingredient, are being challenged – to a point where the legitimacy and proficiency of management regimes and regulatory measures may come to hinge on their ability to include – and attend to – the interests of other legitimate "stakeholders". In some quarters, e.g. the United Nations, the representation and involvement of all relevant stakeholders are now considered a crucial precondition of sustainable management. (Mikalsen and Jentoft 2001: 282)

Mikalsen and Jentoft (2001) use Mitchell, Agle, and Wood (1997) to help distinguish different classes of stakeholders and separate primary from secondary groups, noting that stakeholder theory makes normative (duties to honor legitimate claims of stakeholders), managerial (designing proper structures), and instrumental (positive outcomes) claims upon managers. Some interesting points of their discussion include (i) noting that fisheries need to include groups which have heretofore been overlooked, such as local communities, environmental agencies, consumers, and future generations (Mikalsen and Jentoft 2001: 284); (ii) that managers need to reconsider their status in light of challenges from indigenous groups, local communities, and others which challenge the authority of the state and put pressure to see fisheries management as more of a political coalition and less of a distinct hierarchical organization (285). Acknowledging the tension between trying to include all groups that have legitimate interests and creating structures of dialogue and management that are feasible, the authors note with approval the Canadian Fisheries Resource Conservation Council and the US National Marine Fisheries Service as institutions that exemplify the goals of transparency and inclusion that they believe stakeholder theory entails (289–290). Moving fisheries management systems in this direction not only makes them more normatively legitimate, it also helps to ensure the political viability and effectiveness of their future activities (291).

Other work in the field of the environment and environmental management focuses on the role of science in stakeholder dialogues. Welp, de la Vega-Leinert, Stoll-Kleemann, and Jaeger (2006) note that science plays a critical role in shaping stakeholder dialogues, especially as they pertain to the environment and sustainability. The authors draw from the experience of the European Climate Forum (ECF) to make the case that how we think about science, and the role it plays in dialogues among stakeholders, matters to our approach to the environment. Welp et al. (2006: 173) claim that science-based dialogues have a distinct function (i.e. as compared with other stakeholder dialogues, such as policy, governance, or corporate, that focus on gaining consensus), namely to identify areas of dissent and disagreement – something that may prove immensely valuable to researchers as they decide what questions need to be answered and where further inquiry is needed. The premise of the article is that greater dialogue and understanding among stakeholder groups (e.g. of perceptions, risk judgments, mental models) is needed within the process of scientific inquiry – not just in how science is used to inform the management process (174). Welp et al. (2006) explore three different theoretical frameworks (i.e. rational actor paradigm, Bayesian learning, and organizational learning) to illustrate how one might approach science-based dialogues. Each model provides insights into how stakeholder dialogues might progress and shed light on processes that may be helpful in allowing stakeholders to use science to foster genuine dialogue and mutually beneficial outcomes (181).

Beutler (2005) discusses the involvement of stakeholders in irrigation and drainage district decisions within the California Water Plan. She notes that multi-stakeholder processes (MSPs), when utilized early in a given process, can provide important insights, allow for effective management of expectations and concerns, and assess strategic concerns (including threats and opportunities). Beutler notes that stakeholders are "appropriate parties to engage in situations involving governance and decision making issues," but also points out the challenge of determining who counts as a stakeholder, highlighting the difficulties of including too few and too many groups. She also highlights the fact that the use of stakeholder involvement techniques (e.g. within the Environmental Protection Agency [EPA]) is often done without clear ideas of how such involvement will relate to decision making, creating both confusion and frustration. Beutler makes reference to a grid highlighting how the EPA, in reacting to pressure to define its process better, approaches stakeholder involvement: a 3x3 matrix with the role of the EPA along one axis (with decision maker, partner, and capacity builder as sub-categories) and the role of participants along the other axis (with exchange information, develop recommendations, and develop agreements as sub-categories). She also refers to the methods recommended by the International Association for Public Participation (IAP2) that are tied to "degrees of involvement, increasing level of impact, goals of outreach, public expectations, tools and methods" (Beutler 2005: 1099), which are in turn related to forms of stakeholder engagement that span inform, consult, involve, collaborate, and empower. Beutler argues that, whichever technique is adopted (whether EPA, IAP2, or some other approach), if an agency decides that stakeholder collaboration is appropriate, it should assess eleven specific conditions before moving to implement their process: role and purpose (of collaboration); transparency of decision making; interest-based decision making (i.e. making clear whose interests should count and that relevant groups support the final recommendation); every effort to bring affected stakeholders into the process; stakeholders should represent organized constituencies; up-front exploration of issues; common understanding of problems and joint fact finding; policy and technical expertise; respectful and authentic process; transparency of products; resources. She also notes some best practices from stakeholder engagement processes used by others, as identified by Leach (2004): effective facilitator; focused scope and realistic objectives; tractability of disputes; early successes; early engagement; paying attention to the big picture; pre-work; funding; broad and inclusive participation; adequate scientific and technical information; collaboration skills training; well-defined decision rules and process rules.

Grimble and Wellard (1997) discuss the relevance of stakeholder analysis as a tool to help natural resource managers (NRMs), particularly as they confront a range of different interests and objectives and search for strategic approaches that are efficient, equitable, and sustainable (173). These recite many familiar distinctions mentioned already: the differentiating of stakeholders as primary and secondary, active and passive, as well as in terms of their importance and capacity to exert influence. They emphasize the multiple levels of analysis (global/international; national; regional; local on-site; local off-site) that natural resource managers have to contend with, the various associated interests, and the range of related stakeholders involved. Grimble and Wellard (1997) note that within the NRM context subsistence farmers and "other small-scale resource users" are critical stakeholders to consider, but that they are often overlooked or underappreciated. Stakeholder analysis has a twofold practical function for organizations: (i) improving the selection, efficiency, effectiveness, and evaluation of policies and projects; and (ii) improving the assessment of the distributional, social, and political impacts of the policies and projects (Grimble and Wellard 1997: 177). The authors maintain that certain factors characteristic of NRM contexts make stakeholder analysis a particularly relevant tool: (i) cross-cutting systems and stakeholder interests; (ii) multiple uses and users of the resource; (iii) market failure; iv) subtractability and temporal trade-offs; (v) multiple objectives and concerns; and (vi) poverty and underrepresentation (178–179). The article hails stakeholder analysis as an important tool for addressing NRM-related issues, but also notes its limitations, and the need to address conflicts and trade-offs that may be unavoidable and to tailor approaches to fit the unique circumstances of a given NRM context. They believe that more research should be done to cultivate practical methods, frameworks, analysis, and particular solutions that improve both the process and the outcomes for key stakeholders.

The EPA also discusses stakeholder theory in internal documents that are used by agency officials. One resource, the *Handbook for Developing Watershed Plans to Restore and Protect Our Waters* (2005), outlines an approach to project management that emphasizes engaging stakeholders. The *Handbook* has a variety of web links on the EPA website that provide additional resources and help managers deal with the challenges of watershed projects and outreach with stakeholders.[5] Among the advice to managers are the following: (i) to identify driving forces that motivate the choice to develop a watershed plan; (ii) to be aware of various governmental, community, and regulatory issues and directives relevant to the plan; and (iii) to identify and engage relevant stakeholders ("those who make and implement decisions; those who are affected by the decisions; those who have the ability to assist or impede implementation of the decisions" [3–4]). The *Handbook* then proceeds to help managers develop a strategy and a structure to shape the involvement of stakeholders, recognizing that there is not a one-size-fits-all

[5] See www.epa.gov/owow/watershed/outreach/documents/.

approach: they need to be clear about the role of the stakeholder in question, how decisions will be made, any output they are to produce, and the amount of time commitment expected. In terms of participation the role of stakeholders may vary across such categories as "decision-maker," "advisor," and "supporter." The document also provides some practical advice about stakeholder engagement (e.g. focus on issues that matter to a given stakeholder; be honest; communicate early and often), and the need to start locally but to integrate the plan with input and direction from a number of levels (e.g. state, regional, federal).

Additional work that focused on the use of stakeholder theory in governmental management of environmental issues includes work by Yosie and Herbst (1998). The touchstone of their article is that stakeholder involvement in decisions regarding environment, health, and safety (EHS) issues is growing and inevitable – whether because of a decline in public trust, greater desire for participation by stakeholders, growing expectations for transparency and accountability, or the interest in demonstrating responsiveness to public concerns (643). The authors note that there has been a wide array of initiatives undertaken by governments, particularly via the EPA (e.g. their Common Sense Initiative [CSI], which shifts the focus of regulation), but that not enough work has been done to assess these experiments and develop a useful analytical framework for agencies going forward. Yosie and Herbst (1998) believe that such a framework would include (i) principles and operating procedures; (ii) best practices (specific to given stakeholders, based on past experience); (iii) goals for stakeholder processes and tracking processes to assess effectiveness; (iv) maintaining accountability of participants throughout the process; (v) defining obstacles and strategies to overcome them; (vi) identifying options for designing and managing the stakeholder process; (vii) procedures for decision making; (viii) ensuring transparency and communication throughout the process; and (ix) comparing results against original goals (644–645). They maintain that without a clearer sense of how to develop, manage, and assess specific stakeholder engagement methods, current efforts will produce (at best) mixed results.

Discussion of future directions for stakeholder theory in the environmental policy literature

The use of stakeholder theory in environmental policy literature closely parallels that of public policy; there is a heavy emphasis on analytical techniques and methods of stakeholder participation. Perhaps more than with public policy there is a particularly strong emphasis on engagement with stakeholders and a belief that the larger normative goals to guide organizations are truly things that emerge from the give and take of stakeholder dialogue. An interesting contrast in this literature compared with that of business ethics is the prevalence of the assumption that trade-offs exist in managing natural resources and that stakeholder engagement or dialogue is the most promising method for bringing such conflicts to the surface, creating forms of encounter that allow parties to work through such conflicts, and developing agreements that allow all stakeholders to embrace the resultant management plans. Indeed, reading between the lines, it is the apparent unease with conflict, the confusion about the right normative direction for the organizations overseeing these resources, and the desire for sustainable legitimacy from key groups that seem to drive the interest in stakeholder theory and the strong emphasis on this participatory process. To that extent, engagement risks becoming an end in itself, even as many authors and organizations warn against the blind use of stakeholder engagement and emphasize the need for carefully structured processes that are adapted to fit the context.

Conclusion

This review of the influence of stakeholder theory within law, public policy, health care, and the environment reveals some significant insights relevant to our project. First, stakeholder theory does have a foothold within each of these areas and, within several of them, that foothold is substantial and growing (especially the environment, but also public policy and health care). Second, while there are some notable references to normative stakeholder theory, the vast majority of this research explores the descriptive and instrumental dimensions of stakeholder theory – particularly as a set of techniques to understand the complex array of stakeholders involved in a given organizational context and to formulate strategies to accomplish specific organizational goals. Thus these literatures simply replicate the separation fallacy and the problem of the ethics of capitalism in their specific arenas. Third, while many of the articles on stakeholder theory in each of these four areas make reference to some early stakeholder theories, each area has a number of articles that trace the roots of stakeholder theory back to ideas, theories, and thinkers specific to that area (i.e. law, public policy, health care, the environment). Thus exploring these nonbusiness disciplines provides a larger perspective on stakeholder theory, both what it is and what it is not, as viewed from outside groups. Careful reading of these texts also provides additional resources (i.e. other conceptual resources and theories as well as other specific tools or methods of analysis that are related) that may be of use to stakeholder theorists.

It is clear that each of these disciplines has work that contributes to the larger conversation about stakeholder theory, particularly in terms of empirical tools for stakeholder analysis and engagement. Researchers in management would do well to take note and try to incorporate some of these insights, specific techniques, and best-practice "tools" that may well be applicable to a business context. Considerable attention has been given to an array of techniques for including stakeholders, surveying them, and getting them involved in project management. While some of this work may need to be filtered and adapted to "fit" in a business context, it does provide important material for scholars in management and business ethics.

At the same time it is also clear that each of these areas would do well to move forward, giving greater attention to the integrative considerations of stakeholder theory. To the extent that each domain of research treated these integrative considerations as either unimportant or settled, significant problems were created. First, dubious assumptions were often made about the normative content of stakeholder theory (e.g. in law Jennings and Happel 2002–03; Macey 1991–92), which allowed researchers erroneously to dismiss the value and relevance of this stream of research. Second, and more importantly, this eschewing of normative and integrative considerations allowed researchers to dodge the fundamental normative challenge the stakeholder theory provides: to ask hard questions about the purpose of the organization (or sub-group) and the responsibilities of managers to specific stakeholders. Such a dodge is understandable, given how uncomfortable people are with openly asking such questions, but perhaps the most basic purpose of stakeholder theory is to force managers to address these two questions openly and thoughtfully. Particularly in the context of public administration, health care, and environmental policy – all of which have a "public" dimension – addressing such questions carefully and systematically would be of great value to each of these literatures. We would encourage such a conversation and believe that the existing resources within business ethics and management may provide a useful beginning.

Clement (2005) reviewed twenty years of stakeholder literature and identified five important lessons. Those lessons cut across the business disciplines, and seem to be an appropriate way of ending this chapter:

1. Corporations are feeling increased pressure to be responsive to their stakeholders.
2. Legal systems are expecting higher levels of corporate responsibility to nonshareholder stakeholders.
3. Top executives today are more heavily influenced by social pressures than by the functional business disciplines in which they are first trained.
4. Corporations are responsive to the claims of legitimate and powerful stakeholders, especially when those claims are urgent.
5. Responding to stakeholder concerns can improve the bottom line.

These lessons apply as much to one discipline as to another. They form a foundation for further study both within and across the range of disciplines we have discussed in this chapter as well as in Chapters 4 and 5.

Part III

Stakeholder theory, ethics, and corporate social responsibility

7 Stakeholder theory and business ethics

The distinctive focus of this chapter is on how stakeholder theory has been developed and discussed within the normative business ethics literature as we understand the main work in the discipline.[1] Though it takes many forms, there are many reasons to see stakeholder theory as it has evolved as having a central place in business ethics (and vice versa). Within this literature, we can think of stakeholder theory as providing an effort to address the problem of the ethics of capitalism outlined in Chapter 1 and to integrate it into an understanding of value creation and trade. Partly because of their disciplinary background, and partly due to the momentum of the stakeholder concept, ethicists quickly latched onto stakeholder theory as a powerful way of thinking about the way in which we connect ethics and business.

In order to think in more detail about stakeholder theory as an avenue for addressing the problem of the ethics of capitalism, we identify several themes that underscore the importance of stakeholder theory for business ethics. First, particularly due to its reach into the strategy literature and the wider management literature, stakeholder theory provides a way for ethicists to connect systematically with a wider conversation about business and organizations. No longer just focused on a set of isolated, idiosyncratic problems, the focus of stakeholder theory opens up connections to basic considerations about business, its underlying purposes, its core focus, and its everyday operations. Second, as a "theory," stakeholder theory provides a systematic and specific set of ideas around which one can begin to see what it means for a firm to care about ethics. This holds promise for talking to managers, who often want to know what it means to care about ethics in business, but it may also help ethicists to extend their "normative" work in integrative ways that foster rich empirical ties into an array of literatures on

[1] Once again business ethics is no more purely normative than strategic management is purely descriptive. Saying that it is normative just means that philosophers do business badly. We outline our view on this issue in Chapter 3. For our purposes in this chapter, we shall highlight the idea of "normative."

organizations. Third, discussed and developed as a viewpoint that contrasts with prevailing assumptions about the purpose of business (especially Friedman, but also Jensen), stakeholder theory has provided a contentious context in which ethicists can highlight their work.

As for the importance of business ethics to stakeholder theory, much of the existing work emphasizes that it is the content of business ethics – the core ideas and questions that are its domain – that make stakeholder theory a distinctive and important contribution to the literature on organizations. First, this is evident in terms of its origins. Though early stakeholder theorists were ambiguous as to its distinctive focus, there is little doubt that values, a sense of purpose that goes beyond profitability, and concern for the well-being of stakeholders were critical to the origins of stakeholder theory.[2] Second, if we look at the balance of work that develops stakeholder theory in terms of its normative dimensions, the vast majority of it has come from business ethicists (predominantly doing work in business ethics journals). Many other disciplines have written on stakeholder theory and extended its reach, but most of the theory development that directly addresses and develops the normative content of stakeholder theory has come from business ethics. Certainly, within the literature on management, the normative focus of the theory makes it unique and distinctive. Third, many influential authors claim that normative ethics forms the core of business ethics (see especially Donaldson and Preston 1995). Prominent critics of this claim about stakeholder theory, such as Freeman (1994), nonetheless agree that a critical part of managing a business with integrity and self-reflection requires that managers face the normative questions at the heart of this line of inquiry.

For these reasons it is especially important that we explore the origins of this connection, map out some of the main themes in this part of the literature, and explore its (likely) future directions.

A brief overview of ethics and business ethics

Before we explore in more detail the connections between business ethics and stakeholder theory, we want to provide some background on business ethics.

[2] The evidence for this claim lies in the idea of "enterprise strategy" in Freeman (1984), which is a clear appeal to the idea of values and purpose. See especially Freeman (1984), at 95–99 for a discussion of the role of values, and at 101–110 for a discussion of the clearly ethical idea of enterprise strategy. Walsh (2005) rightly takes Freeman to task for not making these ideas clearer. See our assessment of Freeman (1984) and Walsh's critique in Chapter 2.

As an academic discipline, business ethics has traditionally been conceived as a subfield of ethics and moral philosophy devoted to thinking about ethical issues in a business context. At its core, ethics is a discipline that focuses on wisdom, or what it means to live a good life. We shall isolate three distinct streams of thought that make up ethics. Each represents strands of thought that are an important part of the academic writing on ethics and our practical, commonsensical views of what makes something ethical.

Actions – principles and rules

One part of ethics focuses on actions. Here our thinking is devoted to questions of right and wrong, particularly in terms of rules or principles that one might use to judge a given action (e.g. do not lie, do not cheat or steal, help others when you can). Part of the moral life involves respecting a set of core rules and principles in our conduct. Here the focus is on whether a given action is ethical in and of itself, not because of the outcome of that act, or because of the way in which the act might reflect on the individual character of the person undertaking the action. According to this view, lying is wrong because it violates some core rules of our community (e.g. derived from reason [see Immanuel Kant], natural law, or scriptural authority [see the Bible's Ten Commandments]).

Agents – character

A second part of ethics focuses on the agent. Here we are concerned with questions of character, particularly how we become a good person or create a good community or organization. Part of being a moral person is striving to become someone of good character. Beyond the issue of whether our actions violate a given rule, there lies the question of how our behaviors reflect on us – whether we possess virtues, such as being just, kind, trustworthy, or prudent, rather than vices such as being unfair, unkind, untrustworthy, or foolish. The intellectual tradition most closely identified with Aristotle, the ancient Greek philosopher, asks us to consider questions of character and, in particular, how our behavior over time comes to define who we are and how others view us.

Outcomes – purposes and consequences

The third part of ethics focuses on outcomes. Rather than using rules or questions of character as our focus, we are concerned with the consequences of our actions. Part of what it means to be moral is to carry out actions in the world that create favorable consequences regarding reaching goals that are morally important (e.g. helping your community, taking care of your family, saving lives, fighting a just war, being a good steward of resources placed in your trust). Not all of our actions will produce only good outcomes, but a critical aspect of ethics is trying to create as many positive outcomes (e.g. saving lives, reducing pain, growing resources) as we can while minimizing the negative outcomes (e.g. losing lives, causing pain, shrinking resources). A variety of thinkers have developed the idea that outcomes and consequences are a critical part of the moral life (e.g. Jeremy Bentham, John Stuart Mill).

At its core, business ethics forces us to account for ourselves and our actions – to offer good and defensible reasons for our conduct. When we can offer good reasons we can say that we have acted ethically. When we cannot, or we struggle to do so, we may be said to have acted unethically. What counts as a "good reason" comes from the three traditions mentioned above. We appeal to rules and principles, we discuss issues of character, and we look at consequences that impact important purposes. What is distinct about the subject of business ethics is that we situate these questions firmly within the domain of business.

History of business ethics as a discipline

One can say that business ethics is an ancient discipline with works that go back to the origins of moral philosophy. In another, more technical sense, business ethics is a new field with a relatively short history that dates back only a few decades. While we want to highlight a few of the stronger connections to the intellectual roots of the field, we also want to say a little about the more recent history of this distinct academic discipline, including what brought it into being and what propels it forward. If we go back to ancient Greek philosophy, it doesn't take long to discover that Aristotle was very concerned about economic life as a critical part of what it meant to live well, both as an individual and as a community. We also see considerable attention given to the ethics of economic life in St. Thomas Aquinas, who was particularly concerned about "usury" (loans that involved the charging of interest), and along with Aristotle, considered the idea of making a profit to be deeply immoral. Indeed, before the nineteenth century and the shift to a more "scientific" approach to economics, grounded in a positivist epistemology, most noted economists were also moral philosophers, including the father of

Western-style capitalism, Adam Smith. A. K. Sen's work (1989), among others, notes this connection and laments the fracturing of the two fields in more recent history. Of course, the thematic concern with both ethics and business of an array of distinguished scholars has a long history, but that is significantly different from discussing a group of professionals who are trained in a discipline called "business ethics," who largely have their academic appointments in business schools, who teach and consult directly with business practitioners (in-training), and who see themselves as doing "applied ethics."

Looking more specifically at the more recent field of business ethics, one can note a variety of factors that played a role in the development of a group of professionals who have this as their designation (and disciplinary specialty).

First, the emergence of biomedical ethics as a distinct academic discipline set the trend and opened the door for the creation of other "applied" ethics fields. In response to a series of ethics-related problems that emerged within medicine, there was a rush to find a group of experts who could help medical professionals and regulators think through the array of ethical challenges that began to make headlines and cry out for attention (e.g. the allocation of kidney dialysis in Seattle in the 1960s; see Wicks 1996). Again, much like business ethics, there is a long and rich history of thought concerned with both medicine and ethics, but few before the 1960s who would be inclined to call themselves "bioethicists." Bioethics became a huge industry that has attracted an array of scholars devoted to the study of ethics in medicine. Many of these people either have joint appointments (i.e. in their primary discipline, such as philosophy, and in a professional school) or are employed directly by medical and nursing schools.

Second, business scandals, and the growing media attention to them, created pressure on business and business schools to take action on ethics. In particular, in conjunction with the Association to Advance Collegiate Schools of Business (AACSB), business schools put considerable energy into making sure that something was done about ethics, including offering courses and hiring faculty who could teach them. While the number of schools offering courses was small at first, a large percentage of business schools now have at least one course offering business ethics, and many of the top business schools require a course on the subject.

Third, there were faculty who had an ongoing interest in topics related to business ethics, and once there was demand for their services within business schools, an industry was born. Since this was a new field and no programs offered a doctorate in business ethics, faculty trained in a wide array of related disciplines (e.g. philosophy, religious studies, sociology, political science) found ways to adapt their skill set to do research and to design and teach courses on business ethics. By the mid-1990s we saw the emergence of the first doctoral programs specifically in business ethics in the USA. Though it is still a relatively young field, business ethics has achieved a significant degree of institutional legitimacy and staying power. Indeed, through collaborating with other scholars interested in business and society issues, business ethicists are part of the largest division in the Academy of Management – Social Issues in Management.

Models of business ethics

The previous section sets out some of the basics of what constitutes ethics and, in cursory fashion, situates that field of inquiry in a business context. However, how we resolve the problem of ethics in capitalism – how we see business and ethics as linked, what it means to take ethics seriously in a business setting – is an important matter. We want to offer some possibilities of what that might look like, several of these finding close parallels within the business ethics literature.

Business ethics as a set of specialized problems

One way for managers to think about business ethics is as defined by a specific set of problems that are distinct and largely separable from what managers do day in and day out. Just as they need training in cardiopulmonary resuscitation (CPR) for the rare occasion that someone in the workplace may have a heart attack, so managers need training in such things as sexual harassment, diversity, bribery, and the environment. These are hot topics that can get firms into trouble unless people are on top of them, but if they get the right training, managers can successfully navigate these challenges without destroying shareholder value.

Business ethics as a constraint on self-interest[3]

On this view, business ethics serves as a constraint on the self-seeking behavior of people within the marketplace. Whether drawing from Adam Smith, Oliver Williamson, or Milton Friedman, there are plenty of intellectual

[3] We reject this reading of Friedman in Chapter 1.

resources one can use to see business as fundamentally about self-interest, but not unbridled self-interest. At its core, there is no connection between ethics and self-interest. Rather, the important role that ethics plays is in helping to make sure that actors in a given marketplace do not become so driven by their interests that they begin to take advantage of others – whether by fraud, lying, or theft. Here ethics acts as an extension of the law, a form of external constraint that reins in the excesses of people seeking their own interests. It helps economic self-interest to serve the larger good and make markets realize the constructive ends of the "invisible hand."

Business ethics as corporate social responsibility or charity[4]

Another way to think about business ethics is that it acts as a kind of balance alongside self-interest, not just as a constraint upon it. On this view, managers need corporate social responsibility (or charity) to make self-interest and profit-seeking legitimate. If companies can do positive good – by helping the community, sharing a larger part of the pie with workers, and making safer and more environmentally safe products for consumers – then the fact that they make money isn't so bad. However, it is critical that businesses undertake a variety of initiatives to show that they are responsible – to invest money in these activities even if there is no clear and definite payoff for the company. Indeed, to be seen as CSR, these initiatives need to be things that are unlikely to have a clear bottom-line benefit except in some vague, feel-good, improved public image mechanism. CSR helps take the hard edge off of capitalism and shows that companies can care about more than the rich and powerful shareholders, but largely by abandoning the logic of how they do business and make decisions. It is up to companies to figure out how to do both and get them to coexist, despite the glaring tensions between the logic of CSR and that of "business decisions."

Business ethics as a way of understanding business

In the three models mentioned so far, ethics stands apart from the core of business – as a set of separate issues, as a constraint, or as something done to compensate for the harshness of business. On all these views, ethics fits uncomfortably alongside business. Indeed, it is largely alien to business. However, there is another model of how to think about the relationship of

[4] We analyze this literature in Chapter 8.

ethics and business: ethics becomes a way to think about the core activities of business. On this view, the central features of business are themselves understood as moral values. Unlike the constraint model, this view sees such concepts as self-interest not just as economic, but also as morally based constructs. Seen in the light of Adam Smith's work on moral sentiments, self-interest is best seen as the virtue of prudence (Werhane 1994), something that has moral content through and through, even as its practice has benefits for the self. Other cornerstones of markets – people pursuing their interests within markets, unconstrained by governments – can also be seen as driven by core values like individual freedom, voluntary association, and the desire of people to create value in community with others. When cast in this light, there is no sharp distinction between ethics and economics (or business) (Sen 1995). It is this model, where ethics and business are linked, that holds the most potential for stakeholder theory. Particularly given the centrality of strategy to thinking about the core purpose(s) and function of what corporations do, Freeman sees this as an ideal venue in which to describe a way of thinking where ethics and business go together and are integrally linked (Freeman, Harrison, and Wicks 2007).

Major themes in the literature

There is a rich and evolving literature on stakeholder theory in business ethics. Each theme has had contributions from a number of scholars, and we shall not provide a full review of the literature, rather we shall focus on our overall assessment of the theme, and pay attention to the arguments and subthemes which we believe are most important.

Stakeholder theory versus stockholder theory

Although they were considered radical statements when first published, Milton Friedman's writings on social responsibility and the purpose of the firm have become canonical. Indeed, much of the writing within finance, economics, and management for the past twenty-five years assumes not only that his views – about why firms exist and to whom managers have obligations – are correct, but also that existing US law is built upon them (Donaldson and Preston 1995; Marens and Wicks 1999).

Chapter 1 provides a detailed discussion of the basics of Friedman's argument and the early work of Freeman (e.g. 1984). To summarize that discussion and highlight the themes relevant to this chapter: for Friedman, publicly held corporations exist to make money for their shareholders. The duty of management is strictly and solely to shareholders – to look out for their interests in all that they do. Consideration of any other interests – such as social welfare, corporate responsibility, worker well-being – is morally wrong unless management can show that such consideration coincides with the best interests of shareholders. The core rationale for this view is that shareholders are the owners of the company. It is their money which brought the company into being, and it is for the purpose of serving their interests that managers were hired. Friedman makes clear that management needs to respect widely held ethical customs (e.g. prohibitions against deception or coercion) and the law (e.g. there should be no fraud or violation of other rules of the game), but also that they should be as vigilant as they can be in finding opportunities to make their shareholders as rich as possible.

Friedman is highly critical of calls for social responsibility or any other duty that may be proposed for managers to embrace that would get in the way of their being advocates for shareholders. Looking after the larger social good is a form of socialism, or a subversion of the role and authority that government is supposed to play in a free society. This role for corporations emerges directly from the core values of a free society: that individuals have the liberty that they are due (e.g. freedom from government interference; the rights to private property and to voluntary association) and that enables them to live a prosperous life.

It is in the context of this prevailing view of the corporation that stakeholder theory emerged. There was a long-standing debate about the purpose of the corporation, tied especially to the idea of corporate social responsibility (e.g. Wood 1991). However, early stakeholder theorists provided clear evidence for the idea not only that firms exist to serve not just larger "social" interests, but that firms have a responsibility to serve the interests of particular stakeholder groups beyond shareholders.

The stakeholder paradox

In one of the more famous early debates a group of articles discussed the tensions between the "shareholder view" (i.e. Friedman's view) and the "stakeholder view." Kenneth Goodpaster wrote about his view of this tension, which he dubbed the "stakeholder paradox": "It seems essential, yet in some ways illegitimate, to orient corporate decisions by ethical values that go beyond strategic stakeholder considerations to multi-fiduciary ones" (Goodpaster 1991: 63).

At the heart of the tension lies the idea that consideration of stakeholder interests seems to be what is required by ethics, but it is simultaneously forbidden by the law (i.e. it undermines the fiduciary duty owed to shareholders). For Goodpaster, this conflict boiled down to a choice between business without ethics (the shareholder view) or ethics without business (the stakeholder view). Neither promised to be an attractive alternative. He proposes an alternative that stops short of placing stakeholders on an equal footing with shareholders (i.e. shareholders are the only group to whom management bears fiduciary duties), but does argue that firms need to constrain their activities by moral norms that apply in business conduct (i.e. it is illegitimate to use immoral means to pursue benefit for shareholders).

Boatright wrote a critical reply to Goodpaster, evaluating the basis for his claims and the validity of his "paradox." For him, Goodpaster's claims were unpersuasive because there was a logical gap between the fact that managers had a legal (fiduciary) duty to shareholders and the notion that they had a moral (nonfiduciary) duty to run the firm in the interests of the firm. In short, the legal reality of fiduciary duties left management with considerable discretion in terms of how they ought to run the firm, including the possibility that they ought to consider the interests of other stakeholders (Boatright 1994: 395). Boatright then proceeded to evaluate critically a series of other possible arguments in favor of Goodpaster's view that shareholders had this privileged moral status. Boatright looks at three possible arguments for the paradox: one from contracts, one from agency, and another from public policy. He finds that the first two sources provide minimal support for the paradox. Public policy, or the idea that society at large benefits from a system wherein shareholder interests are treated as paramount by management (i.e. not because there is some inherent special claim they have to this status), does provide some help to sustain the paradox. However, as Boatright claims, this basis makes it far harder to maintain any sharp distinctions between fiduciary and nonfiduciary duties or between shareholders and other stakeholders (403). Indeed, on this view many of the fiduciary duties relate not solely to shareholders, but to other constituents. This leads Boatright to seek an alternative resolution of the stakeholder paradox that relies on singling out those decisions that bear on the fiduciary duties management owes to shareholders and those which do not. In the former case, management must consider nonshareholder stakeholder interests only so far as they appear to benefit shareholders. In the latter, it is incumbent on management to include consideration of ethical values that pertain to wider stakeholder interests (404).

In his reply, written with Holloran (Goodpaster and Holloran 1994), Goodpaster asserts that Boatright gives too technical a reading of his argument and his claims that shareholders retain their "special status" on a moral basis – not just because doing so happens to work best for society on an instrumental basis. Considerations of liberty, fairness, relationship, and community all provide reasons for thinking that shareholders have a special moral claim that justifies protecting their interests against the claims of other stakeholders (427). For them, the stakeholder paradox remains, and the challenge of management is to navigate it rather than hope to eliminate or sidestep it.

Cragg also discusses the stakeholder paradox extensively in his article on stakeholder theory. He believes that much of Goodpaster's perspective is correct, particularly in emphasizing the distinctiveness of fiduciary duties owed to shareholders. However, he maintains that because they are social institutions, corporations have both public and private responsibilities, and it is an appreciation of the array of duties that allows firms to embrace stakeholder theory and see obligations to stakeholders as not in conflict with responsibilities to shareholders (Cragg 2002: 138).

One of the central themes of this discussion is fiduciary duties, particularly the fact that management has a specific fiduciary duty to shareholders while no such duties exist for other stakeholder groups. A range of authors have discussed this issue. Several use it to make the case that shareholders have a distinctive and unique claim on the firm (e.g. Friedman 1970; Sundaram and Inkpen, 2004). Some have taken the view that if we look carefully at the law of corporations, and in particular at the nature of property rights, there is a major problem for the shareholder view. That is, there may be a variety of reasons why there might be a legal fiduciary relationship that might be quite different than the sorts of arguments needed to establish a moral duty to put shareholder interests first (e.g. Boatright 1994; Donaldson and Preston 1995). In addition, shareholders have a difficult time maintaining the idea that their property rights are like other forms of property rights (e.g. owning a car or a baseball bat) – in that they lack possession and use of the property in question – and therefore cannot sustain demands for managements' unwavering commitment to their interests (e.g. Boatright 1994; Donaldson and Preston 1995). Indeed, some claim that there is a stronger case to be made for the idea that managers have a responsibility to the firm's core stakeholders – those stakeholders who are part of the value chain and make the firm a going concern – than for the idea that their duty is only to shareholders (Cragg 2002; Donaldson and Preston 1995). Though there are some nuances to the specific views expressed, the core of both sides of the conversation is the idea that the stakeholder and shareholder views are two singular and distinct philosophies that are to be contrasted with each other. Managers either serve all their core stakeholders or else they serve their shareholders.

An alternative path

Freeman (1994) and Jones and Wicks (1999a) have taken a different view. In his reply to Goodpaster and Holloran (1994) and to Boatright (1994), Freeman argues that the debate between stakeholder theory and shareholder theory is misguided and beside the point. Framing it in terms of two singular views that conflicted – between ethics and business; between serving one group or many – fundamentally gets it wrong. Stakeholder theory is instead a larger view about corporations that encompasses shareholder theory. For Freeman, the introduction of stakeholder theory is not one view of the firm, but an invitation to a conversation that forces managers and the public to examine together two questions that have both ethics and business thoroughly embedded in them: "what is the purpose of the corporation?" and "to whom are managers responsible?" There are many possible answers to these two questions that fall within the boundaries of the law of corporations. Freeman outlines a range of potential answers to the two questions – from the shareholder view to the idea that managers have a duty to all value-chain stakeholders, to stakeholder prioritization based on Rawlsian conceptions of justice, to a feminist conception of the firm. Jones and Wicks (1999a) also build their view of stakeholder theory on this conceptual foundation, arguing that ethicists and management scholars should devote themselves to exploring a range of theories of the firm. They suggest how business and ethics could be integrated into what they call a "convergent stakeholder theory."

Who counts as a stakeholder, and stakeholder legitimacy

A recurring issue for stakeholder theory has been how to understand who stakeholders are and how firms relate to them, and to prioritize among them (i.e. at the level of deciding who has "legitimacy" or deserves broad consideration).

A definition

While Chapter 2 provides a more detailed discussion of this topic, we shall note some of the highlights of the discussion regarding the definition of stakeholders. Different definitions highlight core themes and challenges that various theorists seek to address in their use of the construct. Citing the work of scholars from a variety of theoretical perspectives, Freeman consolidates the existing work that begins to give meaning to the idea of "stakeholders," while making it evident that he is far from the first to use the term. The language and the seeds of the idea came from a number of sources. For Stanford Research Institute (SRI) thinkers, "stakeholder" referred to groups without whose support the organization would cease to exist (e.g. Stewart, Allen, and Cavender 1963).[5] Slinger provides additional perspective on the history of the stakeholder concept, particularly as it was developed at SRI. We noted in Chapter 2 that Slinger was able to determine that the term came to mean all those who had a "stake" in the enterprise – those who contributed to the success of the business.[6]

In addition, there has always been related work in several other fields which gets at something quite similar to the formulation of the stakeholder concept. For example, Ansoff (1965) takes the construct in a notably different direction from SRI, focusing his conception of stakeholders on the objective of the firm and the role of managers in "balancing the conflicting claims."[7] In the organization theory literature, Rhenman (1968) uses the term "stakeholder" to refer to "individuals or groups which depend on the company for the realization of their personal goals and on whom the company is dependent."[8] Clarkson's distinction between primary and secondary stakeholders, which has been much discussed in the literature, emphasizes the role that the former group has in making the firm a "going concern" (noting the interdependence between these groups and the firm) and that the latter group has a more indirect relationship with the firm and is not critical for its survival (Clarkson 1998: 259). Kaler (2002) also discusses definitions of "stakeholder," and notes several streams of definitions: claimant (stakeholders are those groups who make a claim on the firm), influencer (stakeholders are those who can influence, or may be influenced by, the firm), and a combinatory definition (some combination of the claimant and influencer definitions); he opts for the claimant definition as superior. Freeman's definition is widely used:

> A stakeholder in an organization is (by definition) any group or individual who can affect or is affected by the achievement of the organization's objectives. (1984: 46)

[5] See Chapter 2. [6] See Chapter 2. [7] See Chapter 2. [8] See Chapter 2.

The problem of conceptual breadth

While this definition provides some clarity about what might make one a stakeholder, it also raises many questions. Indeed, on this definition, one could imagine virtually anyone, or any organization – including groups who are only incidentally and very indirectly linked to the firm, or whose purposes are explicitly directly at odds with the firm (e.g. some environmental groups want some firms to cease to exist). Given such a wide view of what the term might mean, the notion of stakeholder risks becoming a meaningless designation. If all are stakeholders, then there is no point in using the term. Work needs to be done to pare down and refine what we mean by stakeholders if the term is to prove helpful at a conceptual level or at a practical level. Particularly among scholars concerned with normative issues, the question of to whom the firm has obligations is critical. Since firm resources and abilities are limited, it does not make sense to claim that management has duties to all stakeholders, or that all such duties are equal. The question arises as to how one sorts out duties and assigns them to different groups, and how to fit such theory to our intuitions and commonsense understanding that in for-profit businesses, some groups (e.g. employees, shareholders) and some interests (e.g. the media, competitors) should count more than others. This is an issue that is an important undercurrent in the literature, and a subject that several theorists have explicitly addressed.

The natural environment

One debate that has raged is whether the natural environment is a stakeholder. There are a variety of ways to talk about the environment and get it "on the table." One way is to introduce it as something that various stakeholders share as a concern (e.g. consumers care about protecting the environment, as do many other groups who may or may not have it as a central point of concern). This notion of stakeholder retains a focus on people and organizations made up of people. However, that is far different than saying that the natural environment as such (i.e. a nonhuman entity) is a stakeholder. Here a much stronger claim needs to be made – that the natural environment has the moral status to "count," on its own and irrespective of its connection to human beings – in order to affirm that it is a stakeholder. Mark Starik claims that the natural environment is a stakeholder in the second, stronger, sense of the term. For him, because the environment lacks the "political–economic" voice that other stakeholders have (e.g. to express and protect their interests), and (particularly) because of its inherent moral worth, it is right that we should consider the environment as a stakeholder (Starik 1995). Others take issue with this notion and claim that it makes no sense to talk about the environment, or any other entities, as stakeholders except to the extent that they are manifestations of human agency and interests. Phillips (2003a) is one theorist who takes issue with the idea that the natural environment is a stakeholder. For him, not all moral concerns need to fall within stakeholder theory. The fact that the natural environment might have moral status, or is deserving of moral consideration, is not the same as calling it a "stakeholder." In addition, Phillips claims that providing the extra designation of "stakeholder" in effect does nothing, on its face, to help address the problem of continued environmental destruction. Calling it a stakeholder does not help managers to sort out what they should do with the environment.

Stakeholder legitimacy

The question of what management should do, and who should matter in their decision making, is a central question of stakeholder theory. This presses theorists to address the issue of legitimacy.

A central concern that arises, now that we have identified what makes one a stakeholder, is what management should do based on someone achieving that status. One answer that emerges from the text is that managers should attend to stakeholders because it is in the interest of the organization to do so. However, this does not address the deeper question of "legitimacy," the idea that certain stakeholders – or stakeholder interests – deserve consideration, regardless of whether doing so would clearly benefit the corporation. The former sense of "legitimate" is a "weak" (Freeman 1984: 45) or thin notion that is strictly tied to self-interest. The latter sense is a stronger and more overtly moral concept that suggests that what managers should do encompasses moral considerations that extend beyond pursuing their own self-interest. Some interests, and some groups, may deserve to shape what firms do based on the fact that their claims are, for example, right, meritorious, or just. Freeman identifies this issue, but sidesteps it, focusing solely on the weaker sense of legitimacy (45). Following him, much of the rest of the stakeholder literature finesses or sidesteps the question, noting its importance but not sorting out how one might answer the question of legitimacy in the stronger sense.

Several other answers have been given in the literature. For one, there is a way to read Freeman's book as providing a series of answers to the question of legitimacy.[9] He reviews a variety of stakeholder strategies (e.g. social harmony, specific stakeholder, stockholder, utilitarian, Rawlsian, discussed on 101–107), each of which offers answers as to who are stakeholders and what makes something a legitimate interest. Each of these strategies provides some important criteria for evaluating who and what "counts" at the firm, and what should shape managerial decision making.

Donaldson and Preston (1995) provide a different answer. They claim that stakeholder interests have intrinsic value regardless of their meaning and value to the firm, and that the firm in turn has an obligation to them and their interests. In this sense, they are distinguishing between stakeholders to whom management has an obligation or duty and groups that can affect or who are affected by the firm. Management may need to consider both, but it is only the former group(s) that management need see as "legitimate" and thus have a positive duty to advance their interests.

Phillips (2003a) provides another answer to help pare down and make more specific the meaning of "stakeholder," and particularly which stakeholders "matter." He does so on the basis of the principle of fairness. He claims that stakeholders who "voluntarily accept the benefits of a mutually beneficial cooperative scheme of cooperation" (Phillips 2003a: 92) are the groups who have legitimacy and a claim on the firm (as well as duties owed to it). Given that groups such as employees, customers, stockholders, suppliers, and others, who are part of the "value-chain" of the firm, all voluntarily accept benefits of the firm and help make it a going concern, they have standing in ways that other groups – such as the media, watchdog groups, and so on – do not. Others have used similar ways of sorting out classes of stakeholders. Freeman, following Ackoff (1974), focuses on groups that the firm needs in order to exist – groups "without whose support the firm would fail to exist" – specifically customers, suppliers, employees, financiers, and communities (Dunham, Freeman, and Liedtka 2006: 25). Others have made a similar move, using the designations "primary" and "secondary" to differentiate stakeholders – groups to whom the firm is closely (and formally or officially) tied (and may have special duties towards them that are similar to what is owed to shareholders) from those with more distant ties (and to whom management has no special duties, but to whom they may have regular moral duties, such as not harming) (see, e.g., Carroll 1993: 60; Gibson 2000: 245).

One can interpret much of the existing work on stakeholder theory as providing at least indirect answers to the question of stakeholder legitimacy.

[9] Phillips (2003b) seems to read it this way.

Namely, normative cores (Freeman 1994; Jones and Wicks 1999a) provide some direction and specificity to the interests and stakeholders that should shape decision making at the firm. Finally, Mitchell, Agle, and Wood (1997) outline a theory of stakeholder identification and salience that helps to arrange stakeholders in terms of criteria that may be important for managers in deciding how to spend their time and resources. It is developed as a descriptive theory (which we would predict would be considered by management in decision making) and an instrumental theory (paying attention to certain stakeholders and/or their interests would tend to create beneficial outcomes), but has at least some normative dimensions in it (such as legitimacy).

From the standpoint of thinking about the definitional problem as singular and fixed, we face a seemingly intractable difficulty. No matter how many positive attributes any given candidate may have, no single definition seems to work for all purposes in all situations. All have limitations and weaknesses. From the standpoint of the search for the one correct definition, such a realization creates a real problem. However, one way to think about the role of the definitional problem is to return to the pragmatic perspective when thinking about the issues involved. Rather than seeing the definitional problem as a singular and fixed, admitting of one answer, we instead can see different definitions serving different purposes. Thus what might make one a (legitimate) stakeholder for one company, or for a given research agenda, may vary. While we might have meaningful conversations about what constitutes a poor use of terms and find reasons for settling on particular uses of them for certain purposes, the pragmatic perspective allows us to tolerate a range of definitions to exist under the umbrella of "stakeholder theory." Indeed, given the range of interpretations of stakeholder theory and how it is operationalized by organizations, such flexibility about terms may be an essential attribute to making it relevant and useful.

The distinctions among the parts of stakeholder theory (or not)

Stakeholder theory is discussed and developed across an array of domains and disciplines. Some work has brought us to focus on the distinctiveness of these different contributions and the importance of using methods appropriate to each. In addition, this work has raised the issue of how the various parts of stakeholder theory "fit" together such that various work can be seen to contribute to the literature.

Sharp distinctions across parts of stakeholder theory

Donaldson and Preston (1995) are the first to acknowledge explicitly and discuss systematically the notion that stakeholder theory has three distinct parts: descriptive (research that makes factual claims about managers and what companies actually do), instrumental (research that looks at the outcomes of specific managerial behavior), and normative (research that asks what managers or corporations should do). For them, all three play an important part in the theory, but each has its own particular role and methodology. The first two strands of stakeholder theory are explicitly part of the social sciences and involve matters of fact. The last, the normative dimension, is explicitly moral and is the domain of ethicists. Confusing the three, or failing to identify which type of theory is being used and adopt methods suited to that form of inquiry, leads to muddled research. Donaldson and Preston claim that the normative branch of stakeholder theory is the central core and that the other parts of the theory play a subordinate role. Stakeholder theory is first, and most fundamentally, a moral theory that specifies the obligations that companies have to their stakeholders. Whether companies actually act according to this theory, or whether acting in this way proves financially beneficial, are separate questions that do not bear on the issue of what management should do. Other theorists, particularly within the business ethics literature, have emphasized the normative task of justifying stakeholder theory and sorting out the right moral underpinnings of the theory as their central task (e.g. Cragg 2002; Gibson 2000; Humber 2002).[10]

Weak (or no) distinctions across parts of stakeholder theory

In contrast, Jones and Wicks (1999a) explicitly claim that there is an important connection between the parts of stakeholder theory and that the differences are not as sharp and categorical as Donaldson and Preston suggest. For them, if one looks carefully at the moral obligations of managers to stakeholders, one of the key duties is to take actions that will create benefits over the long term. This means that there is a normative duty to consider the instrumental effects of its normative core, values, and other specific stakeholder duties that extend beyond what common morality may require. They cite Kant's famous dictum, "ought implies can," suggesting that duties that tend to force companies out of business are duties (in general) which should be

[10] Our view of these distinctions is set out in Chapter 3.

viewed as suspect in the context of for-profit corporations. Freeman (1999) explicitly and vehemently rejects the idea that we can distinguish sharply between the three branches of stakeholder theory. He argues that all these forms of inquiry are forms of storytelling and that, conceptually, all three branches have elements of the others embedded within them. Following Quine, Davidson, and others, Freeman claims that there is no value-free language, nor is there epistemological privilege for social science inquiry. At best, we can make pragmatic distinctions among the parts of stakeholder theory. The focus of theorizing needs to be about how to tell better stories that enable people to cooperate and create more value through their activities at the corporation. Creating compelling stories involves all three elements of stakeholder theory, as well as a fourth – that it is managerial. To be a good story, a given normative core has to help managers create value for stakeholders and enable them to live better lives in the real world, not in some imaginary fantasy of philosophers. This approach follows directly from our pragmatist roots, explained in Chapter 3.

Normative cores and ideas driving stakeholder theory

Beyond the broad question of who are stakeholders and who should be considered legitimate, there is a variety of papers that focus on providing core content to stakeholder theory. As outlined by Freeman (1994), normative cores are an explicit effort to answer two questions facing all corporations: what is the purpose of the firm? to whom does management have an obligation? The answer to these two questions necessarily involves moral considerations but, as discussed above, for Freeman it may require other elements of stakeholder theory (e.g. instrumental, descriptive, managerial) to derive a sound normative core. As discussed above in the context of the stakeholder versus stockholder debate, if one rejects the idea that stakeholder theory is a single view of the firm, then one appreciates that there is a whole host of potential answers to Freeman's two questions.

Freeman's original normative cores

Freeman (1984) outlines a series of potential theories or "normative cores" that address his two core questions. He identifies five "generic enterprise level strategies" and envisions a variety of other possibilities that firms can derive to suit their unique situation. Though there is not a specific answer as to how management should choose among them, Freeman does suggest that there should be a "fit" between stakeholders, values, social issues, and the society within which managers operate (101). In addition, managers should engage in extensive planning and strategic activities, including stakeholder audits, to identify various social issues and values, as well as to help monitor performance and keep score with stakeholders over time.

Kantian capitalism

In the widely cited article "A stakeholder theory of the modern corporation: Kantian capitalism," Evan and Freeman (1993) maintain that management has a fiduciary duty to stakeholders – specifically to those who make investments (not just financial, but in terms of their labor, their future) in its ongoing operations, such as suppliers, employees, customers, shareholders, and the local community. The job of management is to keep stakeholder interests "in balance." Evan and Freeman cite Kant's notion that people should be treated as an end, never as a mere means, as a central reason why management has this fiduciary duty. Taking this Kantian ideal seriously means that managers have a duty to look out for their interests and to give them (or their representatives) voice in the decision-making process. Another dimension to their argument is that taking a stakeholder approach is actually the best method of generating the maximum financial return emphasized by Friedman, but that this can only happen by focusing on stakeholders and their well-being. Thus, even if one shares Friedman's goals and his concern with shareholder benefit, one is drawn to adopt a stakeholder approach. Others who take a similar perspective, particularly in seeing stakeholders as investors and therefore as entitled to the same kind of consideration as shareholders, include Blair (1998), Schlossberger (1994), and Etzioni (1998). Blair argues that core stakeholders, not just shareholders, have core assets tied up in the corporation and bear significant risks and are therefore owed consideration. Schlossberger uses dual investor theory, one which focuses on specific capital, the other on opportunity capital (provided by society – existing knowledge, infrastructure, education, etc.). Given that firms depend on opportunity capital, they therefore have a duty to society and to consider the interests of stakeholders as part of their corporate purpose (Schlossberger 1994: 462). Etzioni (1998) emphasizes the notion of the corporation as a community, and claims that all those groups who make up the community of the firm invest in it and deserve consideration in decision making as well as the right to participate in corporate governance.

Personal projects

In contrast to Freeman's earlier book, Freeman and Gilbert (1988) take an overtly normative view of stakeholder theory and lay out a variety of ways of thinking about enterprise strategy. Here ethics provides the clear core of stakeholder theory, and while the examples used are meant to illustrate the viability and strategic appeal of the theory, the authors lean heavily on moral persuasion as its core appeal. Managers should embrace stakeholder theory because it is a better way to live, it allows us to be authentic, and it enables cooperation with other stakeholders such that, over time, everybody wins. In this view the personal projects enterprise strategy is a way of understanding stakeholder theory (and strategy) that puts human beings and individual rights at the center of economic activity. The corporation is viewed as a vehicle for individuals to pursue their own personal projects, and companies should be organized and run in ways that allow stakeholders to do precisely that, in cooperation with other stakeholders.

Feminist theory

Wicks, Freeman, and Gilbert (1994) use feminist theory and extensive work on cooperation to argue that there is a distinctive way to understand stakeholder theory. Given the changes in the nature of the business environment – particularly related to the pace of change, the importance of networks, the need to share information, and the value of getting the most from people in their labor, all of which are prominent themes in this literature – feminist theory becomes a powerful lens through which to consider organizations. Here stakeholders are thought of in terms of a web of interconnected relationships, or networks, that reshape our conception of the firm (i.e. it is more organic and extended, and is built around relationships rather than just formal structures and clear lines of demarcation). The job of management is to extend care to stakeholders and maintain the web of cooperation that allows the firm to thrive and create value for stakeholders (493). To succeed, managers need to find a way to excel at managing relationships, finding the right networks, and getting people to work together to create value.

Burton and Dunn (1996) provide additional resources for thinking about the connections between feminist theory and stakeholder theory, noting that the distinctive value of feminist theory is that it provides a compelling alternative to economic theory as a grounding for stakeholder theory, in that it is morally compelling and emphasizes the concept of the interrelatedness of individuals and groups that make up the firm. It also has a practical orientation, emphasizing particular ways of relating to others, processes for making decisions, and the way in which stakeholders get along in real organizations.

Doctrine of fair contracts

In Freeman's article, "The politics of stakeholder theory: Some future directions" (1994), he lays out what he means by a normative core, lists several examples within the literature, and then articulates his own take on a specific normative core which he terms the "doctrine of fair contracts." This particular normative core lays out a liberal interpretation of fairness among stakeholders, drawing particularly on Rawls, and, in effect, lays out the conditions for developing a specific normative core. These principles include principles for entry and exit, governance, externalities, contracting costs, agency, and limited immortality (417). Thus one could interpret this section as providing broader parameters for evaluating specific normative cores (or as conditions that would have to be met to constitute a morally legitimate normative core), rather than providing a separate and specific version of one. Indeed, it is here that Freeman makes clear that he sees stakeholder theory as more than just a single theory, rather as a "genre" of theories, all of which explicitly address the central questions he poses: (i) what is the purpose of the corporation? (ii) to whom does the corporation have responsibilities?

Critical theory and Habermas

Reed's work on stakeholder theory, "Stakeholder management theory: A critical theory perspective" (1999), is explicitly postmodern, drawing on critical theory, particularly the work of Jürgen Habermas. Reed shares an emphasis on the centrality of normative stakeholder theory, and he develops normative claims that emerge out of three different kinds of stake: legitimacy (political equality), morality (fair economic opportunity), and ethics (authenticity). Reed does discuss some priority rules for sorting out different claims that emerge for managers, but there is some degree of ambiguity here, and while these factors place significant emphasis on the importance of stakeholders Reed also gives a prominent role to shareholders because of the importance of their property rights. At the same time Reed wants to give stakeholders considerable latitude to engage in discourse and come to agreements about the running of the corporation and the terms for stakeholder cooperation.

Convergent stakeholder theory

In their article "Convergent stakeholder theory in management research" (1999a), Jones and Wicks focus primarily on the criteria for developing a sound normative core, but they do develop part of a normative core that they claim has both normative and instrumental justification. The authors take particular note of the interest in stakeholder theory taken by both normative ethicists and social scientists, and search for common ground within the theory to bring their efforts together to provide support for stakeholder theory. For them, managers ought to develop a relatively trusting relationship with stakeholders at the corporation – something for which they try to show both compelling reasons found in moral theory and solid evidence that behaving in such a way would enable a firm to create sustainable value over time. Jones and Wicks claim that there are compelling reasons within stakeholder theory to value both normative and instrumental support as vital to any normative core that would seek justification – because of both the Kantian idea of "ought" implies "can" and the idea that for stakeholders to receive benefits, managers have to act in such a way as to keep the firm a going concern. Neither the focus on instrumental benefits or sound moral norms should dominate – indeed, both should work together and reinforce each other. A series of response papers to this article, published alongside it, by other prominent authors (Donaldson 1999a; Freeman 1999; Treviño and Weaver 1999b; Gioia 1999b) take issue with some of the core insights and emphasize different themes and directions for stakeholder theory. Donaldson (1999a) argues that the linkages provided by Jones and Wicks to combine the normative and instrumental strands of theory are insufficiently strong and that researchers need to explore managerial "as if" statements to better connect normative commitments and instrumental outcomes. Freeman (1999) argues that rather than focusing on theory that converges, researchers should be more focused on divergence, particularly in generating a wide array of narrative accounts which can show that corporations can thrive via stakeholder cooperation. Treviño and Weaver (1999b) focus their attention on the claims made about the integration of normative and instrumental inquiry, arguing that Jones and Wicks overstate their case and do not provide integrated theory. Gioia (1999b) shares the skepticism of Treviño and Weaver regarding claims of integration, and also argues that the claims of stakeholder theory lack credibility with real managers, as they come over as idealistic and impractical.

Fairness

In his book Phillips (2003a) lays out his vision of stakeholder theory in detail. In this sense, while he may disagree with efforts to depict his approach to stakeholder theory as one of a series of normative cores, it can be described in that way. As discussed above, on Phillips's view, stakeholder theory can be thought of as a cooperative scheme wherein the participants incur obligations to others through the taking and giving of the benefits of the scheme. Their connections to the organization are related to their receipt of the benefits.

Libertarian stakeholder theory

Freeman and Phillips (2002) argue that stakeholder theory has organic roots in libertarian political theory. They demonstrate that, when read in light of the core libertarian principles of personal freedom, voluntary association, and individual responsibility, stakeholder theory has a particularly robust underpinning. Of special importance is the notion that this libertarian reading helps to emphasize that stakeholder theory is fundamentally about how we understand value creation and trade – the foundations of capitalism – rather than offering an ethical revision of the "standard account" of business as shareholder profit maximization. Freeman and Phillips claim that five core libertarian principles capture the shift from "stakeholder theory" to a libertarian stakeholder capitalism that embraces the injunction to be "managerial," while simultaneously combining the normative and the instrumental. These principles are (i) the principle of stakeholder cooperation (stakeholders jointly satisfy each other's needs through voluntary agreements); (ii) the principle of stakeholder responsibility (parties to an agreement take responsibility for their actions); (iii) the principle of complexity (human beings have a multitude of motivations and values); (iv) the principle of continuous creation (people use organizations as a vehicle for constantly searching for new ways of creating value); and (v) the principle of emergent competition (competition is a secondary effect, not a primary driver, in a context of cooperative schemes devoted to value creation in a free society).[11]

Community

Both Argandoña (1998) and Hartman (1996) emphasize the notion of the common good as a way to think about the corporation and its obligations to

[11] We use these principles below in Chapter 9 to articulate stakeholder capitalism.

stakeholders (see also Etzioni 1998). Argandoña notes the weakness of existing "theoretical foundations" within stakeholder theory (1998: 1100) and the arbitrariness of any duties that emerge. He claims that the notion of the common good can provide the robustness required of any such candidate for undergirding stakeholder theory and that it can help to determine the various rights and duties of the stakeholders involved. Hartman specifically eschews the language of stakeholder theory, but he does develop a way of thinking about individual stakeholders and the good life in the context of the corporation, drawing especially on the work of Aristotle, Rawls, and Rorty. His approach to the subject is complementary to stakeholder theory, as he sees the corporation as a community of persons, each of whom has certain rights and responsibilities, a notion of the good that is more personal, and a larger notion of the good that is tied to the community that is the firm, and his project is to think about how people can jointly find a way forward that makes everyone better off. Both works provide a noteworthy set of ideas that may be used to think about stakeholder theory and its role in shaping our understanding of the corporation.

Integrative social contracts theory

In their landmark book on integrative social contracts theory (ISCT), Donaldson and Dunfee (1999) go to great lengths to show the connections between stakeholder theory and their theory. Indeed, they make the claim that the vantage point of ISCT actually is helpful in thinking about how particular normative cores are developed in a global context. ISCT provides a powerful tool for thinking about the moral sub-structure of economic life – the idea that there is a set of explicit and implicit norms that govern exchange, the cooperation of individuals, the operation of firms, and the function of markets. ISCT offers a way of thinking about norms that operate in a highly specific context (e.g. in the markets of Verona, Italy), while also thinking about norms across contexts (e.g. when a firm in Verona does business with a company in San Diego, California) – both to understand such norms (i.e. to understand them in a factual manner) and to think about what kinds of norms can be justified (i.e. to offer a normative defense of them). Donaldson and Dunfee emphasize the importance of individuals and groups being able to negotiate the terms of their association, but within constraints imposed by moral norms, including "hypernorms" that provide universal, baseline conditions for moral behavior. The authors believe that ISCT provides the moral resources needed by managers in order to wrestle with moral questions that are not provided by stakeholder theory (e.g. Phillips, Freeman, and Wicks 2003, and their view that stakeholder theory is not a comprehensive moral doctrine), including guidance on the priority of different norms that may prove relevant to a given decision, and a clearer idea of which obligations may be required, permitted, or prohibited (Donaldson and Dunfee 1999: 256–261). They believe that the ISCT-based approach to stakeholder theory is more compelling than that developed by some theorists because it does not presuppose the universality of certain moral ideas (e.g. Kantian capitalism) and allows communities the respect and latitude they need to develop their own accounts of stakeholder theory.

Normative justification of stakeholder theory or of business

One way to think about the work developed under the banner of stakeholder theory is to see it as providing a normative justification for the theory and its associated activities. Such an activity is the domain of philosophers, who seek to develop complex and sophisticated arguments to show that a given idea or activity can be defended using normative reasons – notions of what "should be" the case. Of particular import is the notion that stakeholder theory is viewed (exclusively or primarily) as a moral theory. One could easily see Donaldson and Preston (1995), Goodpaster (1991), and Boatright as engaged in this quest – to find a moral basis to support this theory and to show its superiority to that of shareholder theory. Hendry (2001b) is also focused on the project of the normative justification for stakeholder theory (159), even as he notes the practical difficulties of adopting several versions of the theory and encourages those producing future work to do a better job of creating "realistic" versions of the theory. Indeed, in another paper (2001a) Hendry develops a different "foundation" for stakeholder theory, based on social relationships, arguing that it is more effective as a mechanism to provide justification for the theory. Gibson (2000) takes as his core project the determination of whether there is "any moral justification for stakeholder theory," claiming that he finds that there is one version (based on deontological theory) that supports the general thesis of stakeholder theory (255).

Another way to think about the work done by stakeholder theory is to provide a justification for business. On this view, business is a morally suspect activity – a view that has a long history, particularly if we associate the term "business" with the profit-seeking activities of individuals and corporations of our current era (see, e.g., Aristotle and St. Thomas Aquinas, who both thought of such persons as parasites). The only way to make business an acceptable activity is to find a way of mapping an alternative path that has "values" and "ethics" at its core – the driver to legitimate what corporations do, to distinguish sharply how decisions are made from more traditional accounts where profits and instrumental considerations drive decision making.

While there are a number of ways to categorize existing work in stakeholder theory, this grouping will best fit theories that are intent on sharply distinguishing stakeholder theory from shareholder theory, particularly because shareholder theory (i.e. traditional "business") is viewed as morally suspect and/or indefensible. One can read Kaler's work (2003) in this light, as he sees stakeholder theory as providing "basically a reformist stance toward capitalism, seeking … to move it in the direction of greater equity" (71). He also notes that a critical part of the normative merit is that any such objective for the firm would need to be devoted to "serving more than shareholder interests" (Kaler 2006: 264).

A note on enterprise strategy

To close this section on normative cores, it is important to tie this concept to the enterprise strategy concept developed earlier by Freeman (1984). Particularly if we are to reject the idea that research in this field is (primarily) about providing normative justification for stakeholder theory or business, enterprise strategy becomes an important concept to bring us back to the core focus of the theory – how we understand capitalism. This is an activity that is not the primary domain of philosophers, and as a result, forces researchers to move on to unfamiliar and daunting territory. Philosophers provide an important voice and have a critical role to play in developing compelling accounts of business, but through how they help us to understand the activity of business rather than by importing ethical concepts into business, offering wholesale critiques of capitalism, or seeing the primary challenge of research as to normatively "prop up" either stakeholder theory or business.

As articulated by Freeman (1984), Freeman and Gilbert (1988), and Freeman, Harrison, and Wicks (2007), enterprise strategy answers the question, "what do we stand for?" (Freeman 1984: 90). It is about the larger notions (e.g. mission, values, and principles) and the particular practices of how a company defines itself and lives that out systematically through its activities and engagement with stakeholders. Enterprise strategy represents a way of thinking about how business and ethics go together, the "conjunction of ethical and strategic thinking" (Freeman and Gilbert 1988: 71) in an intentional and forward-looking way. On this view value-laden ideas are integrally involved in the economic activities of the firm and the ongoing association of stakeholders. Taking enterprise strategy seriously involves clarifying priorities, seeing what the "trump cards" are within a given business, and seeing how an enterprise comes together to make everyone better off (Freeman and Gilbert 1988: 71). Thus normative cores need to be viewed in terms of their potential to serve as candidates for an enterprise strategy, something that could order and direct the activities of a corporation and the managers who run it.

The separation thesis[12]

A central topic that has emerged from conversations about stakeholder theory is the separation thesis. As first articulated by Freeman, the separation thesis posits the following: "The discourse of business and the discourse of ethics can be separated so that sentences like 'x is a business decision' have no moral content, and 'x is a moral decision' have no business content" (Freeman 1994: 412). The concept was first developed in the context of an article in which Freeman saw scholars languishing in the midst of Goodpaster's "stakeholder paradox" and recognized the need to keep stakeholder theory from veering off course. The separation thesis provided a way of highlighting the fundamental connections between ethics and business captured in enterprise strategy and to repudiate efforts by philosophers to turn stakeholder theory into either moral philosophy (e.g. a normative justification for stakeholder theory and business) or amoral business. Wicks (1996) extended Freeman's argument and demonstrated how deeply embedded the assumptions of the separation thesis were in the business ethics and business and society literatures. He also provided some directions on how it was necessary for research to change to avoid these problematic assumptions and move in a more constructive direction. Other work has extended discussion of the separation thesis and its relevance for research (e.g. Freeman 2000; Freeman, Wicks, and Parmar 2004; Martin and Freeman 2004).

More recent work revisits the separation thesis and discusses both its core meaning(s) and its relevance for research. Sandberg (2008a) argues that the

[12] While we have referred to this idea in a variety of ways, such as the separation fallacy or the problem of the ethics of capitalism, it has taken on a separate life in the business ethics literature. Our analysis in Chapter 1 is of one of the main causes of why the problem of the ethics of capitalism has arisen, and in Chapter 3, of one of the main culprits in the increasing irrelevance of business schools.

separation thesis, as articulated by Freeman, is equivocal and open to a wide array of possible interpretations – he specifically explores nine different meanings in the paper. Most of the nine interpretations are distinguished across "descriptive" and "normative" categories. Among the more notable themes explored in the paper, Sandberg notes Margolis and Walsh's (2001: 25) interpretation of the separation thesis as meaning that the demands of business pursuits and the demands of morality are "inherently antithetical," and Kaler's (2002) take, that the demands of business and the pursuit of ethical objectives are different and often conflict. Sandberg concludes by reasserting the lack of precision surrounding the separation thesis, the importance of the issues that the various meanings raise, and the need to offer supporting reasons to defend the claims of the separation thesis (whether for or against).

In response, Harris and Freeman (2008) argue that the separation thesis is impossible to maintain. They agree with Sandberg that it is integrally linked to the fact/value dichotomy and that such an interpretation of this thesis is unsustainable under critical scrutiny. They further illustrate the problems in our thinking (both in research and management) resulting from adopting the mindset of the separation thesis, particularly since we enact the world we create with our theories (e.g. Ghoshal 2005). Given the tendency of researchers to operate from the standpoint of the separation thesis (see, e.g., Harris and Freeman 1994; Sen 1987; Wicks 1996), Harris and Freeman argue that there is an urgent need for researchers to come to grips with the separation thesis and to adopt modes of theorizing that get beyond it – opening up more complex and creative modes of theorizing that allow for collaboration across an array of disciplines. In his response, Wempe (2008) emphasizes what he takes as the core message from Freeman's initial development of the separation thesis – the admonition that research in business ethics cannot or should not be done from either a purely economic or purely normative (i.e. moralizing) point of view. Dienhart (2008) talks about the separation thesis in terms of the identity thesis (namely, "every business decision is an ethical decision") and uses it as a reference to think about how best to direct future inquiry to more nuanced understandings and avoid the pitfalls of the separation thesis. He concurs that Sandberg has done a valuable service in highlighting the various meanings of the separation thesis and pointing out the futility of finding any single meaning of the concept. Sandberg (2008b) has the last word and reaffirms his belief that there are important issues embedded in the variety of meanings he finds associated with the separation thesis. He also notes that Harris and Freeman do not provide specific arguments why the separation thesis should be rejected – instead only offering lists of the dangers associated with it (2008b: 564).

Managerial relevance and direction

Two core works of the ethics literature on stakeholder theory, Freeman (1994) and Donaldson and Preston (1995), claim that stakeholder theory is relevant to management and can help managers in their day-to-day decision making. The question remains, what does that mean and to what extent does stakeholder theory deliver on it?

Our answer is clear. Stakeholder theory is explicitly a managerial theory. Indeed, it was developed precisely to help managers acknowledge and deal with the complex reality they faced more effectively than other prevailing theories. Particularly in the context of the array of techniques for developing their theory of the firm, implementing it, and assessing it, speaking to and guiding the activity of managers was a core concern of all the early stakeholder theorists.

However, much of the literature has focused more on broad concepts and normative ideals than on detailed direction. As one example, Evan and Freeman's notion of stakeholder theory involves seeing all value-chain stakeholders as having equal status as fiduciaries.[13] The firm should be run in their interest. While in some sense this is as helpful and directive as shareholder theory, it creates new problems that beg for resolution for fear that managers will be lost as to whether they have enacted stakeholder theory or not. If all these groups are fiduciaries, then how can a manager resolve conflicts between them – something that appears inevitable, at least in the short term and possibly even in the long term? The authors offer up the notion of King Solomon as a useful guide and reinforce the idea that there needs to be "balance" among their interests, but others have argued this is too broad and not realistic. We suggest that the whole idea of "fiduciary" in today's world is not terribly useful.

Jensen claims that it is not possible for the firm to have multiple constituencies for whom they have to maximize returns. He claims that conceptually it is not possible, leaving the shareholder theory as the sole viable theory to drive managerial behavior. Sundaram and Inkpen (2004) make a similar claim in their critique of stakeholder theory and defense of the shareholder view. For

[13] For a stakeholder approach to understanding the value chain see Freeman and Liedtka (1997).

them, the theory is unable to direct managerial behavior in a coherent way. This, in turn, rules it out as potentially relevant, since if it cannot help direct managerial behavior, there can be no relevance that is meaningful or helpful to managers.

Donaldson and Preston (1995) make the claim that until their article, much of the stakeholder literature was too unfocused and general, thereby undermining its academic coherence and its ability to be useful to managers. They claimed that their theory pushed us a step in the right direction and provided some metrics according to which we could assess stakeholder theory as a managerial theory (i.e. their breaking stakeholder theory into three parts, all of which were important to the theory and should work together to make the case for it).

Elms, Berman, and Wicks (2002) argued that stakeholder theory, even as revised by Donaldson and Preston, did not go far enough. Using the example of health care and the complex array of incentives influencing key stakeholders (e.g. especially, health-care practitioners and providers) that in order to be useful and directive, stakeholder theory had to get closer to the world of practice. That is, unless there was another layer of theorizing that connected (meta)theory and practice, stakeholder theory risked being so broad as to provide effectively no help for managers trying to sort out what to do in the context of some difficult problems in health care. These authors argued that theorists should recognize the import of incentives in shaping behavior and developing theory which helps to address these incentives and enable managers to envision and act according to the tenets of stakeholder theory (Elms et al. 2002: 426).

Related claims are made by Donaldson and Dunfee (1994) in their work on integrative social contracts theory. For them, stakeholder theory remains fatally generic and unable to incorporate the kind of detail necessary to provide insight that is directive and to account for the features of the situation required for that direction to be relevant (255). In a later work that fleshes out the details of ISCT in book form, they revise their earlier critique. They then suggest that their theory is fully compatible with stakeholder theory, and indeed, can provide important guidance for managers trying to operate according to stakeholder theory in a global economy (Donaldson and Dunfee, 1999, ch. 9).

In their reply to Sundaram and Inkpen (2004), Freeman, Wicks, and Parmar (2004b) attempt to rebut the idea that stakeholder theory is too broad. Sundaram and Inkpen (2004) argue for the primacy of shareholder theory. Three of their arguments for shareholder theory suggest problems with using stakeholder theory that reinforce concerns about its conceptual breadth: (i) that the shareholder value model "creates the appropriate incentives for managers to assume managerial risks" (and, implicitly, that the stakeholder model does not); (ii) "having more than one objective will make governing difficult, if not impossible" (i.e. a direct attack on stakeholder theory for being too broad and messy); and (iii) "it is easier to make shareholders out of stakeholders than vice versa" (353). In their reply, Freeman et al. (2004b) offer several arguments. First, they claim that addressing and resolving stakeholder concerns that arise are not unique to stakeholder theory. Any effort to resolve such conflicts in ways that systematically benefit shareholders at the expense of other key stakeholders will fail. Indeed, stakeholder theory provides a more realistic view of business. It suggests that stakeholders count and are critical for creating outstanding performance – it provides not only resources, but language and action to help stakeholders see that they are important and that their commitment is critical to creating outstanding value (365). Second, stakeholder theory does provide direction for managers in ways that allow them to create value (i.e. direct response to points (i) and (ii)). At its core, stakeholder theory is about business – about putting together a deal in which "suppliers, customers, employees, communities, managers, and shareholders all win continuously over time" (365). Specifically in terms of creating new value and taking risks, if such deals do not take into account stakeholder interests and see them as fundamentally joint, there will be an exodus and another venture will be formed which does so (365; see also Venkataraman 2002). Third, evidence from many of the biggest and most successful companies show that stakeholder theory, particularly as practiced by real companies, is specific and directive enough. Companies such as Merck, 3M, Johnson & Johnson, and Motorola have all managed the problem of considering multiple constituencies and use their notions of stakeholder theory to create outstanding value over time. Finally, they point out that shareholders already are stakeholders, thereby undercutting the idea that there is an antagonism and separation to begin with.

Misunderstandings and misuses of stakeholder theory

Stakeholder theory has been used in a variety of different ways – by critics and "friends" alike. We shall look at some of the more prominent misunderstandings and focus on one article that discusses this issue in depth. Phillips, Freeman, and Wicks (2003) isolate an array of ways in which stakeholder theory has been misread.

Stakeholder theory is an excuse for managerial opportunism

The core claim put forward by Jensen (2000), Marcoux (2000), and Sternberg (2000) is that by providing more groups who, management argues, benefit from their actions, stakeholder theory makes it far easier to engage in self-dealing and to defend it than if shareholder theory were the sole purpose. In short, by having so many different masters, managers in fact have none and can effectively do what they want and find a rationale that their choices benefit at least one group and are therefore defensible. In contrast, Jensen, Marcoux, and Sternberg argue that if managers have a duty only to shareholders, it makes it easier to judge their performance and clearer whether they have done well (or not). Phillips, Freeman, and Wicks (2003) offer two replies: first, much of the current managerial opportunism has been done under the banner of shareholder maximization (e.g. Enron, Worldcom) and they specifically criticize the actions of Al Dunlap, who grossly mismanaged a number of companies to create his own financial benefit; and, second, this is an issue for any theory of organization and does not put stakeholder theory in a worse light because of it (484). Indeed, the authors argue, there are good reasons to see stakeholder theory as creating more accountability from managers as they have more obligations and duties of care to more constituencies, and are therefore less likely to engage in self-dealing.

Stakeholder theory cannot provide a sufficiently specific objective function for the corporation

Jensen (2000) and Sundaram and Inkpen (2004), and others who offer this critique, maintain that having a singular objective for the corporation is essential – both because it provides an objective foundation for evaluating performance and because without such a clear and specific objective management is unable to determine a clear and coherent course of action. Without the clarity and precision of profit maximization, managers are lost. Phillips, Freeman, and Wicks (2003) counter that these criticisms are misplaced for several reasons. First, stakeholder theory in the abstract is incapable of answering questions about specific management decisions, since one needs a particular normative core (or corporate mission) to dig into decision making. Asking for such precision from stakeholder theory writ large is to miss the point of the theory. Second, this critique could be applied to any relevant theory and used to find them wanting – given any standard for management decision making (whether singular or plural), there are potentially innumerable methods of implementing it. In keeping with this view, the business judgment rule provides managers with just such flexibility and implicitly recognizes that there are a variety of paths for serving the interests of the organization. Third, advocates of the shareholder view (e.g. Jensen and Sternberg) seem to embrace stakeholder theory as a viable method for creating the instrumental benefits they advocate for shareholders – in seeming contradiction to the core critique that was initially offered. Fourth, managers (and theorists) should not seek more simplicity than is necessary in an objective function. Having such narrow and specific criteria may delude managers about their core activities and create undue confidence in their choices. Fifth, stakeholder theory is fully compatible with long-term value maximization (i.e. not maximizing shareholder wealth or share price). The tension between stakeholder theory and shareholder theory only appears to arise when managers single out shareholders as the primary (or exclusive) beneficiary of the profits.

Stakeholder theory is primarily concerned with distribution of financial outputs

This view, put forward by Marcoux (2000), depicts stakeholder theory as primarily about who benefits from the resources of the organization, and poses a stark and inherent conflict between shareholders and other stakeholders in terms of who gets what. If one begins with the idea of the firm as having a fixed pie of surplus (i.e. profits) to distribute, and views stakeholder theory and shareholder theory as providing different schemes for distributing that wealth, then the contrast between them appears to be sharp and stark. Freeman, Wicks, and Parmar (2004a) claim that distribution is only part of the story, namely that a critical part of stakeholder theory is about process and procedural justice – that stakeholders deserve a say in how resources are allocated, that such involvement affects how they view the distribution of resources, and that their involvement can also create new opportunities for value creation (i.e. enlarging the pie). They cite research which shows that stakeholders are more accepting of outcomes when they perceive the process as fair. They also mention that distribution involves more than just financial resources – that information is something which can be shared among stakeholders and does not pit shareholders against other stakeholders (487–488).

All stakeholders must be treated equally

Though several versions of what it means to treat stakeholders equally (e.g. egalitarianism, equalitarianism) are offered by Gioia (1999), Marcoux (2000), and Sternberg (2000), the core point is that critics have focused on the notion of treating stakeholders equally, particularly around the language of "balance" that has been prominent in discussions of what it means to manage on behalf of stakeholders. The first reply to this criticism is that they create "straw men" and do not tackle arguments put forward by specific theorists. The authors argue that there is a variety of ways of understanding stakeholder theory, and that these more complex understandings make this criticism, even in its more sophisticated forms, largely irrelevant. Phillips, Freeman, and Wicks (2003) also claim that one can use forms of meritocracy (e.g. using Phillips's notion of fairness in benefits given being in proportion to those received), that meaningful distinctions among stakeholders can be made by theorists (see the discussion above of legitimacy and normative cores), and that each firm may handle this issue differently, depending on its own particular version of stakeholder theory. This criticism also compounds the mistake of confusing stakeholder theory as primarily or exclusively about the distribution of financial outputs rather than about process and consideration in decision making.

Stakeholder theory requires changes to current law

Some, including Hendry (2001a, 2001b) and Van Buren (2001), have argued that the law needs to be changed, either to overcome the concern that doing anything other than shareholder management is illegal or to make it easier to practice stakeholder theory (i.e. making it more transparent that using stakeholder theory to manage does not violate core principles of business law). For example, Humber (2002) takes the view that Freeman "seems to advocate passage of enabling legislation which will force corporations to be managed in the interests of stakeholders" (208). The core reply offered is that while there may be reasons to consider various changes to the legal system, stakeholder theory contains no requirement that the law be changed to allow firms to practice it. Marens and Wicks (1999) show that the business judgment rule allows firms to use stakeholder theory without fear of running afoul of the theory or practice of the law. Enacting specific changes in the law that force management to consider stakeholders (e.g. corporate constituency statutes) may prove useful, but they are not to be confused with the core of what constitutes stakeholder theory, or to be seen as essential concomitants to embracing the theory.

Stakeholder theory is socialism and refers to the entire economy

This view has been put forward by Barnett (1997), Hutton (1995), and Rustin (1997). In the UK and other parts of Europe there is talk of a "stakeholder economy" (it is a term used by the former British prime minister Tony Blair). Phillips et al. (2003) argue that stakeholder theory is first and foremost a theory of organizations, not a theory of political economy. In addition, while there may be some merit in drawing from stakeholder theory discussions of economies within a political context, doing so makes truly problematic the concerns raised about the breadth of the theory and for what purposes it is being used (491–492). Stakeholder theory has been developed as a system of voluntary exchange for individuals within a capitalist economy. It is decidedly not a form of socialism or a set of social policies to be enforced by the state.[14]

Stakeholder theory is a comprehensive moral doctrine

Orts and Strudler (2002) put forward this argument. In his discussion of what constitutes a comprehensive moral doctrine, John Rawls (1993) claims that it is a theory which can address the full array of moral questions that arise without reference to any other theory. According to Phillips et al. (2003), stakeholder theory is not a comprehensive doctrine. Rather, it is a theory of organizations that does not even cover all the moral questions relevant to a business context, let alone the rest of the moral world. Indeed, if one examines Friedman's shareholder theory, one finds that he specifically mentions that the profit maximization activities of companies need to occur within the rules set by legal precedent and widely shared ethical custom – two additional sources of moral guidance that exist apart from his theory of the firm. Phillips et al. (2003) specifically mention violation of hypernorms in a given business context as an important moral issue that may come up for a given business, specifically noting that hypernorms come from moral philosophy and not stakeholder theory (494).

Stakeholder theory applies only to corporations

Some critics, including Donaldson and Preston (1995), maintain that stakeholder theory applies solely to corporations. Though Phillips et al. (2003) go out of their way to help draw boundaries to their theory, they also argue that limiting it solely to publicly traded corporations is a mistake that misses some of the potential richness of stakeholder theory. Though specific issues may arise in determining what aspects of the theory can be applied, and under what conditions, they see it as potentially relevant to "small or family owned

[14] See our distinctly libertarian view in Chapter 9 below.

businesses, privately owned concerns of any size, partnerships, non-profit and governmental organizations" (495).

Talk of "paradigms" and links to the management literature

In assessing its overall significance, some have termed stakeholder theory a potential "paradigm" for the field of business ethics (or business and society); others have pushed theorists to consider its reach into the wider management literature and how this concept might take the conversations among business ethicists and extend them to other theories and concepts discussed in the management literature.

Paradigms

Tom Jones, in his work on stakeholder theory (Jones 1995) and in other writings on business and society, has explicitly talked about paradigms (e.g. Kuhn 1970) and their importance for creating legitimacy and providing a foundation for good research. Jones has lamented the lack of an organizing framework within which to ground work on business and society, as well as the resulting incoherence and atheoretical work that has resulted. Without the kind of simplifying assumptions and widespread agreement found in other fields (e.g. economics), business and society research appeared to be permanently stuck in a no-win situation. One of the most appealing parts of stakeholder theory was, to his mind, the opportunity to provide such a unifying framework within which to ground work in ethics (and business and society, more broadly). Thus, rather than a single theory, to be compared alongside management theories such as resource dependence, stakeholder theory was far more ambitious and fundamental in its reach.

Links to management theory

We believe that stakeholder theory, in some form, is inescapable for all theories of organization, particularly management theory. While much existing work claims to be neutral or indifferent regarding ethics and questions of the purpose of the firm, we believe that it is bad faith to make such claims and not recognize that assumptions – either implicit or explicit – are being made all the time by theorists of organization (see Wicks and Freeman 1998; Freeman 1994). One of the key insights of stakeholder theory is to make evident that management theory, in its current form, is ethics done badly – precisely because it does not recognize the ethics questions embedded in any discussion of organizations and it systematically tries to exclude them as part of theoretical inquiry.

For Jones and Wicks (1999a), stakeholder theory represents an important new trend in management theory, serving as a bridge between the normative analysis of the philosopher and the empirical or instrumental investigation of the management scholar. By being at once explicitly moral and requiring support from instrumental analysis, stakeholder theory offers a new way of thinking about management theory. To provide a defensible normative core, researchers need to be able to show that it is simultaneously defensible in a normative (i.e. it embodies a set of defensible moral norms and principles) and an instrumental (i.e. that enacting these norms and principles is likely to help the firm generate economic value and enable the firm to remain a sustainably profitable enterprise) sense. Such an agenda gives researchers on both sides of the ethics/social-science divide an important role in the future development of stakeholder theory. This new focus also addresses the concern that existing management theory is amoral and provides little room for ethics to become integral to the conversation. For Jones and Wicks (1999a), stakeholder theory is part of management theory and should explicitly draw upon management theory and methods, but it is equally a part of ethics and moral theory. Stakeholder theory should be used as a model for expanding and critiquing existing theories of organization.

Conclusion

There is a diverse array of literature on stakeholder theory within business ethics. Indeed, one can readily make the case that stakeholder theory is currently one of the most important parts of the business ethics literature. This chapter provides a way of understanding the larger objectives of the business ethics literature and, within that context, to see how stakeholder theory emerged as a natural and important extension of the inquiry that is distinctive to business ethics researches and how it has evolved over time. Given the larger objective of thinking about how ethics and business are connected in a systematic way, stakeholder theory has become a powerful vehicle for thinking about the way in which ethics becomes central to the core operations of the firm and how managing is a morally laden activity – rather than a strictly formalistic and amoral quest for economic gain. Along with discussions of CSR, charity, and the ethical duties to society of companies, stakeholder theory provides an important conceptual innovation that gives expression to these concerns while simultaneously refocusing attention on business and the value-creating activity of corporations. In short, it addresses the problem of the ethics of capitalism, while also drawing in discussion of the problem of value creation and trade.

Within this broad frame of reference, the chapter highlights an array of distinctive conversations about what stakeholder theory is, how it relates to other theories of the firm (e.g. shareholder theory), how it provides direction for managers in organizations, and what kinds of connections there are between ethics and the practice of business. Many of these conversations are ongoing and show no signs of diminishing in relevance. However, while many of the rudimentary questions about stakeholder theory (e.g. defining stakeholders, sorting out to whom managers have obligations, overcoming the stakeholder paradox) continue to gain attention from some scholars, much of the conversation has pushed forward and moved to newer ground. Particularly as researchers have tried to see stakeholder theory as a theory of managing (rather than primarily as a moral theory), more attention has been paid to thinking about connections to the management literature and seeing it as a theory of organizations that spans a wide variety of disciplines. Of particular note are the widespread influence of stakeholder theory outside the domain of ethics and the SIM division of the Academy of Management, the cultivation of various stakeholder engagement techniques to help firms improve their performance, the increased attention to the development of specific normative cores and approaches of specific companies as versions of stakeholder management, and the capitulation of iconic figures from the shareholder theory camp to embracing stakeholder theory (e.g. Michael Jensen). In short, while stakeholder theory has a long way to go and much to do, a great deal has been accomplished and many of the early battles have been won. Perhaps stakeholder theorists should declare victory for stakeholder theory – both in the sense of changing the conversation from a stakeholder vs. a shareholder theory of the firm (i.e. the stakeholder paradox is a mistake), and in the sense of showing how stakeholder theory captures the best of what is embedded in shareholder theory and provides more compelling ideas and practices that make corporations richer communities and better able to create value over time.

And, while there is still a wide variety of ways in which theorists talk and think about stakeholder theory, there is a good deal of agreement as well, particularly that it underscores the inescapable moral dimensions of firm purpose and managerial responsibility, that it expands the conversation beyond consideration solely of shareholders, and that theory development needs to take into account the complex array of phenomena that stakeholder theory incorporates (e.g. descriptive, instrument, normative, managerial).

Remaining concerns exist about the temptation to make stakeholder theory more than it is or can be. This chapter documents numerous efforts, many of them well intentioned, to get stakeholder theory to provide more guidance than it is capable of (as a theory), to apply in contexts where it is not equipped to provide relevant insights, or to address (moral) questions it simply is not capable of addressing. Future research needs to focus on the promise of stakeholder theory, while practicing restraint and being mindful of its limitations

8 Stakeholder theory and corporate social responsibility

This chapter focuses on the connections between stakeholder theory and the corporate social responsibility (CSR) literature. After more than half a century of research and debate, there is not a single widely accepted definition of CSR. Researchers in the field of CSR have claimed that "the phrase 'corporate social responsibility' has been used in so many different contexts that it has lost all meaning" (Sethi 1975: 58). There are many different ideas, concepts, and practical techniques that have been developed under the umbrella of CSR research, including *corporate social performance* (Carroll 1979; Wartick and Cochran 1985; Wood 1991); *corporate social responsiveness* (Ackerman 1975; Ackerman and Bauer 1976; Sethi 1975); *corporate citizenship* (Wood and Logsdon 2001; Waddock 2004); *corporate governance* (Jones 1980; Freeman and Evan 1990; Evan and Freeman 1993; Sacconi 2006); *corporate accountability* (Zadek, Pruzan, and Evans 1997); *sustainability*, *triple bottom line* (Elkington 1994); and *corporate social entrepreneurship* (Austin, Stevenson, and Wei-Skillern 2006). All these are different nuances of the CSR concept that have been developed in the last fifty years – and beyond.[1] Each of these diverse efforts shares a common aim in the attempt to broaden the obligations of firms to include more than financial considerations. This literature wrestles with and around questions of the broader purpose of the firm and how it can deliver on those goals.

[1] Although there seems to be some consensus in setting the date of the first relevant contributions in the CSR literature in the 1950s, it has also been noted that writings by Andrew Carnegie and others at the beginning of the twentieth century were already explicitly dealing with the relationship between business and society (see, e.g., Freeman 1984; Windsor 2001; Carroll 2006). Nevertheless, the landmark beginnings of CSR literature are usually traced back to the writings of Howard R. Bowen, who published his *Social Responsibilities of the Businessman* in 1953; quite emphatically, Archie Carroll argues that Bowen "should be called the father of corporate social responsibility" (Carroll 2006: 5). Of course this is a Western and specifically US perspective. The connections between business and society in other traditions are much older. See Chapple and Moon (2005) for an overview of CSR in Asia; Welford (2005) for a comparison of CSR in Europe, North America, and Asia; Arora and Puranik (2004) and Panda (2008) for a review of CSR in India; Qu (2007) for a Chinese perspective on CSR; and Demise (2005, 2006) for Japan.

This chapter does not aim to give a comprehensive review of the rich body of literature that comprises CSR research.[2] The intent here is different: we shall examine a number of distinctive concepts and related streams of research which originated within the CSR literature, and discuss their meaning, their evolution, and their connections with the main ideas of stakeholder theory.

By reviewing some of the key contributions to the development of the CSR literature, this chapter will demonstrate how the stakeholder idea can and should be used as a foundational unit of analysis for the ongoing conversation around CSR, and how stakeholder theory can add value to the future development of CSR, by better specifying and integrating financial and social concerns. Our view is that intentions behind corporate social responsibility are better satisfied if we think about *company stakeholder responsibility*.

First we introduce the main ideas within the CSR literature that illustrate, in our view, the key stages in the development of the concept and its linkages with stakeholder theory.

The concept of CSR

The major development of the modern concept of corporate social responsibility can be traced back primarily to the contributions by a number of prominent business and society scholars in the 1960s and 1970s.

Davis (1960, 1967, 1973) contributed to the emerging conversation about CSR by stating that in order to talk meaningfully about CSR, managers need to look for something more than legal compliance and something beyond the traditional way of managing the corporation according to the profit maximization logic. In his 1960 article, Davis argued that social responsibility refers to "businessmen's decisions and actions taken for reasons *at least partially beyond* the firm's direct economic or technical interest" (Davis, 1960: 70, emphasis added). Recognizing the difficulties in providing a substantive definition of what the social responsibilities of business might include, Davis suggests a definition of the concept in negative terms: a firm cannot be said to be socially responsible "if it merely complies with the minimum requirements of the law, because this is what any good citizen would do" (Davis 1973: 313). There are social obligations, argues Davis, that push the firm to go beyond the requirements of the law. He therefore articulated CSR as the firm's consideration of, and response to, "issues beyond the narrow economic, technical and

[2] For a historical examination of the evolution of the CSR concept see Carroll (1999) and Frederick (2006).

legal requirements of the firm" (312). The blunt interpretation of Friedman's view – that the corporation should care only for profit maximization and do nothing more than comply with the legal requirements – is explicitly rejected by Davis. This argument is not based on philosophical considerations, but is developed in managerial (risk-management) terms: to ignore social obligations seemed to Davis a very dangerous corporate strategy.[3] This is because of the "iron law of responsibility," which states that when society grants legitimacy and power to business, "In the long run, those who do not use power in a manner which society considers responsible will tend to lose it" (314).

We can see some seeds of stakeholder theory in Davis's approach to CSR, particularly in the idea that corporations have broader obligations than solely to stockholders. He also recognizes the instrumental value of broadening corporate obligations, and could be read as saying that it is essential for the firm's success that managers lead the corporation by taking into account these broader obligations: "to the extent businessmen do not accept social responsibility obligations as they arise, other groups eventually will step in to assume those responsibilities and the power that goes with them." (Davis 1973: 314).

In addition to the obligations of the firm, CSR scholars articulated the process by which these obligations should be managed. Post (1978, 1981) offered other important contributions to the development of the CSR concept, by analyzing the rationale and the practical processes through which corporations should – and those most forward-looking actually do – engage in the "management of public issues." Post saw this as a necessary corporate strategy in order to respond successfully to an uncertain and continuously changing economic, social, and political environment. In his writings we can find the roots of an idea that has been recently fully developed within stakeholder theory by Venkataraman (2002)[4] – that the strategic management of the firm works basically as an "equilibrating mechanism" designed continuously to find solutions that systematically take into consideration and constantly strive to *balance* the interests of all the corporation's stakeholders.

Post explicitly argues that CSR involves some mechanism for balancing stakeholders' interests – even if, of course, the word "stakeholder" was not (yet) part of his vocabulary: "constituencies" and "publics" were the terms he used. He argued that the degree of interpenetration between firm and society

[3] To support his point, Davis quotes the famous economist Paul Samuelson, who argued that "a large corporation these days not only may engage in social responsibility, it had damn well better try to do so" (Davis 1973, quoted in Carroll 1977: 35).

[4] See our analysis in Chapter 1.

determined the need for organizations to respond to stakeholders (Post 1978). Given the importance of these relationships, the corporation needs to measure its ability to respond effectively to "the publics with which it interacts." This was seen by Post not as an option but as an essential part of strategic management, otherwise some other mechanisms (e.g. public regulation) would have intervened. No manager could afford to let the gap between public expectations of performance and the firm's actual performance become too large: if this happened, the corporation would risk losing its social legitimacy, and "either corporate action or public action would have to occur in order to narrow the expectations/performance gap" (Post 1978: 218). Through the analysis of a number of case studies, Post concluded that *adaptive* and *proactive* approaches adopted by corporations could not be effective if they continued to be "ad hoc" tactics to deal with external change: there was a need for managers to embrace more *innovative* thinking and adopt *strategic* approaches to coping with change (as the title of his concluding chapter claimed). In light of this conclusion, we think that Post is one of the first scholars who saw how the concept of CSR should be a central component of the strategy and policy formulation process, and not an "add-on" to a given, profit-making corporate strategy.

Bill Frederick (1994) nicely summarizes the early development of CSR. In this phase, which he refers to as "CSR_1," scholars aim to work out the normative implications for the central idea that corporations have obligations to society. In Frederick's view this concept has created four interrelated debates: (i) What does CSR mean – how can one judge if a corporate act is socially responsible? (ii) What are the appropriate mechanisms for CSR? Should companies rely on market forces, government redistribution, or some hybrid, to create value for society? (iii) What are the trade-offs between economics and social good, and how should they be balanced? And (iv) what are the moral foundations of the CSR idea? Is there a moral principle from which corporate obligations to society can be derived?

From concept to capabilities

While some authors were mainly involved in the discussion concerning the definition and meaning of the concept of CSR, others took a different approach and shifted their focus to empirical investigation of CSR (Ackerman 1975; Ackerman and Bauer 1976; Sethi 1975; Frederick 1978, 1987, 1998; Carroll 1979, 1991; Wartick and Cochran 1985; Ullman 1985; Epstein 1987; Wood 1991).

As Carroll noted, these authors felt that the CSR model, by focusing exclusively on "the notion of business obligation and motivation," had fundamentally "overlooked the dimension of corporate action and performance" (Carroll 1991: 40). Therefore there was a need to shift attention from corporate social responsibility to the concept of corporate social *responsiveness*, a capability that emphasized "corporate action, pro-action, and implementation of a social role" (40).

As Frederick (1978, 1994) defined it, corporate social responsiveness (or "CSR_2," to differentiate it from CSR_1 – corporate social responsibility) is "the capacity of a corporation to respond to social pressures. The key questions are: Can the company respond? Will it? Does it? How does it? To what extent? And with what effect?" (Frederick 1994: 154). In a deliberate turn from the normative, CSR_2 takes a descriptive approach to understanding the process of corporate social responsibility.

Sethi (1975) was among the first to discuss the several dimensions that differentiate the concept of CSR_2 from CSR_1, including: the relationship of the firm's management and the prevailing "*ethical norms*" (social responsiveness requires managers to "take a definite stance on issues of public concerns" and not "consider business value-neutral"); the "*operating strategy*" (adopting a proactive strategy not only to respond, but also to anticipate future social changes); and the firm's "*response to social pressure*," urging the management to move from a conciliatory approach to become willing to disclose information and "discuss corporate activities with outside groups" (Sethi 1975: 63, emphasis added). This call for managers to place a greater emphasis on the "outside groups" of the corporation resonates with the stakeholder idea that management is about balancing stakeholder needs and expectations, emphasizing in this case the need for information on corporate strategies and actions. Another interesting linkage with stakeholder theory lies in Sethi's statement that "corporate social performance is "culture-bound," that is, since the social, cultural, and political contexts are constantly evolving, "a specific action is more or less socially responsible only within the framework of time, environment and the nature of the parties involved" (Sethi 1975: 59).

Subsequently, Carroll (1979) provided an important three-dimensional model to define corporate social performance (CSP) and its relationship with CSR. Carroll's CSP model was built upon three elements of a business organization's CSR configuration: (i) the definition of the firm's "corporate responsibility categories," including economic, legal, ethical, and discretionary (later on, Carroll called these philanthropic) responsibilities; (ii) the identification of the "social issues involved" in the firm's management; and (iii) the specification of the "philosophy of corporate responsiveness" adopted by the organization. It contributed to the CSR literature in two important ways.

First, it entered into the debate around the conceptual definition of CSR, by distinguishing four different categories of social responsibility corresponding to various expectations from society. These four categories comprise:

(a) *economic responsibilities*: the basic obligations of business "*to produce goods and services that society wants and to sell them at a profit*";
(b) *legal responsibilities*: the idea that corporations should respect – as part of the "social contract" between business and society – "*the ground rules – the laws and regulations – under which business is expected to operate*";
(c) *ethical responsibilities*: beyond economic and legal requirements, business should consider "*additional behavior and activities that are not necessarily codified into law but nevertheless are expected of business and society's members*"; and
d) *discretionary responsibilities*, defined as those responsibilities that are "at business discretion" – such as making a philanthropic contribution – since they do not respond to a clearly defined need or expectations by society (avoiding donating to a charity would not be considered a violation of an ethical norm), but still do respond to general societal expectations (Carroll 1979: 500).

Carroll's second contribution, built upon the work of Ackerman and Bauer (1976), emphasizes the view that if CSR is to be based on societal expectations, to respond to these by a mere assumption of responsibility is not a satisfactory attitude: "Responding to social demands is much more than deciding what to do. There remains the management task of doing what one has decided to do, and this task is far from trivial" (Carroll 1979: 498). Therefore Carroll articulated his three-dimensional model by adding to the "social responsibilities" axis two additional dimensions: the type of behavioral attitude taken by corporations in responding to societal demands – the philosophy of social responsiveness – and the specific social issues involved in the relationship. The model aimed to help managers to visualize how different social issues – environmental concerns, product safety, human right issues, and so on – can be tackled by the corporation using different attitudes – namely in a reacting, defensive, accommodating, or proacting behavior – according to their understanding of where each specific issue can be positioned in the continuum of the firm's economic, legal, ethical, and discretionary responsibilities.

Similarly, Wartick and Cochran highlight the integrative nature of the CSP model, able to reflect the "the underlying interaction among the principles of social responsibility, the process of social responsiveness and the policies developed to address social issues" (Wartick and Cochran 1985: 758). They pointed out that the third element of the model – issue management – was not sufficiently developed in Carroll's model, as it was simply indicated as "issue areas." To implement an effective issue management process, they suggested, organizations need to engage in a process of (i) issue identification; (ii) issue analysis; and (iii) response development. They conclude by making an explicit reference to the potentially beneficial role of stakeholder theory for the issue of management literature – in particular, by referring to the usefulness of the framework presented in Freeman's 1984 book: "issues analysis, the critical linkage between issues identification and effective response development, is being significantly enhanced by 'stakeholder analysis' (Freeman 1984) and social cognition theory" (Wartick and Cochran 1985: 766).

The concept and capabilities of CSR, which rely on a separation between business and society and also a separation of business and ethics, fall short in addressing the three problems that stakeholder theory aims to solve. The problem of value creation and trade does not fall within the scope of CSR, unless the way in which a company creates value affects society negatively. CSR has nothing to say about how value is created, because ethics is an afterthought in the value-creation process.

By adding a social responsibility to the existing financial responsibilities of the firm, CSR only exacerbates the problem of capitalism and ethics. The recent financial crises show the consequences of separating ethics from capitalism. The large banks and financial services firms all had CSR policies and programs, but because they did not see ethics as connected to what they do – to how they create value – they were unable to fulfill their basic responsibilities to their stakeholders and ended up destroying value for the entire economy.

Managers need a way of thinking about these issues that is closely tied to their day-to-day activities. The discourse of CSR is abstracted from managerial concerns and does not embed ethics in the fabric of management. It keeps the description of capitalism and business as amoral and tries to add an ethical safeguard too late in the process. Without redescribing the managerial function as a moral function, the CSR literature perpetuates the interpretation of business that allows moral concerns to be marginalized.

In the next section we shall explore various subthemes in the CSR literature and make explicit the role stakeholder perspective has played in that conversation.

Major themes in CSR research and the role of stakeholder theory

Stakeholder theory and the meaning of corporate social responsibility

Many scholars have turned to stakeholder theory to specify better and operationalize the concepts of CSR. Donna Wood's work on CSR provides a crucial linkage with stakeholder theory. Wood for the first time clearly formulated the idea that CSR is challenging the *purpose* of the corporation, shifting from the shareholder view – the vision according to which the purpose of the corporation (and "its only social responsibility," as Friedman famously stated) is to maximize profits – to a "social" view, where the corporation's purpose needs to include some larger social interests. But she did more than this. In fact, this was only a first step in the direction of stakeholder theory, and to complete the transition one further step was needed. As we have argued earlier, the move towards the stakeholder approach to strategic management requires abandoning the idea that shareholder value maximization is the unique or predominant purpose of the corporation, and embracing the idea that the interests of *specific* stakeholder groups (i.e. those who can affect or are affected by the corporate activities) have to be considered in defining the purpose of the corporation. This is not to say that the shareholder view is to be neglected, but rather that it has to be embedded in the wider stakeholder view of the corporation.

Wood (1991) revisited the concept of CSP, trying to develop further the model originally articulated by Carroll (1979) and revised by Wartick and Cochran (1985). Wood saw three distinct problems limitations with these models. First, they defined CSP as "interaction" between the different components, overlooking the fact that CSP has to be defined in terms of *action* and *outcomes*, rather than interaction. Second, they tended to identify social responsiveness with a single process, whereas there can be many different processes through which the corporation responds to societal issues. Third, and most important, Wartick and Cochran assigned to the third element of their model – the *policies* – a too restrictive role, therefore failing to recognize that a wider range of corporate actions, behaviors, and programs, beyond written, formal policies, can improve the social performance of the organization: "if a policy does not exist, it cannot be inferred that no social performance exists" (Wood 1991: 693).

In light of these three clarifications, Wood suggested a revised definition of CSP as "a business organization's configuration of the principles of social responsibility, processes of social responsiveness and the policies, programs, and observable outcomes as they relate to the firm's societal relationships" (Wood 1991: 693). The advantages of such definitions are, according to Wood, twofold: on the one hand, it "does not isolate CSP as something completely distinct from business performance." At the same time, it provides us with a "construct for evaluating business outputs that must be used in conjunction with *explicit values* about appropriate business–society relationships" (694, emphasis added).

Similarly, Windsor (2001) offers a nice history of the CSR concept. He is particularly critical of the wealth creation movement in management which aims to increase social welfare through profit maximization. He also claims that it is difficult to distinguish between normative and instrumental motives for CSR, and that the link between financial performance and social responsibility is confused at best. The central claim of his paper is that a broader sense of responsibility that goes beyond wealth creation is needed, if CSR is to flourish in the future. In a 2006 paper Windsor argues that the ethical responsibility and the economic responsibility viewpoint have competing moral frameworks and have not been integrated well, and that the corporate citizenship literature does not effectively synthesize the two concerns. He outlines an instrumental citizenship interpretation of social responsibility which views philanthropy as a strategic decision to increase the firm's reputation and market opportunities. He integrates the stakeholder view with his positions by saying,

> A negative externality impacting a stakeholder or society constitutes real cost. Negative externalities can distort production and/or consumption to the detriment of general welfare. Such burdens must be addressed by the affected party through complaint or lawsuit or change in public policy. (Windsor 2006: 105)

While Windsor acknowledges the effects on stakeholders that a firm can have, he sees governmental intervention as the major means of mediating this problem rather than managerial discretion and proaction.

Pedersen (2006) begins his argument by pointing out that there is no accepted definition of CSR or stakeholders, and proceeds to describe how companies translate the abstract concepts of CSR into practice. He states, "The important matter is that the definition of CSR acknowledges the close ties to stakeholder theory and accepts the eclectic nature of CSR by refraining from limiting itself to specific strategies, specific stakeholders, and/or specific social and environmental issues" (Pedersen 2006: 138). He outlines five levels of engagement for stakeholder dialogue: inclusion, openness, tolerance, empowerment, and transparency, which are affected by such factors as consciousness, commitment, capacity, and consensus.

Munilla and Miles (2005) depict a CSR continuum that has three modes of engagement with stakeholders: compliance, where CSR expenditures are perceived as the cost of doing business; strategic, where CSR is seen as an investment in the firm's competencies; and forced, where CSR is seen as a tax imposed by external stakeholders. They argue that both compliance and forced modes weaken the firm's ability to create strategic advantage.

Carson offers a version of stakeholder theory that he believes addresses the social objectives of business more robustly than previous formulations by Goodpaster that resemble too closely Friedman's view of social responsibility. He says,

> Business executives have positive duties to promote the interest of all stakeholders (these are prima facie duties). But the duties to some stakeholders are more important than the duties to other stakeholders. Thus, sometimes the lesser interests of more important stakeholders take precedence over the greater interests of less important stakeholders. Positive duties to stakeholders are constrained by negative duties not to lie or break the law, etc. (Carson 1993: 174)

While Carson does not outline a criterion by which the importance of a stakeholder group can be evaluated, the value proposition of a firm can be one important starting place.

Each of these approaches aims to clarify further the concept of CSR by addressing how companies interact with specific stakeholders.

Stakeholder theory and the link between corporate social performance and corporate financial performance

In addition to the project of understanding how some managers address specific social obligations, researchers have sought to understand better the consequences of social performance – specifically on the financial performance of the firm. As Ackerman stated, there was a clear underlying hope in this research project – namely to be able to prove empirically that the "social" was compatible with the "economic" dimension of business: "In the long run, the more successful corporations will be those that can achieve both social responsiveness and good economic performance" (Ackerman 1973: 88).

A prominent example of this genre of research is Waddock and Graves (1997). They hypothesize that better financial performance leads to better social performance and that better social performance increases financial performance. They constructed an index of eight social responsibility indicators using data from Standard & Poor's and the Kinder, Lydenberg, Domini (KLD) index for 430 companies in the year 1990. They controlled for company size, risk, and industry, and measured financial performance using return on equity, return on assets, and return on sales. They found a small positive relationship between corporate social performance (CSP) and corporate financial performance (CFP). In order to operationalize variables that measure social responsibility, researchers such as Graves and Waddock turn to metrics that focus on specific stakeholders. For example, the KLD index used by Graves and Waddock (1994) rates companies on positive metrics such as community, employee relations, environment, product, and diversity.

Barnett argues that heterogeneity in the CSP–CFP link is due to differences in a firm's stakeholder influence capacity – or its ability to identify, act on, and profit from opportunities to improve stakeholder relationships through CSR (Barnett 2007: 803). He develops a set of propositions that show how a firm's specific set of stakeholder relationships can affect the link between CSP and CFP for that firm.

Margolis and Walsh (2001) provide an impressive and valuable analysis of this research stream. They analyze ninety-five empirical studies that examine the relationship between CSP and CFP, concluding that the positive relationship claimed in over 50 percent of CSP–CFP studies is questionable at best. They claim that this instability in the results is due to a variance in the way in which these studies were conducted, specifically variance in the samples of firms used by researchers, the operationalization of CSP and CFP, and in control measures. For example, in order to test the relationship between CSP and CFP some researchers relied on firms featured in *Fortune*'s most admired companies, or focused only on one industry or firm size, to generalize across firms. CSP was operationalized by using metrics like the KLD index, the total amount of charity engaged in by the firm, and from content analyses of the company's annual report. CFP was measured using accounting measures such as return on assets (ROA), market measures such as stock price, or a mix of the two.

Margolis and Walsh also set a new agenda for CSR research (2003). Their view, as we understand it, is as follows. There are significant social problems in the world that need attention. According to an economic logic, firms need to maximize their profits, therefore attempts to legitimize corporate social activities have tried to appease this economic logic by (i) discovering an empirical relationship between CSP and CFP, and (ii) retaining an instrumentalist logic. The tension between financial and normative social demands on the firm are real and need to be examined in greater detail. Margolis and Walsh adopt a decision-making framework in order to understand better

> how companies extract and appraise the stimuli for action; how companies generate response options; how companies evaluate these options and select a course of action; how the selected course is implemented; and, finally, what consequences follow from corporate efforts to ameliorate social ills. (Margolis and Walsh 2003: 285)

We agree with Margolis and Walsh on several counts, first and foremost that there are issues such as human rights abuses, environmental concerns, and poverty that need immediate attention in our world today. We disagree, however, on the best way to address these problems. While it is true that corporations are asked to help alleviate these ills, we are not convinced that every company can and should do so. We see the firm as a tool to achieve morally rich human ends – including financial sustainability, human thriving, and the pursuit of the firm's specific value proposition. Specific companies evolve and are designed to meet their specific value proposition in a variety of ways; some of them are successful at achieving the strategic alignment of capabilities and stakeholder engagement required to perform well and some are not. In short, companies are tools for doing specific things. Depending on the specific company, its value proposition, and its specific capabilities, it may be better or worse at addressing the kinds of social problems that we and Margolis and Walsh care about. Instead of asking all companies to contribute to alleviating poverty, or addressing AIDS in Africa, we believe that managers and concerned citizens should take into account how well a specific tool can help to achieve those goals. It may be better to design other tools with the specific purpose of addressing those problems. To us, Margolis and Walsh's approach seems like using a wrench to pound nails into a falling wall because you can't find a hammer. Using the wrong tools can damage the tool and create more problems than the one you are trying to fix. We propose designing better hammers – or specifically companies and organizations that can address those specific purposes. That does not mean that we should not study how firms currently address or fail to address "social" issues in the hopes of learning how to design better responses.

We also agree with Margolis and Walsh that on many occasions different stakeholder interests around an issue will conflict and managers will need a well-thought-out justification for the way in which they will address these tensions and trade-offs. We would add that trade-offs are not completely objective. They are crafted and shaped by the way in which stakeholders and managers make sense of their situation and the available alternatives. Instead of simply taking a trade-off at face value, it would help the firm to achieve its rich value proposition if managers were to reflect on how they and their stakeholders have constructed that trade-off, and imagine and innovate ways of constructing it that can reduce or remove that trade-off. We acknowledge that this strategy will not always be effective and some trade-offs cannot be reconstructed, but without trying to dissolve some of these either-or choices, managers will make more than they have to and potentially destroy value in the process.

Finally, Margolis and Walsh depict stakeholder theory as preoccupied with consequences – financial consequences in particular. They claim that this instrumentalist logic obscures stakeholders who are not salient or whose contributions or treatment is less clear, and therefore normative reasons are required for firms to engage in socially responsible actions. They say,

> [A] preoccupation with instrumental consequences renders a theory that accommodates economic premises yet sidesteps the underlying tensions between social and economic imperatives that confront organizations. Such a theory risks omitting the pressing descriptive and normative questions raised by these tensions, which, when explored, might hold great promise for new theory, and even for addressing practical management challenges. (Margolis and Walsh 2003: 280)

We think that any set of actions, for any stakeholder, has a blend of financial and moral consequences. One can increase wealth for shareholders or serve the community for instrumental and moral reasons. So the issue is not just when purely "financial" and purely "social" tensions conflict, but when specific stakeholder conceptions which have both financial and social dimensions conflict with each other. Even firms and nonprofits that exist to address "social" concerns will have to be cognizant of financial concerns and how they use resources efficiently. Therefore it makes little sense to us to separate out social from financial concerns.

Margolis and Walsh's deeper point is about the distinction between instrumental vs. normative logic, and their perception that stakeholder theory is more instrumental than normative. We are more cautious about drawing such a firm line between instrumental and normative claims and only selecting one of the two for companies to use. These types of reason can be mutually reinforcing and need to be used together. It may turn out that normative logic is most useful when the relevant cause–effect relationships needed to apply instrumental logic cannot be made sense of or are unacceptable. For example, today (thankfully) we have a normative principle to respect human dignity, but in the past it was acceptable to determine the price of slaves, and there were mathematical functions to calculate the specific dollar worth of a human being. To prevent people from thinking about those kinds of calculations, a normative principle is needed. But this practice of respecting normative prescriptions can be taken too far. By not thinking about the consequences of following a principle, one may create unfavorable situations, as in the case of the man who, refusing to lie, tells the murderer where his wife is. Reliance on principles without reflection can leave valuable opportunities on the table, as in the case of those early doctors who disregarded the principle of respect for the dead in order to study the human body. Without their work, we would not enjoy the quantity and quality of life we have today.

When following any principle, one can always ask, why are you following this principle and not others? And usually the answer is: because of the consequences for the outside world and for one's own character that arise from following the principle. Similarly, when applying an instrumental logic one can ask, why did you assign this or that value to a certain outcome or action? That answer is usually tied to a set of values or principles. Therefore it is hard to separate out instrumental from normative logic, and our view has always been that firms need to think through both in order to craft better responses. Take, for example, the case of Merck and Mectizan – the drug to cure river blindness. Under stakeholder theory, it is justifiable for Merck to pursue the distribution of Mectizan, given Merck's goal of reducing human suffering caused by disease, even though there may be significant financial reasons to avoid doing so. In order to enact this strategy derived from a normative principle, Merck, like all companies, had to weigh the consequences of acting one way or another.

Despite our subtle differences with Margolis and Walsh, we support the further exploration and inquiry into how companies make sense of and enact issues that are traditionally labeled "social." While Margolis and Walsh would like to carve out a separate niche for examining the trade-offs between financial and social concerns, we interpret this as an interesting and useful branch of stakeholder research to pursue, rather than a new logic for CSR. Margolis and Walsh cast themselves in the tradition of CSR when they look for a one-size-fits-all approach to CSR to remedy the ills of an instrumental shareholder-based theory. Stakeholder theory is a more nuanced view of how firms create both social and financial value and the inseparable role of ethics and morality in this process.

Stakeholder theory, corporate social responsibility, and corporate governance[5]

A number of scholars have approached the concept of CSR from a corporate governance (CG) perspective. This perspective shifts the focus of the research from the juxtaposition of "business" and "society" to a more interesting discussion around the ways to govern a complex system such as the firm. Naturally, this perspective addresses a relevant dimension of one of the key problems of stakeholder theory – the problem of value creation and trade. Since corporate governance is defined as the "the system by which companies are directed and controlled" (Cadbury 1992: 14), it essentially deals with the organization of the relationships between shareholders, boards of directors, management, and other stakeholders of the corporation. By analyzing and discussing the kind of obligations that corporations owe to *stakeholders* – not just to their shareholders – these scholars articulated the concept of corporate social responsibility as a *method* for corporate governance. We discuss below some key contributions in this stream of research and their key linkages with stakeholder theory.

Jones was the first to articulate the concept of corporate social responsibility as a *method* for corporate governance – or a form for self-control. In the light of raising criticism towards the business system, accompanied by concerns around "the power and privilege associated with large corporations" (Jones 1980: 59), Jones argued that CSR could serve as an appealing form of self-control to deal with the pitfalls of previously attempted modes of control of business in corporate America. In front of the criticism of those who were pointing out the vagueness inherent in the social responsibility concept, Jones replied that "CSR ought not to be seen as a set of outcomes, but as a process" (65). In this perspective, one could reasonably ask socially responsible corporations to integrate their decision-making processes with some mechanisms to take social concerns into full consideration, in order to develop appropriate responses. Jones criticized CSR scholars who prescribed managers to develop their corporate social policy based on a generic principle of "public responsibility," mirroring the government's public policy. This approach in fact cannot be useful at all, precisely because in many crucial areas there is no social consensus around what are the appropriate policy measures. Therefore, Jones argued, managers cannot find useful guidance by adopting public policy as their unique CSR criterion. On the other hand, when

[5] See Chapter 4 for our view on stakeholder theory, strategic management, and corporate governance. These ideas are obviously connected.

managers conceive corporate social responsibility as a *means*, and not as a set of *ends*, they naturally recognize the importance of identifying the interests of the various groups (other than the shareholders) who are affected by their actions and take them into consideration in their decision-making processes.

Another significant contribution to the debate on CSR, corporate governance, and its linkages with stakeholder theory is what Evan and Freeman present as their "stakeholder interpretation" of corporate governance and of the theory of the firm (Evan and Freeman 1993; Freeman and Evan 1990). The authors build their model on Oliver Williamson's transaction cost economics[6] that conceptualizes the firm as a governance mechanism for a set of multilateral contracts over time with different stakeholders. An effective model of corporate governance, according to Williamson, defines the "rules of the game" that govern these interactions. Evan and Freeman suggest adding another dimension to Williamson's analysis – namely, the *fairness* of the governance mechanism. They point out that, in order to be able to promote mutual collaboration by all the organization's stakeholders with their diverse and specific assets (the employees with their knowledge and skills, the suppliers with their goods and services, the financiers with their capital, etc.), the contracts governing stakeholder interactions need to be *fair*. The model the authors suggest in order to understand the concept of contract fairness is John Rawls's hypothetical choice under the veil of ignorance, where rational and free individuals design such a contract that they "would agree to it in ignorance of their actual stakes." Therefore Evan and Freeman argue that an effective corporate governance mechanism should be designed according to *fair* rules, otherwise it would not be effective in promoting the mutual collaboration by all the organization's stakeholders. Their "principle of corporate governance" in fact argues that the procedures for changing the rules of the game must be agreed by unanimous consent (Evan and Freeman 1993).

A similar conclusion was reached by Jones and Goldberg (1982), who nevertheless still looked at government as the best solution to ensure stakeholder representation in the corporate governance mechanism. Their rationale is that, for an issue of democracy, appointed public directors would be the most appropriate response to "three corporate governance problems: (1) the vagueness of the social responsibility doctrine; (2) the legitimacy of corporate social decision making; and (3) the compatibility of corporate governance with democratic principles" (Jones and Goldberg 1982: 603).

[6] We discuss our overall view of Williamson in Chapter 1.

More recently, the debate investigating the concept of CSR under the perspective of corporate governance has been reinvigorated by new contributions by scholars working from a law and economics perspective.

Blair (1995), Zingales (1998), and Blair and Stout (1999) have rejected the principle of shareholder supremacy and the reductive principal–agent view of the firm, where managers bear fiduciary duties only towards the shareholders. These authors suggest that, in approaching corporate governance, we must consider that numerous stakeholder groups may make firm-specific investments and that the "owner" of these assets and the outputs (surplus) created are not the shareholders, but the corporation itself.

Sacconi (2006) recently suggests a reconceptualization of CSR as a *model* of corporate governance. Sacconi's approach combines the economic analysis of organizations – drawing in particular from the neo-institutional theory of Oliver Williamson (1975), Hart and Moore (1990), Grossman and Hart (1986), Hansmann (1996) – with the philosophical perspective of social contract theory – building upon the work on rational bargaining by Harsanyi (1977) and the idea put forward by Gauthier (1986) and Binmore (1991, 1994, 1997) that moral norms can arise from rational agreements. Sacconi elaborated the following definition for CSR: corporate social responsibility is a model of extended corporate governance whereby a firm (entrepreneurs, directors, and managers) has responsibilities that range from fulfillment of fiduciary duties towards the owners to fulfillment of analogous fiduciary duties towards all the firm's stakeholders (Sacconi 2006: 262).

In this perspective, CSR, corporate governance, and stakeholder theory seem to converge: the firm is defined as a multi-stakeholder organization, where the individual groups collaborate (as in Evan and Freeman 1993) as long as they can rely on a fair exercise of the discretionary power by the management or, in other words, as long as the corporate governance mechanisms are fair.

Stakeholder theory, corporate social responsibility, and the practice of social and ethical accounting, auditing, and (sustainability) reporting

A distinct research stream within corporate social responsibility began to emerge during the 1990s and is nowadays a well-established practice within the business community. Initially known as "social auditing" or "social accounting," it came to be labeled "social and ethical accounting, auditing and reporting," or SEAAR, at the end of the 1990s (Zadek, Pruzan, and Evans 1997). Often it is also referred to as *sustainability reporting*, recognizing that the boundaries between "social" and "environmental," and between "social" and "economic," are often overlapping. Since its beginning, research on SEAAR was characterized by the close collaboration between academicians and practitioners in the struggle to develop internationally accepted, standardized approaches and methodologies for measuring and reporting the social, ethical, and environmental dimensions of corporate performance. They felt that the concept of CSR could not be usefully adopted in managerial practice if its advocates were not able to develop reliable, systematic ways of translating it into accountable measurements: "Accounting for the social and ethical dimensions of an organisation's activities is therefore a precondition for the development of socially and ethically responsible business" (Pruzan 1998: 1390). While, as we have seen, already in the 1960s there have been various attempts to define and measure the concept of corporate social performance, this new stream of research took a much more practical, practice-oriented focus. In other words, it was CSR in its most *managerial* manifestation. As Zadek (1994) argued in the early stages of the development of the field, the key, distinctive element of this approach was its explicit emphasis on the point of view of the organization's stakeholders in order to obtain a comprehensive assessment of the organization's performance: "social auditing is the process of defining, observing, and reporting measures of the ethical behavior and social impact of an organization in relation to its aims and those of its stakeholders" (Zadek 1994: 632). Companies such as Traidcraft (a UK fair-trade organization), SbN (a Danish bank), Ben and Jerry's (USA, ice-cream manufacturers), and the Body Shop (UK, cosmetics) were among the pioneering organizations contributing to this new practice in the early 1990s, by publishing a new form of public statements – aimed at complementing their financial statements – under the various names of Social Audit, Ethical Accounting Statement, Social Statement, and Values Report, respectively. A number of scholars (Gray, Owen, and Adams 1996; Gray, Dey, Owen, Evans, and Zadek 1997; Zadek, Pruzan, and Evans 1997; Wheeler and Sillanpää 1997; Elkington 1997; Zadek 1998; Pruzan 1998; Gray 2001), often involved both at the academic and at the practitioner level, contributed to the emergence of SEAAR. As Zadek, Pruzan and Evans (1997) explain, the definition of the discipline highlights the three distinct dimensions that characterize the SEAAR process: (i) accounting – the creation of a "social book-keeping" system, consisting of both quantitative and qualitative indicators, in order to capture the "social, ethical and environmental footprints" of the organization; (ii) auditing – the idea that the veridicality and accuracy of the whole process of information gathering and reporting is evaluated by an independent third-party organization performing an "external verification" (later called "assurance"); and (iii) reporting – the production of a public report by means of which the organization communicates to its stakeholders the results of the SEAAR process. The establishment of SEAAR as an internationally recognized methodology was strengthened by the creation, in 1996, of the Institute of Social and Ethical AccountAbility, a professional, nonprofit organization which in 1999 launched AccountAbility 1000 (AA1000), an open-source standard indicating quality principles for the process of SEAAR and also setting guidelines for the profession of the "social and ethical auditor" – further developed with the publication of the AA1000 Assurance Standard.[7] AA1000, as well as other international standards promoting social and environmental reporting – such as the GRI Sustainability Reporting Guidelines – emphasize the need for an extension of the traditional financial accounting to a more comprehensive balance sheet, including measures of social, economic, and environmental performance (or "triple bottom-line accounting"). Parallel to the extension from financial to nonfinancial reporting (or, as recently introduced by the Danish pharmaceutical company NovoNordisk, the adoption of a unique, integrated economic, social, and environmental statement)[8] is the shift from a mono-stakeholder (i.e. the shareholders) to a multi-stakeholder model for strategic management (of which reporting is an essential part).

Stakeholder theory has clearly contributed to the development of the SEAAR concept and practice. The shift of the focus from "social responsibility" to organizational "accountability" is clearly based on the acknowledgement of the centrality of the stakeholder approach: accountability is in fact defined as "identifying what one is responsible for and then providing information about that responsibility to *those who have rights to that information*" (Gray 2001: 11, emphasis added). As Gray illustrates, the concept of the stakeholder (in particular, stakeholder engagement) is at the core of the SEAAR process, and stakeholder theory "can be used to help define the social account" (9), first of all by informing the process of stakeholder identification, and then breaking down the general stakeholder categories into their "constituent parts – for example, the different categories of employees, including past employees and possibly employees' families" (12).

Wheeler and Sillanpää (1997) and Sillanpää (1998) provide a forward-looking example of how the stakeholder approach could be translated into real management practice through a SEAAR process, not only at the strategic

[7] See www.accountability21.net. [8] See www.novonordisk.com/sustainability/reports/reports.asp.

level, but also in the day-to-day processes. They developed a model for a "stakeholder corporation" based on their experience as executives at the Body Shop, one of the pioneering organizations in the field of SEAAR. Their model clearly supports Freeman's (1984) view that the stakeholder approach should be integrated into strategic management. They argue that companies that take stakeholder interests into account are more likely to be sustainable over time. Companies that always put shareholders' short-term interests first are not likely to prosper for long (Wheeler and Sillanpää 1997).

In conclusion, the theoretical reflection and practical experiences that have been produced in the field of SEAAR have the merit of being able to tackle the problem of value creation and trade in a very pragmatic way. We believe that this is one of the most important avenues of future research within CSR, and for stakeholder theory as well.

Stakeholder theory and corporate citizenship

The corporate citizenship literature[9] aims to show that corporate actors are more than autonomous individual actors, and are situated in a community that places obligations and responsibilities upon them.[10] Logsdon and Wood (2002) sketch out a view of business citizenship that depicts organizations as citizens of a community and as such subject to societal controls and limits on their actions. They distinguish between local and global business citizenship to delineate where the efforts of the firm are focused, and show how a business citizenship perspective integrates political, moral, and strategic analyses. They explicitly incorporate stakeholder concerns into their conception of business citizenship, which has three elements:

> Business will be a primary driver of global human rights enforcement, and it can best do this through a clear, operationalizable, and fundamental definition of business citizenship. Such a definition will require businesses to affirm their primary mission as agents of their stakeholders, and to structure their policies, processes, incentives, and control systems accordingly. Such a definition will require human stakeholders to affirm their responsibility as "principals" of business organizations, to monitor their agents' behavior, and to provide appropriate incentives so that desired goals are achieved and undesired effects are avoided. (Logsdon and Wood 2002: 156–157)

[9] For one view of the connection of stakeholder theory to this literature, see Phillips and Freeman (2008).

[10] Scherer and Palazzo (2008) is an up-to-date and thorough resource on the current corporate citizenship literature.

Similarly, Carroll (2003) outlines the four faces of corporate citizenship, which comprise financial responsibilities, legal responsibilities, ethical responsibilities, and philanthropy. He argues that these responsibilities are to be fulfilled simultaneously rather than sequentially and that doing so will enhance the stakeholder environment of the future.

Matten and Crane offer a nice history of the corporate citizenship literature and synthesize a definition:

> Corporate citizenship describes the role of the corporation in administering citizenship rights for individuals. Such a definition reframes corporate citizenship away from the notion that the corporation is a citizen in itself (as individuals are) and toward the acknowledgement that the corporation administers certain aspects of citizenship for other constituencies. These include traditional stakeholders, such as employees, customers, or shareholders, but also include constituencies with no direct transactional relationship to the company. (Matten and Crane 2005: 174)

They go on to delineate various social, civil, and political rights of which the corporation is respectively a provider, enabler, and channel. Their view embraces the idea that a stakeholder has multiple stakes in a firm. Responsibilities exist at the business, social, civil, and political levels.

In a similar fashion Waddock (2004) defines corporate citizenship as "manifested in the strategies and operating practices a company develops in operating practices, in operationalizing its relationships with and impacts on stakeholders and the natural environment" (Waddock 2004: 9). Zadek (2007) argues that corporate citizenship requires that companies take into account not only their financial performance but their social and environmental performance as well. The essential civil corporations for Zadek are companies that are empowered to enact our best thinking on how to create the conditions for sustainable development.

Approaches to corporate citizenship are the latest effort to broaden the responsibilities of the firm but, like other CSR efforts, they need to supplement their breadth with depth and detail about to whom the firm is responsible and the nature of those responsibilities.

Stakeholder theory and globalization

As more corporations expand their operations and activities beyond national boundaries, more complicated issues arise about how best to manage the diversity of interests, norms, laws, and expectations. In recognition of business as a driving force in globalization, the UN introduced a strategic policy

Human rights

- Principle 1: Businesses should support and respect the protection of internationally proclaimed human rights; and
- Principle 2: make sure that they are not complicit in human rights abuses.

Labor standards

- Principle 3: Businesses should uphold the freedom of association and the effective recognition of the right to collective bargaining;
- Principle 4: the elimination of all forms of forced and compulsory labor;
- Principle 5: the effective abolition of child labor; and
- Principle 6: the elimination of discrimination in respect of employment and occupation.

Environment

- Principle 7: Businesses should support a precautionary approach to environmental challenges;
- Principle 8: undertake initiatives to promote greater environmental responsibility; and
- Principle 9: encourage the development and diffusion of environmentally friendly technologies.

Anti-corruption

- Principle 10: Businesses should work against corruption in all its forms, including extortion and bribery.

Figure 8.1. UN Global Compact Ten Principles
Source: www.unglobalcompact.org/AboutTheGC/TheTenPrinciples/index.html.

initiative to help ensure that advances in the commercial sector also benefit societies. It drafted a set of ten Global Compact Principles (Figure 8.1), which are built around human rights, labor, the environment, and anti-corruption. These principles can be seen as codifying the responsibilities of a variety of groups including employees, suppliers, customers, shareholders, and the larger community. In the same spirit as the larger CSR conversation, these global principles seek to expand the responsibilities of business beyond financial concerns. Similarly, the Caux Round Table, an international group promoting more responsible capitalism, has adopted a more explicit stakeholder approach in drawing up its Principles for Responsible Business (Caux Round Table 2009). Principle 1, titled "Respect Stakeholders beyond Shareholders," outlines specific stakeholder principles, and guideline 1 of the attached Stakeholder Management Guidelines states that "[a] responsible business treats its customers with respect and dignity. Business therefore has a responsibility to:

a. Provide customers with the highest quality products and services consistent with their requirements.

b. Treat customers fairly in all aspects of business transactions, including providing a high level of service and remedies for product or service problems or dissatisfaction.
c. Ensure that the health and safety of customers is protected.
d. Protect customers form harmful environmental impacts of products and services.
e. Respect the human rights, dignity and the culture of customers in the way products and services are offered, marketed, and advertised."

Both the Caux Round Table Principles and the UN Global Compact attest to the need for business conduct to be held to a higher standard. Either implicitly or explicitly, these standards come from the variety of stakeholders affected by a business.

Bridging social and financial concerns

In the previous sections we have reviewed some of the key contributions and themes in the CSR literature. If we look back at the development of CSR from the perspective of stakeholder theory, it is possible to identify at least two distinct (although not monolithic) lines of thought for the integration of financial and social concerns that seem to proceed in parallel and still coexist in ongoing academic research and managerial practice. These strategies are depicted in Table 8.1.

The *residual* view of CSR is the initial view on CSR that was developed by the early scholars back in the 1960s and 1970s, and is still predominant in today's academic and business conversations around CSR, particularly in the American context. This view conceptualizes CSR as a residual (i.e. nonstrategic) activity, summarized by the "giving back to society" proposition, that is, the idea that there is a moral obligation and/or a number of good practical reasons for corporations to give back to society some of the value they have created. Under this view CSR is not integrated with the most important value-creating activities of the firm. In other words, this perspective focuses on ex-post profit distribution. For corporations (and scholars) embracing residual CSR, being socially responsible means to "add on" a social role to business, without challenging the traditional understanding of business that sees the economic purpose – profit maximization – as the primary (and, according to Friedman, the only morally legitimate) social responsibility of the corporation.

The redistribution of profits can be pursued for normative reasons – as an end in itself, as in the case of firms that believe that the welfare of society writ

Table 8.1. Residual and integrated approaches to corporate social responsibility

	Residual CSR	*Integrated CSR*
CSR definition	Giving back to society (after profits are made)	Integration of economic with ethical, social, and environmental decision-making criteria
Stakeholder focus	Shareholders first, then communities, or others	All stakeholders have moral standing
Economic focus	Profit redistribution (after profits are maximized)	Value creation
Purpose of CSR	Sustain legitimacy of business	Contribute to overall success of the corporation
CSR business model	Being responsive to societal claims	Building partnerships with stakeholder groups
CSR processes	Communication; public relations	Stakeholder engagement
CSR activities	Corporate philanthropy; sponsorships	Integration of "nonfinancial reporting" into traditional corporate reporting

large is more important than the financial performance of the firm. These firms see profits as a means to improving society. Ben and Jerry's provides a good example. Similarly, Matten and Moon (2008) offer a distinction between implicit and explicit CSR, which represent European and American approaches respectively. They argue that because of institutional differences and cultural norms, CSR strategies are different in different regions. The implicit (European) model is characterized by a culture of collective effort on the part of business to better society. The underlying assumption is that the firm exists to benefit society. Of course, not all European firms make this assumption.

Managers can also subscribe to the residual view for more instrumental reasons. The redistribution of profits to society can be seen as a means of allowing the firm to continue to make its profit. This is exemplified by earlier CSR scholars like Davis and in the blunt interpretation of Friedman's article, where CSR is read as a series of ad hoc strategies to keep groups satisfied enough to prevent trouble for the firm. These strategies are not integrated into the firm's value proposition, nor are they engaged in for principled or well-articulated reasons. An example would be when firms "contribute" to NGOs to keep them off their back.

At the other end is the *integrated* view of CSR. It conceptualizes CSR as the integration of social, ethical, and environmental concerns into the management criteria for corporate strategy. This view is clearly embraced by scholars in management and business ethics who see that the core idea of stakeholder theory is "to integrate ethics and social issues directly into strategy," as we pointed out in Chapter 2. This approach simply sees CSR as part of core management concepts and processes; it posits their evolution into a more robust decision-making framework, more adequate to take into account and deal with both the complexity of human nature and the challenges of the external environment. In other words, it embraces the key ideas of the stakeholder approach and it acknowledges that the management of any economic organization includes, by definition, the management of the relationship with its stakeholders. The integrated CSR approach does not view CSR as the imposition of additional duties on a "business as usual" model, but, on the contrary, it points out the need for a redefinition of the corporations' "political and legal status, and for the scope of their managerial responsibilities" (Post, Preston, and Sachs 2002a: 11). Therefore this perspective focuses on ex-ante value creation, not on profit distribution.

Firms can integrate their CSR strategy with the larger value proposition of the business for many reasons. Managers may believe that it produces efficiencies to integrate strategies for addressing social concerns with those that create value. Even though some firms integrate their processes, they still place financial concerns above social concerns, but understand the need to address social concerns efficiently and coherently. For example, Michael Porter's recent work on "strategic charity" recognizes that a number of philanthropic activities are being chosen by corporations in a much more careful way, in order to create positive linkages with their core business or the key interests of their key stakeholders: "No business can solve all of society's problems or bear the cost of doing so. Instead, each company must select issues that intersect with its particular business" (Porter and Kramer 2002: 5–16). Matten and Moon (2008) argue that American firms typically adopt an explicit CSR strategy to gain individual firm-level benefits. This strategy works in light of the assumption that the "real" purpose of the firm is to maximize profits.

Beyond financial and social

In the previous section we described two strategies to integrate social and financial obligations for the firm. Both corporate financial performance and corporate social performance make a category mistake. They aim to define the role of the corporate at too abstract and general a level. Managers, who are charged with increasing financial or social performance, have to use a more fine-grained vocabulary to understand what this value is, and how it can be created. Stakeholder theory enters in the CSR debate by suggesting that the managers of the corporations have a responsibility not simply (and vaguely) to serve the *general interests* of society (which society? In today's global economy, where even small firms have dealings involving partners in several countries, with different social, legal, and ethical contexts, the definition of "society" as if it was a unique entity becomes very problematic), but rather to serve the interests of the *corporation's stakeholders* – that is, those specific individuals and groups that

(1) *make* the firm, or explain how a firm comes into existence, in first instance – in a Schumpeterian view of the entrepreneur's action, as pointed out by Venkataraman (1997);
(2) *contribute* to its success, with their cooperative efforts aimed at generating value that can be mutually beneficial – as indicated by Phillips's (2003) principle of stakeholder fairness; and
(3) *bear* the consequences of its activities – what managers need to take into account, for any "private" cooperative agreement might generate external consequences, as pointed out by Dewey (1927).

Wood's 1991 article has the merit of explicitly recognizing this link between the stakeholder approach and corporate social responsibility; as she pointed out, "Freeman's definition of stakeholders ... brought the abstract idea called society closer to home" (Wood 1991: 697). She further articulated this view by emphasizing that the stakeholder approach enables managers to understand how, in practice, "society grants and takes away corporate legitimacy." In other words, it is by looking at its relationships with specific stakeholders that the corporation can secure its "license to operate," by generating performance levels that satisfy its shareholders, selling products that meet the expectations of customers, providing career opportunities and salaries able to attract and retain its employees, and so forth.

We would add that it also enables managers to understand how financial value is created in practice. Indeed, stakeholder theory rejects the hard separation of financial and social value. We believe that a large body of work in CSR supports a view of business that is fundamentally "detached" from society. In other words, the residual view of CSR perpetrates the separation fallacy, according to which economics and ethics are two separate spheres of decision making (see our discussion of the separation thesis in Chapter 1). Freeman (1984) emphasized the need for a conceptual framework enabling the analysis of social and economic forces influencing the success of the corporation in a new, *integrative* fashion: "Isolating 'social' issues as separate from the economic impact which they have, and conversely isolating economic issues as if they had no social effect, misses the mark both managerially and intellectually" (Freeman 1984: 40). And Freeman and Liedtka (1991: 92) pointed out a number of reasons why "the concept of CSR should be abandoned," being a "dangerous idea" that did not deliver on its promise. Other scholars agree that the concept of CSR is not useful, and advocate its dismissal. For example, Enderle critically analyzes various formulations of the concept of CSR and recommends "drop[ping] the term 'CSR' entirely and us[ing] instead 'corporate responsibility' including economic, social, and environmental tasks" (Enderle 2006: 118).

On the other hand, we acknowledge that the motives driving CSR research are respectable. Business should consider more than the bottom line, but it does no better to swing the pendulum in the opposite direction and emphasize social metrics rather than financial metrics. Managers and researchers need a way to think about these concerns together.

Over the past thirty years, the stakeholder idea has entered and shaped the CSR literature – by contributing to the emergence and wider diffusion of a more integrated CSR approach. As we have noted, a clear turning point in favor of integrated CSR was provided by Donna Wood (1991), who clearly made explicit the link between the "social" of CSR and the stakeholder approach. Since then, research on CSR has moved into a new stage, recognizing the centrality of the stakeholder idea for the concept itself of CSR.

The future of corporate social responsibility

Embracing and integrating the stakeholder idea within the CSR discourse enables us to better deliver on the motivations of CSR research. Assume that the CEO of firm A is asked the following: "Well, I know that your company makes products that consumers like, and that those products make their lives better. And I know that suppliers want to do business with your company because they benefit from this business relationship. I also know that employees really want to work for your company, and are satisfied with their remuneration and professional development. And let's not forget that you're a good citizen in the communities where you are located;[11] among other things, you pay taxes on the profits you make. You compete hard but fairly.

[11] We admit that there are many ways of being a good corporate citizen.

You also make an attractive return on capital for shareholders and other financiers. However, are you socially responsible?"

We confess to having absolutely no idea what "socially responsible" could mean here. If a firm is doing all the things that firm A does, then it deserves to be applauded and offered as an example for other firms, large and small, to emulate. If it is not doing these things as satisfactorily as we think it ought to, then we could perhaps offer to help it do them better, rather than appeal to actions and responsibilities that might lie outside the domain of its day-to-day activities. In summary, by talking of business and social responsibility as if they were two separate things, we might unintentionally be promoting the idea that they involve discrete thought processes and activities. In our opinion, the challenge is to promote a different way of doing business that integrates considerations of business, ethics, and society.

Herein lies the problem with corporate social responsibility. Corporate social responsibility reinforces the "separation thesis," or the idea that we should separate "business" from "ethics or society."[12] This separation is an idea that reaches very deeply into Western culture. It is reinforced by the disciplines of business, by our major theoretical frameworks in management, and by executives and business thinkers themselves. At its worst it generates an absolutely destructive idea of capitalism – that is, that capitalism is about "anything goes." After all, the theory says, "it's just business." Viewed in this way, corporate social responsibility becomes an "add-on" to ameliorate the supposedly harsh consequences of this view of capitalism.

Let us go back to the example of our firm A, and examine its decision to hire employees. Has it done something that is "for the business"? We believe that the answer to that question is a resounding and unqualified "yes." Has it done something that is "for society"? We believe that the answer to that question is also a resounding and unqualified "yes." So, how do matters of employment count – in the social ledger or the business ledger? A similar argument can be made for customers and communities and for suppliers and financiers as well. All these individuals and organizations are full-fledged members of society, as well as being stakeholders in firm A. If they benefit in their dealings with firm A, then society benefits too, both directly and in a number of indirect ways.

Corporate social responsibility is often about seeming to "do good works." And, while there is certainly nothing wrong with doing more good, there can be an implication that companies need to do good works because the

[12] See Chapters 1 and 7 for an explanation. We are indebted to Professor Rama Velamuri for his ideas in this section.

underlying structure of business is not good, or morally neutral. We believe that this is a destructive idea, because it fails to recognize the central role business has played in improving the well-being and prosperity of hundreds of millions of people around the world. And it often causes companies to act in bad faith and get involved in matters in which they have little expertise.

This is not Milton Friedman's argument that the only social responsibility is to increase profits; rather it is a practical matter, that giving money to the opera does not make up (in any moral sense) for shortchanging customers or communities. The focus needs to be on how value is created in the basic business proposition. How does this company make customers, suppliers, communities, employees, and financiers better off? Capitalism is a system of social cooperation – a system of how we work together to create value for each other. Seeing it in any other way can lead to dangerous social policies, and to the tarnishing of the one institution – business – that still has to play a central role in lifting hundreds of millions of more people out of poverty in Asia, Africa, and Latin America.

The second problem with CSR is that it is focused on "corporate" social responsibility. Why is it not called business social responsibility? The focus on "corporate" implies that corporations, due to their size and success and perhaps their shareholding pattern, have to shoulder responsibilities that smaller and more closely held businesses do not. Why? It could be argued that large and successful corporations have a greater responsibility to society than small and less successful ones because they have greater resources to shoulder society's burdens, and "can" implies "ought." However, we believe that talking of responsibilities that are contingent on size and success is highly problematic.

In short, our argument is that if you take a "creating value for stakeholders" approach to business, and if you acknowledge that ethics and values are as important in these relationships as they are in our other relationships with our fellow human beings, then the idea of "corporate social responsibility" is superfluous. There is nothing natural about categories such as "economic," "political," "social," and so on, and we want to suggest that such a conceptual scheme – that separates the social responsibilities of a corporation from its business responsibilities – has long outlived its usefulness.

We propose to replace "corporate social responsibility" with an idea we call "company stakeholder responsibility." This is not just semantics, but a new interpretation of the very purpose of CSR. "Company" signals that all forms of value creation and trade, all businesses and nonprofits need to be involved. "Stakeholder" goes back to the idea of this book and suggests that the main goal of CSR is to create value for key stakeholders and fulfill our responsibilities to them. And "responsibility" implies that we cannot separate business from ethics.[13] We have argued that taking a stakeholder approach to business is ideally suited to integrate business, ethics, and societal considerations. Stakeholder theory is about value creation and trade – it is a managerial theory about how business works. It does not subscribe to the separation thesis, so it asks at the same time business and ethics questions about each stakeholder relationship.

This new approach to CSR – namely the idea of company stakeholder responsibility – looks at business and society as intertwined, and it looks not just at corporations, but at many different forms of organizations, and promotes a pragmatic focus on managing the relations with all the organization's stakeholders as a primary task for success. This requires a detailed understanding of to whom exactly a firm is responsible and the nature of those responsibilities. Firms address these questions in a variety of ways, but each time they need the language of stakeholders to get to a more actionable level of specificity.

[13] Note that we are using "ethics" in its broadest sense to encompass obligations to employees and other stakeholders. This is sometimes referred to as an "American" usage, whereby the "European" usage is much narrower. CSR is our broad term here, and we think it is more specific and more useful than distinguishing "ethical" from "social." We are grateful to Dr. Valeria Fazio for many conversations on this issue.

Part IV

Stakeholder theory: some future possibilities

9 Stakeholder theory and capitalism[1]

We live in the age of markets. While they have been around for thousands of years, we are just beginning to understand their power for organizing society and creating value. In the last two hundred years markets have unleashed a tremendous amount of innovation and progress in the West. The industrial revolution, the rise of consumerism, and the dawn of the global marketplace have each in their own way made life better for millions of people. Many of us now know comforts, skills, and technologies that our ancestors could only dream of.

Alongside these great strides forward are a set of deeply troubling issues. Capitalism, understood in the sense of "how markets work," has also notoriously increased the divide between rich and poor, both within and across nations. We have become blind to some of the consequences of our actions that are harmful to others, such as environmental degradation, dominance of less privileged groups, and the inequitable distribution of opportunities. The seeds from these deeply troubling issues are beginning to germinate. Global warming, global financial crises, and global terrorism threaten to destabilize our world. It is more imperative than ever to study carefully and understand the power of markets and capitalism, and begin the construction of a new narrative about how capitalism can be a force for good in the world.

We have suggested that we need a new story, a new narrative, about business, and the previous chapters can be thought of as an assessment or progress report on the construction of the new narrative that is unfolding. We have argued that if stakeholder theory comes to occupy a central place in the disciplines of business, we shall have a more useful account of business. We shall be able to address the problems of value creation and trade, the ethics of capitalism, and the mindsets of managers. If we put stakeholder theory at the

[1] Some of the ideas in this chapter have appeared earlier, in Freeman (2000), Freeman and Phillips (2002), and Freeman, Martin, and Parmar (2006). We are grateful to the editors and publishers for their permission to recast here some of the ideas in these papers.

center of our thinking about business we can avoid the mindless pursuit of gains for shareholders at the expense of other stakeholders, a pursuit which ultimately destroys both shareholder and stakeholder value. In this chapter we suggest that putting stakeholder theory at the center of our thinking about business leads to a new understanding of capitalism. We shall propose that what is emerging can be called by a variety of names: creative capitalism, responsible capitalism, conscious capitalism,[2] or, as we prefer, stakeholder capitalism. We shall outline the principles of stakeholder capitalism and describe how this view rejects problematic assumptions in the current narratives of capitalism.

Traditional narratives of capitalism rely on assuming that competition, limited resources, and a winner-takes-all mentality are fundamental to business and economic activity. These approaches leave little room for ethical analysis, take a simplistic view of human beings, and focus on value capture rather than value creation. In short, these assumptions are inadequate for understanding the twenty-first-century world, and they create the very problems that we have argued form the raison d'être of stakeholder theory. We shall begin the reframing of the narrative of capitalism around the concepts of stakeholder theory.[3] If we think about how a society can sustain a system of voluntary value creation and trade that creates value for multiple stakeholders, then capitalism can once more become a useful concept.

Our strategy is as follows. First, we present five contemporary narratives of capitalism and show that each privileges the rights of one group over the others. In addition, all five narratives share a common set of assumptions about markets and capitalism that we believe to be counterproductive. Our claim is that the great strides forward and the deeply concerning issues about markets and capitalism are connected to these assumptions. The majority of current conversations about capitalism are not about these fundamental assumptions but about designing the best enforcement mechanisms. We are told that institutions and legal structure can solve the troubling consequences that arise in a market. Are property rights enforced? Transaction costs reduced? Designing good rules for markets to work does help to foster good behavior on the part of market participants. Institutional structure and the

[2] This is the phrase preferred by many businesses surrounding entrepreneurs such as John Mackey of Whole Foods Market.

[3] We can only begin such a reframing here. There is much more to be said about all the issues that we raise in this chapter, and there is much more literature than we present here. Take this chapter as a promissory note on a more fully worked out version of stakeholder capitalism. We are most grateful to our colleague, Professor Kirsten Martin of Catholic University, who is our collaborator in thinking about stakeholder capitalism.

rules of the game do matter. We want to add that the way we talk about markets and the assumptions we make about value creation also play a role in creating the outcomes we want as well those we do not.

In the final section of this chapter we offer a new narrative of capitalism, based on the ideas from earlier chapters, one that builds in morality and ethics from the foundations, and acknowledges stakeholders as essential to value creation and trade, rather than trying to put the rights of one group beyond discussion. Stakeholder capitalism is one way to resolve some of the deep tensions within capitalism, and to better foster the powerful innovations that can help us all to live better.

The narratives of capitalism

In this section we examine five contemporary narratives of capitalism that dominate academic, political, and practitioner discourse and thinking. Each of these current narratives falls short in addressing the concerns of a broad set of stakeholders, and makes a series of assumptions that perpetuate many of the problems of capitalism.[4] The classic narratives of capitalism – labor, government, investor, managerial, and entrepreneurial – retell the story of value creation and trade from the perspective of one stakeholder, whose views become inseparable from and ultimately stand in for the larger story.

Labor capitalism

Since the revolutionary writings of Marx and Engels, the term capitalism has been tied to class division, specifically the self-aggrandizement of the capitalist at the expense of the proletariat. The division of society into capitalist and labor has always played a central role in Marxist writings, from examinations of the American Civil War to detailed investigations of pricing. Marxism, and its political derivatives socialism and communism, turn on the dialectic between the capitalists (or bourgeoisie) who own property and the means of production and the laborers (or proletariat) who own no property and are obligated to sell their labor to the bourgeoisie to gain subsistence (Marx and Engels 1847a, 1847b). For Marx and Engels, this labor market is inherently

[4] We fully acknowledge that our discussion does not represent a complete survey of thought on capitalism. We have chosen these views because they are most prevalent in modern discourse, and we are indebted to their authors for furthering our thinking and that of countless other academics on the subject.

fraught with tension, since the interests of the capitalist and the laborer are diametrically opposed. Within these competing interests, those of the laborer dominate Marx and Engels' view of capitalism. Engels points out in the *Principles of Communism*, which later became the foundation for the *Communist Manifesto*, that

> To say that "the worker has an interest in the rapid growth of capital" means only this: that the more speedily the worker augments the wealth of the capitalist, the larger will be the crumbs which fall to him, the greater will be the number of workers that can be called into existence, the more can the mass of slaves dependent upon capital be increased. (Marx and Engels 1847a)

Ethics and moral language are obscured when viewed through the Marxist lens. Noted Marx scholar David McLellan comments on the apparent paradox in his introduction to *Socialism and Morality*:

> Morality has been viewed by Marxists as a form of ideology reflective of class interests and of changing social patterns. Such a stance ruled out appeal to moral principles by Marxism, which was viewed as a science of society and therefore as indifferent to morality as was, say, the science of biology. On the other hand, the works of Marxists from Marx himself onwards have contained bitter condemnations of the injustices of capitalism, and have been shot through with moral terms such as "alienation" and "exploitation". (McLellan and Sayers 1990: 1)

The Marxist version of capitalism tells a story in which the opposing groups of labor and capital fight over the fixed resources of productive assets. Economic and business activity itself is amoral and the only inevitable solution is for labor to take control of those productive assets by force.

Government capitalism

Born the year Marx died, economist John Maynard Keynes was concerned with the vagaries of the labor market, specifically the stability in national unemployment rates. In his acclaimed *General Theory of Employment, Interest and Money* (Keynes 1936), Keynes traced the connections between unemployment, consumption, and investment (Stewart 1999). Keynes's revolutionary shift of economic thought from a micro view (pricing and cost mechanisms) to a macro view (national income and employment) has had tremendous policy implications for political economists and theoretical implications for business academics (Romano and Leiman 1970). To the requisite institutions of capitalism he added the idea that capitalism could and should be managed by government.

For Keynes the world was far too complex for individuals to bring about the necessary changes for a good society. Since Keynes believed that a government that heavily regulated economic affairs could achieve optimal levels of wealth and employment, we credit him with the creation of *government capitalism*, where the government and its rights dominate the needs of all other stakeholders in the narrative of capitalism.

Although Keynesian economics has become less popular in the post-cold war period (although experiencing a resurgence in 2008 and 2009 with the various debates on how to address the worldwide economic crisis), Keynes's deeper view of capitalism still holds strong among liberals and academics. It is explicit in Keynes's views that capitalism without interventions by the government would lead society astray from "ideal values." In fact, capitalism, according to Keynes, fosters a counterproductive love of money:

> The love of money as a possession – as distinguished from the love of money as a means to the enjoyments and realities of life – will be recognized for what it is, a somewhat disgusting morbidity, one of those semi-criminal, semi-pathological propensities which one hands over with a shudder to the specialists in mental disease. (Hoover 2003: 84)

The metaphor in this narrative is of a garden, that capitalism left to its own devices would produce chaos and unchecked dominance through a love of money. The government is seen as the gardener, who through his skill, knowledge, and wise management keeps the productive powers of capitalism under control, and creates a utopia by enacting policies that keep growth and weeds in balance.

Keynes's view of utopia and ideal values were heavily influenced by the moral philosopher G. E. Moore. Both viewed certain mental states as morally good in themselves. It was these states that Keynes hoped to foster in the American public through his economic policies. A closer look at these mental states shows "Keynes's belief in the rationality of ends and the homogeneity of values"; in short, for Keynes there was a finite moral answer, which he believed everyone should attain (Skidelsky 1995). Ethics in this view becomes about one person's interpretation of the good that is made to stand for everyone and thus becomes unattainable in a diverse and changing world. Furthermore, ethics is imposed by government through the amoral tool of economic policies – to regulate a system that is seen as actively leading society astray from the good.

Keynes's view of capitalism is conflicted – the system can do good, but this requires government intervention:

> I think that capitalism, wisely managed, can probably be made more efficient for attaining economic ends than any alternative system yet in sight, but that in itself it is

in many ways extremely objectionable. Our problem is to work out a social organization which shall be as efficient as possible without offending our notions of a satisfactory way of life. (Romano and Leiman 1970: 119)

The concept of the welfare state is a descendant of Keynes's vision for capitalism. Today, many echo Keynes's distrust of capitalism and reassure their faith in the government to solve problems created by the market.

Investor capitalism

In direct opposition to many of Keynes's conclusions, Milton Friedman advocates a return to laissez-faire economic policies and a reliance on the market mechanisms to achieve "fair" distributions. Economic freedom – the ability to buy and sell without interference from the government – becomes central to Friedman's vision. It is important to note that Friedman believes in economic freedom for particular groups, namely shareholders. To facilitate this view, Friedman limits the role and rights of the government in his narrative about how capitalism should function. In Friedman's view, government's role should be relegated to eliminating monopolies, reforming the tax laws in favor of corporations, and maintaining law and order.

As Friedman shifts focus away from government and its regulation of capital, he focuses on a new dominant group: investors. In fact the whole of commercial business activity has one specific purpose: "to use its resources and engage in activities designed to increase its profits, so long as it stays within the rules of the game, which is to say, engages in free and open competition, without deception or fraud" (Friedman 1962: 133). This goal is the investor's goal, and it is assumed to be in competition with alternative stakeholders' goals. In Friedman's view shareholders who are better off will continue to invest in the market and produce better results for all. Friedman and those who give priority to the concerns of investors above and beyond the concerns of other stakeholders, subscribe to *investor capitalism.*

Friedman's writings suggest that he views the inner workings of capitalism as amoral. His analysis and description of capitalism is given in monetary terms and in the language of economics, a grammar that avoids "non-factual" value distinctions (Romano and Leiman 1970). Nevertheless, ethics and morality play a large role in justifying Friedman's claims about the importance of free enterprise and actions against a centrally mandated economy:

The fundamental threat to freedom is power to coerce, be it in the hands of a monarch, a dictator, an oligarchy, or a momentary majority. The preservation of freedom requires the elimination of such concentration of power to the fullest possible extent and the dispersal and distribution of whatever power cannot be eliminated. (Friedman 1962: 17)

Managerial capitalism

For scholars studying capitalism and the corporation, the owner of the private property is in control. Keynes, Marx, and Friedman all assume that the investor (or stockholder) is the owner of the means of production and has responsibility for and control over its use. Managerial capitalism, on the other hand, clearly differentiates the managers of the organization from the investors and other stakeholders. Berle and Means (1932) see traditional economic theory as inadequate in handling the newly differentiated roles between ownership and control of assets. To them we are now dealing with distinct functions: ownership on the one side, control on the other. This control tends to move further and further away from ownership and ultimately to lie in the hands of the management itself, a management capable of perpetuating its own position. These distinct functions of ownership and control now lie in the hands of opposing groups with competing interests.

Similarly, Marris (1964) positions managers as separate and distinct from all other stakeholders including investors. Managers, as those who both control and have responsibility for the corporation, are the dominant group of interest for this view of modern capitalism. This line of scholarship is continued through the literature on agency theory, where owners of corporations are seen as property holders of the organization and managers are the agents of those stockholders. Managers have a contractual or fiduciary duty to shareholder interests above and beyond any other relationship in managing the shareholder's property (the organization in this case). Continuing within this narrative, agency theory positions the managers' interests to be in competition with other stakeholders.

Managerial capitalism's view on business ethics is more complicated. As Berle and Means state, "Neither the claims of ownership nor those of control can stand against the paramount interests of the community" (Berle and Means 1932). While acknowledging the community interests as an important consideration for the functioning of the firm, the authors also believe it essential for the "control" (or management) of the corporation to develop into a purely neutral technocracy. As with Friedman, the process of business is considered amoral, with a reconciliation with morality or community interests required.

Marris continues by stating that directors or managers who pay attention to competing social interests to the detriment of profits may be popular. However, he also believes that managers have growth and productivity as primary goals and constraints for their actions. Marris's view of morality and motivation outlines the financial motivations of managers in their role as controllers of the corporation. Marris does, however, find the rules of the game to be open and flexible, giving managers the opportunity to pursue alternative goals to those which are financial.

Entrepreneurial capitalism

The entrepreneur is missing from many of the views of capitalism outlined above. Yet the entrepreneur becomes an important stakeholder to ignore, as she epitomizes the role of value creation in the capitalist system. Within modern theory, economists such as Schumpeter (1942), Kirzner (1979), and more recently Baumol (1990) emphasize the role of the entrepreneur within capitalism and epitomize what we are calling *entrepreneurial capitalism*. For these authors, the entrepreneur functions as the dominant player within the capitalist system, who shapes economic power (Kirzner 1985).

Schumpeter (1942) argues that the entrepreneur is part of the process of *creative destruction* – the destruction of the current market to introduce a new market. In doing so, Schumpeter posits the entrepreneur in opposition to the status quo interests of other stakeholders and in competition over resources. Others, within this same narrative, do not take such a view. Kirzner allows for the entrepreneur to be a part of *creative discovery* and focuses on a more positive vision of capitalism within the "Austrian" tradition of modern economic thought. Such a narrative of capitalism leaves open the possibility of a strong role for business ethics. However, such a role is not explicitly stated by these scholars.

Each author differentiates the entrepreneur and singles her out from capitalists, property owners, managers, and laborers. Entrepreneurs for these economists are decidedly different – and each has their own interpretation of that difference. Something that is common to all, however, is the importance of the role of the entrepreneur in the capitalist system as the agitator who leads all others away from the status quo.

The current financial crisis offers an interesting case study on these partial narratives. Many have suggested that it is investor capitalism which has led to the current set of problems. However, at the same time, it is these very "investors" who have lost so much of their wealth through the financial crisis.

It is tempting to combine the five narratives and say that things have gotten out of balance. Some commentators have suggested that labor has proportionately too much power in key industries such as automobiles, while others have suggested that we need more government controls on this investor capitalism. Still others have argued that we need a return to a more entrepreneurial economy to work our way out of the difficulties. And there is the age-old argument about managerial control. In today's crisis this argument is found in endless editorials about top management compensation and corporate governance effectiveness. We believe that these calls for trade-offs and balance miss the underlying issues.

Problems with the traditional narratives

All five narratives make a similar set of assumptions about markets and capitalism that we believe to be counterproductive. Each narrative assumes that market participants have a naïve version of self-interest (that one's self-interest is not connected to, or does not take into account, the self-interests of others), that morality is separate from (or even antithetical to) economic prosperity, and that competition for limited resources (value as a zero-sum game) is the dominant mode of prosperity. These assumptions yield several new aspects of the three problems that stakeholder theory tries to solve.

The problem of value creation and trade: competition

By pitting individuals against one another within the survival-of-the-fittest atmosphere, narrators of the traditional approach to capitalism foster the notion of competition as a *prerequisite* to capitalist society. Competition is necessary, it is argued, because of the many individuals fighting over the same resources. Other individuals are seen as a threat to survival rather than as potential partners for value creation, and capitalists are left with the problem of resolving competitor demands and threats. Capitalism is to be defined primarily by the assumption of scarcity. And value creation and trade are to be defined primarily, on this view, through the lens of competition.

This focus on competition rather than cooperation is mistaken on two counts. First, focusing on how to beat stakeholders and retain power in any relationship leaves out those many instances where collaboration is necessary in order to survive. For many entrepreneurial ventures, strong collaborational relationships are necessary to create sustainable organizations. According to

Sarasvathy (2001), entrepreneurs rely on noncompetitive stakeholder relationships to navigate the perils of extreme uncertainty and to bolster their legitimacy. Those creating markets for future goods and services (Shane and Venkataraman 2000) simply cannot ignore value-creating relationships as a means of creating a sustainable competitive advantage. While entrepreneurs are the lifeblood of capitalism, the traditional story of capitalism does not tell their story of collaboration and mutually beneficial relationships for survival. Using their imagination to create sustainable collaborative relationships can lead managers to be more effective even within highly competitive markets. Large gains in prosperity throughout history are associated more with mutually beneficial trade (which creates value) than with dominance (which tries to capture value).

The problem of value creation and trade: the dominant group

This competitive framing of capitalism leads to debates over who is the "dominant" group in a market – the ideas of competition tumble over to those intimately involved in the organization. The focus is on the conflicting needs and demands of labor, government, investors, and managers in the hope of resolving the "inherent" conflicts. As such, one group must dominate in order to win the conflict and thereby prioritize its demands. The ensuing relationships are "fraught with tension" (Freeman, Martin, and Parmar 2006).

The problem of the dominant group is that there must be one group whose rights trump the rights of others. The wishful thinking behind this view goes something like, "If only we were all to follow the right leading group and align our interests with theirs, the ills of capitalism would be solved, and we would become more prosperous."

For Keynes, the government's rights and responsibilities supersede all others. For Marx, the laborers' rights have been ignored for too long. Berle and Means' major contribution was in securing separate rights for management. Friedman's focus on investor rights diminished the role of all other stakeholders including government. After securing dominant rights, each narrative positions the organization in existence to serve the needs of the corresponding dominant group. Not only must the goals of the dominant group become the goal of the organization, but all organizational decisions must then take into account the rights of this dominant group.

These narratives do not simply ignore other stakeholders. Rather, each narrative presumes that by focusing on the interests and rights of their dominant group, all other stakeholders will benefit. Friedman is particularly pointed when he argues that in allowing investors to prosper, all others will benefit as a result. We see many benefits in meeting the needs of a dominant group in these narratives, including the following:

- The economy is prevented "from falling into a rut and precludes those who constitute the economy from falling into lethargy" (Baumol).
- Society is led towards ideal values (Keynes).
- All other stakeholders see better results (Friedman).
- Economic growth rises (Friedman, Schumpeter).
- Income is distributed fairly to other stakeholders (Berle and Means).
- Alternative, nonproductive interests are kept in balance (Marx, Berle and Means).

Though such a paternalistic treatment of stakeholders acknowledges the existence of stakeholders and their need to thrive, it subsumes stakeholders' interests to those of the dominant group. Each of these views improperly focuses on one group to the detriment of all others. We may encounter specific instances where the needs of one group – for example the investor – trumps those of others. However, entering every decision-making situation with this type of a priori prioritization leads academics and practitioners to make decisions that can hurt the long-term value creation of the company. In practice, placing stakeholders in opposition to one another leads to a focus on winning and losing as opposed to working together. Situations are analyzed with an either/or mentality, since the requirements of the different groups are assumed to be in opposition.

The problem of the ethics of capitalism

In Chapter 1 we suggested that stakeholder theory has emerged to solve, in part, the problem of the ethics of capitalism. We see this even more clearly in the current narrative of capitalism, where individuals are in a constant survival mode with value being "distributed" rather than "created." Ethics is assumed to have a limited (and even detrimental) role in capitalism. We are faced with a continual "ethics crisis" as we have mistakenly taught managers that business within capitalism is by its very nature amoral.[5] Individuals are in competition with others for limited resources and societal rules are assumed to be of limited value. The traditional models of capitalism

[5] In our relatively brief careers we can remember the calls for corporate social responsibility in the late 1960s and early 1970s; the associated scandals such as Lockheed, Firestone 500, and others; the insider trading scandals of the 1980s; the excesses of the Internet boom of the 1990s; the Enron, WorldCom, Adelphia, Parmalat, second Firestone tire scandal, and so on; and, now, the current financial scandals.

needlessly separate it from ethics by making the foundations of capitalism competition and autonomy.

The problem of the ethics of capitalism is that ethics is left out of the story of capitalism, just as in Chapter 1 we suggested that it was left out of our understanding of business. Rather than acknowledging the moral dimensions of every decision – whether in business or not – academics and practitioners have created a separate sphere of norms, rules, and morals, naming it "capitalism," where competition and winning dictate the rules of the game.

Ironically, the arguments against acknowledging values or morality within a survival of the fittest narrative of capitalism ignores the fact that moral concepts such as relationships, mutually beneficial agreements, teams, trust, honesty, and care are necessary in those instances when the survival of the individual, group, or organization is at stake. As Daniel Dennett (1995) illustrates, evolutionary theory or jungle metaphors do not negate ethics and morality in themselves. Mutually beneficial agreements (versus opportunism), group focus (versus individualism), and empathy (versus narcissism) foster surviving and thriving. This approach guides managers to ignore the ethical implications of their decisions. It does not, however, make their decisions amoral; rather, it causes managers to "do ethics badly" (Wicks and Freeman 1998). Business ethicists are left to add ethics back into the story of capitalism, but, as we argued in Chapters 3 and 7, they often do so at their own peril of accepting the dominant narratives about business.

The problems of value creation and trade and the ethics of capitalism: business in a liberal democracy

When we fail to address adequately the problems we have outlined, we also generate the corresponding role for government to fix them. This creates the issue of the proper role of business in a liberal democracy. It usually results in creating larger, more intrusive government in a system that is founded on a liberal democracy.

The state has three primary roles in relation to the problems created above. First, the government *resolves conflicts* between stakeholders. With winners, losers, and limited resources (the problem of competition) comes the role of the referee to resolve those conflicts. Rather than allowing organizations and individuals to create their own relationships, the state becomes the place where conflict is resolved, because individuals "cannot be trusted to find solutions that will benefit society."

Second, the state *legislates the morality* of capitalism. If capitalism is seen as amoral, then it necessitates the legislation of morality for business, organizations, and individuals. This is most commonly seen through the legal system, where the boundaries of propriety are laid out, clear as night and day. It is assumed that individuals and organizations are allowed to move freely and with moral norms within the bounds set by legislators.

Third, the state *redistributes resources*. When one group is assumed to dominate all others in the acquisition of resources, the government is called upon to redistribute those resources when they become too unbalanced. One group is assumed to be constantly taking from all others, and the government exists to protect these disadvantaged groups and redistribute the resources through a tax code.

Ironically, these roles for the state are self-perpetuating. As government fulfills its role, the consequence is a continuation of a problem rather than a solution. If we set up rules governing the morality of individuals and organizations, we absolve those agents of their responsibility to conduct business according to community norms. That is now the government's job. Individuals and organizations in a capitalist society are expected to behave poorly and without a personal value-system as long as they stay within the moral code as legislated – Keynes noted that capitalism without government intervention would lead society astray from ideal values. As Berle and Means state, the role of the organization is "balancing a variety of claims by various groups in the community and assigning to each a portion of the income stream on the basis of public policy rather than private cupidity" (Berle and Means 1932: 313). But, as Ghoshal has suggested, we act out our theories of how the world works. So we actually find capitalists who justify or at least excuse their actions by asserting that "in the end the market will correct unethical behavior."

If we rely on the state to redistribute wealth, we find that it will inevitably make mistakes and create a further need to reredistribute wealth. Milton Friedman, the Nobel laureate in economics, warns, "In fiscal policy as in monetary policy, all political considerations aside, we simply do not know enough to be able to use deliberate changes in taxation or expenditures as a sensitive stabilizing mechanism. In the process of trying to do so, we almost surely make matters worse" (Friedman, quoted in Romano and Leiman 1970: 58).

If we rely on the state to resolve stakeholder conflicts, individuals and organizations would never develop the imagination required to create different, mutually beneficial relationships. In addition, the parties are not expected to learn how to resolve issues themselves when the court system was created for such a purpose.

Further, individuals and organizations game and manipulate the legislative system to their advantage. As evidenced by the proliferation of civil court cases, the lobbying for favorable legislation, and industry writing its own regulations (later enforced by the state), businesses have not allowed government to be the dictator of capitalism. However, the involvement of business with government also enlarges and perpetuates the role of government. Collusion and civil lawsuits become strategic tools.

This view of government omits a role for the state as a part of value creation. Rather than solving disputes and reallocating resources, the state could be a player in the capitalist system in knocking down barriers to value creation and trade. However, as it stands, government is too busy solving problems that need not exist.

Stakeholder capitalism

We wish to sketch a new vision of capitalism – stakeholder capitalism – founded on libertarian and pragmatist lines. Stakeholder capitalism is not based solely on private property, self-interest, competition, and free markets – such a view requires constant justification based on achieving good outcomes or avoiding authoritarian alternatives.

We argue that we do not need to justify capitalistic systems based on the outcome or the alternatives – the principles of capitalism are worthy goals in and of themselves. Rather, stakeholder capitalism is "based on freedom, rights, and the creation by consent of positive obligations."

First, adults have *freedom* to do what they want, including making voluntary agreements that are sustainable over time. Rather than focusing on individuals in competition over limited resources as in traditional narratives of capitalism, stakeholder capitalism focuses on individuals voluntarily working together to create sustainable relationships in the pursuit of value creation.

Second, individuals have *rights* protecting them in those agreements. One group's rights do not prima facie dominate the narrative of capitalism. Rather, each stakeholder should be protected within their voluntary agreements.

Finally, those individuals can decide to cooperate and *obligate themselves* to others through those voluntary agreements. These obligations can take the form of formal written contracts or social contracts with assumed responsibilities. The relationships are sustainable when these obligations and responsibilities are upheld.

With freedom comes responsibility. Indeed, we believe that most people are responsible for themselves. Equal liberty for all makes no sense if one person may do whatever she likes to another. The libertarian must assume that people are capable of controlling their actions so that they do not harm others. Second, when such boundary crossings or harms occur, the offending party must make some attempt at reparation. The alternative to this strong notion of individual responsibility is to make some collective, such as the state, responsible for repairing any damage that is done; but the whole point of the minimal state is that such "collective responsibility" carries severe "freedom denying" penalties. So, libertarians do or ought to accept some variant responsibility as inextricable from liberty.[6]

We offer six principles that together build a framework for our value creation and trade that infuses ethics at the foundations, respects the complexity of human beings, fosters innovation, and can help us move beyond the problems outlined above. These principles are not offered in any kind of foundationalist sense, given our philosophical commitments, but as guides to the way in which many people who engage in business and value creation can, should, and do think about capitalism. Our argument is that if people on the ground make sense of their activities and their system of value creation in this way, they will act in ways that will make our capitalism more responsible and more resilient.

Principles of stakeholder capitalism

1. The principle of stakeholder cooperation

"Value can be created, traded, and sustained because stakeholders can jointly satisfy their needs and desires by making voluntary agreements with each other that for the most part are kept."

Rather than assume that we are all first and foremost self-interested and out to maximize our own benefit, this principle highlights the social nature of value creation. Value is not "discovered" lying around in the market, but created through shared assumptions and beliefs in a community. Value, any value, is a social phenomenon. We must create value in a context, with the help of others and with others who value what we create. This principle

[6] We might call this kind of libertarian ethics "responsible libertarianism." We are grateful to John Mackey and Michael Strong for inspiring this label, though they may not approve of it.

acknowledges that business activity is explicitly social and uses that to enhance the process of value creation. Foregrounding the social nature of business gives us insight into the problem of value creation and trade, because it puts the focus on human relationships and the shared sense making that creates value.

2. The principle of stakeholder engagement

"To successfully create, trade, and sustain value, a business must engage its stakeholders. Almost every business transaction involves customers, suppliers, communities, employees, and financiers. Other stakeholders such as media, additional civil society representatives, NGOs, and so on are often affected or can affect value creation."

Rather than argue over whose rights trump whose, this principle acknowledges that a large cast of stakeholders is necessary to sustain value creation. As often as possible, the needs of multiple stakeholders must be met. There may be specific situations in which privileging the rights of one group can benefit others in the long term, but this is not clear prima facie, and must be decided upon by the effected parties. Recognizing the role of a multitude of stakeholders in the value-creation process diminishes the problem of the dominant group. Instead of trying to find and create arguments for one group's right to trump the rest, engaging stakeholders in creating as many win–win situations as possible lies at the heart of creating sustainable value.

3. The principle of stakeholder responsibility

"Value can be created, traded, and sustained because parties to an agreement are willing to accept responsibility for the consequences of their actions. When third parties are harmed, they must be compensated, or a new agreement must be negotiated with all of those parties who are affected."

This principle rejects the view that business is amoral or even immoral. If business is a social process, then morality is at its center. Scandals and selfish behavior are a breach of the trust and transparency that is the norm for business to flourish. We can all think of notable lapses in managerial responsibility, but the successes are less visible. Being proactive about effects on others, rather than waiting for government recourse, will help managers build stakeholder trust and loyalty, both of which will help create more sustainable business. The stakeholder responsibility principle brings ethics into the heart of capitalism and reduces the problem of ethics and capitalism. It also helps to resolve the problem of business in a liberal democracy, because if ethics is inherent to business, then the role of government as an "ethics watchdog" is lessened. Responsible business does not need the external imposition of morality. Finally, this redescription of capitalism helps managers to embed ethics in the way they think about their day-to-day activities.

4. The principle of complexity

"Value can be created, traded, and sustained because human beings are complex psychological creatures capable of acting from many different values and points of view." Individuals are socially situated and their values are connected to their social context.

This principle rejects the cardboard view of human nature at the heart of the current narratives of capitalism. People are complex; they act for a variety of reasons. Their actions benefit themselves and others, and people usually take that into account. It is also important to note that since we are complex, we are able to differentiate consequences based on who is being affected. It is part of human nature to care more about consequences that affect those we are close to rather than others. The view of human nature that we hold has a tendency to become a self-fulfilling prophecy – when we expect managers to be self-interested they meet those expectations. By raising the bar for human complexity in business we allow for a broader conceptualization of "value" and create more space for ethics. That is another reason why the principle of stakeholder responsibility is important. It helps to balance our natural tendency to discriminate and reminds us that despite our differences and separation we still can have profound effects on each other.

Based on these principles, capitalism becomes "the voluntary associations of fair, responsible, cooperation, consenting, and complex adults" and does not include competition or self-interest as foundational assumptions.

5. The principle of continuous creation

"Business as an institution is a source of the creation of value. Cooperating with stakeholders and motivated by values, businesspeople continuously create new sources of value."

Self-interest is not the only source of innovation or progress. Working with others and for others can be a stronger motivation to enhance the pace of progress. Managers will encounter difficult trade-offs in this process, but with transparency and imagination they may be able to dissolve those trade-offs as well. This kind of innovation typically comes from engaging with stakeholders to generate new ideas and understanding how they will evaluate the new alternatives. This principle also sheds light on the problem of ethics and capitalism, because as managers see the value of acting with integrity and responsibility, they will be better able to incorporate those strategies into their actions. Business is a source of innovation, and it can be a source of moral innovation as well.

6. The principle of emergent competition

"Competition emerges from a relatively free society so that stakeholders have options. Competition is an emergent property rather than a necessary assumption to capitalism."

This principle also highlights the ways in which our assumption of competition can affect our behavior. Not every interaction is a zero-sum game and not every interaction has a win–win solution. We should do our best to look for the win–win before jumping to other sub-optimal solutions. By backgrounding competition in our description of capitalism, we reduce the potential of the problem of the dominant group to hijack value creation. Choice is an important element in markets, but choice does not always lead to zero-sum solutions.

Finally, these principles and the stakeholder capitalism view do not claim to be a panacea. There will always be a small minority who are focused on their own self-interest at the expense of others. Our claim is that we should set the bar for capitalism at the best we can achieve, not limit it by trying only to avoid the worst. Talking about capitalism this way can foster behavior along these lines. Those who choose to exploit the trust of their stakeholders for their own gain are doing so at their own peril.

We are not claiming that by adopting these principles we shall remove conflict from capitalism and from then on things will be easy. In some ways explicitly dealing with stakeholders is harder than ignoring them. Participants in the value-creation process will have to have a thick skin and patience, and be comfortable with conflict and change. These things are not easy. But creating value necessitates them. They provide the opportunity for real leadership.

The recent credit crisis offers an illustration of how forgetting these basic principles can jeopardize the entire global economy. The seventeen-year increase in house prices was fueled by the perverse incentives to maximize short-term profits by executives of banks, analysts, rating agents, mortgage brokers, home appraisers, and many others, who forgot their obligations to broader stakeholder groups. The harm to third parties of these actions was wished away in a system which selected for irresponsibility. As new debt instruments and mortgage-backed securities were created, the basic consequences were dismissed (e.g. what would happen if house prices fell?) and their broad effects on other stakeholders and on the long-term viability of the economy were blatantly ignored. To restore confidence in the markets will take more than just an infusion of money – increasing the throughput in a corrupt system will only increase the amount of corruption. Lasting confidence will require that responsibility to stakeholders be placed back at the heart of what we mean by value creation and trade.

Conclusion

In the social sciences the way we talk affects what we see and how we live. The theories we create and the stories we tell become self-fulfilling. We argue that the same process is at work in our discussions of capitalism. The current narratives of capitalism assume naïve self-interest, the separation of business and morality, and the limited nature of valuable resources. These assumptions form the core of four problems that we currently face: competition, business ethics, dominant groups, and business in a liberal democracy. If we are to overcome these problems, we shall have to change the way we talk about business as well as the way we actually conduct it. The stories we tell and the assumptions we make about business affects how business is actually carried out. By making these assumptions explicit and optional rather than implicit and mandatory, we hope that we can move a step closer to overcoming the deeply troubling issues that surface in our current practice of value creation.

Business should be about the best that we can create together, rather than about avoiding the worst. If we critically embrace a new set of assumptions about how value is created, the practice of business will soon follow. We do not have to sacrifice the great strides forward to solve some of the deeply troubling issues with capitalism. We need to think critically, acknowledge the social nature of value creation, and work with an insatiable passion to create value for our stakeholders.

10 Questions on the horizon

The argument in the preceding chapters is that the body of work that we have called stakeholder theory can be seen as articulating a different and morally rich way of thinking about the disciplines of business. We have suggested in Chapter 9 that it offers no less than a thoroughgoing revision of our understanding of business and capitalism. Whether or not stakeholder theory fulfills these promises will be determined more by the work of the next thirty years than by the work that has already been done. Therefore we want to set out briefly a set of research questions and themes that point stakeholder theory and the researchers who work in this area towards what we see as some fruitful areas of inquiry. We do this in the pragmatic spirit of experimentalism. We should explore many more areas than the ones suggested here, keep what works, and discard the projects that lead to dead ends.

In Chapter 1 we argued that the language of stakeholders has been developed to address three important and interrelated questions about business: how value is created, the nature of the relationship between ethics and capitalism, and how managers can best think about their day-to-day practices.

The pursuit of these questions raises many more. We believe that the vocabulary of stakeholders is not only good for addressing these three purposes, but for creating new opportunities for practical and theoretical development as well. Stakeholder language opens more intellectual design space. We organize the generative capacities of stakeholder thinking into three interrelated themes. First, if we take the ideas of stakeholder theory seriously, we require some *richer descriptions* – things we want to know more about; second, we require some *redescriptions* – things we need to think differently about, given the assumptions that motivate stakeholder thinking; and, finally, we point to opportunities for innovating theory by *relating descriptions* to other bodies of knowledge and ways of talking.

The format that we are going to use is simply to set out a number of questions within a theme. These ideas are at an early stage of inception, so we leave them open to interpretation to increase their potential for sparking insight and imagination. Work on many of these questions is already under way, and we have outlined it in the chapters of this book. The purpose of this chapter is to combine some of the most important questions we have uncovered as we have reviewed the very diverse body of work on the stakeholder concept with some questions that have received scant, if any, treatment. These thirty-six questions should be taken as food for thought. Hopefully they will stimulate our research colleagues to ask even better and deeper ones.

Richer description

The stakeholders of stakeholder theory would be better served if we can craft compelling answers to the following questions. The first set of questions has to do with describing better how firms manage their relationships with stakeholders. The management and marketing disciplines have been the focal point of research on this topic to date, but there is much work to be done.

1. What are some industry best practices that illustrate stakeholder management? Can we build theory around these practices to show how and why they create value, specifically connecting purposes and values to specific practices?
2. Can we create a database of stakeholder engagement strategies?
3. How and why do these stakeholder engagement strategies change over time?
4. Can we tell some interesting stories from the company's and the stakeholders' points of view?

Other important questions deal with the nature of relationships between firms and stakeholders and their combined or divergent interests. Organizational behavior scholars may currently have the best set of tools to work with in examining these questions, although the answers are important to all areas.

5. What are the key dimensions of each stakeholder relationship and how do we observe them? Some useful starting points may be transaction costs, interaction frequency, interaction quality, interaction quantity, relevance to value proposition, generation of value-creation possibilities, and degree of shared values and assumptions. How do these dimensions change over time and what are the effects of these changes?
6. What are some common disruptions in stakeholder relationships, and how can those disruptions be minimized?
7. How do managers think about appropriate metrics for stakeholder relationships? How do they and should they design metrics to foster the robust

value proposition of the firm? What are the challenges and opportunities to doing this?

8. How do we conceptualize the interaction effects of stakeholders – the jointness of stakeholder interests?
9. What are the underlying mechanisms of the way in which stakeholder interests are coordinated? The negotiation and sense-making literature can be a helpful starting point here. What are the mechanisms that managers use to bring interests together and how can they do it better?

Accountability also surfaced as a key issue to address, especially in light of societal demands for more business accountability. Environmental protection reflected in the "greening" of business and the popularity of sustainability reporting, as well as political and legal trends towards higher levels of oversight and regulation, make this issue very important:

10. In today's business climate, firms can be held accountable for their stakeholders' actions. How do companies find stakeholders who act responsibly or get them to do so?

"Value" is another topic that came up repeatedly in our review of the strategic management, business, and related disciplines. If, in fact, the superordinate goal of stakeholder theory is to explain value creation, then there are a number of questions on this topic that need to be addressed.

11. What does "value" mean for a particular group of stakeholders and how do firms create these different types of "value" for stakeholders?
12. How do we measure the value created by the behaviors recommended by stakeholder theory?
13. How can we measure the different value that a firm creates for stakeholders, beyond accounting and financial measures?
14. What types of values should we include? What is the scope of this metric?
15. In what contexts do firms and communities need a single generalizable metric and where do they need multiple stakeholder specific metrics?
16. How do managers think about redistributing value created by the firm? To what implicit theories of justice do they subscribe?

Finally, we need a richer description of one of the most fundamental topics in the stakeholder literature – identification of stakeholders and their interests. These questions have been explored since the inception of the stakeholder discussion, but there is much work yet to be done:

17. How do executives make sense of who is or is not a stakeholder?
18. What are the relevant categories of stakeholder that managers use, and what happens when the common categories of customer, supplier, shareholder, and so on break down?

19. What does it mean to balance stakeholder interests? Are there different types of balance and compromise? Which types are best for which circumstances?
20. How do stakeholders make sense of equity and fairness?
21. If we turn CSR into company stakeholder responsibility, as we argued in Chapter 8, what are "company customer responsibility," "company employee responsibility," and so on, and what are the analogous concepts of "employee company responsibility," etc. by which we mean to understand how a stakeholder acts responsibly towards a company.

Redescription

Stakeholder theory also provides an opportunity to redescribe many concepts and narratives that are closely connected to it. These concepts and narratives are found in the literatures on business ethics, economics, public administration, finance, philosophy, and management, to name a few examples. Future work can make sense of these related theories in ways that allow managers and academics to create better business practices and results.

22. Can other organizations and institutions be better described using stakeholder language? For example, schools and governments? What is similar or different about the stakeholder view in these different contexts?
23. If stakeholder theory depends on seeing stakeholders as fully moral – as persons – what is our idea about persons in the modern world? If we take some kind of relational psychology seriously, is there something like a stakeholder theory of the person?
24. If we get rid of the separation fallacy, how do we redescribe the traditional disciplines or narratives about business so that we see stakeholders as fully moral beings? For instance, marketing may become about promises to customers. We may come to see the idea of markets in economics and finance as morally rich, working only when participants have a clear idea about responsibility (what Adam Smith called "men of justice"). We may conceptualize production and operations management as consisting of communities of complex persons joined together in collaborative tasks.
25. If we come to see capitalism as the way in which companies create value for stakeholders, can we reexamine the history of capitalism in a useful way?
26. Can we reconceptualize capitalism as creating value for stakeholders, where ethics, corporate responsibility, and sustainability are at the center of the conversation?

27. Can we rethink the basics of ethics, having given up the separation fallacy, and redescribe ethics to include the idea that human beings are value creators and traders?
28. Can we replace stock options with stake options?
29. How can we understand the background narratives about business and how they affect the ability of stakeholders to create value and trade? What is the role of mediating institutions in reinforcing background narratives?
30. How are we to understand key features of most stakeholder relationships, such as collaboration and the use of collaborative strategies such as conversation, obedience to authority, and so on?

Relating descriptions

One of the really fruitful developments in many of the academic disciplines has been a call for work of an interdisciplinary nature. There is so much that disciplines can learn from each other and, of course, the stakeholder concept is sufficiently broad to facilitate such collaborative efforts. A few of many possible questions are offered as examples of the types of issue that might be addressed.

31. What are the crossovers between stakeholder theory and other domains – how can it be a vehicle for talking about different types of organization – generating insights from a variety of conversations?
32. What new disciplines can we bring to bear on the understanding of business?
33. How do we break out of traditional disciplines and stakeholder roles? Are employees who are customers like employees and like customers – or something else?
34. Can we think about stakeholder theories along the following lines: a stakeholder theory of (i) large corporate MNEs; (ii) family enterprises large and small, by generation, by gender involvement, by culture; (iii) SMEs; (iv) micro businesses; (v) partnerships and other legal forms? Could we then say what are the similarities and differences between these kinds of stakeholder theory?
35. What are the consequences of stakeholder management for the larger economy? If firms stop trying to externalize costs of negative consequences and work with stakeholders to create internal solutions, can we model the changes to the larger economy? Agent-based simulations may offer insights here.

36. Structural equation modeling can offer a useful tool for examining the interconnections between stakeholders. Theorists can ask how value created for one stakeholder affects others in the system. Can we develop a more nuanced understanding of the ripple effects of interacting with any one stakeholder?

Conclusion

We have argued that the three problems outlined in Chapter 1 can best be solved by moving stakeholder theory to the center of our thinking about business. We need to see value creation and trade, first and foremost, as creating value for stakeholders. Understanding the economics of markets is important, but at the center of starting, managing, and leading a business is a set of stakeholder relationships which define the business. We have detailed how the scholars working in the disciplines of business can and are redefining value creation and trade within their disciplines in terms of stakeholder theory.

We have suggested that it is easier to address the problem of the ethics of capitalism with integrative ideas of creating value for stakeholders. By appealing to some principle of responsibility, eschewing the separation fallacy, and simply realizing that stakeholders and businesspeople share a common humanity, we can build more effective methods of value creation. Indeed, we can even build a better story about capitalism based on these principles of responsibility and freedom. Finally, if we adopt what we called in Chapter 3 pragmatic experimentalism, we can make our ideas about business more useful and hence worthy of being taught to managers and future managers.

It is presumptuous to write a conclusion. Stakeholder theory is a living "Wiki" constantly evolving, as stakeholder theorists attempt to invent more useful ways of describing, redescribing, and relating our multiple conceptions of ourselves and our institutions such as business. As pragmatists we believe in encouraging a diversity of ideas. Some of them will undoubtedly lead to dead ends, but many will bear fruit.

The challenge before us is large, yet the progress made by an increasingly large group of researchers and business thinkers is quite real. We can be the generation that remakes business and capitalism, putting ethics at the center of business, and business at the center of ethics, creating a way of understanding business in the world of the twenty-first century. Surely this is a task that is worthy of our efforts.

Bibliography

Aaltonen, K., Kujala, J. and Oijala, T. 2008. Stakeholder salience in global projects. *International Journal of Project Management* 26 (5): 509–516.

Abrams, F. 1951. Management responsibilities in a complex world. *Harvard Business Review* 29 (5): 29–34.

Achterkamp, M. C. and Vos, J. F. J. 2008. Investigating the use of the stakeholder notion in project management literature, a meta-analysis. *International Journal of Project Management* 26 (7): 749–757.

Ackerman, R. W. 1973. How companies respond to social demands. *Harvard Business Review* 51 (4): 88–98.

1975. *The Social Challenge to Business.* Cambridge, MA: Harvard University Press.

Ackerman, R. W. and Bauer, R. A. 1976. *Corporate Social Responsiveness.* Upper Saddle River, NJ: Prentice-Hall.

Ackoff, R. L. 1970. *A Concept of Corporate Planning.* New York: John Wiley & Sons.

1974. *Redesigning the Future.* New York: John Wiley & Sons.

Acquier, A., Gand, S. and Szpirglas, M. 2008. From stakeholder to stakeholder management in crisis episodes: A case study in a public transportation company. *Journal of Contingencies and Crisis Management* 16 (2): 101–114.

Adams, C. A. 2004. The ethical, social and environmental reporting-performance portrayal gap. *Accounting, Auditing and Accountability Journal* 17 (5): 731–757.

Adler, R. W. 2002. Stakeholders' perceptions of organizational decline. *Accounting Forum* 26 (1): 31–45.

Adler, R. W. and Chaston, K. 2002. Stakeholders' perceptions of organizational decline. *Accounting Forum* 26 (1): 31–45.

Agle, B. R., Mitchell, R. K. and Sonnenfeld, J. A. 1999. Who matters to CEOs? An investigation of stakeholder attributes and salience, corporate performance, and CEO values. *Academy of Management Journal* 42 (5): 507–525.

Ahlstedt, L. and Jahnukainen, I. 1971. *A Business Organization as a Management System.* Tapiola: Weilin & Goos.

Albinger, H. S. and Freeman, S. J. 2000. Corporate social performance and attractiveness as an employer to different job seeking populations. *Journal of Business Ethics* 28 (3): 243–253.

Aldrich, H. E. and Whetten, D. A. 1981. Organization sets, action sets, and networks: Making the most of simplicity. In P. C. Nystrom and W. H. Starbuck (eds.), *Handbook of Organizational Design.* Oxford and New York: Oxford University Press. 385–408.

Alkhafaji, A. F. 1989. *A Stakeholder Approach to Corporate Governance: Managing in a Dynamic Environment.* Westport, CT: Quorum Books.

Allen, D. 2003. All for one and one for all. *Financial Management* July/August: 12.

Allen, F., Carletti, E. and Marquez, R. 2007. Stakeholder capitalism, corporate governance and firm value. European Corporate Governance Institute (ECGI) Finance Working Paper no. 190/2007. Knowledge@wharton Working Paper. http://knowledge.wharton.upenn.edu/papers/1344.pdf (accessed Feb. 2, 2009).

Allison, G. 1971. *Essence of Decision: Explaining the Cuban Missile Crisis.* Boston: Little, Brown.

Allison, G. and Zelikow, P. 1999. *The Essence of Decision.* 2nd edn. New York: Longman.

Al-Mudimigh, A. S., Zairi, M. and Ahmed, A. M. M. 2004. Extending the concept of supply chain: The effective management of value chains. *International Journal of Production Research* 87 (3): 309–321.

Alvarez-Gil, J., Berrone, P., Husillos, F. J. and Lado, N. 2007. Reverse logistics, stakeholders' influence, organizational slack, and managers' posture. *Journal of Business Research* 60: 463–473.

Ambler, T. and Wilson, A. 1995. Problems of stakeholder theory. *Business Ethics: A European Review*, 4 (1): 30–5.

American Bar Association, Committee on Corporate Laws. 1990. Other Constituencies Statutes: Potential for Confusion. *Business Law* 45: 2253.

Andreadis, N. A. 2002. Leadership for civil society: Implications for global corporate leadership development. *Human Resource Development International* 5 (2): 143–149.

Andrews, K. 1980. *The Concept of Corporate Strategy.* 3rd edn. Homewood, IL: R. D. Irwin.

Andriof, J., Waddock, S., Husted, B. and Rahman, S. S. (eds.). 2002. *Unfolding Stakeholder Thinking. 1: Theory, Responsibility and Engagement.* Sheffield: Greenleaf Publishing.

Ansoff, H. I. 1965. *Corporate Strategy: An Analytic Approach to Business for Growth and Expansion.* New York: McGraw-Hill.

1979. The changing shape of the strategic problem. *Journal of General Management* 4 (4): 42–58.

1991. Critique of Henry Mintzberg's "The design school: reconsidering the basic premises of strategic management." *Strategic Management Journal* 12: 449–461.

Argandoña, A. 1998. The stakeholder theory and the common good. *Journal of Business Ethics* 17 (9): 1093–1102.

Argenti, J. 1993. *Your Organization: What Is It for?* New York: McGraw-Hill.

1997. Stakeholders: The case against. *Long Range Planning* 30 (3): 442–445.

Armstrong, J. S. 1982. The value of formal planning for strategic decisions: Review of empirical research. *Strategic Management Journal* 3 (3): 197–211.

Arnold, S. J. and Luthra, M. N. 2000. Market entry effects of large format retailers: A stakeholder analysis. *International Journal of Retail and Distribution Management* 28 (4/5): 139–154.

Arora, A. and Alam, P. 2005. CEO compensation and stakeholders' claims. *Contemporary Accounting Research* 22 (3): 519–547.

Arora, B. and Puranik, R. 2004. A review of corporate social responsibility in India. *Development* 47 (3): 93–100.

Ashbaugh, H. and Warfield, T. D. 2003. Audits as a corporate governance mechanism: Evidence from the German market. *Journal of International Accounting Research* 2: 1–21.

Astley, W. G. 1984. Toward an appreciation of collective strategy. *Academy of Management Review* 9 (3): 526–535.

1985. Administrative science as socially constructed truth. *Administrative Science Quarterly* 30 (4): 497–513.

Atkinson, A. A., Waterhouse, J. H. and Wells, R. B. 1997. A stakeholder approach to strategic performance measurement. *MIT Sloan Management Review* 38 (3): 25–37.

Aupperle, K. E., Carroll, A. B. and Hatfield, J. D. 1985. An empirical examination of the relationship between corporate social responsibility and profitability. *Academy of Management Journal* 28 (2): 446–463.

Austin, J., Stevenson, H. and Wei-Skillern, J. 2006. Social and commercial entrepreneurship: Same, different, or both? *Entrepreneurship Theory and Practice* 30 (1): 1–22.

Austin, J. L. 1962. *How to Do Things with Words*. Oxford: Clarendon Press.

Baele, L., De Jonge, O. and Vander Vennet, R. 2007. Does the stock market value bank diversification? *Journal of Banking and Finance* 31 (7): 1999–2023.

Bainbridge, S. M. 1993. Independent directors and the ALI corporate governance project. *George Washington Law Review* 61: 1034–1083.

Baker, C. R. and Owsen, D. M. 2002. Increasing the role of auditing in corporate governance. *Critical Perspectives on Accounting* 13 (5/6): 783–796.

Ball, R., Kothari, S. P. and Robin, A. 2000. The effect of international institutional factors on properties of accounting. *Journal of Accounting and Economics* 29 (1): 1–51.

Balmer, J. M. T. 2008. Identity-based views of the corporation: Insights from corporate identity, organisational identity, social identity, visual identity, corporate brand identity and corporate image. *European Journal of Marketing* 42 (9/10): 879–906.

Bamonte, T. 1995. The meaning of the "corporate constituency" provision of the Illinois Business Corporation Act. *Loyola University Chicago Law Journal* 27: 1–25.

Bansal, P. 2005. Evolving sustainability: A longitudinal study of corporate sustainable development. *Strategic Management Journal* 26 (3): 197–218.

Barnard, C. I. 1938. *Functions of the Executive*. Cambridge, MA: Harvard University Press.

Barnett, A. 1997. Towards a stakeholder democracy. In G. Kelly, D. Kelly, and A. Gamble (eds.), *Stakeholder Capitalism*. London: Macmillan. 82–95.

Barnett, M. L. 2007. Stakeholder influence capacity and the variability of financial returns to corporate social performance. *Academy of Management Review* 32 (3): 794–816.

Barney, J. B. 1986. Types of competition and the theory of strategy: Toward an integrative framework. *Academy of Management Review* 11 (4): 791–800.

1991. Firm resources and sustained competitive advantage. *Journal of Management* 17 (1): 99–120.

Barney, J. B. and Arikan, A. M. 2001. The resource-based view: Origins and implications. In M. A. Hitt, R. E. Freeman, and J. S. Harrison (eds.), *Handbook of Strategic Management*. Oxford: Blackwell. 124–188.

Barney, J. B. and Ouchi, W. G. 1986. *Organizational Economics*. San Francisco, CA: Jossey-Bass.

Baron, D. P. 1995. The nonmarket strategy system. *Sloan Management Review* 37 (1): 73–85.

Barringer, B. R. and Harrison, J. S. 2000. Walking a tightrope: Creating value through interorganizational relationships. *Journal of Management* 26 (3): 367–404.

Barton, S. L., Hill, N. C. and Sundaram, S. 1989. An empirical test of stakeholder theory predictions of capital structure. *Financial Management* 18 (1): 36–44.

Bartov, E., Goldberg, S. R. and Kim, M. 2005. Comparative value relevance among German, US and international accounting standards: A German stock market perspective. *Journal of Accounting, Auditing and Finance* 20 (2): 95–119.

Baskerville-Morley, R. F. 2004. Dangerous, dominant, dependent, or definitive: Stakeholder identification when the profession faces major transgressions. *Accounting and the Public Interest* 4: 24–42.

Baucus, M. S. 1995. Halo-adusted residuals: Prolonging the life of a terminally ill measure of corporate social performance. *Business and Society* 34 (2): 227–235.

Bauer, R. A. and Fenn, D. H., Jr., 1972. *The Corporate Social Audit.* New York: Russell Sage Foundation.

Baum, J. A. C. and Oliver, C. 1991. Institutional linkages and organizational mortality. *Administrative Science Quarterly* 36 (2): 187–218.

Baumhart, R. 1968. *An Honest Profit – What Businessmen Say about Ethics in Business.* New York: Holt, Rinehart & Winston.

Baumol, W. J. 1990. Entrepreneurship: productive, unproductive, and destructive. *Journal of Political Economy* 98 (5): 893–921.

1994. *Entrepreneurship, Management, and the Structure of Payoffs.* Boston: MIT Press.

Baysinger, B. D. and Butler, H. 1985. Corporate governance and the board of directors: performance effects of changes in board composition. *Journal of Law, Economics and Organization* 1 (1): 101–134.

Beasley, M. S., Chen, A., Nunez, K. and Wright, L. 2006. Working hand in hand: Balanced scorecards and enterprise risk management. *Strategic Finance* 87 (9): 49–55.

Beasley, M. S. and Frigo, M. L. 2007. Strategic risk management: Creating and protecting value. *Strategic Finance*, 88 (11): 25–53.

Beer, M., Spector, B., Lawrence, P., Quinn Mills, D. and Walton, R. 1984. *Managing Human Assets.* New York: Free Press.

Berle, A. A., Jr. 1954. *The Twentieth Century Capitalist Revolution.* New York: Harcourt, Brace.

Berle, A. A., Jr., and G. C. Means. 1932. *The Modern Corporation and Private Property.* New York: Macmillan.

Berman, S. L., Wicks, A. C., Kotha, S. and Jones, T. M. 1999. Does stakeholder orientation matter? The relationship between stakeholder management models and firm financial performance. *Academy of Management Journal* 42 (5): 488–506.

Beutler, L. 2005. Involving stakeholders in irrigation and drainage district decisions: Who, what, when, where, why, how? *California Water Plan Update* 4: 1095–1105.

Bhattacharya, C. B. and Korschun, D. 2008. Stakeholder marketing: Beyond the four Ps and the customer. *Journal of Public Policy and Marketing* 27 (1): 113–116.

Bhimani, A. and Soonawalla, K. 2005. From conformance to performance: The corporate responsibilities continuum. *Journal of Accounting and Public Policy* 24 (3): 165–174.

Biancalana, J. 1990. Defining the proper corporate constituency: Asking the wrong question. *University of Cincinnati Law Review* 59: 425, 429–30.

Biehl, M., Kim, H. and Wade, M. 2006. Relationships among the academic disciplines: A multi-method citation analysis. *Omega* 34 (4): 359–371.

Binmore, K. 1991. *Fun and Games: A Text on Game Theory.* Lexington, MA: D. C. Heath.

1994. *Game Theory and the Social Contract.* Cambridge, MA: MIT Press.

1997. Rationality and Backward Induction, *Journal of Economic Methodology* 4: 23–41.

Bishop, John Douglas (ed.). 2000. *Ethics and Capitalism*. Toronto: University of Toronto Press.

Blair, J. and Buesseler, J. 1998. Competitive forces in the medical group industry: A stakeholder perspective. *Health Care Management Review* 23 (2): 7–27.

Blair, J. and Fottler, M. 1990. *Challenges In Health Care Management: Strategic Perspectives for Managing Key Stakeholders*. San Francisco, CA: Jossey-Bass.

Blair, J., Fottler, M. and Whitehead, C. 1996. Diagnosing the stakeholder bottom line for medical group practices: Key stakeholders' potential to threaten and/or cooperate. *Medical Group Management Journal* 43 (2): 40, 42–8, 50–1.

Blair, J., Rock, T., Rotarius, T., Fottler, M., Bosse, G. and Driskill, J. 1996. The problematic fit of diagnosis and strategy for medical group stakeholders – including IDS/Ns. *Health Care Management Review* 21 (1): 7–28.

Blair, J., Savage, G. and Whitehead, C. 1989. A strategic approach for negotiating with hospital stakeholders. *Health Care Management Review* 14 (1): 13–23.

Blair, J. and Whitehead, C. 1988. Too many on the seesaw: Stakeholder diagnosis and management for hospitals. *Hospital and Health Services Administration* 33 (2): 153–166.

Blair, M. 1995. Whose interests should be served?" In M. Clarkson (ed.), *Ownership and Control: Rethinking Corporate Governance for the Twenty First Century*. Washington, DC: The Brookings Institution. 202–234.

Blair, M. M. 1998. For whom should corporations be run? An economic rationale for stakeholder management. *Long Range Planning* 31 (2): 195–200.

Blair, M. M. and Stout, L. 1999. A team production theory of corporate law. *Virginia Law Review* 85 (2): 248–328.

Blodgett, J. G., Long-Chuan, L., Rose, G. M. and Vitell, S. J. 2001. Ethical sensitivity to stakeholder interests: A cross-cultural comparison. *Journal of the Academy of Marketing Science* 29 (2): 190–202.

Boatright, J. R. 1994. Fiduciary duties and the shareholder-management relation: Or, what's so special about shareholders? *Business Ethics Quarterly* 4 (4): 393–407.

2000. *Ethics and the Conduct of Business*. 3rd edn. Upper Saddle River, NJ: Prentice-Hall.

2002. Contractors as stakeholders: Reconciling stakeholder theory with the nexus-of-contracts firm. *Journal of Banking and Finance* 26 (9): 1837–1852.

Boesso, G. and Kumar, K. 2007. Drivers of corporate voluntary disclosure. *Accounting, Auditing and Accountability Journal* 20 (2): 269–296.

Bosse, D. A., Phillips, R. A. and Harrison, J. S. 2009. Stakeholders, reciprocity and firm performance. *Strategic Management Journal* 30 (4): 447–456.

Bourgeois, L. J. III. 1984. Strategic management and determinism. *Academy of Management Review* 9 (4): 586–596.

Boutilier, R. G. 2007. Social capital in firm-stakeholder networks. *Journal of Corporate Citizenship* 26: 121–134.

Bowen, H. 1953. *Social Responsibilities of the Businessman*. New York: Harper & Row.

Bowen, R. M., Johnson, M. F., Shevlin, T. and Shores, D. 1992. Determinants of the timing of quarterly earnings announcement. *Journal of Accounting, Auditing and Finance* 7 (4): 395–422.

Bowie, N. E. 1998. A Kantian theory of capitalism. *Business Ethics Quarterly*. The Ruffin Series, Special Issue 1: 37–60. Charlottesville, VA: Philosophy Documentation Center.

1999. *Business Ethics: A Kantian Perspective*. Oxford: Blackwell.

Bradley, N. 2003. How to measure and analyze corporate governance. *International Financial Law Review*, special issue on corporate governance: 40–47. www.iflr.com/Article.aspx?ArticleID=2026778 (accessed Feb. 4, 2009).

Braudel, Fernand. 1982. *Civilization and Capitalism: 15th–18th Century*, Vol. 2, *The Wheels of Commerce*. New York: Harper & Row.

Brenner, S. N. 1993. The stakeholder theory of the firm and organizational decision making: Some propositions and a model. In J. Pasquero and D. Collins (eds.), *Proceedings of the Fourth Annual Meeting of the International Association for Business and Society*. San Diego. 205–210.

1995. Stakeholder theory of the firm: Its consistency with current management techniques. In J. Näsi (ed.), *Understanding Stakeholder Thinking*. Helsinki: LSR-Julkaisut Oy. 75–96.

Broehl, W. G. 1999. *Tuck and Tucker: The origin of the Graduate Business School*. Hanover: University Press of New England.

Brown, B. and Perry, S. 1995. Halo-removed residuals of Fortune's "Responsibility to the community and environment": A decade of data. *Business and Society* 34 (2): 199–215.

Brugha, R. and Varvasovszky, Z. 2000. Stakeholder analysis: A review. *Health Policy and Planning* 15 (3): 239–246.

Bryson, J. 2004. What to do when stakeholders matter. *Public Management Review* 6 (1): 21–53.

Bryson, J., Cunningham, G. and Lokkesmoe, K. 2002. What to do when stakeholders matter: The case of problem formulation for the African American Men Project of Hannepin County Minnesota. *Public Administration Review* 62 (5): 568–584.

Bryson, J., Freeman, R. E. and Roering, W. 1986. Strategic planning in the public sector: Approaches and future directions. In B. Checkoway (ed.), *Strategic Perspectives on Planning Practice*. Boston: Lexington Books. 65–85.

Bryson, N. and Mobolurin, A. 1996. An action learning evaluation procedure for multiple criteria decision making problems. *European Journal of Operational Research* 96 (2): 379–386.

Buchanan, J. M. and Tullock, G. 1965. *The Calculus of Consent: Logical Foundations of Constitutional Democracy*. Ann Arbor, MI: University of Michigan Press.

Buchheit, S., Collins, D. and Reitenga, A. 2002. A cross-discipline comparison of top-tier academic journal publication rates: 1997–1999. *Journal of Accounting Education* 20 (2): 123–130.

Buchholz, R. A. 1989. *Fundamental Concepts and Problems in Business Ethics*. Englewood Cliffs, NJ: Prentice-Hall.

Buchholz, R. A. and Rosenthal, S. B. 2000. *Rethinking Business Ethics: A Pragmatic Approach*. New York: Oxford University Press.

Burgstahler, D. and Dichev, I. 1997. Earnings management to avoid earnings decreases and losses. *Journal of Accounting and Economics* 24 (1): 99–126.

Burke, M. J., Borucki, C. C. and Hurley, A. E. 1992. Reconceptualizing psychological climate in a retail service environment: A multiple-stakeholder perspective. *Journal of Applied Psychology* 77 (5): 717–729.

Burton, B. K. and Dunn, C. P. 1996. Collaborative control and the commons: Safeguarding employee rights. *Business Ethics Quarterly* 6 (3): 277–288.

Burton, R. M. and Naylor, T. H. 1980. Economic theory in corporate planning. *Strategic Management Journal* 1 (3): 249–262.

Buysse, K. and Verbeke, A. 2003. Proactive environmental strategies: A stakeholder perspective. *Strategic Management Journal* 24 (5): 453–470.

Byrne, M. R. and Polonsky, M. J. 2001. Impediments to consumer adoption of sustainable transportation alternative fuel vehicles. *International Journal of Operations and Production Management* 21 (12): 1521–1538.

Cadbury, A. 1992. *Report of the Committee on the Financial Aspects of Corporate Governance*. London: The Committee on the Financial Aspects of Corporate Governance and Gee and Co. Ltd./Burgess Science Press.

Calton, J. M. 1991. The dark side of commitment: Is the literature on organizational commitment an ideological black hole? In K. Paul (ed.), *Contemporary Issues in Business Ethics and Politics*. Lewiston, NY: Edwin Mellen Press. 69–99.

Calton, J. M. and Kurland, N. B. 1995. A theory of stakeholder enabling: Giving voice to an emerging postmodern praxis of organisational discourse. In D. M. Boje, R. P. Gephart, and T. J. Thatchenkery (eds.), *Postmodern Management and Organization Theory*. London: Sage. 154–177.

Calton, J. M. and Lad, L. J. 1995. Social contracting as a trust-building process: Of network governance. *Business Ethics Quarterly* 5 (2): 271–295.

Cameron, K. 1980. Critical questions in assessing organizational effectiveness. *Organizational Dynamics* 9 (2): 66–80.

1984. Effectiveness as paradox: Consensus and conflict in conceptions of organizational effectiveness. *Management Science* 32 (5): 539–553.

Campbell, A. 1997. Stakeholders: The case in favour. *Long Range Planning* 30 (3): 446–449.

Campbell, A. and Yeung, S. 1991. Brief case: Mission, vision and strategic intent. *Long Range Planning* 24 (4): 145–147.

Campbell, D., Moore, G. and Shrives, P. 2006. Cross-sectional effects in community disclosure. *Accounting, Auditing and Accountability Journal* 19 (1): 96–114.

Campbell, J. L. 2007. Why would corporations behave in socially responsible ways? An institutional theory of corporate social responsibility. *Academy of Management Review* 32 (3): 946–967.

Carey, J. M., Beilin, R., Boxshall, A., Burgman, M. A. and Flander, L. 2007. Risk-based approaches to deal with uncertainty in a data-poor system: Stakeholder involvement in hazard identification for marine national parks and marine sanctuaries in Victoria, Australia. *Risk Analysis: An International Journal* 27 (1): 271–281.

Carrigan, M. 1995. Positive and negative aspects of the social marketing concept: Stakeholder conflicts for the tobacco industry. *Journal of Marketing Management* 11 (5): 469–485.

Carroll, A. B. (ed.). 1977. *Managing Corporate Social Responsibility*. Boston: Little, Brown.

1979. A three-dimensional conceptual model of corporate social performance. *Academy of Management Review* 16 (4): 497–505.

1991. The pyramid of corporate social responsibility: Toward the moral management of organizational stakeholders. *Business Horizons* 34 (4): 39–48.

1993. *Business and Society: Ethics and Stakeholder Management*. 2nd edn. Cincinnati, OH: South-Western Publishing.

1999. Corporate social responsibility: Evolution of a definitional construct. *Business and Society* 38 (3): 268–295.

2003. The four faces of corporate citizenship. *Business and Society Review* 100 (101): 1–7.

2006. Corporate social responsibility: A historical perspective. In M. Epstein and K. Hanson (eds.), *The Accountable Corporation*, Vol. 3. Westport, CT: Praeger Publishers. 3–30.

Carroll, A. B. and Hoy, F. 1984. Integrating corporate social policy into strategic management. *Journal of Business Strategy* 4 (3): 48–57.

Carroll, A. B. and Näsi, J. 1997. Understanding stakeholder thinking: Themes from a Finnish conference. *Business Ethics* 6 (1): 46–51.

Carroll, D. S. A. 1983. Managing relations with government and society: The business perspective. *Long Range Planning* 16 (2): 10–14.

Carson, T. L. 1993. Does the stakeholder theory constitute a new kind of theory of social responsibility? *Business Ethics Quarterly* 3 (2): 171–176.

Carter, S. M. 2006. The interaction of top management group, stakeholder, and situational factors on certain corporate reputation management activities. *Journal of Management Studies* 43 (5): 1145–1176.

Caux Round Table. 2009. Principles for Responsible Business. www.cauxroundtable.org/index.cfm?&menuid=8.

Chakravarthy, B. S. 1986. Measuring strategic performance. *Strategic Management Journal* 7 (5): 437–458.

Chandler, A. D. 1962. *Strategy and Structure: Chapters in the History of the American Industrial Enterprise*. Cambridge, MA: MIT Press.

Chang, Y.-H., Yeh, C.-H. and Wang, S.-Y. 2007. A survey of optimization-based evaluation of development strategies for the air cargo industry. *International Journal of Production Economics* 106 (2): 550–562.

Chapple, W. and Moon, J. 2005. Corporate social responsibility in Asia. *Business and Society* 44 (4): 415–441.

Charan, R. and Freeman, R. E. 1980. Planning for the business environment of the 1980s. *Journal of Business Strategy* 1 (2): 9–19.

Chatterjee, C. and Bergh, D. D. 2003. Failed takeover attempts, corporate governance and refocusing. *Strategic Management Journal* 24 (1): 87–100.

Chatterjee, C. and Harrison, J. S. 2001. Corporate governance. In M. A. Hitt, R. E. Freeman, and J. S. Harrison (eds.), *Handbook of Strategic Management*. Oxford: Blackwell. 543–563.

Chemla, G. 2005. Hold-up, stakeholders and takeover threats. *Journal of Financial Intermediation* 14 (3): 376–397.

Chen, L., Carson, E. and Simnett, R. 2007. Impact of stakeholder characteristics on voluntary dissemination of interim information and communication of its level of assurance. *Accounting and Finance* 47 (4): 667–691.

Chen, Y. C. K. and Sackett, P. J. 2007. Return merchandize authorization stakeholders and customer requirements management – high-technology products. *International Journal of Production Research* 45 (7): 1595–1608.

Child, J. W. and Marcoux, A. M. 1999. Freeman and Evan: Stakeholder theory and the original position. *Business Ethics Quarterly* 9 (2): 207–224.

Chinyio, E. A. and Akintoye, A. 2008. Practical approaches for engaging stakeholders: Findings from the UK. *Construction Management and Economics* 26 (6): 591–599.

Chou, T.-Y., Chou, S.-C. T. and Tzeng, G.-H. 2006. Evaluating IT/IS investments: A fuzzy multi-criteria decision model approach. *European Journal of Operational Research* 173 (3): 1026–1046.

Christensen, R., Andrews, K. and Bower, J. 1980. *Business Policy: Text and Cases*. Homewood, IL: R. D. Irwin.

Christopher, M., Payne, A. and Ballantyne, D. 1991. *Relationship Marketing: Bringing Quality, Customer Service and Marketing Together*. Oxford: Butterworth-Heinemann.

2002. *Relationship Marketing: Creating Stakeholder Value*. 2nd edn. Oxford: Butterworth-Heinemann.

Chung, W., Chen, H. and Reid, E. 2009. Business stakeholder analyzer: An experiment of classifying stakeholders on the Web. *Journal of the American Society for Information Science and Technology* 60 (1): 59–74.

Churchman, C. W. 1968. *The Systems Approach*. New York: Delacorte Press.

1971. *The Design of Inquiring Systems: Basic Concepts of Systems and Organizations*. New York: Basic Books.

Churchman, C. W., Ackoff, R. L. and Wax, M. (eds.). 1947. *Measurement of Consumer Interest*. Philadelphia: University of Pennsylvania Press.

Clark, R. 1986. *Corporate Law*. Boston: Little, Brown.

Clarke, L. L. and Lyons, E. C. 2007. The corporate common good: The right and obligation of managers to do good to others. *University of Daytona Law Review* 32: 273–299.

Clarke, T. 1998. The stakeholder corporation: A business philosophy for the information age. *Long Range Planning* 31(2): 182–194.

Clarkson, M. B. E. 1988. Corporate social performance in Canada, 1976–86. In L. E. Preston (ed.), *Research in Corporate Social Performance and Policy*, Vol. 12. Greenwich, CT: TM Press. 331–358.

1991. Defining, evaluating and managing corporate social performance: A stakeholder management model. In J. E. Post (ed.), *Research in Corporate Social Performance and Policy*, Vol. 12. Greenwich, CT: JAI Press. 331–358.

1994. *A Risk-Based Model of Stakeholder Theory*. Toronto: Centre for Corporate Social Performance and Ethics.

1995. A stakeholder framework for analyzing and evaluating corporate social performance. *Academy of Management Review* 20 (1): 92–117.

1998. *The Corporation and Its Stakeholders: Classic and Contemporary Readings*. Toronto: University of Toronto Press.

Clarkson Centre for Business Ethics. 1999. *Principles of Stakeholder Management*. Toronto: University of Toronto. (Reproduced in 2002, *Business Ethics Quarterly*, 12 (1): 256–264.)

Clegg, S. R., Pitsis, T. S., Rura-Polley, T. and Marosszeky, M. 2002. Governmentality matters: Designing an alliance culture of inter-organizational collaboration for managing projects. *Organization Studies* 23 (3): 317–337.

Cleland, D. I. and Ireland, L. R. 2002. *Project Management: Strategic Design and Implementation*. New York: McGraw-Hill.

Clement, R. W. 2005. The lessons from stakeholder theory for US business leaders. *Business Horizons* 48 (3): 255–264.

Cloninger, D. O. 1995. Managerial goals and ethical behavior. *Financial Practice and Education* 5 (1): 50–59.

1997. Share price maximization, asymmetric information and ethical behavior: A comment. *Financial Practice and Education* 7 (2): 82–84.

Clulow, V. 2005. Futures dilemmas for marketers: Can stakeholder analysis add value? *European Journal of Marketing* 39 (9/10): 978–997.

Coase, R. H. 1937. The nature of the firm. *Economica* 4 (16): 386–405.

Cochran, P. L. and Wood, R. A. 1984. Corporate social responsibility and financial performance. *Academy of Management Journal* 27 (1): 42–56.

Coff, R. W. 1999. When competitive advantage doesn't lead to performance: The resource-based view and stakeholder bargaining power. *Organization Science* 10 (2): 119–133.

Coffee, J. 1988. The uncertain case for takeover reform: An essay on stockholders, stakeholders, and bust-ups. *Wisconsin Law Review* 435–465.

Colakoglu, S., Lepak, D. P. and Hong, Y. 2006. Measuring HRM effectiveness: Considering multiple stakeholders in a global context. *Human Resource Management Review* 15: 209–218.

Collier, P. M. 2008. Stakeholder accountability. *Accounting, Auditing and Accountability Journal* 21: 933–954.

Collins, J. and Porras, J. I. 1997. *Built to Last: Successful Habits of Visionary Companies.* New York: HarperCollins.

Coman, A. and Ronen, B. 1995. Information technology in operations management: A theory-of-constraints approach. *International Journal of Production Research* 33 (5): 1403–1415.

Connolly, T., Conlon, E. J. and Deutsch, S. J. 1980. Organizational effectiveness: A multiple-constituency approach. *Academy of Management Review* 5 (2): 211–217.

Conway, T. and Whitelock, J. 2007. Relationship marketing in the subsidised arts: The key to a strategic marketing focus? *European Journal of Marketing* 41 (1/2): 199–213.

Coombs, J. E. and Gilley, K. M. 2005. Stakeholder management as a predictor of CEO compensation: Main effects and interactions with financial performance. *Strategic Management Journal* 26 (9): 827–840.

Copulsky, W. 1991. Balancing the needs of customers and shareholders. *Journal of Business Strategy* 12 (6): 44–47.

Córdoba, J.-R. and Midgley, G. 2006. Broadening the boundaries: An application of critical systems thinking to IS planning in Colombia. *Journal of the Operational Research Society* 57 (9): 1064–1080.

Cornell, B. and Shapiro, A. C. 1987. Corporate stakeholders and corporate finance. *Financial Management* 16 (1): 5–14.

Covey, S. M. R. and Merrill, R. R. 2006. *The Speed of Trust: The One Thing that Changes Everything.* New York: Free Press.

Cragg, W. 2002. Business ethics and stakeholder theory. *Business Ethics Quarterly* 12 (2): 113–142.

Crane, A. 1998. Exploring green alliances. *Journal of Marketing Management* 14 (6): 559–579.

Cummings, J. F. 2001. Engaging stakeholders in corporate accountability programmes: A cross-sectoral analysis of UK and transnational experience. *Business Ethics: A European Review* 10 (1): 45–52.

Cyert, R. M. and March, J. G. 1963. *A Behavioral Theory of the Firm.* Englewood Cliffs, NJ: Prentice-Hall.

Daft, R. L. 1992. *Organization Theory and Design.* 4th edn. St. Paul, MN: West Publishing.

Daft, R. L. and Marcic, D. 2001. *Understanding Management.* Fort Worth: Southwestern Publishing.

Daily, C. M. 1995. CEO and director turnover in failing firms: an illusion of change? *Strategic Management Journal* 16 (5): 393–400.

1996. Governance patterns in bankruptcy reorganizations. *Strategic Management Journal* 17 (5): 355–375.

Daily, C. M. and Dalton, D. R. 1994. Corporate governance and the bankrupt firm: An empirical assessment. *Strategic Management Journal* 15 (8): 643–654.

Dalton, D. R., Daily, C. M., Ellstrand, A. E. and Johnson, J. L. 1998. Meta-analytic reviews of board composition, leadership structure, and financial performance. *Strategic Management Journal* 19 (3): 269.

Davis, J. J. 1992. Ethics and environmental marketing. *Journal of Business Ethics* 11 (2): 81–87.

Davis, K. 1960. Can business afford to ignore social responsibilities? *California Management Review* 2 (3): 70–76.

1967. Understanding the social responsibility puzzle: What does the businessman owe to society? *Business Horizons* 10 (4): 45–50.

1973. The case for and against business assumption of social responsibilities. *Academy of Management Journal* 16 (2): 312–322.

Davis, P. and Freeman, R. E. 1978. Technology assessment and idealized design: An application to telecommunications. In Elton, M. C. J., Lucas, W. A. and Conrath, D. W. (eds.), *Evaluating New Telecommunications Services*. New York: Plenum Press. 325–344.

Deakin, S. and Slinger, G. 1997. Hostile takeovers, corporate law, and the theory of the firm. *Journal of Law and Society* 24 (1): 124–51.

De Lopez, T. 2001. Stakeholder management for conservation projects: A case study of Ream National Park, Cambodia. *Environmental Management* 28 (1): 47–60.

Demise, N., 2005. Business ethics and corporate governance in Japan. *Business and Society* 44 (2): 211–217.

2006. CSR in Japan: A historical perspective. www.ctwcongress.de/ifsam/download/track_19/pap00478.pdf (accessed Jan. 30, 2009).

den Hengst, M., de Vreed, G-J. and Maghnouji, R. 2007. Using soft OR principles for collaborative simulation: A case study in the Dutch airline industry. *Journal of the Operational Research Society* 58 (5): 669–682.

Denis, D. J., Denis D. K. and Sarin, A. 1997. Agency problems, equity ownership, and corporate diversification. *Journal of Finance* 52 (1): 135–160.

Dennett, D. 1995. *Darwin's Dangerous Idea: Evolution and the Meanings of Life*. New York: Simon & Schuster.

Derkinderen, F. G. J. and Crum, R. L. 1979. *Projects Set Strategies*. Boston: Martinus Nijhoff.

Dermer, J. 1990. The strategic agenda: Accounting for issues and support. *Accounting, Organizations and Society* 15 (1/2): 67–76.

Dewey, J. 1927. *The Public and Its Problems*. New York: Ohio University Press Books.

Dey, P. K., Hariharan, S. and Clegg, B. T. 2006. Measuring the operational performance of intensive care units using the analytic hierarchy process approach. *International Journal of Operations and Production Management* 26 (8): 849–865.

Dienhart, J. 2008. The separation thesis: Perhaps nine lives are enough. *Business Ethics Quarterly* 18 (4): 555–559.

Dierickx, I. and Cool, K. 1989. Asset stock accumulation and sustainability of competitive advantage. *Management Science* 35 (12): 1504–1511.

Dill, W. R. 1958. Environment as an influence on managerial autonomy. *Administrative Science Quarterly* 2 (4): 409–443.

1975. Public participation in corporate-planning: Strategic management in a kibitzer's world. *Long Range Planning* 8 (1): 57–63.

DiMaggio, P. and Powell, W. 1983. The iron cage revisited: Institutional isomorphism and collective rationality in organizational fields. *American Sociological Review* 48 (2): 147–160.

Dimovski, B. and Brooks, R. 2004. Stakeholder representation on the boards of Australian initial public offerings. *Applied Financial Economics* 14 (17): 1233–1238.

Dipboye, R. L. 2007. Eight outrageous statements about HR science. *Human Resource Management Review* 17 (2): 96–106.

Dodd, E. M., Jr. 1932. For whom are corporate managers trustees? *Harvard Law Review* 45 (7): 1145–1163.

Donaldson, T. 1999. Response: Making stakeholder theory whole, *Academy of Management Review* 24 (2): 237–241.

Donaldson, T. and Dunfee, T. W. 1994. Towards a unified conception of business ethics: Integrative social contracts. *Academy of Management Review* 19 (2): 252–284.

1999. *Ties that Bind: A Social Contracts Approach to Business Ethics.* Boston: Harvard Business School Press.

Donaldson, T. and Preston, L. E. 1995. The stakeholder theory of the corporation: Concepts, evidence, and implications. *Academy of Management Review* 20 (1): 65–91.

Donaldson, T. J. and Freeman, R. E. (eds.). 1994. *Business as a Humanity.* New York: Oxford University Press.

Dray, W. H. 1964. *Philosophy of History.* Englewood Cliffs, NJ: Prentice-Hall.

Drisco, C. and Stank, M. 2004. The primordial stakeholder: Advancing the conceptual consideration of stakeholder status for the natural environment. *Journal of Business Ethics* 49 (1): 55–74.

Drucker, P. 1980. *Managing in Turbulent Times.* New York: Harper & Row.

Duncan, T. and Moriarty, S. E. 1998. A communication-based marketing model for managing relationships. *Journal of Marketing* 62 (2): 1–13.

Dunham, L., Freeman, R. E. and Liedtka, J. 2006. Enhancing stakeholder practice: A particularized exploration of community. *Business Ethics Quarterly* 16 (1): 23–42.

Dyer, J. H. and Hatch, N. W. 2004. Using supplier networks to learn faster. *MIT Sloan Management Review* 45 (3): 57–63.

Dyer, J. H. and Nobeoka, K. 2000. Creating and managing a high-performance knowledge-sharing network: The Toyota case. *Strategic Management Journal* 21 (3): 345–367.

Dyer, J. H. and Singh, H. 1998. The relational view: Cooperative strategy and sources of inter-organizational competitive advantage. *Academy of Management Review* 23 (4): 660–679.

Dymond, S., Nix, T., Rotarius, T. and Savage, G. 1995. Why do key integrated delivery stakeholders really matter? Assessing control, coalitions, resources and power. *Medical Group Management Journal* 42 (6): 27–38.

Edmunds, D. and Wollenberg, E. 2001. A strategic approach to multistakeholder negotiations. *Development and Change* 32 (2): 231–253.

Elias, A. A., Cavana, R. Y. and Jackson, L. S. 2002. Stakeholder analysis for R&D project management. *R&D Management* 32 (4): 301–320.

Elkington, J. 1994. Towards the sustainable corporation: Win-win-win business strategies for sustainable development. *California Management Review* 36 (2): 90–100.
1997. *Cannibals with Forks: The Triple Bottom Line of 21st Century Business*. Oxford: Capstone Publishing.
Elms, H., Berman, S. and Wicks, A. 2002. Ethics and incentives: An inductive development of stakeholder theory in the health care industry. *Business Ethics Quarterly* 12 (4): 413–432.
Ely, K. M. and Pownall, G. 2002. Shareholder- versus stakeholder-focused Japanese companies: Firm characteristics and accounting valuation. *Contemporary Accounting Research* 19 (4): 615–636.
Emanuel, E. 1999. Choice and representation in health care. *Medical Care Research and Review* 56 (1): 113–140.
Emery, F. E. and Trist, E. L. 1965. The causal texture of organizational environments. *Human Relations* 18 (1): 21–32.
Emshoff, J. and Freeman, R. E. 1981. Stakeholder management: A case study of the US brewers and the container issue. In R. Schultz (ed.), *Applications of Management Science*, Vol. 1. Greenwich, CT: JAI Press. 57–90.
Emshoff, J. R. 1980. *Managerial Breakthroughs*. New York: AMACOM.
Emshoff, J. R. and Finnel, A. 1979. Defining corporate strategy: A case study using strategic assumptions analysis. *Sloan Management Review* 20 (3): 41–52.
Enderle, G. 2006. Corporate responsibility in the CSR debate. In J. Wieland and G. Brenkert (eds.), *Unternehmensethik im Spannungsfeld der Kulturen und Religionen*. Stuttgart: Kohlhammer. 108–124.
Environmental Protection Agency (EPA). 1998. Stakeholder involvement: Action plan. www.epa.gov/publicinvolvement/siap1298.htm.
2005. *Handbook for Developing Watershed Plans to Restore and Protect Our Waters*. EPA 841-B-05-005. www.epa.gov/owow/nps/pubs.html.
Epstein, E. M. 1969. *The Corporation in American Politics*. Englewood Cliffs, NJ: Prentice-Hall.
1980. Business political activity: Research approaches and analytical issues. In L. E. Preston (ed.), *Research in Corporate Social Performance*, II. Greenwich, CT: JAI Press. 1–55.
1987. The corporate social policy process: Beyond business ethics, corporate social responsibility, and corporate social responsiveness. *California Management Review* 29 (3): 99–114.
Etzioni, A. 1964. *Modern Organizations*. Englewood Cliffs, NJ: Prentice-Hall.
1996. *The New Golden Rule. Community and Morality in a Democratic Society*. New York: Basic Books.
1998. A communitarian note on stakeholder theory. *Business Ethics Quarterly* 8 (4): 679–691.
Evan, W. M. 1966. The organization-set: Toward a theory of inter-organizational relations. In J. D. Thompson (ed.), *Approaches to Organizational Design*. Pittsburgh: University of Pittsburgh Press. 174–190.
Evan, W. M. and Freeman, R. E. 1993. A stakeholder theory of the modern corporation: Kantian capitalism. In T. L. Beauchamp and N. E. Bowie (eds.), *Ethical Theory and Business*. Englewood Cliffs, NJ: Prentice-Hall. 97–106.
Eyles, J., Brimacombe, M., Chaulk, P., Stoddart, G., Pranger, T. and Moase, O. 2001. What determines health? To where should we shift resources? Attitudes towards the determinants of health among multiple stakeholder groups in Prince Edward Island, Canada. *Social Science and Medicine* 53 (12): 1611–1619.

Fairfax, L. 2006. The rhetoric of corporate law: The impact of stakeholder rhetoric on corporate norms. *Journal of Corporate Law* 31 (3): 675–719.

Fama, E. F. 1970. Efficient capital markets: A review of theory and empirical work. *Journal of Finance* 25 (5): 383–417.

1980. Agency problems and the theory of the firm. *Journal of Political Economy* 88 (2): 288–307.

Fama, E. F. and Jensen, M. C. 1983. Separation of ownership and corporate control. *Journal of Law and Economics* 26 (2): 301–325.

Fassin, Y. 2008. Imperfections and shortcomings of the stakeholder model graphical representation. *Journal of Business Ethics* 80 (4): 879–888.

Ferguson, J., Collison, D., Power, D. and Stevenson, L. 2005. What are recommended accounting textbooks teaching students about corporate stakeholders? *British Accounting Review* 37 (1): 23–46.

2007. Exploring lecturers' perceptions of the emphasis given to different stakeholders in introductory accounting textbooks. *Accounting Forum* 31 (2): 113–127.

Ferraro, F., Pfeffer, J. and Sutton, R. I. 2005. Economics language and assumptions: How theories can become self-fulfilling. *Academy of Management Review* 30 (1): 8–24.

Ferrell, O. C. and Ferrell, L. 2008. A macromarketing ethics framework: Stakeholder orientation and distributive justice. *Journal of Macromarketing* 28 (1): 24–32.

Feyerabend, P. K. 1975. *Against Method: Outline of an Anarchistic Theory of Knowledge.* London: Humanities Press.

Fiedler, L. and Kirchgeorg, M. 2007. The role concept in corporate branding and stakeholder management reconsidered: Are stakeholder groups really different? *Corporate Reputation Review* 10 (3): 177–188.

Fineman, S. and Clark, K. 1996. Green stakeholders: Industry interpretations and response, *Journal of Management Studies* 33 (6): 715–30.

Firouzabadi, A. K., Henson, B. and Barnes, C. 2008. A multiple stakeholders' approach to strategic selection decisions. *Computers and Industrial Engineering* 54 (4): 851–865.

Fischer, E. and Reuber, R. 2007. The good, the bad and the unfamiliar: The challenges of reputation facing new firms. *Entrepreneurship Theory and Practice* 31 (1): 53–75.

Flak, L., Moe, C. and Sæbø, Ø. 2003. On the evolution of e-government: The user imperative. *Proceedings of the 2nd International Conference on e-Government.* Prague: 139–142.

Florida, R. and Goodnight, J. 2005. Managing for creativity. *Harvard Business Review* 83 (7/8): 124–131.

Fogarty, T. J. and Markarian, G. 2007. An empirical assessment of the rise and fall of accounting as an academic discipline. *Issues in Accounting Education* 22 (2): 137–161.

Fombrun, C. 2001. Corporate reputations as economic assets. In M. A. Hitt, R. E. Freeman, and J. S. Harrison (eds.), *Handbook of Strategic Management.* Oxford: Blackwell. 289–312.

Fombrun, C. and Astley, W. G. 1983. Beyond corporate strategy. *Journal of Business Strategy* 3 (4): 47–54.

Fombrun, C. and Shanley, M. 1990. What's in a name? Reputation building and corporate strategy. *Academy of Management Journal* 33 (2): 233–258.

Fort, T. 1997. The corporation as mediating institution: An efficacious synthesis of stakeholder theory and corporate constituency statutes. *Notre Dame Law Review* 73 (1): 173–203.

Fort, T. and Schipani, C. 2000. Corporate governance in a global environment: The search for the best of all worlds. *Vanderbilt Journal of Transnational Law* 33 (4): 829–876.

Foster, D. and Jonker, J. 2003. Third generation quality management: The role of stakeholders in integrating business into society. *Managerial Auditing Journal* 18 (4): 323–333.

Fottler, M. and Blair, J. 2002. Introduction: New concepts in health care stakeholder management theory and practice. *Health Care Management Review* 27 (2): 50–51.

Fottler, M. D., Blair, J. D., Whitehead, C. J., Laus, M. D. and Savage, G. T. 1989. Assessing key stakeholders: Who matters to hospitals and why? *Hospital and Health Services Administration* 34 (4): 525–547.

Frank, R. H. 1988. *Passions within Reason: The Strategic Role of Emotions.* New York: W. W. Norton.

Frank, R. H., Gilovich, T. and Regan, D. T. 1993. Does studying economics inhibit cooperation? *Journal of Economic Perspectives* 7: 159–171.

Frederick, W. C. 1978. From CSR1 to CSR2: The maturing of business and society thought. Working Paper no. 279, Graduate School of Business, University of Pittsburgh.

1986. Toward CSR3: Why ethical analysis is indispensable and unavoidable in corporate affairs. *California Management Review* 28 (2), 126–155.

1987. Theories of corporate social performance. In S. P. Sethi and C. M. Falbe (eds.), *Business and society: Dimensions of Conflict and Cooperation.* Lexington, MA: Lexington/D. C. Heath. 142–161

1994. From CSR1 to CSR2. *Business and Society* 33 (2): 150–165.

1998a. Creatures, corporations, communities, chaos, complexity: A naturological view of the corporate social role. *Business and Society* 37 (4): 358–389.

1998b. Moving to CSR4: What to pack for the trip. *Business and Society* 37 (1): 40–59.

2006. *Corporation Be Good! The Story of Corporate Social Responsibility.* Dog Ear Publishing Inc.

Frederick, W. C., Post, J. E. and Davis, K. 1988. *Business and Society: Corporate Strategy, Public Policy, Ethics.* 6th edn. New York: McGraw-Hill.

Frederiksen, H. D. and Mathiassen, L. 2005. Information-centric assessment of software metrics practices. *IEEE Transactions on Engineering Management* 52 (3): 350–362.

Freedman, M. and Stagliano, A. J. 1992. European unification, accounting harmonization and social disclosures. *International Journal of Accounting* 27 (2): 112–122.

Freeman, R. E. 1984. *Strategic Management: A Stakeholder Approach.* Boston: Pitman.

1994. The politics of stakeholder theory: Some future directions. *Business Ethics Quarterly* 4 (4): 409–421.

1998. Poverty and the politics of capitalism. In Patricia H. Werhane (ed.), *New Approaches to Business Ethics*, The Ruffin Series of the Society for Business Ethics 1. 31–35.

1999. Response: Divergent stakeholder theory. *Academy of Management Review* 24 (2): 233–236.

2000. Business ethics at the millennium. *Business Ethics Quarterly* 10 (1): 169–180.

2004. The stakeholder approach revisited. *Zeitschrift für Wirtschafts-und Unternehmensethik* 5 (3): 228–241.

2005. The development of stakeholder theory: An idiosyncratic approach. In K. Smith and M. A. Hitt (eds.), *Great Minds in Management.* Oxford: Oxford University Press. 417–435.

Freeman, R. E., Bryson, J. and Roering, W. 1986. Strategic planning in the public sector: Approaches and future directions. In B. Checkoway (ed.), *Strategic Perspectives on Planning Practice.* Boston: Lexington Books. 65–85.

Freeman, R. E. and Emshoff, J. 1979. Who's butting into your business? *Wharton Magazine* 4 (Fall): 44–48, 58–59.

Freeman, R. E. and Evan. W. 1990. Corporate governance: a stakeholder interpretation. *Journal of Behavioral Economics* 19 (4): 337–59.

Freeman, R. E. and Gilbert, D. R. 1987. Managing stakeholder relationships. In S. P. Sethi and G. M. Falbe (eds.), *Business and Society: Dimensions of Conflict and Cooperation*. Lexington, MA: Lexington Books. 397–423.

1988. *Corporate Strategy and the Search for Ethics*. Englewood Cliffs, NJ: Prentice-Hall.

1992. Business ethics and society: a critical agenda. *Business and Society* 31 (1): 9–17.

Freeman, R. E., Harrison, J. S. and Wicks, A. C. 2007. *Managing for Stakeholders: Business in the 21st Century. Managing for Stakeholders: Survival, Reputation, and Success*. New Haven: Yale University Press.

Freeman, R. E. and Liedtka, J. 1991. Corporate social responsibility: A critical approach. *Business Horizons* 34 (4): 92–98.

1997. Stakeholder capitalism and the value chain. *European Management Journal* 15 (3): 286–296.

Freeman, R. E. and Lorange, P. 1985. Theory building in strategic management. In R. Lamb and P. Shrivastava (eds.), *Advances in Strategic Management*, Vol. 3, Greenwich, CT: JAI Press, 9–38.

Freeman, R. E. and McVea, J. 2001. Stakeholder theory: The state of the art. In M. A. Hitt, R. E. Freeman, and J. S. Harrison (eds.), *Handbook of Strategic Management*. Oxford: Blackwell. 189–207.

Freeman, R. E., Martin, K. and Parmar, B. 2006. Ethics and capitalism. In M. Epstein and K. Hanson (eds.), *The Accountable Corporation*, Vol. 2, *Business Ethics*. Westport: Praeger. 193–208.

Freeman, R. E. and Newkirk, D. 2008a. Business school research: Some preliminary suggestions. 1st IESE Conference, *Humanizing the Firm and Management Profession*, Barcelona, IESE Business School.

2008b. Business as a human enterprise: Implications for education? In Samuel Gregg and James R. Stoner, Jr. (eds.), *Rethinking Business Management*. Princeton, NJ: Witherspoon Institute. 131–148.

Freeman, R. E. and Phillips, R. 2002. Stakeholder theory: A libertarian defense. *Business Ethics Quarterly* 12 (3): 331–350.

Freeman, R. E. and Reed, D. L. 1983. Stockholders and stakeholders: A new perspective on corporate governance. *California Management Review* 15 (3): 88–106.

Freeman, R. E., Wicks, A. and Parmar, B. 2004. Stakeholder theory and "the corporate objective revisited." *Organization Science* 15 (3): 364–369.

Freeman, R. E., Wicks, A. C., Parmar, B. and McVea, J. 2004. Stakeholder theory: The state of the art and future perspectives. *Politeia* Anno XX, No.74. 9–22.

Fried, C. 1981. *Contract as Promise: A Theory of Contractual Obligation*. Cambridge, MA: Harvard University Press.

Friedman, A. L. 2002. Developing stakeholder theory. *Journal of Management Studies* 39 (1): 1–21.

Friedman, A. L. and Miles, S. 2001. Socially responsible investment and corporate social and environmental reporting in the UK: An exploratory study. *British Accounting Review* 33 (4): 523–548.

2006. *Stakeholders: Theory and Practice*. Oxford and New York: Oxford University Press.
Friedman, A. L. and Phillips, M. 2005. Model for governance of professional associations. *Nonprofit Management and Leadership* 15 (2): 187–204.
Friedman, D. 1973. *The Machinery of Freedom: Guide to a Radical Capitalism*. New York: Arlington House.
Friedman, M. 1962. *Capitalism and Freedom*. Chicago: University of Chicago Press and Phoenix Books.
1970. The social responsibility of business is to increase its profits. *New York Times* September 13: 33.
Friedman, M. T. and Mason, D. 2004. A stakeholder approach to analyzing economic development decision making: Public subsidies for professional sport facilities. *Economic Development Quarterly* 18 (3): 236–254.
2005. Stakeholder management and the public subsidization of Nashville's coliseum. *Journal of Urban Affairs* 27 (1): 93–118.
Friedman, S. D. and Olk, P. 1995. Four ways to choose a CEO: Crown heir, horse race, coup d'état, and comprehensive search. *Human Resource Management* 34 (1): 141–164.
Frooman, J. 1999. Stakeholder influence strategies. *Academy of Management Review* 24 (2): 191–205.
Frost, F. A. and Mensik, S. 1991. Balancing minerals development and environmental protection. *Long Range Planning* 24 (4): 58–73.
Froud, J., Haslam, C., Suckdev, J., Shaoul, J. and Williams, K. 1996. Stakeholder economy? From utility privatisation to new labour. *Capital and Class* 60 (Autumn): 119–134.
Fry, M. L. and Polonsky, M. J. 2004. Examining the unintended consequences of marketing. *Journal of Business Research* 57 (11): 1303–1314.
Fryxell, G. E. and Wang, J. 1994. The Fortune corporate reputation index: Reputation for what? *Journal of Management* 20 (1): 1–14.
Fubini, D. G., Price, C. and Zollo, M. 2006. The elusive art of postmerger leadership. *McKinsey Quarterly* 4: 28–37.
Gallo, G. 2004. Operations research and ethics: Responsibility, sharing and cooperation. *European Journal of Operational Research* 153 (2): 468–476.
Gamble, G. and Kelly, G. 1996. Stakeholder capitalism and one nation socialism. *Renewal* 4 (1): 23–32.
Garavan, T. N. 1995. Stakeholders and strategic human resource development. *Journal of European Industrial Training* 19 (10): 11–15.
Gauthier, D. 1986. *Morals by Agreement*. New York: Oxford University Press.
Gelis, A. 2003. The reaction of stakeholders to the role of the Brazilian Federal Agency for Health Plans. *Clinical Research and Regulatory Affairs* 20: (1): 59–66.
George, B. 2003. *Authentic Leadership: Rediscovering the Secrets to Creating Lasting Value*. Hoboken, NJ: Jossey-Bass.
Ghonkrokta, S. S. and Lather, A. S. 2007. Identification of role of social audit by stakeholders as accountability tool in good governance. *Journal of Management Research* 7(1): 18–26.
Ghoshal, S. 2005. Bad management theories are destroying good management practices. *Academy of Management Learning and Education* 4 (1): 75–91.
Gibson, J. L., Ivancevich, J. M., Donnelly, J. H., Jr. and Konopaske, R. 2003. *Organizations: Behavior Structure Processes*. 11th edn. New York: McGraw-Hill Higher Education.
Gibson, K. 2000. The moral basis of stakeholder theory. *Journal of Business Ethics* 26 (3): 245–257.

Gilligan, C. 1982. *In a Different Voice*. Cambridge, MA: Harvard University Press.

Gilmartin, M. and Freeman, R. E. 2002. Business ethics and health care: A stakeholder perspective. *Health Care Management Review* 27 (2): 52–65.

Gioia, D. A. 1999a. Practicability, paradigms and problems in stakeholder theorizing. *Academy of Management Review* 24 (2): 228–232.

1999b. Gioia's reply to Jones and Wicks, *Academy of Management Review* 26 (4): 624–625.

Glaskiewicz, J. 1994. *Advances in Social Network Analysis: Research in the Social and Behavioral Sciences*. Thousand Oaks, CA: Sage.

Gonin, M. 2007. Business research, self-fulfilling prophecy, and the inherent responsibility of scholars. *Journal of Academic Ethics* 5(1): 33–58.

González-Benito, J. and González-Benito, O. 2006. The role of stakeholder pressure and managerial values in the implementation of environmental logistics practices. *International Journal of Production Research* 44 (7): 1353–1373.

Goodpaster, K. 1991. Business ethics and stakeholder analysis. *Business Ethics Quarterly* 1 (1): 53–73.

Goodpaster, K. and Holloran, T. 1994. In defense of a paradox. *Business Ethics Quarterly* 4 (4): 423–430.

Gordon, R. A. and Howell, J. E. 1959. *Higher Education for Business*. New York: Columbia University Press.

Gowthorpe, C. and Amat, O. 1999. External reporting of accounting and financial information via the Internet in Spain. *European Accounting Review* 8 (2): 365–371.

Granovetter, M. 1985. Economic action and social structure: The problem of embeddedness. *American Journal of Sociology* 91 (3): 481–510.

Graves, S. B. and Waddock, S. A. 1990. Institutional ownership and control: Implications for long-term corporate performance. *Academy of Management Executive* 37 (4): 1034–1046.

1994. Institutional owners and corporate social performance. *Academy of Management Journal* 37 (4): 75–83.

Gray, R. 2001. Thirty years of social accounting, reporting, and auditing: What (if anything) have we learnt? *Business Ethics: A European Review* 10 (1): 9–15.

Gray, R., Dey, C., Owen, D., Evans, R. and Zadek, S. 1997. Struggling with the praxis of social accounting: Stakeholders, accountability, audits and procedures. *Accounting, Auditing and Accountability Journal* 10 (3): 325–364.

Gray, R., Kouhy, R. and Lavers, S. 1995. Corporate social and environmental reporting: A review of the literature and a longitudinal study of UK disclosure. *Accounting, Auditing and Accountability Journal* 8 (2): 47–75.

Gray, R., Owen, D. and Adams, C. 1996. *Accounting and Accountability: Changes and Challenges in Corporate Social and Environmental Reporting*. London: Prentice-Hall.

Greenhalgh, L. 2001. *Managing Strategic Relationships*. New York: Free Press.

Greening, D. W. and Turban, D. B. 2000. Corporate social performance as a competitive advantage in attracting a quality workforce. *Business and Society* 39 (3): 254–280.

Greenley, G. E. and Foxall, G. R. 1996. Consumer and nonconsumer stakeholder orientation in U.K. companies. *Journal of Business Research* 35 (2): 105–116.

1997. Multiple stakeholder orientation in UK companies and the implications for company performance. *Journal of Management Studies* 34 (2): 259–284.

1998. External moderation of associations among stakeholder orientations and company performance. *International Journal of Research in Marketing* 15 (1): 51–69.

Greenley, G. E., Hooley, G. J., Broderick, A. and Rudd, J. M. 2004. Strategic planning differences among different multiple stakeholder orientation profiles. *Journal of Strategic Marketing* 12 (3): 163–182.

Greenwood, M. R. and Simmons, J. 2004. A stakeholder approach to ethical human resource management. *Business and Professional Ethics Journal* 23 (3): 3–23.

Gregory, A. 2007. Involving stakeholders in developing corporate brands: The communication dimension. *Journal of Marketing Management* 23 (1–2): 59–73.

Gregory, R. and Keeney, R. L. 1994. Creating policy alternatives using stakeholder values. *Management Science* 40 (8): 1035–1048.

Griffin, J. J. 1998. Using technology to understand stakeholders. *Business and Society* 37 (1): 107–110.

Grimble, R., Aglionby, J. and Quan, J. 1994. *Tree Resources and Environmental Policy: A Stakeholder Approach.* NRI Socioeconomics Series 7. Chatham: Natural Resources Institute.

Grimble, R. and Chan, M. 1995. Stakeholder analysis for natural resource management in developing countries. *Natural Resources Forum* 19 (2): 113–124.

Grimble, R. and Wellard, K. 1997. Stakeholder methodologies in natural resource management: A review of principles, contexts, experiences and opportunities. *Agricultural Systems* 55 (2): 173–193.

Grinyer, J. R., Sinclair, C. D. and Ibrahim, D. N. 1999. Management objectives in capital budgeting. *Financial Practice and Education* 9 (2): 12–22.

Grossman, S. J. and Hart, O. 1986. The costs and benefits of ownership: A theory of vertical and lateral integration. *Journal of Political Economy* 94: 691–719.

Guild, W. L. 2002. Relative importance of stakeholders: Analysing speech acts in a layoff. *Journal of Organizational Behavior* 23 (7): 837–852.

Gulati, R. and Singh, J. H. 1998. The architecture of cooperation: Managing coordination costs and appropriation concerns in strategic alliances. *Administrative Science Quarterly* 43 (4): 781–814.

Gunther, M. 2004. Money and morals at GE. *Fortune*. November 15: 178.

Gupta, A. 1995. A stakeholder analysis approach for interorganizational systems. *Industrial Management and Data Systems* 95: (6): 3–7.

Gutting, G. 1999. *Pragmatic Liberalism and the Critique of Modernity.* Cambridge: Cambridge University Press.

Habermas, J. 1978. *Knowledge and Human Interests*, trans. J. J. Shapiro. 2nd edn. Boston: Beacon Press.

1984. *The Theory of Communicative Action.* Boston: Beacon Hill.

1987. Philosophy as stand-in and interpreter. In K. Baynes, J. Bohman, and T. McCarthy (eds.), *After Philosophy.* Cambridge, MA: MIT Press.

1989. *The Structural Transformation of the Public Sphere: An Inquiry into a Category of Bourgeois Society*, trans. T. Burger. Cambridge, MA: MIT Press.

1990. *Moral Consciousness and Communicative Action.* Cambridge: Polity.

1993. *Justification and Application: Remarks on Discourse Ethics.* Cambridge, MA: MIT Press.

1996. *Between Facts and Norms: Contributions to a Discourse Theory of Law and Democracy.* Cambridge, MA: MIT Press.

Hall, A. T., Blass, F. R., Ferris, G. R. and Massengale, R. 2004. Leader reputation and accountability in organizations: Implications for dysfunctional leader behavior. *Leadership Quarterly* 15 (4): 515–536.

Hall, J. and Vredenburg, H. 2005. Managing stakeholder ambiguity. *MIT Sloan Management Review* 47 (1): 11–13.

Hambrick, D. C. 2007. The field of management's devotion to theory: Too much of a good thing? *Academy of Management Journal* 50 (6): 1346–1352.

Hampton-Turner, C. and Trompenaars, A. 1993. *The Seven Cultures of Capitalism.* New York: Doubleday Dell Publishing Group.

Hanks, J. 1991. Playing with fire: Nonshareholder constituency statutes in the 1990s. *Stetson Law Review* 21: 97, 111.

Hansmann, H. 1996. *The Ownership of the Enterprise.* Cambridge, MA: Harvard University Press.

Hardy, C., Phillips, E. and Lawrence, T. B. 2003. Resources, knowledge and influence: The organizational effects of interorganizational collaboration. *Journal of Management Studies* 40 (2): 321–347.

Hargreaves, B. J. A. and Dauman, J. 1975. *Business Survival and Social Change: A Practical Guide to Responsibility and Partnership.* New York: John Wiley & Sons.

Harris, J. and Bromiley, P. 2007. Incentives to cheat: The influence of executive compensation and firm performance on financial misrepresentation. *Organization Science* 18 (3): 350–367.

Harris, J. and Freeman, R. E. 2008. The impossibility of the separation thesis. *Business Ethics Quarterly* 18 (4): 541–548.

Harris, P. and Rees, P. 2005. *Stakeholder Marketing.* London: Sage.

Harrison, J. S. 1996. Managing and partnering with external stakeholders. *Academy of Management Executive* 10 (2): 46–60.

Harrison, J. S. and Fiet, J. O. 1999. New CEOs pursue their own self-interests by sacrificing stakeholder values. *Journal of Business Ethics* 19 (3): 301–308.

Harrison, J. S. and St. John, C. H. 1994. *Strategic Management of Organizations and Stakeholders: Concepts and Cases.* St. Paul, MN: West Publishing.

1998. *Strategic Management of Organizations and Stakeholders: Concepts and Cases.* 2nd edn. Cincinnati, OH: South-Western Publishing.

Harsanyi, J. C., 1977. *Rational Behavior and Bargaining Equilibrium in Games and Social Situations.* Cambridge: Cambridge University Press.

Hart, O. 1995. *Firms, Contracts, and Financial Structure.* Oxford: Oxford University Press.

Hart, O. and Holmstrom, B. 1986. The theory of contracts. Working Paper no. 418, Massachusetts Institute of Technology (MIT), Department of Economics.

Hart, O. and Moore, J. 1990. Property rights and the nature of the firm. *Journal of Political Economy* 98 (6): 1119–1158.

Hart, S. L. and Sharma, S. 2004. Engaging fringe stakeholders for competitive imagination. *Academy of Management Executive* 18 (1): 7–18.

Hartman, E. 1996. *Organizational Ethics and the Good Life.* New York: Oxford University Press.

Haselhoff, F. 1976. A new paradigm for the study of organizational goals. In Ansoff, I., Declerk R. and Hayes, R. (eds.), *From Strategic Planning to Strategic Management*. New York: John Wiley & Sons. 15–27.

Hasnas, J. 1998. The normative theories of business ethics. A guide for the perplexed. *Business Ethics Quarterly* 8 (1): 19–42.

Hausman, D. M. 2002. Trustworthiness and self-interest. *Journal of Banking and Finance* 26 (9): 1767–1783.

Hayek, F. von 1974. The pretence of knowledge. In *Nobel Lectures: Economic Sciences 1969–1980*. Singapore: World Scientific Publishing. 179–189.

1979. *Law, Legislation, Liberty*, Vol. 3, *The Political Order of a Free People*. Chicago: University of Chicago Press.

Hayes, R. H. and Abernathy, W. J., 1980. Managing our way to economic decline. *Harvard Business Review* 58 (4): 67–77.

Heenan, D. and Perlmutter, H. 1979. *Multinational Organizational Development*. Reading, MA: Addison-Wesley.

Heller, F. 1997. Leadership and power in a stakeholder setting. *European Journal of Work and Organizational Psychology* 6 (4): 467–479.

Hellriegel, D., Slocum, J. W., Jr. and Woodman, R. W. 2001. *Organizational Behavior*. 9th edn. Cincinnati, OH: South-Western College Publishing.

Hemmati, M. 2002. *Multi-Stakeholder Processes for Governance and Sustainability – Beyond Deadlock and Conflict*. London: Earthscan.

Hendry, J. 2001a. Economic contacts versus social relationships as a foundation for normative stakeholder theory. *Business Ethics: A European Review* 10 (3): 223–232.

2001b. Missing the target: Normative stakeholder theory and the corporate governance debate. *Business Ethics Quarterly* 11 (1): 159–176.

Henn, A. and Patz, R. 2007. A multicriteria approach for corporate decisions in sustainable planning policy. *International Transactions in Operational Research* 14 (1): 14–23.

Henriksen, E., Johansen, M., Deraas, T. and Arild, E. 2005. Difficulties in moving routine medical checks from the specialist level to the general practitioner level. *Journal of Telemedicine and Telecare* 11 (S2): 47–50.

Heugens, P. P. M. A. R., Van Den Bosch, F. A. J. and Van Riel, C. B. M. 2002. Stakeholder integration: Building mutually enforcing relationships. *Business and Society* 41 (1): 36–60.

Hilary, G. 2003. Accounting behavior of German firms after an ADR issuance. *International Journal of Accounting* 38 (3): 355–377.

Hill, C. W. L. and Jones, T. M. 1992. Stakeholder–agency theory. *Journal of Management Studies* 29 (2): 131–154.

Hillman, A. J. and Dalziel, T. 2003. Boards of directors and firm performance: Integrating agency and resource dependence perspectives. *Academy of Management Review* 28 (3): 383–396.

Hillman, A. J. and Keim, G. D. 2001. Shareholder value, stakeholder management, and social issues: What's the bottom line? *Strategic Management Journal* 22 (2): 125–139.

Hirschman, A. O. 1970. *Exit Voice and Loyalty: Response to Decline in Firms, Organizations and States*. Cambridge, MA: Harvard University Press.

Hitt, M. A. 2005. Spotlight on strategic management. *Business Horizons* 48 (5): 371–377.

Hitt, M. A., Freeman, R. E. and Harrison, J. S. (eds.). 2001. *Handbook of Strategic Management*, Oxford: Blackwell.

Hitt, M. A., Harrison, J. S. and Ireland, R. D. 2001. *Mergers and Acquisitions: A Guide to Creating Value for Stakeholder*. New York: Oxford University Press.

Hitt, M. A., Keats, B. W. and DeMarie, S. M. 1998. Navigating in the new competitive landscape: Building strategic flexibility and competitive advantage in the 21st century. *Academy of Management*, 12 (4): 22–42.

Hjortsø, C. N. 2004. Enhancing public participation in natural resource management using soft OR – an application of strategic option development and analysis in tactical forest planning. *European Journal of Operational Research* 152: 667–683.

Hoek, J. and Maubach, N. 2005. A model for addressing stakeholders' concerns about direct-to-consumer advertising of prescription medicines. *European Journal of Marketing* 39 (9–10): 1151–1169.

Hofer, C. W., Murray, E. A., Jr., Charan, R. and Pitts, R. A. 1980. *Strategic Management: A Casebook in Business Policy and Planning*. St. Paul, MN: West Publishing.

Hofer, C. W. and Schendel, D. E. 1978. *Strategy Formulation: Analytical Concepts*. St. Paul, MN: West Publishing.

Holder, M. E., Langrehr, F. W. and Hexter, J. L. 1998. Dividend policy determinants: An investigation of the influences of stakeholder theory. *Financial Management* 27 (3): 73–82.

Honore, A. M. 1961. Ownership. In A. G. Guest (ed.), *Oxford Essays in Jurisprudence*. Oxford: Clarendon Press.

Hoover, K. R. 2003. *Economics as Ideology*. Lanham, MD: Rowman & Littlefield.

Hosmer, L. T. 1994. Strategic planning as if ethics mattered. *Strategic Management Journal* 15 (Special Issue): 17–34.

Hosseini, J. and Brenner, S. N. 1992. The stakeholder theory of the firm: A methodology to generate value matrix weight. *Business Ethics Quarterly* 2 (2): 99–119.

Hrebiniak, L. G. and Joyce, W. F. 1985. Organizational adaptation: Strategic choice and environmental determinism. *Administrative Science Quarterly* 30 (3): 336–349.

Humber, J. M. 2002. Beyond stockholders and stakeholders: A plea for corporate moral autonomy. *Journal of Business Ethics* 36 (3): 207–221.

Huss, W. R. 1988. A move toward scenarios. *International Journal of Forecasting* 4 (3): 377–388.

Hussain, Z. and Hafeez, K. 2008. Changing attitudes and behavior of stakeholders during an information systems-led organizational change. *Journal of Applied Behavioral Science* 44 (4): 490–513.

Hussey, D. and Langham, M. 1978. *Corporate Planning: The Human Factor*. Oxford: Pergamon Press.

Hutton, W. 1995. *The State We're In*. London: Jonathan Cape.

IASC (International Accounting Standards Committee). 1989. *Framework for the Preparation and Presentation of Financial Statements*. New York: IASC.

Ibarra, H. and Hunter, M. 2007. How leaders create and use networks. *Harvard Business Review* 85 (1): 40–48.

Ilinitch, A. Y., Soderstrom, N. S. and Thomas, T. E. 1998. Measuring corporate environmental performance. *Journal of Accounting and Public Policy* 17 (4/5): 383–407.

Ippolito, R. A. and James, W. H. 1992. LBOs, reversions and implicit contracts. *Journal of Finance* 47 (1): 139–167.

Ireland, P. 1996. Corporate governance, stakeholding, and the company: Towards a less degenerate capitalism? *Journal of Law and Society* 23 (2): 287–320.

Ireland, R. D. and Hitt, M. A. 2005. Achieving and maintaining strategic competitiveness in the 21st century: The role of strategic leadership. *Academy of Management Executive* 19 (4): 63–77.

Ireland, R. D., Hitt, M. A. and Vaidyanath, D. 2002. Managing strategic alliances to achieve a competitive advantage. *Journal of Management* 28 (3): 413–446.

Islam, M. A. and Deegan, C. 2008. Motivations for an organisation within a developing country to report social responsibility information. *Accounting, Auditing and Accountability Journal* 21 (6): 850–874.

Istaitieh, A. and Rodriquez-Fernandez, J. M. 2006. Factor-product markets and firm's capital structure: A literature review. *Review of Financial Economics* 15 (1): 49–75.

Jackson, J. 2001. Prioritising customers and other stakeholders using the AHP. *European Journal of Marketing* 35 (7/8): 858–871.

Jallat, F. and Wood, E. 2005. Exploring "deep" and "wide" stakeholder relations in service activity. *European Journal of Marketing* 39 (9/10): 1013–1024.

Jamal, T. and Eyre, M. 2003. Legitimation struggles in national park spaces: The Banff Bow Valley Round Table. *Journal of Environmental Planning and Management* 46 (3): 417–441.

Jamal, T., Stein, S. and Harper, T. 2002. Beyond labels: Pragmatic planning in multistakeholder tourism-environmental conflicts. *Journal of Planning Education and Research* 22 (2): 164–177.

James, W. 1907. Pragmatism, a new name for some old ways of thinking. *Popular Lectures on Philosophy*. New York: Longman Green.

Jansen, E. and Von Glinow, M. A. 1985. Ethical ambivalence and organizational rewards systems. *Academy of Management Review* 10 (4): 814–830.

Jawahar, I. M. and McLaughlin, G. L. 2001. Towards a descriptive stakeholder theory: An organizational life cycle approach. *Academy of Management Review* 26 (3): 3397–3414.

Jennings, M. M. and Happel, S. 2002–3. The post-Enron era for stakeholder theory: A new look at corporate governance and the Coase Theorem. *Mercer Law Review* 54: 873–938.

Jensen, M. C. 1989. The evidence speaks loud and clear. *Harvard Business Review* 67 (6): 186–188.

2000. Value maximization and the corporate objective function. In M. Beer and N. Nohria (eds.), *Breaking the Code of Change*. Boston: Harvard Business School Press. 37–58.

2001. Value maximization, stakeholder theory, and the corporate objective function. *European Financial Management* 7(3): 297–317.

2002. Maximization, stakeholder theory, and the corporate objective. *Business Ethics Quarterly* 12 (2), 235–256.

Jensen, M. C. and Meckling, W. 1976. Theory of the firm: Managerial behavior, agency costs and capital structure. *Journal of Financial Economics* 3 (4): 305–360.

Johnson, J. L., Daily, C. M. and Ellstrand, A. E. 1996. Boards of directors: A review and research agenda. *Journal of Management* 22 (3): 409–438.

Johnson, R. W. 1947. *Or Forfeit Freedom.* New York: Doubleday.

Jones, E. 1964. *The Life and Times of Sigmund Freud.* London: Penguin Books.

Jones, M. T. and Kunz, P. 2005. Competitive advantage through nonmarket strategy: Lessons from the Baywatch experience. *The Business Review* 3 (2): 271–283.

Jones, R. E. 1990. Managing the political context in PMS organizations. *European Journal of Operational Research* 49 (1): 60–67.

Jones, T. M. 1980. Corporate social responsibility revisited, redefined. *California Management Review* 22 (2): 59–67.

1995. Instrumental stakeholder theory: A synthesis of ethics and economics. *Academy of Management Review* 20 (2): 404–437.

Jones, T. M., Felps, W. and Bigley, G. A. 2007. Ethical theory and stakeholder-related decisions: The role of stakeholder culture. *Academy of Management Review* 32 (1): 137–155.

Jones, T. M. and Goldberg, L. 1982. Governing the large corporation: More arguments for public directors. *Academy of Management Review* 7 (4): 603–611.

Jones, T. M. and Wicks, A. C. 1999a. Convergent stakeholder theory in management research. *Academy of Management Review* 24 (2): 206–221.

1999b. Letter to AMR regarding "Convergent Stakeholder Theory." *Academy of Management Review* 26 (4): 621–623.

Jørgensen, T. H., Remmen, A. and Mellado, M. D. 2006. Integrated management systems – three different levels of integration. *Journal of Cleaner Production* 14 (8): 713–722.

Joseph, G. 2007. Implications of a stakeholder view on corporate reporting. *Accounting and the Public Interest* 7: 50–65.

Kale, J. R. and Shahrur, H. 2008. Corporate leverage and specialized investments by customers and suppliers. *Journal of Applied Corporate Finance* 20 (4): 98–104.

Kale, P., Dyer, J. and Singh, H. 2001. Value creation and success in strategic alliances: Alliancing skills and the role of alliance structure and systems. *European Management Journal* 19 (5): 463–471.

Kaler, J. 2002. Morality and strategy in stakeholder identification. *Journal of Business Ethics* 39 (1/2): 91–99.

2003. Differentiating stakeholder theories. *Journal of Business Ethics* 46 (1): 71–83.

2006. Evaluating stakeholder theory. *Journal of Business Ethics* 69 (3): 249–268.

Kane, E. J. 2004. Continuing dangers of disinformation in corporate accounting reports. *Review of Financial Economics* 13 (1/2): 149–164.

Kanter, R. M. 1994. Collaborate advantage: The art of alliances. *Harvard Business Review* 72 (4): 96–108.

Kaptein, M. 2008. Developing a measure of unethical behavior in the workplace: A stakeholder perspective. *Journal of Management* 34 (5): 978–1008.

Karlsen, J. T. 2002. Project stakeholder management. *Engineering Management Journal* 14 (4): 19–24.

Katz, D. and Kahn, R. L. 1978. *The Social Psychology of Organizations.* 2nd edn. New York: John Wiley & Sons.

Katz, D., Kahn, R. L. and Adams, S. 1980. *The Study of Organizations.* New York: John Wiley & Sons.

Keasey, K. and Wright, M. 1993. Issues in corporate accountability and governance: An editorial. *Accounting and Business Research* 23 (91A): 291–303.

Keeley, M. 1978. A contingency framework for performance evaluation. *Academy of Management Review* 3 (3): 428–439.

Keeney, R. L. 1988. Structuring objectives for problems of public interest. *Operations Research* 36 (3): 396–405.

Keeney, R. L. and McDaniels, T. L. 1999. Identifying and structuring values to guide integrated resource planning at BC Gas. *Operations Research* 47 (5): 651–662.

Kenny, G. K. 2001. *Strategic Factors*. Mosman, Australia: President Press.

Kent, B., Kaval, P., Berry, J., Retzlaff, M., Hormaechea, D. and Shields, D. 2003. A role for stakeholder objectives in USDA Forest Service plan revisions: A case study on the White River National Forest. *International Transactions in Operational Research* 10 (5): 515–542.

Keynes, J. M. 1936. *The General Theory of Employment, Interest, and Money*. London: Macmillan.

Kiechel, W., III. 1979. Playing by the rules of the corporate strategy game. *Fortune* September 24: 24–26.

King, W. and Cleland, D. 1978. *Strategic Planning and Policy*. New York: Van Nostrand Reinhold Co.

Kingdon, J. 1984. *Agendas, Alternatives and Public Policies*. Boston: Little, Brown.

Kirzner, I. M. 1979. *Perception, Opportunity and Profit*. Chicago: University of Chicago Press.

1985. *Discovery and the Capitalist Process*. Chicago: University of Chicago Press.

Klassen, R. D. 1993. The integration of environmental issues into manufacturing: Toward an interactive open-systems model. *Production and Inventory Management Journal* 34 (1): 82–88.

Klemm, M., Sanderson, S. and Luffman, G. 1991. Mission statements: Selling corporate values to employees. *Long Range Planning* 24 (3): 73–78.

Kochan, T. A. and Dyer, L. 1993. Managing transformational change: The role of human resource professionals. *International Journal of Human Resource Management* 4 (3): 569–590.

Kochan, T. A. and Rubenstein, S. A. 2000. Toward a stakeholder theory of the firm: The Saturn partnership. *Organization Science* 11 (4): 367–386.

Kolk, A. and Pinkse, J. 2007. Towards strategic stakeholder management? Integrating perspectives on sustainability challenges such as corporate responses to climate change. *Corporate Governance: The International Journal of Effective Board Performance* 7 (4): 370–378.

Kotler, P. 2003. *Marketing Management*. 11th edn. Upper Saddle River, NJ: Prentice-Hall.

2005. The role played by the broadening of marketing movement in the history of marketing thought. *Journal of Public Policy and Marketing* 24 (1): 114–116.

Kotter, J. and Heskett, J. 1992. *Corporate Culture and Performance*. New York: Free Press.

Kreitner, R. and Kinicki, A. 2008. *Organizational Behavior*. 8th edn. Boston: McGraw-Hill Irwin.

Kruchten, P., Woo, C., Monu, K. and Sotoodeh, M. 2008. A conceptual model of disasters encompassing multiple stakeholder domains. *International Journal of Emergency Management* 5 (1/2): 25–56.

Krucken, L. and Meroni, A. 2006. Building stakeholder networks to develop and deliver product-service systems: Practical experiences on elaborating pro-active materials for communication. *Journal of Cleaner Production* 14 (17): 1502–1508.

Kuhn, T. S. 1962. *The Structure of Scientific Revolutions*. Chicago: University of Chicago Press.
1970. *The Structure of Scientific Revolutions*. 2nd edn. Chicago: University of Chicago Press.

Kumar, K. and Subramanian, R. 1998. Meeting the expectations of stakeholders. *SAM Advanced Management Journal* 63 (2): 31–41.

Kumar, Y., Chaudhury, N. and Vasudev, N. 1997. *Stakeholder Analysis: The Women's and Children's Health Project in India*. Technical Report no. 13. Bethesda, MD: Partnerships for Health Reform, Abt. Associates, Inc.

Labib, N. and Appelbaum, S. H. 1993. Strategic downsizing: A human resources perspective. *Human Resource Planning* 16 (4): 69–93.

Lado, A. A., Boyd, N. G. and Hanlon, S. C. 1997. Competition, cooperation and the search for economic rents: A syncretic model. *Academy of Management Review* 22 (1): 110–141.

Lamberg, J.-A., Pajunen, K., Parvinen, P. and Savage, G. T. 2008. Stakeholder management and path dependence in organizational transitions. *Management Decision* 46 (6): 846–863.

Langtry, B. 1994. Stakeholders and the moral responsibilities of the firm. *Business Ethics Quarterly* 4 (4): 431–43.

Laplume, A. O., Sonpar, K. and Litz, R. A. 2008. Stakeholder theory: Reviewing a theory that moves us. *Journal of Management* 34 (6): 1152–1189.

Lavie, D. 2006. The competitive advantage of interconnected firm: An extension of the resource-based view. *Academy of Management Review* 31 (3): 638–658.

Lawrence, P. R. and Lorsch, J. W. 1967. Differentiation and integration in complex organizations. *Administrative Science Quarterly* 12 (1): 1–47

Lea, D. 2004. The imperfect nature of corporate responsibilities to stakeholders. *Business Ethics Quarterly* 14 (2): 201–217.

Leach, W. 2004. *Public Involvement and Facilitation Assistance*. Center for Collaborative Policy, Sacramento State University.

Learned, E. P., Christensen, C. R., Andrews, K. R. and Guth, W. D. 1965. *Business Policy: Text and Cases*. Homewood, IL: R. D. Irwin.

Le Cardinal, G., Guyonnet, J.-F., Pouzoullic, B. and Rigby, J. 2001. Intervention methodology for complex problems: The FAcT-mirror method. *European Journal of Operational Research* 132 (3): 694–702.

Letza, S., Sun, X. and Kirkbride, J. (2004). Shareholding versus stakeholding: A critical review of corporate governance. *Corporate Governance* 12 (3): 242–262.

Lewis, M., Young, B., Mathiassen, L., Rai, A. and Welke, R. 2007. Business process innovation based on stakeholder perceptions. *Information Knowledge Systems Management* 6 (1/2): 7–27.

Liebl, F. 2002. The anatomy of complex societal problems and its implications for OR. *Journal of the Operational Research Society* 53 (2): 161–183.

Lim, G., Ahn, H. and Lee, H. 2005. Formulating strategies for stakeholder management: A case-based reasoning approach. *Expert Systems with Applications* 28 (4): 831–840.

Lim, S. S. and Wang, H. 2007. The effect of financial hedging on the incentives for corporate diversification: The role of stakeholder firm-specific investments. *Journal of Economic Behavior and Organization* 62 (4): 640–656.

Lindblom, C. 1959. The science of muddling through. *Public Administration Review* 19: 78–88.

Lindfelt, L.-L. and Törnroos, J.-A. 2006. Ethics and value creation in business research: Comparing two approaches. *European Journal of Marketing* 40 (3/4): 328–351.

Logsdon, J. and Wood, D. 2002. Business citizenship: From domestic to global level of analysis. *Business Ethics Quarterly* 12 (2): 155–187.

Long, D. M. and Rao, S. 1995. The wealth effects of unethical business behavior. *Journal of Economics and Finance* 19 (2): 65–73.

Lorange, P. 1983. Strategic control. In R. Lamb (ed.), *Latest Advances in Strategic Management: A New View of Business Policy and Planning.* Boston: Little, Brown.

Lorange, P., Roos, J. and Bronn, P. S. 1992. Building successful strategic alliances. *Long Range Planning* 25 (6): 10–17.

Lorca, P. and Garcia-Diez, J. 2004. The relation between firm survival and the achievement of balance among its stakeholders: An analysis. *International Journal of Management* 21 (1): 93–99.

Lorigan, T. 2006/2007. Marketing, schmarketing! *NZ Business* 20 (11): 12.

Lowendahl, B. and Revang, O. 1998. Challenges to existing strategy theory in a postindustrial society. *Strategic Management Journal* 19 (8): 755–769.

Lozano, R. 2006. Incorporation and institutionalization of SD into universities: Breaking through barriers to change. *Journal of Cleaner Production* 14 (9–11): 787–796.

Lubatkin, M. 2007. One more time: What is a realistic theory of corporate governance? *Journal of Organizational behavior* 28 (1): 59–67.

Luk, C.-L., Yau, O. H. M., Tse, A. C. B., Sin, L. Y. M. and Chow, R. P. M. 2005. Stakeholder orientation and business performance: The case of service companies in China. *Journal of International Marketing* 13 (1): 89–110.

Luoma, P. and J. Goodstein. 1999. Stakeholders and corporate boards: Institutional influences on board composition and structure. *Academy of Management Journal* 42 (5): 553–563.

McCraw, Thomas K. (ed.). 2003. *Creating Modern Capitalism.* Cambridge, MA: Harvard University Press.

Macey, J. R. 1999. Fiduciary duties as residual claims: Obligations to nonshareholder constituencies from a theory of the firm perspective. *Cornell Law Review* 84: 1266–1281.

1991–2. An economic analysis of the various rationales for making shareholders the exclusive beneficiaries of corporate fiduciary duties. *Stetson Law Review* 21: 23–44.

Macey, J. R. and Miller, G. P. 1993. Corporate stakeholders: A contractual perspective. *University of Toronto Law Journal* 43: 401–424.

McGuire, J. B., Sundgren, A. and Schneeweis, T. 1988. Corporate social responsibility and firm financial performance. *Academy of Management Journal* 31 (4): 854–872.

McHale, R. 2006. Relationship capital. *Financial Management* April: 38–39.

McLellan, D. and Sayers, S. (eds.). 1990. *Socialism and Morality.* London: Macmillan.

McManus, J. 2002. The influence of stakeholder values on project management. *Management Services* 46 (6): 8–16.

MacMillan, I. C. 1974. Business strategies for political action. *Journal of General Management* 2 (1): 51–63.

1978. *Strategy Formulation: Political Concepts.* St. Paul, MN: West Publishing.

1982. Seizing competitive initiative. *Journal of Business Strategy* 2 (4): 43–57.

1983. Corporate ideology and strategic delegation. *Journal of Business Strategy* 3 (3): 71–76.

McNerney, D. 1994. Competitive advantage: Diverse customers and stakeholders. *HR Focus* 71 (6): 9–10.

McQuater, R. E., Peters, A. J., Dale, B. G., Spring, M., Rogerson, J. H. and Rooney, E. M. 1998. The management and organisational context of new product development: Diagnosis and self-assessment. *International Journal of Production Economics* 55 (2): 121–131.

Magness, V. 2006. Strategic posture, financial performance and environmental disclosure: An empirical test of legitimacy theory. *Accounting, Auditing and Accountability Journal* 19 (4): 540–563.

Mahon, J. F. 1982. Public affairs structures and activities in large American corporations. *Academy of Management Proceedings* 366–370.

Mahon, J. R. and Murray, E. A., Jr. 1981. Strategic planning for regulated companies. *Strategic Management Journal* 2 (3): 251–262.

Mahoney, J. T. 2005. *Economic Foundations of Strategy*. Thousand Oaks, CA: Sage.

Maignan, I., Ferrell, O. C. and Ferrell, L. 2005. A stakeholder model for implementing social responsibility in marketing. *European Journal of Marketing* 39 (9/10): 956–977.

Maksimovic, V. and Titman, S. 1991. Financial policy and reputation for product quality. *Review of Financial Studies* 4 (1): 175–200.

Malekzadeh, A. R. and Nahavandi, A. 1987. Merger mania: Who wins? Who loses? *Journal of Business Strategy* 8 (1): 76–79.

Malvey, D., Fottler, M. and Slovensky, D. 2002. Evaluating stakeholder management performance using a stakeholder report card: The next step in theory and practice. *Health Care Management Review* 27 (2): 66–79.

Manring, S. L. and Moore, S. B. 2006. Creating and managing a virtual inter-organizational learning network for greener production: A conceptual model and case study. *Journal of Cleaner Production* 14 (9–11): 891–899.

March, J. and Simon, H. 1958. *Organizations*. New York: John Wiley & Sons.

Marcoux, A. M. 2000. Balancing act. In DesJardins, J. R. and McCall, J. J. (eds.), *Contemporary Issues in Business Ethics*. 4th edn. Belmont, CA: Thomson Wadsworth. 92–100.

2003. A fiduciary argument against stakeholder theory. *Business Ethics Quarterly* 13 (1): 1–24.

Marens, R. and Wicks, A. C. 1999. Getting real: Stakeholder theory, managerial practice, and the general irrelevance of fiduciary duties owed to shareholders. *Business Ethics Quarterly* 9 (2): 272–293.

Margolis, J. D. and Walsh, J. P. 2001. *People and Profits: The Search for a Link Between a Company's Social and Financial Performance*. Mahwah, NJ: Lawrence Erlbaum.

2003. Misery loves companies: Rethinking social initiatives by business. *Administrative Science Quarterly* 48 (2): 268–305.

Marris, R. 1964. *The Economic Theory of "Managerial" Capitalism*. Glencoe, IL: Free Press.

Martin, K. and Freeman, R. E. 2004. The separation of technology and ethics in business ethics. *Journal of Business Ethics* 53 (4): 353–364.

Marx, K. and Engels, F. 1847a. *The Principles of Communism*. www.marxists.org/archive/marx/works/1847/11/prin-com.htm.

1847b. *Wage and Labor Capital*. www.marxists.org/archive/marx/works/1847/wage-labour/ch08.htm.

Mason, D. S. and Slack, T. 1996–7. Appropriate opportunism or bad business practice? Stakeholder theory, ethics, and the franchise relocation issue. *Marquette Sports Law Journal* 7: 399–426.

Mason, R. and Mitroff, I. 1982. *Challenge Strategic Planning Assumptions*. New York: John Wiley & Sons.

Matten, D. and Crane, A. 2005. Corporate citizenship: Toward an extended theoretical conceptualization. *Academy of Management Review* 30 (1): 166–179.

Matten, D. and Moon, J. 2008. "Implicit" and "Explicit" CSR: A conceptual framework for a comparative understanding of corporate social responsibility. *Academy of Management Review* 33 (2): 404–424.

Mattingly, J. 2004. Redefining the corporation: Stakeholder management and organizational wealth (book review). *Academy of Management Review* 29 (3): 520–523.

Maull, R., Hughes, D., Childe, S., Weston, N., Tranfield, D. and Smith, S. 1990. A methodology for the design and implementation of resilient CAPM systems. *International Journal of Operations and Production Management* 10 (9): 27–36.

Meek, G. K. and Gray, S. J. 1988. The value added statement: An innovation for US companies? *Accounting Horizons* 2 (2): 73–81.

Mendelow, A. L. 1983. Setting corporate goals and measuring organizational effectiveness – a practical approach. *Long Range Planning* 16 (1): 70–76.

Mikalsen, K. and Jentoft, S. 2001. From user-groups to stakeholders? The public interest in fisheries management. *Marine Policy* 25 (4): 281–292.

Miller, R. L. and Lewis, W. F. 1991. A stakeholder approach to marketing management using the value exchange models. *European Journal of Marketing* 25 (8): 55–68.

Millon, D. 1991. Redefining corporate law. *Indiana Law Review* 24: 223.

Mills, R. W. and Chen, G. 1996. Evaluating international joint ventures using strategic value analysis. *Long Range Planning* 29 (4): 552–561.

Minnow, N. 1991–2. Shareholders, stakeholders, and boards of directors. *Stetson Law Review* 21: 197–243.

Mintzberg, H. 1971. Patterns in strategy formation. *Management Science* 24 (9): 934–948.

1978. Managerial work: Analysis from observation. *Management Science* 18 (2): B97–B110.

1993. The pitfalls of strategic planning. *California Management Review* 36 (1): 32–47.

1994. *The Rise and Fall of Strategic Planning: Re-conceiving Roles for Planning, Plans, and Planners*. New York: Free Press.

2004. *Managers Not MBAs: A Hard Look at the Soft Practice of Managing and Management Development*. San Francisco, CA: Berrett-Koehler Publishers.

Mitchell, L. 1992. A theoretical and practical framework for enforcing constituency statutes. *Texas Law Review* 70: 579–643.

Mitchell, R., Agle, B. R. and Wood, D. J. 1997. Toward a theory of stakeholder identification and salience: Defining the principles of who and what really counts. *Academy of Management Review* 22 (4): 853–886.

Mitnick, B. M. 1980. *The Political Economy of Regulation: Creating, Designing, and Removing Regulatory Forms*. New York: Columbia University Press.

Mitroff, I. 1983a. Archetypal social systems analysis: On the deeper structure of human systems. *Academy of Management Review* 8 (3): 387–397.

1983b. *Stakeholders of the Organizational Mind*. San Francisco, CA: Jossey-Bass.

Mitroff, I. and Emshoff, J. 1979. On strategic assumption-making. *Academy of Management Review* 4 (1): 1–12.

Mitroff, I., Emshoff, J. and Kilmann, R. 1979. Assumptional analysis: a methodology for strategic problem solving. *Management Science* 25 (6): 583–593.

Mitroff, I. and Mason, R. O. 1980. Structuring ill-structured policy issues: Further explorations in a methodology for messy problems. *Strategic Management Journal* 1 (4): 331–342.

Moerman, L. and van der Laan, S. 2005. Social reporting in the tobacco industry: All smoke and mirrors? *Accounting, Auditing and Accountability Journal* 18 (3): 374–389.

Moffat, A. and Auer, A. 2006. Corporate environmental innovation: A government initiative to support corporate sustainability leadership. *Journal of Cleaner Production* 14 (6/7): 589–600.

Mohanty, R. P., Agarwal, R., Choudhury, A. K. and Tiwari, M. K. 2005. A fuzzy ANP-based approach to project selection: A case study. *International Journal of Production Research* 43 (24): 5199–5216.

Moneva, J. M. and Llena, F. 2000. Environmental disclosure in the annual reports of large companies in Spain. *European Accounting Review* 9 (1): 7–29.

Morelli, N. 2006. Developing new product service systems: Methodologies and operational tools. *Journal of Cleaner Production* 14 (17): 1495–1501.

Morgan. G. 1986. *Images of Organization*. Newbury Park, CA: Sage.

Morgan, R. and Matlock, M. 2008. A collaborative learning matrix for combining science with stakeholder involvement to prioritize watershed implementation in Arkansas' nonpoint source state management plan. *Journal of Environmental Assessment Policy and Management* 10 (3): 307–331.

Moskowitz, M. 1972. Choosing socially responsible stocks. *Business and Society* 1: 71–75.

MSH (Management Sciences for Health) and UNICEF. 2005. Stakeholder analysis. http: //erc.msh.org/quality/ittools/itstkan.cfm (accessed Feb. 4, 2009).

Munilla, L. and Miles, M. 2005. The corporate social responsibility continuum as a component of stakeholder. *Business and Society Review* 110 (4): 371–387.

Murillo-Luna, J. L., Garcés-Ayerbe, C. and Rivera-Torres, P. 2008. Why do patterns of environmental response differ? A stakeholders' pressure approach. *Strategic Management Journal* 29 (11): 1225–1240.

Murphy, B., Maguiness, P., Pescott, C., Wislang, S., Ma, J. and Wang, R. 2005. Stakeholder perceptions presage holistic stakeholder relationship marketing performance. *European Journal of Marketing* 39 (9/10): 1049–1059.

Murray, E. A., Jr. 1976. Limitations on strategic choice. *Academy of Management Proceedings* 140–144.

Näsi, J. 1979. Yrityksen suunnittelun perusteet. Yrityksen taloustieteen ja yksityisoikeuden laitoksen julkaisuja A 1: 15. Tampere: Tampereen yliopisto.

1982. Towards a deeper comprehension of the social responsibility of firms: Some philosophical, conceptual and methodological frameworks for scientific research. In *Social Responsibility of Marketing*. Publication of the Turku School of Economics and Business Administration. Series A-2. Turku.

1995a. *Understanding Stakeholder Thinking*. Helsinki: LSR-Julkaisut Oy.

1995b. What is stakeholder thinking? A snapshot of social theory of the firm. In J. Näsi (ed.), *Understanding Stakeholder Thinking*. Helsinki: LSR-Julkaisut Oy. 19–32.

Neligan, C. 2003. *Increasing Accountability Through External Stakeholder Engagement*. London: One World Trust.

Nelson, J. A. 2006. *Economics for Humans*. Chicago: University of Chicago Press.

Neugebauer, G. P., III. 2003. Indigenous peoples as stakeholders: Influencing resource-management decisions affecting indigenous community interests in Latin America. *New York University Law Review* 78: 1227–1261.

Neville, B. A., Bell, S. J. and Mengüc, B. 2005. Corporate reputation, stakeholders and the social performance–financial performance relationship. *European Journal of Marketing* 39 (9/10): 1184–1198.

Newman, W. H. 1979. Commentary. In D. E. Schendel and C. W. Hofer, *Strategic Management: A New View of Business Policy and Planning*. Boston: Little, Brown. 44–47.

Nobes, C. W. 1992. A political history of goodwill in the UK: An illustration of cyclical standard setting. *Abacus* 28 (2): 142–167.

Noddings, N. 1984. *Caring: A Feminine Approach to Ethics and Moral Education*. Berkeley, CA: University of California Press.

Nozick, R. 1974. *Anarchy, State and Utopia*. Oxford: Blackwell.

Nunamaker, J. F., Applegate, L. M. and Konsynski, B. R. 1988. Computer-aided deliberation: Model management and group decision support. *Operations Research* 36 (6): 826–248.

Nutt, P. C. 2004. Expanding the search for alternatives during strategic decisions-making. *Academy of Management Executive* 18 (4): 13–28.

Nwankwo, S. and Richardson, B. 1996. Organizational leaders as political strategists: A stakeholder management perspective. *Management Decision* 34 (10): 43–50.

Nystrom, P. C. and Starbuck, W. H. (eds.). 1981. *Handbook of Organizational Design*. Oxford and New York: Oxford University Press.

ODA. 1995a. Guidance note on how to do stakeholder analysis of aid projects and programmes (July). London: Social Development Department, Overseas Development Administration. www.dfid.gov.uk/Pubs/files/sddstak.pdf (accessed February 4, 2009).

1995b. Guidance note on indicators for measuring and assessing primary stakeholder participation (July). London: Social Development Department, Overseas Development Administration. www.dfid.gov.uk/Pubs/files/sddstak.pdf (accessed February 4, 2009).

O'Dwyer, B. 2005a. The construction of a social account: A case study in an overseas aid agency. *Accounting, Organizations and Society* 30 (3): 279–296.

2005b. Stakeholder democracy: Challenges and contributions from social accounting. *Business Ethics: A European Review* 14 (1): 28–41.

O'Dwyer, B. and Hession, E. 2005. User needs in sustainability reporting: Perspectives of stakeholders in Ireland. *European Accounting Review* 14 (4): 759–787.

O'Dwyer, B. and Owen, D. L. 2005. Assurance statement practice in environmental, social and sustainability reporting: A critical evaluation. *British Accounting Review* 37 (2): 205–229.

O'Dwyer, B., Unerman, J. and Bradley, J. 2005. Perceptions on the emergence and future development of corporate social disclosure in Ireland: Engaging the voices of nongovernmental organizations. *Accounting, Auditing and Accountability Journal* 18 (1): 14–43.

Ogden, S. and Watson, R. 1999. Corporate performance and stakeholder management: Balancing shareholder and customer interests in the U.K. privatized water industry. *Academy of Management Journal* 42 (5): 526–536.

Ohman, P., Hackner, E., Jansson, A. and Tschudi, F. 2006. Swedish auditors' view of auditing: Doing things right versus doing the right things. *European Accounting Review* 15 (1): 89–114.

Olander, S. 2007. Stakeholder impact analysis in construction project management. *Construction Management and Economics* 25 (3): 277–287.

Olian, J. D. and Rynes, S. L. 1991. Making total quality work: Aligning organizational processes, performance measures, and stakeholders. *Human Resource Management* 30 (3): 303–333.

Oliver, C. 1991. Strategic responses to institutional processes. *Academy of Management Review* 16 (1): 145–179.

O'Neill, H. M. 1989. Board members, corporate social responsiveness and profitability: Are tradeoffs necessary? *Journal of Business Ethics* 8 (5): 353–357.

Oral, M., Kettani, O. and Cinar, U. 2001. Project evaluation and selection in a network of collaboration: A consensual disaggregation multi-criterion approach. *European Journal of Operational Research* 130 (2): 332–346.

Orlitzky, M. and Benjamin, J. D. 2001. Corporate social performance and firm risk: A meta-analytic review. *Business and Society* 40 (4): 369–396.

Orlitzky, M., Schmidt, F. L. and Rynes, S. L. 2003. Corporate social and financial performance: A meta-analysis. *Organization Studies* 24 (3): 403–441.

Orts, E. W. 1992. Beyond shareholders: Interpreting corporate constituency statutes. *George Washington Law Review* 61 (1): 14–135.

1997. A North American legal perspective on stakeholder management theory. In F. M. Patfield (ed.), *Perspectives on Company Law.* The Hague: Kluwer Law International. II, 165–179.

Orts, E. W. and Strudler, A. 2002 The ethical and environmental limits of stakeholder theory. *Business Ethics Quarterly* 12 (2): 215–34.

Osheroff, M, 2006. SOX as opportunity. *Strategic Finance* 87 (10): 19–20.

Ostas, D. T. 1995. Religion and the business enterprise: An American perspective. *Journal of Human Values* 1 (1): 27–35.

O'Sullivan, P. and Murphy, P. 1998. Ambush marketing: The ethical issues. *Psychology and Marketing* 15 (4): 349–366.

Oswald, L. J. 1998. Shareholders v. stakeholders: Evaluating corporate constituency statutes under the takings clause. *Journal of Corporation Law* 24 (1): 1–29.

O'Toole, J. 1979. What's ahead for the business-government relationship. *Harvard Business Review* 57 (2): 94–105.

Owen, D. L., Swift, T. and Hunt, K. 2001. Questioning the role of stakeholder engagement in social and ethical accounting, auditing and reporting. *Accounting Forum* 25 (3): 264–282.

Page, C. G. 2002. The determination of organization stakeholder salience in public health. *Journal of Public Health Management and Practice* 8 (5): 76–84.

Pagell, M., Krumwiede, D. W. and Sheu, C. 2007. Efficacy of environmental and supplier relationship investments – moderating effects of external environment. *International Journal of Production Research* 45 (9): 2005–2028.

Palmer, M. and Quinn, B. 2005. Stakeholder relationships in an international retailing context: An investment bank perspective. *European Journal of Marketing* 39 (9/10): 1096–1117.

Panda, S. K. 2008. *Corporate Social Responsibility in India: Past, Present, and Future.* Delhi: Eastern Book Corporation.

Payne, A., Ballantyne, D. and Christopher, M. 2005. A stakeholder approach to relationship marketing strategy: The development and use of the "six markets" model. *European Journal of Marketing* 39 (7/8): 855–871.

Pearce, J. A., III 1982. The company mission as a strategic tool. *Sloan Management Review* 23 (3): 15–24.

Pedersen, E. R. 2006. Making corporate social responsibility (CSR) operable: How companies translate stakeholder dialogue into practice. *Business and Society Review* 11 (2): 137–163.

Pennings, J. M. 1981. Strategically interdependent organizations. In P. C. Nystrom and W. H. Starbuck (eds.), *Handbook of Organizational Design*. Oxford and New York: Oxford University Press.

Penrose, E. 1959. *The Theory of the Growth of the Firm*. Oxford: Blackwell.

Pensions and Investment Research Consultants (PIRC). 1999. *The 1999 Survey of Environmental Reporting at FTSE 350 Companies*. London: PIRC.

Peters, M. H. and Austin, M. J. 1995. The impact of JIT: A critical analysis. *Industrial Management and Data Systems* 95 (1): 12–17.

Pfeffer, J. and Fong, C. T. 2002. The end of business schools? Less success than meets the eye. *Academy of Management Learning and Education* 1 (1): 78–95.

Pfeffer, J. and Salancik, G. R. 1978. *The External Control of Organizations: A Resource Dependence Perspective*. New York: Harper & Row.

Phillips, R. 1997. Stakeholder theory and a principle of fairness. *Business Ethics Quarterly* 7 (1): 51–66.

2003a. *Stakeholder Theory and Organizational Ethics*. San Francisco, CA: Berrett-Koehler Publishers.

2003b. Stakeholder legitimacy. *Business Ethics Quarterly* 13 (1): 25–41.

Phillips, R. and Freeman, R. E. 2008. Corporate citizenship and community stakeholders. In A. G. Scherer and G. Palazzo (eds.), *Handbook of Research on Global Corporate Citizenship*. Northampton, MA: Edward Elgar. 99–115.

Phillips, R., Freeman, R. E. and Wicks, A. C. 2003. What stakeholder theory is not. *Business Ethics Quarterly* 13 (4): 479–502.

Phillips, R. and Reichart, J. 1998. The environment as a stakeholder: A fairness-based approach. *Journal of Business Ethics* 23 (2): 185–197.

Pirson, M. and Malhotra, D. 2008. Unconventional insights for managing stakeholder trust. *MIT Sloan Management Review* 49 (4): 43–50.

Podnar, K. and Jancic, Z. 2006. Towards a categorization of stakeholder groups: An empirical verification of a three-level model. *Journal of Marketing Communications* 12 (4): 297–308.

Poindexter, G. C. 1995–6. Addressing morality in urban brownfield redevelopment: Using stakeholder theory to craft legal process. *Virginia Environmental Law Journal* 15 (1): 37–76.

Polonsky, M. J. 1995. A stakeholder theory approach to designing environmental marketing strategy. *Journal of Business and Industrial Marketing* 10 (3): 29–46.

2001. Strategic bridging within firm-environmental group alliances: Opportunities and pitfalls. *Journal of Marketing Theory and Practice* 9 (1): 38–47.

Polonsky, M. J., Carlson, L. and Fry, M.-L. 2003. The harm chain – a public policy development and stakeholder perspective. *Marketing Theory* 3 (3): 345–360.

Polonsky, M. J. and Hyman, M. R. 2007. A multiple stakeholder perspective on responsibility in advertising. *Journal of Advertising* 36 (2): 5–13.

Polonsky, M. J. and Ottman, J. 1998. Stakeholders' contribution to the green new product development process. *Journal of Marketing Management* 14 (6): 533–537.

Polonsky, M. J., Schuppisser, D. S. W. and Beldona, S. 2002. A stakeholder perspective for analyzing marketing relationships. *Journal of Market-Focused Management* 5 (2): 109–126.

Polonsky, M. J. and Scott, D. 2005. A quantitative examination of the freeman stakeholder strategy matrix. *European Journal of Marketing* 39 (9/10): 1199–1215.

Polonsky, M. J., Suchard, H. T. and Scott, D. R. 1999. The incorporation of an interactive external environment: An extended model of marketing relationships. *Journal of Strategic Marketing* 7 (1): 41–55.

Popper, K. 1968. *The Logic of Scientific Discovery*. New York: Harper & Row.

Porter, M. 1980. *Competitive Strategy*. New York: Free Press.

1985. *Competitive Advantage*. New York: Free Press.

Porter, M. and Kramer, M. K. 2002. The competitive advantage of corporate philanthropy. *Harvard Business Review* 80 (12): 55–69.

2006. Strategy and society: The link between competitive advantage and corporate social responsibility. *Harvard Business Review* 84 (12): 78–92.

Post, J. 1978. *Corporate Behavior and Social Change*. Reston, VA: Reston Publishing Company.

1981. Research in business and society: Current issues and approaches, presented at AACSB Conference on Business Environment/Public Policy and the Business School of the 1980s, Berkeley, CA.

Post, J., Preston, L. and Sachs, S. 2002a. *Redefining the Corporation: Stakeholder Management and Organizational Wealth*. Stanford, CA: Stanford University Press.

2002b. Managing the extended enterprise: The new stakeholder view. *California Management Review* 45 (1): 6–28.

Preston, L. 1986. *Social Issues and Public Policy in Business and Management: Retrospect and Prospect*. College Park, MD: Center for Business & Public Policy.

Preston, L. and Sapienza, H. J. 1990. Stakeholder management and corporate performance. *Journal of Behavioral Economics* 19 (4): 361–375.

Preston, L. E. and Post, J. E. 1975. *Private Management and Public Policy: The Principle of Public Responsibility*. Englewood Cliffs, NJ: Prentice-Hall.

Priem, R. L. and Butler, J. E. 2001. Is the resource-based "view" a useful perspective for strategic management research? *Academy of Management Review* 26 (1): 22–40.

Primack, D. 2008. *PE Week Wire*. October 17, 2008. http://hosting.mansellgroup.net/enable-mail/ThomsonNewLetter/HostedWires/NewsLetters/oct17-08.htm.

Provan, K. and Milward, H. B. 2001. Do networks really work? A framework for evaluating public-sector organizational networks. *Public Administration Review* 61 (4): 414–423.

Pruzan, P. 1998. From control to values-based management and accountability. *Journal of Business Ethics* 17 (13): 1379–1394.

Puccini, D. S. and Marley-Clarke, B. W. G. 1979. The management of offshore resources: Some implications of the 200-mile limit. *Long Range Planning* 12 (5): 8–15.

Puncheva, P. 2008. The role of corporate reputation in the stakeholder decision-making process. *Business and Society* 47 (3): 272–290.

Putnam, H. 2002. *The Collapse of the Fact–Value Dichotomy*. Cambridge, MA: Harvard University Press.

Qu, R. 2007. Corporate social responsibility in China: Impact of regulations, market orientation and ownership structure. *Chinese Management Studies* 1 (3): 198–207.

Quagli, A. 1995. Knowledge in the system of the firm's intangible resources. *European Accounting Review* 4 (2): 393–396.

Quine, W. V. 1951. *Mathematical Logic*. Cambridge, MA: Harvard University Press.

1960. *Word and Object*. Cambridge, MA: MIT Press.

1961. Two dogmas of empiricism. In W. V. O. Quine, *From a Logical Point of View*. 2nd edn. Cambridge, MA: Harvard University Press. 20–46.

Rahman, M. Z. 1990. The local value added statement: A reporting requirement for multinationals in developing host countries. *International Journal of Accounting* 25 (2): 87–97.

Rappaport, A. 1986. *Creating Shareholder Value: A Guide for Managers and Investors*. New York: Free Press.

Rawls, J. 1993. *Political Liberalism*. New York: Columbia University Press.

Raymond, T. J. C. and Greyser, S. A. 1978. The business of managing the arts. *Harvard Business Review* 56 (4): 123–132.

Reed, D. 1999. Stakeholder management theory: A critical theory perspective. *Business Ethics Quarterly* 9 (3): 453–483.

2002. Employing normative stakeholder theory in developing countries. *Business and Society* 41 (1): 166–207.

Reich, M. 1994. *Political Mapping of Health Policy: A Guide for Managing the Political Dimension of Health Policy*. Boston: Harvard School of Public Health.

Reuer, J. J. and Leiblein, M. J. 2001. Real options: Let the buyer beware. In J. Pickford (ed.), *Financial Times Mastering Risk*. London: FT Prentice-Hall.

Rhenman, E. 1964. *Företagsdemokrati och företagsorganisation*. Stockholm: Thule.

1968. *Industrial Democracy and Industrial Management: A Critical Essay on the Possible Meanings and Implications of Industrial Democracy*. London: Tavistock.

1973. *Organization Theory for Long-Range Planning*. New York: John Wiley & Sons.

Rhenman, E. and Stymne, B. 1965. *Företagsledning i en Föränderlig Värld*. Stockholm: Aldus/Bonniers.

Riahi-Belkaoui, A. 1991. Organizational effectiveness, social performance and economic performance. *Research in Corporate Social Performance and Policy* 12: 143–153.

Ribstein, L. E. 2005–6. Accountability and responsibility in corporate governance. *Notre Dame Law Review* 81: 1431–1494.

Richardson, H. S. 1997. *Practical Reasoning about Final Ends*. New York: Cambridge University Press.

Richardson, V. J. 2000. Information asymmetry and earnings management: Some evidence. *Review of Quantitative Finance and Accounting* 15 (4): 325–347.

Riis, J. O., Dukovska-Popovska, I. and Johansen, J. 2006. Participation and dialogue in strategic manufacturing development. *Production Planning and Control* 17 (2): 176–188.

Ringbakk, K. 1976. Strategic planning in a turbulent international environment. *Long Range Planning* 9 (3): 2–11.

Rivera-Camino, J. 2007. Re-evaluating green marketing strategy: A stakeholder perspective. *European Journal of Marketing* 41 (11/12): 1328–1340.

Robbins, J. 2003. Stakeholders and conflict management corporate perspectives on collaborative approaches. In J. Andriof, S. Waddock, B. Husted, and S. Sutherland Rahman (eds.),

Unfolding Stakeholder Thinking 2: Relationships, Communication, Reporting and Performance. Sheffield: Greenleaf Publishing. 162–180.

Roberts, N. and Bradley, T. 1991. Stakeholder collaboration and innovation: A study of public policy initiation at the state level. *Journal of Applied Behavioral Science* 27 (2): 209–227.

Roberts, N. and King, P. J. 1989. Stakeholder audit goes public. *Organizational Dynamics* 17 (3): 63–79.

Roberts, R. W. 1992. Determinants of corporate social responsibility disclosure: An application of stakeholder theory. *Accounting, Organizations and Society* 17 (6): 595–612.

Roberts, R. W. and Mahoney, L. 2004. Stakeholder conceptions of the corporation: Their meaning and influence in accounting research. *Business Ethics Quarterly* 14 (3): 399–431.

Robilotti, M. 1997. Codetermination, stakeholder rights, and hostile takeovers: A reevaluation of the evidence from abroad. *Harvard International Law Journal* 38: 536–538.

Rodgers, W. and Gago, S. 2004. Stakeholder influence on corporate strategies over time. *Journal of Business Ethics*, 52 (4): 349–363.

Romano, R. and Leiman, M. 1970. *Views on Capitalism*. Beverly Hills: Glencoe Press.

Roper, S. and Davies, G. 2007. The corporate brand: Dealing with multiple stakeholders. *Journal of Marketing Management* 23 (1/2): 75–90.

Rorty, R. 1979. *Philosophy and the Mirror of Nature*. Princeton: Princeton University Press.

1982. *Consequences of Pragmatism*. Minneapolis, MN: University of Minnesota Press.

1986. Beyond realism and anti-realism. In L. Nagl and R. Heinrich (eds.), *Wo steht die analytische Philosophie heute?* Vienna: R. Oldenbourg Verlag.

1989. *Contingency, Irony, and Solidarity*. Cambridge: Cambridge University Press.

1998. *Truth and Progress: Philosophical Papers III*. Cambridge: Cambridge University Press.

1999. *Philosophy and Social Hope*. Harmondsworth: Penguin.

Rosenthal, S. and Buchholz, G. 2000. *Rethinking Business Ethics: A Pragmatic Approach*. New York: Oxford University Press.

Rostow, Eugene V. 1959. To whom and for what ends are corporate managements responsible? In E. S. Mason (ed.), *The Corporation in Modern Society*. Cambridge, MA: Harvard University Press. 46–84.

Rothschild, W. 1976. *Putting It All Together*. New York: AMACOM.

Rowe, A. J., Mason, R. O. and Dickel, K. E. 1985. *Strategic Management and Business Policy: A Methodological Approach*. Reading, MA: Addison-Wesley.

Rowley, T. J. 1997. Moving beyond dyadic ties: A network theory of stakeholder influences. *Academy of Management Review* 22 (4): 887–910.

Rubenstein, D. B. 1992. Bridging the gap between great accounting and black ink. *Accounting, Organizations and Society* 17 (5): 501–508.

Rudner, R. 1953. The scientist *qua* scientist makes value judgments. *Philosophy of Science* 20: 1–6.

Rueda-Manzanares, A., Aragón-Correa, J. A and Sharma, S. 2008. The influence of stakeholders on the environmental strategy of service firms: The moderating effects of complexity, uncertainty and munificence. *British Journal of Management* 19 (2): 185–203.

Ruf, B. M., Muralidhar, K., Brown, R. M, Janney, J. J. and Paul, K. 2001. An empirical investigation of the relationship between change in corporate social performance and financial performance: A stakeholder theory perspective. *Journal of Business Ethics* 32 (2): 143–156.

Ruffat, J. 1983. Strategic management of public and non-market corporations. *Long Range Planning* 16 (2): 74–84.

Russo, M. V. and Fouts, P. A. 1997. A resource-based perspective on corporate environmental performance and profitability. *Academy of Management Journal* 40 (3): 534–559.

Rustin, M. 1997. Stakeholding and the public sector. In G. Kelly, D. Kelly, and A. Gamble (eds.), *Stakeholder Capitalism*. London: Macmillan. 72–81.

Ryan, C. 2002. Equity, management, power sharing and sustainability – issues of the "new tourism." *Tourism Management* 23 (1): 17–26.

Sacconi, L. 2006. A social contract account for CSR as an extended model of corporate governance (I): Rational bargaining and justification. *Journal of Business Ethics* 68 (3): 259–281.

Sachdeva, R. 2007. Mixing methodologies to enhance implementation of healthcare operational research. *Journal of the Operational Research Society* 58 (2): 159–167.

Sachdeva, R., Williams, T. and Quigley, J. 2007. Mixing methodologies to enhance the implementation of healthcare operational research. *Journal of the Operational Research Society* 58 (2): 159–167.

Sandberg, J. 2008a. Understanding the separation thesis. *Business Ethics Quarterly* 18 (2): 213–232.

2008b. The tide is turning on the separation thesis? *Business Ethics Quarterly* 18 (4): 561–565.

Sandoval, M. C., Veiga, M. M., Hinton, J. and Sandner, S. 2006. Application of sustainable development concepts to an alluvial mineral extraction project in Lower Caroni River, Venezuela. *Journal of Cleaner Production* 14 (3/4): 415–426.

Sarasvathy, S. 2001. Causation and effectuation: Toward a theoretical shift from economic inevitability to entrepreneurial contingency. *Academy of Management Review* 26 (2): 243–288.

Saravanamuthu, K. 2004. What is measured counts: Harmonized corporate reporting and sustainable economic development. *Critical Perspectives on Accounting* 15 (3): 295–302.

Sarig, O. H. 1998. The effect of leverage on bargaining with corporation. *Financial Review* 33 (1): 1–16.

Sass, S. A. 1982. *The Pragmatic Imagination: A History of the Wharton School, 1881–1981*. Philadelphia: University of Pennsylvania Press.

Sauter, E. T. and Leisen, B. 1999. Managing stakeholders – a tourism planning model. *Annals of Tourism Research* 26 (2): 312–328.

Savage, G., Taylor, R., Rotarius, T. and Buesseler, J. 1997. Governance of integrated delivery systems/networks: A stakeholder approach. *Health Care Management Review* 22 (1): 7–20.

Schankar, V., Urban, G. L. and Sultan, F. 2002. Online trust: A stakeholder perspective, concepts, implications, and future directions. *Journal of Strategic Information Systems* 11 (3): 325–344.

Schelling, T. 1960. *The Strategy of Conflict*. Cambridge, MA: Harvard University Press.

1978. *Micromotives and Macrobehavior*. New York: W. W. Norton.

Schendel, D. E. and Hatten, K. J. 1972. Business policy or strategic management: A broader view for an emerging discipline. Paper presented at the annual meeting of the Academy of Management National Meeting, Minneapolis, MN.

Schendel, D. E. and Hofer, C. W. 1979. *Strategic Management: A New View of Business Policy and Planning*. Boston: Little, Brown.

Scherer, A. G. and Palazzo, G. (eds). 2008. *Handbook of Research on Global Corporate Citizenship*. Northampton, MA: Edward Elgar.

Schilling, M. A. 2000. Decades ahead of her time: Advancing stakeholder theory through the ideas of Mary Parker Follett. *Journal of Management History* 6 (5): 224–242.

Schlossberger, E. 1994. A new model of business: Dual-investor theory. *Business Ethics Quarterly* 4 (4): 459–474.

Schneider, A., Church, B. and Ely, K. 2006. Non-audit services and auditor independence: A review of the literature. *Journal of Accounting Literature* 25: 169–211.

Schneider, M. 2002. A stakeholder model of organizational leadership. *Organization Science* 13 (2): 209–220.

Schoemaker, P. J. H. 1993. Multiple scenario development: Its conceptual and behavioral basis. *Strategic Management Journal* 14 (3): 193–213.

1995. Scenario planning: A tool for strategic thinking. *Sloan Management Review* 36 (2): 25–40.

Scholes, E. and Clutterbuck, D. 1998. Communication with stakeholders: An integrated approach. *Long Range Planning* 31 (2): 227–238.

Schonberger, R. J. 1980. MIS design: A contingency approach. *MIS Quarterly* 4 (1): 13–20.

Schreuder, H. and Ramanathan, K. 1984. Accounting and corporate accountability: A post-script. *Accounting, Organizations and Society* 9 (3/4): 421–423.

Schumpeter, J. A. 1942. *Capitalism, Socialism, and Democracy*. London: Allen & Unwin.

Scott, J. E. M., McKinnon, J. L. and Harrison, G. L. 2003. Cash to accrual and cash to accrual: A case study of financial reporting in two NSW hospitals 1857 to post-1975. *Accounting, Auditing and Accountability Journal* 16 (1): 104–125.

Scott, S. G. and Lane, V. R. 2000. A stakeholder approach to organizational identity. *Academy of Management Review* 25 (1): 43–62.

Seal, W. 2006. Management accounting and corporate governance: An institutional interpretation of the agency problem. *Management Accounting Research* 17 (4): 389–408.

Searle, J. 1964. How to derive "ought" from "is." *Philosophical Review* 73 (1): 43–58.

Selznick, P. 1966. *TVA and the Grassroots*. New York: Harper Torch Books.

Sen, A. 1987. *On Ethics and Economics*. Oxford: Blackwell.

1989. *Hunger and Public Action*. Oxford: Clarendon Press.

1995. *Inequality Reexamined*. Cambridge, MA: Harvard University Press.

Sen, S., Bhattacharya, C. B. and Korschun, D. 2006. The role of corporate social responsibility in strengthening multiple stakeholder relationships: A field experiment. *Journal of the Academy of Marketing Science* 34 (2): 158–166.

Sethi, S. P. 1970. *Business Corporations and the Black Man: An Analysis of Social Conflict: The Kodak-Fight Controversy*. Scranton, PA: Chandler Publishing Company.

1975. Dimensions of corporate social performance: An analytic framework. *California Management Review* 17 (3): 58–64.

Shaffer, B., Quasney, T. J. and Grimm, C. M. 2000. Firm-level performance implications of nonmarket actions. *Business and Society* 39 (2): 126–143.

Shah, A. K. 1995. Accounting policy choice: The case of financial instruments. *European Accounting Review* 4 (2): 397–399.

Shah, S. and Bhaskar, A. S. 2008. Corporate stakeholder management: Western and Indian perspectives: An overview. *Journal of Human Values* 14 (1): 73–93.

Shane, P. B. and Spicer, B. H. 1983. Market response to environmental information produced outside the firm. *Accounting Review* 58 (3): 521–536.

Shane, S. and Venkataraman, S. 2000. The promise of entrepreneurship as a field of research. *Academy of Management Review* 25 (1): 217–226.

Shankman, N. A. 1999. Reframing the debate between agency and stakeholder theories of the firm. *Journal of Business Ethics* 19 (4): 319–334.

Sharma, S. and Henriques, I. 2005. Stakeholder influence on sustainability practices in the Canadian forest products industry. *Strategic Management Journal* 26 (2): 159–180.

Sharma, S. and Starik, M. 2004. *Stakeholders, the Environment and Society*. Cheltenham: Edward Elgar.

Shortell, S. 1988. The evolution of hospital systems: Unfulfilled promises and self-fulfilling prophesies. *Medical Care Review* 45 (2): 177–214.

Silbert, T. H. 1952. Financing and factoring accounts receivable. *Harvard Business Review* 30 (1): 39–54.

Sillanpää, M. 1998. The Body Shop Values Report: Towards integrated stakeholder auditing. *Journal of Business Ethics* 17 (13): 1443–1456.

Simon, H. A. 1947. *Administrative Behavior: A Study of Decision-Making Processes in Administrative Organizations*. New York: Macmillan.

Sisodia, R., Wolfe, D. B. and Sheth, J. 2007. *Firms of Endearment: How World-Class Companies Profit from Passion and Purpose*. Upper Saddle River, NJ: Wharton School Publishing.

Skidelsky, R. 1995. The role of ethics in Keynes' economics. In S. Brittan and A. Hamilton (eds.), *Market Capitalism and Moral Values*. Brookfield: Edward Elgar.

Slatter, S. S. 1980. Strategic planning for public relations. *Long Range Planning* 13 (3): 57–69.

Slinger, G. 1998. Spanning the gap: The theoretical principles connecting stakeholder policies to business performance. Working Paper, Centre for Business Research, Department of Applied Economics, University of Cambridge.

1999. Essays on stakeholding, Ph.D. dissertation, Department of Applied Economics, University of Cambridge.

Smith, A. 1986. The theory of moral sentiments. In R. L. Heilbroner (ed.), *The Essential Adam Smith*. New York: W. W. Norton. 57–148.

Smith, A. M. and Fishbacher, M. 2005. New service development: A stakeholder perspective. *European Journal of Marketing* 39 (9/10): 1025–1048.

Smith, H. J. 2003. The shareholders vs. stakeholders debate. *MIT Sloan Management Review* 44 (4): 85–90.

Smith, H. J. and Hasnas, J. 1999. Ethics and information systems: The corporate domain. *MIS Quarterly* 23 (1): 109–127.

Smith, J. V., Adhikari, A. and Tondkar, R. H. 2005. Exploring differences in social disclosures internationally: A stakeholder perspective. *Journal of Accounting and Public Policy* 24 (2): 123–151.

Smith, M. 1993. *Pressure, Power and Policy: State Autonomy and Policy Networks in Britain and the United States*. Hemel Hempstead: Harvester Wheatsheaf.

Sperling, K. L. 2006. The employer's role in reforming the US health care system. *Journal of Applied Corporate Finance* 18 (1): 108–116.

Spicer, B. H. 1978. Investors, corporate social performance and information disclosure: An empirical study. *Accounting Review* 53 (1): 94–111.

Starik, M. 1995. Should trees have managerial standing? Towards stakeholder status for non-human nature. *Journal of Business Ethics* 14 (3): 207–217.

Stead, W. E. and Stead, J. G. 1992. *Management for a Small Planet: Strategic Decision Making and the Environment.* Newbury Park, CA: Sage.

2004. *Sustainable Strategic Management.* London: M. E. Sharpe.

Steadman, M., Albright, T. and Dunn, K. 1996. Stakeholder group interest in the new manufacturing environment. *Managerial Auditing Journal* 11 (2): 4–20.

Steadman, M. E., Zimmerer, T. W. and Green, R. F. 1995. Pressures from stakeholders hit Japanese companies. *Long Range Planning* 28 (6): 29–37.

Stearns, J. M., Walton, J. R., Crespy, C. T. and Bol, J. W. 1996. The role of moral obligations to stakeholders in ethical marketing decision making. *Journal of Marketing Management* 6 (2): 34–47.

Stearns, L. B. and Mizruchi, M. S. 1993. Board composition and corporate financing: The impact of financial institution representation on borrowing. *Academy of Management Journal* 36 (3): 603–618.

Sternberg, E. 1996. Stakeholder theory exposed. *Corporate Governance Quarterly* 2 (1): 4–18.

2000. *Just Business.* New York: Oxford University Press.

Sternberg, R. J. 2007. A systems model of leadership. *American Psychologist* 62 (1): 34–42.

Stewart, D. W. 1984. Managing competing claims: An ethical framework for human resource decision making. *Public Administration Review* 44 (1): 14–22.

Stewart, M. 1999. *Keynes and After.* Harmondsworth: Penguin.

Stewart, R. F., Allen, J. K. and Cavender, J. M. 1963. The strategic plan. Research Report 168, Stanford Research Institute, Long Range Planning Service, Industrial Economics Division.

Stout, D. E. and West, R. N. 2004. Using a stakeholder-based process to develop and implement an innovative graduate-level course in management accounting. *Journal of Accounting Education* 22 (2): 95–118.

Strand, R. 2008. The stakeholder dashboard. *Greener Management Journal* 54: 23–36.

Strong, K. C., Ringer, R. C. and Taylor, S. A. 2001. THE* rules of stakeholder satisfaction (*timeliness, honesty, empathy). *Journal of Business Ethics* 32 (3): 219–230.

Sturdivant, F. D. 1979. Executives and activists: Test of stakeholder management. *California Management Review* 22 (1) 53–60.

Stymne, B. 2004. Travelling in the borderline of academy and industry. In N. Adler, A. B. Shani, and A. Styhre (eds.), *Collaborative Research in Organizations: Foundations for Learning, Change, and Theoretical Development.* London: Sage. 37–53.

Subrahmanyam, A. and Titman, S. 2001. Feedback from stock prices to cash flows. *Journal of Finance* 56 (6): 2389–2415.

Sundaram, A. K. and Inkpen, A. C. 2004. The corporate objective revisited. *Organization Science* 15 (3): 350–363.

Sundkvist, A. and Finnveden, G. 2007. Stakeholder needs study on indicators for integrated product policy. *Journal of Cleaner Production* 15 (4): 323–326.

Sussland, W. A. 2001. Creating business value through intangibles. *Journal of Business Strategy* 22 (6): 23–28.

Sutherland-Rahman, S., Waddock, S., Andriof, J. and Husted, B. 2002. *Unfolding Stakeholder Thinking: Theory, Responsibility and Engagement.* Sheffield: Greenleaf Publishing.

Svendsen, A. 1998. *The Stakeholder Strategy: Profiting from Collaborative Business Relations.* San Francisco, CA: Berrett-Koehler Publishers.

Svendsen, A. and Laberge, M. 2006. Beyond consultation: A co-creative approach to stakeholder engagement. CoreRelation Consulting. www.sfu.ca/cscd/cli/beyondconsultation.pdf (accessed Feb. 4, 2009).

Swanson, D. L. 1999. Towards an integrative theory of business and society: A research strategy for corporate social performance, *Academy of Management Review* 24 (3): 506–524.

Sweeney, L. and Coughlan, J. 2008. Do different industries report corporate social responsibility differently? An investigation through the lens of stakeholder theory. *Journal of Marketing Communications* 14 (2): 113–124.

Sweetser, A. G. and Petry, G. H. 1972. A history of the seven academic finance associations and their contributions to development of the discipline. *Financial Management* 10 (2): 46–70.

Taylor, B. 1971. The future development of corporate strategy. *Journal of Business Policy* 2 (2): 22–38.

1977. Managing the process of corporate development. In B. Taylor and J. Sparkes (eds.), *Corporate Strategy and Planning.* New York: John Wiley & Sons.

1995. The new strategic leadership – driving change, getting results. *Long Range Planning* 28 (5): 71–81.

Taylor, B. and Sparkes, J. 1977. *Corporate Strategy and Planning.* London: Heinemann.

Tesch, D. and Klein, G. 2003. The impact of information system personnel skill discrepancies on stakeholder satisfaction. *Decision Sciences* 34 (1): 107–129.

Theys, M. and Kunsch, P. L. 2004. The importance of co-operation for ethical decision-making with OR. *European Journal of Operational Research* 153 (2): 485–488.

Thomas, P. and Palfrey, C. 1996. Evaluation: Stakeholder-focused criteria. *Social Policy and Administration* 30 (2): 125–142.

Thomas, T., Schermerhorn, J. R., Jr. and Dienhart, J. W. 2004. Strategic leadership of ethical behavior in business. *Academy of Management Executive* 18 (2): 56–66.

Thompson, J. D. 1967. *Organizations in Action.* New York: McGraw-Hill.

Titman, S. 1984. The effect of capital structure on a firm's liquidation decision. *Journal of Financial Economics* 13 (1): 137–151.

Topping, S. and Fottler, M. 1990. Improved stakeholder management: The key to revitalizing the HMO movement? *Medical Care Review* 47 (3): 365–393.

Treviño, L. K. and Weaver, G. R. 1999a. The stakeholder research tradition: Converging theorists – not convergent theory. *Academy of Management Review* 24 (2): 222–227.

1999b. Treviño and Weaver's reply to Jones and Wicks. *Academy of Management Review* 24 (4): 623–624.

Trigeorgis, L. 1993. Real options and interactions with financial flexibility. *Financial Management* 22 (3): 202–224.

1997. *Real Options.* Cambridge, MA: MIT Press.

Trist, E. 1981. *The Evolution of Socio-Technical Systems: A Conceptual Framework and Action Research Program.* Toronto: Ontario Ministry of Labour.

Tsai, P. C. F., Yeh, C. R., Wu, S.-L. and Huang, I.-C. 2005. An empirical test of stakeholder influence strategy models: Evidence from business downsizing in Taiwan. *International Journal of Human Resource Management* 16 (10): 1862–1885.

Tsui, A. S. 1990. A multiple-constituency model of effectiveness: An empirical examination at the human resource subunit level. *Administrative Science Quarterly* 35 (3): 458–483.

Tullock, G. and Buchanan, J. M. 1962. *The Calculus of Consent: Logical Foundations of Constitutional Democracy*. Ann Arbor: University of Michigan Press.

Turban, D. B. and Greening, D. W. 1996. Corporate social performance and organizational attractiveness to prospective employees. *Academy of Management Journal* 40 (3): 658–672.

Turnbull, S. 1997. Stakeholder governance: A cybernetic and property rights analysis. *Corporate Governance* 5 (1): 180–205.

Ullman, A. 1985. Data in search of a theory: A critical examination of the relationship among social performance, social disclosure and economic performance. *Academy of Management Review* 10 (3): 540–577.

Ulmer, R. R. 2001. Effective crisis management through established stakeholder relationships. *Management Communication Quarterly* 14 (4): 590–611.

Ulrich, D. 1989. Assessing human resource effectiveness: Stakeholder, utility, and relationship approaches. *Human Resource Planning* 12 (4): 301–315.

Unerman, J. and Bennett, M. 2004. Increased stakeholder dialogue and the Internet: Towards greater corporate accountability or reinforcing capitalist hegemony? *Accounting Organizations and Society* 29 (7): 685–707.

Van Buren, H. J. 2001. If fairness is the problem, is consent the solution? Integrating ISCT and stakeholder theory. *Business Ethics Quarterly* 11 (3): 481–499.

Vancil, R. F. and Lorange, P. 1975. Strategic planning in diversified companies. *Harvard Business Review* 53 (1): 81–90.

Van Der Weide, M. 1996. Against fiduciary duties to corporate stakeholders. *Delaware Journal of Corporate Law* 21: 27–41.

Van de Ven, A. H., Emmett, D. and Koenig, R., Jr. 1975. Frameworks for inter-organizational analysis. *Organization and Administrative Sciences*. 6 (1). Repr. in Negandhi, A. (ed.). 1975. *Inter-Organization Theory*. Ohio: Kent State University Press.

Van de Ven, A. H. and Joyce, W. F. (eds.). 1981. *Perspectives on Organization Design and Behavior*, New York: Wiley Interscience.

Van Raak, A., Paulus, A. and Mur-Veeman, I. 2005. Why do health and social care providers co-operate? *Health Policy* 74 (1): 13–23.

Van Wezel Stone, K. 1991. Employees as stakeholders under state nonshareholder constituency statutes. *Stetson Law Review* 21: 54–71.

Varvasovszky, Z. and Brugha, R. 2000. How to do (or not to do) … a stakeholder analysis. *Health Policy and Planning* 15 (3): 338–345.

Venkataraman, S. 1997. The distinctive domain of entrepreneurship research: An editor's perspective. In J. Katz and R. Brokhous (eds.), *Advances in Entrepreneurship, Firm Emergence, and Growth*. Greenwich, CT: JAI Press.

2002. Stakeholder value equilibration and the entrepreneurial process. In R. E. Freeman and S. Venkataraman (eds.), *Ethics and Entrepreneurship*. Ruffin Series 3. Charlottesville, VA: Philosophy Documentation Center. 45–57.

Vicarelli, Fausto. 1984. *Keynes: The Instability of Capitalism*. Philadelphia: University of Pennsylvania Press.

Vickers, M. R. 2005. Business ethics and the HR role: Past, present and future. *Human Resource Planning* 28 (1): 26–32.

Vilanova, L. 2007. Neither shareholder nor stakeholder management: What happens when firms are run for their short-term salient stakeholder? *European Management Journal* 25 (2): 146–162.

Vincent, D. R. 1988. Understanding organizational power. *Journal of Business Strategy* 9 (2): 40–44.

Von Neumann, J. and Morgenstern, O. 1946. *The Theory of Games and Economic Behavior*. 2nd edn. New York: John Wiley & Sons.

Votaw, D. 1964. *The Six-Legged Dog*. Berkeley, CA: University of California Press.

Wack, P. 1985. Scenarios: Uncharted waters ahead. *Harvard Business Review* 63 (5): 72–89.

Waddock, S. 2004. Parallel universes: Companies, academics and the progress of corporate citizenship. *Business and Society Review* 109 (1): 5–42.

Waddock, S. and Graves, S. 1997. The corporate social performance–financial performance link. *Strategic Management Journal* 18 (4): 303–319.

Walker, D., Bourne, L. and Shelley, A. 2008. Influence, stakeholder mapping and visualization. *Construction Management and Economics* 26 (6): 645–658.

Wallace, J. S. 2003. Value maximization and stakeholder theory: Compatible or not? *Journal of Applied Corporate Finance* 15 (3): 120–127.

Walsh, J. P. 2005. Book review essay: Taking stock of stakeholder management. *Academy of Management Review* 30 (2): 426–452.

Walters, D. 2005. Performance planning and control in virtual business structures. *Production Planning and Control* 16 (2): 226–239.

Wang, H., Barney, J. B. and Reuer, J. J. 2003. Stimulating firm-specific investment through risk management. *Long Range Planning* 36 (1): 49–58.

Wartick, S. L. and Cochran, P. L. 1985. The evolution of the corporate social performance model. *Academy of Management Review* 10 (4): 758–769.

Weaver, G. R. and Cochran, P. L. 1999. Integrated and decoupled corporate social performance: Management commitments, external pressures and corporate ethics practices. *Academy of Management Journal* 42 (5): 539–552.

Weaver, G. R. and Treviño, L. K. 1994. Normative and empirical business ethics. *Business Ethics Quarterly* 4 (2): 129–144.

Weetman, P. 1999. *Financial and Management Accounting: An Introduction*. London: Pitman.

Weick, K. 1979. *The Social Psychology of Organizing*. 2nd edn. New York: McGraw-Hill.

1989a. Organized improvisation: 20 years of organizing. *Communication Studies* 40 (4): 241–248.

1989b. Theory construction as disciplined imagination. *Academy of Management Review* 14 (4): 516–531.

1993. The collapse of sensemaking in organizations: The Mann Gulch disaster. *Administrative Science Quarterly* 38 (4): 628–652.

Weinberger, M. G. and Romeo, J. B. 1989. The impact of negative product news. *Business Horizons* 32 (1): 44–50.

Weiner, P. P. 1973–74. Pragmatism. In P. P. Weiner (ed.), *The Dictionary of the History of Ideas: Studies of Selected Pivotal Ideas*. New York: Charles Scribner's Sons. III, 551–570.

Weiss, J. W. 2003. *Business Ethics: A Stakeholder and Issues Management Approach*. 3rd edn. Mason, OH: Thomson South-Western.

Welford, R. J. 2005. Corporate social responsibility in Europe, North America and Asia: 2004 results. *Journal of Corporate Citizenship* 17: 33–52.

Welp, M., de la Vega-Leinert, A., Stoll-Kleemann, S. and Jaeger, C. 2006. Science-based stakeholder dialogues: Theories and tools. *Global Environmental Change* 16 (2): 170–181.

Wempe, B. 2008. Understanding the separation thesis: Precision after the decimal point. *Business Ethics Quarterly* 18 (4): 549–553.

Werhane, P. H., 1994. The normative/descriptive distinction in methodologies of business ethics. *Business Ethics Quarterly* 4 (2): 175–180.

1999. *Moral Imagination and Management Decision-Making*. New York: Oxford University Press.

Werhane, P. H., Spencer, E., Mills, A. and Rorty, M. 2000. *Organization Ethics in Health Care*. New York: Oxford University Press.

Wernerfelt, B. 1984. A resource-based view of the firm. *Strategic Management Journal* 5 (2): 171–180.

Westbrook, R. B. 1991. *John Dewey and American Democracy*. Ithaca, NY: Cornell University Press.

Weyer, M. V. 1996. In an ideal world. *Management Today* September: 34–39.

Wharton School. 2000. The Wharton century: A century of perspectives on business education. Philadelphia: Wharton School. http://hbrsrv.com/jenia/files/flashPaper/WhartonCentury.swf (accessed March 26, 2009).

Wheeler, D. and Sillanpää, M. 1997. *The Stakeholder Corporation: The Body Shop Blueprint for Maximizing Stakeholder Value*. London: FT Pitman.

1998. Including the stakeholders: The business case. *Long Range Planning* 31 (2): 201–210.

Wheeler, S. 1997. Works councils: Towards stakeholding? *Journal of Law and Society* 24 (1): 44–64.

1999. Fraser and the politics of corporate governance. *Journal of Law and Society* 26 (2): 240–251.

Whysall, P. 2000. Addressing ethical issue in retailing: A stakeholder perspective. *International Review of Retail, Distribution and Consumer Research* 10 (3): 305–318.

2005. Retailers' press release activity: Market signals for stakeholder engagement? *European Journal of Marketing* 39 (9/10): 1118–1131.

Wicks, A. 1996. Overcoming the separation thesis: The need for a reconsideration of SIM research. *Business and Society* 35 (1): 89–118.

1998. How Kantian a Kantian theory of capitalism? *Business Ethics Quarterly*. Charlottesville, VA: Philosophy Documentation Center. Special Issue no. 1: 61–74.

In press. *Business ethics in an era of corporate crisis*. Darden School Working Paper.

Wicks, A. C. and Freeman, R. E. 1998. Organization studies and the new pragmatism: Positivism, anti-positivism, and the search for ethics. *Organization Science* 9 (2): 123–140.

Wicks, A. C., Freeman, R. E. and Gilbert, D. R. 1994. A feminist reinterpretation of the stakeholder concept. *Business Ethics Quarterly* 4 (4): 475–497.

Wijnberg, N. M. 2000. Normative stakeholder theory and Aristotle: The link between ethics and politics. *Journal of Business Ethics* 25 (4): 329–342.

Williamson, O. E. 1975. *Markets and Hierarchies: Analysis and Antitrust Implications*. New York: Free Press.

1984a. Corporate governance. *Yale Law Journal* 93 (7): 1197–1230.

1984b. *The Economic Institutions of Capitalism*. New York: Free Press.

Williamson, O. E. and Bercovitz, J. 1996. The modern corporation as an efficiency instrument: The comparative contracting perspective. In C. Kaysen (ed.), *The American Corporation Today*. New York: Oxford University Press. 327–359.

Windsor, D. 2000. Moral activism and value harmonization in an integrating global economy. *Proceedings, 7th Annual International Conference Promoting Business Ethics*, 2 vols. I, 300–312.

2001. The future of corporate social responsibility. *International Journal of Organizational Analysis* 9 (3), 225–256.

2006. Corporate social responsibility: Three key approaches. *Journal of Management Studies* 43 (1): 93–113.

Windsor, D. and Getz, K. A. 2000. Multilateral cooperation to combat corruption: Normative regimes despite mixed motives and diverse values. *Cornell International Law Journal* 33: 731–772.

Winston, C. C. K. and Sharp, D. 2005. Power and international accounting standard setting: Evidence from segment reporting and intangible assets projects. *Accounting, Auditing and Accountability Journal* 18 (1): 74–99.

Wisdom, A. J. T. D. 1957. *Philosophy and Psychoanalysis.* Oxford: Blackwell.

Wittgenstein, L. 2001. *Philosophical Investigations.* 3rd edn, trans. G. E. M. Anscombe. Oxford: Blackwell.

Wokutch, R. E. and Spencer, B. A. 1987. Corporate saints and sinners: The effects of philanthropic and illegal activity on organizational performance. *California Management Review* 19 (2): 62–73.

Wommack, W. W. 1979. Responsibility of the board of directors and management in corporate strategy. *Harvard Business Review* 57 (5): 48–62.

Wood, D. and Ross, D. G. 2006. Environmental social controls and capital investments: Australian evidence. *Accounting and Finance* 46 (4): 677–695.

Wood, D. J. 1991. Corporate social performance revisited. *Academy of Management Review* 16 (4): 691–718.

1995. The Fortune database as a CSP measure. *Business and Society* 24 (2): 1997–1999.

Wood, D. J. and Logsdon, J. M. 2001. Theorising business citizenship. In J. Andriof and M. McIntosh (eds.), *Perspectives on Corporate Citizenship*. Sheffield: Greenleaf. 83–103.

Wooldridge, B. and Weistroffer, H. R. 2004. Supporting government performance by capturing the values and expertise of key stakeholders: A delphi/decision support system approach to local revenue planning. *Journal of Public Budgeting, Accounting and Financial Management* 16 (3): 362–376.

Worthy, J. C. 1984. *Shaping an American Institution: Robert E. Wood and Sears, Roebuck.* Urbana: University of Illinois.

Wright, P. and Ferris, S. P. 1997. Agency conflict and corporate strategy: The effect of divestment on corporate value. *Strategic Management Journal* 18 (1): 77–90.

Yau, O. H. M., Chow, R. P. M., Sin, L. Y., Tse, A. C., Luk, C. K. and Lee, J. S. Y. 2007. Developing a scale for stakeholder orientation. *European Journal of Marketing* 41 (11/12): 1306–1320.

Yehning, C., Weston, J. F. and Altman, E. I. 1995. Financial distress and restructuring models. *Journal of the Financial Management Association* 24 (2): 57–75.

Yosie, T. and Herbst, T. 1998. Managing and communicating stakeholder-based decision making. *Human and Ecological Risk Assessment* 4 (3): 643–646.

Zadek, S. 1994. Trading ethics: Auditing the market. *Journal of Economic Issues* 28 (2): 631–645.

1998. Balancing performance, ethics, and accountability. *Journal of Business Ethics* 17 (13): 1421–1441.

2007. Inconvenient but true. *Fortune International* 156 (9): 56.

Zadek, S., Pruzan, P. and Evans. R. (eds.). 1997. *Building Corporate Accountability: Emerging Practices in Social and Ethical Accounting and Auditing.* London: Earthscan Publications.

Zald, M. 1993. Organization studies as a scientific and humanistic enterprise: Toward a reconceptualization of the foundations of the field. *Organization Science* 4 (4): 513–528.

Zingales, L. 1998. Corporate governance. In P. Newman (ed.), *The New Palgrave Dictionary of Economics and the Law.* London: Palgrave Macmillan. 497–503.

2000. In search of new foundations. *Journal of Finance* 55 (4): 1623–1653.

Zinkhan, G. M. 2002. Relationship marketing: Theory and implementation. *Journal of Market-Focused Management* 5 (2): 83–89.

Index

Printed in the United States
By Bookmasters